Coalitional behaviour in theory and practice

The theoretical approaches to coalition studies are strongly in need of rethinking, particularly with respect to contextual factors which influence coalitional behaviour. Also, until recently, coalition politics has been a somewhat neglected area in political science – surprisingly so for Western Europe, where governments have tended as a rule to be coalitions. This volume attempts to marry theory and practice by avoiding the pure abstraction of the formal coalition theories on the one hand and the over-descriptiveness of some of the empirical work on the other. Too often in the past, there has been a separation between abstract theory and empirical work on the subject; and, in particular, there has been little effort to relate work on coalitional behaviour to the study of party systems in Western Europe.

This collection of theoretical or comparative chapters and national case-studies presents and applies an inductive model for coalitional behaviour in the form of a multi-dimensional framework based on the hypothesis of political parties as the central actors in coalition politics. These dimensions are as follows: historical, institutional, motivational, horizontal/vertical (including centre-periphery relations), internal party, socio-political and environmental/external. They both elaborate those aspects most examined by previous research, and also draw attention to neglected variables in coalition politics. In developing this approach, the book aims at encouraging a new direction in work on coalitional behaviour by focussing on it as a continuous and dynamic process rather than one confined to the formation of coalitions as well as at helping to overcome the isolation of coalition studies. It also broaches the virtually unexplored field of local coalitional behaviour and includes neglected country studies like Spain, France and also Italy. Some of the contributors have long been involved in work on coalition theory, while nearly all of them have been engaged in research on their countries' party systems or coalition politics independently of this volume.

T0381625

Edited by
GEOFFREY PRIDHAM

Coalitional behaviour in theory and practice:
an inductive model for Western Europe

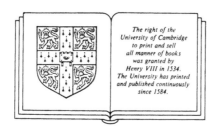

The right of the
University of Cambridge
to print and sell
all manner of books
was granted by
Henry VIII in 1534.
The University has printed
and published continuously
since 1584.

CAMBRIDGE UNIVERSITY PRESS

Cambridge
London   New York   New Rochelle
Melbourne   Sydney

CAMBRIDGE UNIVERSITY PRESS
Cambridge, New York, Melbourne, Madrid, Cape Town, Singapore,
São Paulo, Delhi, Dubai, Tokyo

Cambridge University Press
The Edinburgh Building, Cambridge CB2 8RU, UK

Published in the United States of America by Cambridge University Press, New York

www.cambridge.org
Information on this title: www.cambridge.org/9780521125567

First published 1986
This digitally printed version 2009

A catalogue record for this publication is available from the British Library

Library of Congress Cataloguing in Publication data

Coalitional behaviour in theory and practice.
Includes bibliographies and index.
1. Political parties – Europe – Addresses, essays,
lectures. 2. Coalition governments – Europe – Addresses,
essays, lectures. I. Pridham, Geoffrey, 1942–
JN94.A979C63   1986   324.24   86–23260

ISBN 978-0-521-30537-2 Hardback
ISBN 978-0-521-12556-7 Paperback

Contents

Illustration

Tables

Notes on the contributors

Patricia Brearey is currently researching into West German local politics in the School of European Studies at the University of Bradford.

David Broughton is currently completing his doctoral thesis on the impact of religion upon voting patterns in the Federal Republic of Germany and Canada at the University of Essex. He has also studied at the Universities of Sussex, Konstanz and Strathclyde. Amongst his current interests are the liberal parties of Western Europe, general comparative politics and survey research methodology.

Eric C. Browne is Professor of Political Science at the University of Wisconsin, Milwaukee. He has published articles in many scholarly journals, including the *American Political Science Review*, the *American Journal of Political Science*, the *British Journal of Political Science*, *Comparative Politics* and *Comparative Political Studies*. He is coeditor and a contributor to the anthology *Government Coalitions in Western Democracies*, and his research interests centre on coalition theory and behaviour and the stability of cabinet governments.

Jordi Capo Giol is Full Professor of Constitutional Law and Political Science in the University of Barcelona. He studied at this University, reaching the degree of Doctor in Law (1981), and completed his training at the Institut d'Etudes Politiques in Paris.
   He has published *Partits i parlamentaris a la Catalunya d'avui (1977–1979)* (1980, written in collaboration) and *La institucionalización de las Cortes Generales* (1983), besides numerous articles in specialised books and reviews like *Revista de Estudios Políticos* and *Revista Española de Sociología*.

John Fitzmaurice works in Brussels and has written widely on European politics. Among his several books are *The Party Groups in the European Parliament* (1975), *The European Parliament* (1978), *Politics in Denmark* (1981) and *The Politics of Belgium* (1983).

Dennis W. Gleiber is Assistant Professor of Political Science at Memphis State University. His research interests include comparative political behaviour and research methodology. His publications include articles in the *British Journal of Political Science* and *Publius*.

Michael D. Higgins, Statutory Lecturer in Political Science and Sociology in University College, Galway. Chairman of the Irish Labour party since 1978, he has been a member of parliament for Galway West and currently represents the National University of Ireland in Seanad Eireann

He is the author of a number of articles on clientelism, migration and social policy. He has studied at the National University of Ireland in Galway, Indiana University and Manchester University.

Ursula Hoffmann-Lange. Member of the Faculty of Social Sciences, University of Mannheim, since 1980, and formerly study director, Zentrum für Umfragen, Methoden and Analysen, Mannheim. Her interests are elite research and political parties in the field of political sociology, and she is co-author of *Konsens und Konflikt zwischen Führungsgruppen in der Bundesrepublik Deutschland* (with Helga Neumann and Bärbel Steinkemper). She now teaches at the University of Texas at Austin.

Jan M. de Jong is Assistant Professor at the Department of Public Administration of the Erasmus University in Rotterdam (Netherlands). His main publications are on political parties and the Dutch party system. One of the topics he is currently doing research on concerns the impact of party politics on (energy) policies in the Netherlands.

Emil Kirchner has been a lecturer in the Department of Government at the University of Essex since 1974. He is the director of the MA programme in Western European politics and amongst his recent publications are *The European Parliament: performance and prospects* (1984) and *Public Service Unions and the European Community* (1983). His interests focus on the European Community, especially the parliament, German and French politics and theories of political integration.

Michael Laver is Professor of Political Science and Sociology at University College, Galway. He is author of several books, and a range of articles on rational-choice theories of politics, coalitions and party competition. He is currently coordinating an international project involving the empirical analysis of government coalition policy in Europe.

Colin Mellors is Senior Lecturer in Politics in the School of European Studies at the University of Bradford. He is author of *The British MP* (1978) and, besides his work on local coalitions, is currently interested in the subjects of privacy and data protection, and military conscription and conscientious objection. He has published on these and other subjects in contributions to books and academic journals, including *Parliamentary Affairs*, *Political Quarterly*, *Public Administration* and *West European Politics*.

Bert Pijnenburg was a member of the Department of Political and Social Sciences at the University Institution of Antwerp (Belgium) until 1980. Since 1981 he has been attached as Assistant Professor to the Department of Political Science at the Erasmus University in Rotterdam, Netherlands. His present research is focussed on political participation at the grass-roots level (particularly its subculture-related dimension and the social movement type of behaviour). Recent publications have been centred around the problems of pillarisation and deconfessionalisation of Catholics and Protestants in present-day Dutch politics.

Geoffrey Pridham. Reader in European Politics at Bristol University.

His books include *Christian Democracy in Western Germany: the CDU/CSU in government and opposition, 1945–1976* (1977), *Transnational Party Cooperation and European Integration: the process towards direct elections* (1981), *The Nature of the Italian Party System: a regional case-study* (1981) and (editor) *The New Mediterranean Democracies: regime transition in Spain, Greece and Portugal* (1984).

He is writing a book on *Political Parties and Coalitional Behaviour in Italy: an interpretative study* (to be published by Croom Helm). Further work is in the fields of Italian politics, comparative Mediterranean studies and comparative coalitional behaviour in Western Europe.

Chris Rudd. Lecturer in Politics at the University of Essex. He is currently carrying out doctoral research on the Belgian party system. He has published articles in such journals as the *European Journal for Political Research*, *Political Quarterly* and *Electoral Studies*.

Preface

This volume is the outcome of the workshop on 'Political Parties and Coalitional Behaviour in Western Europe' held during the sessions of the European Consortium for Political Research (ECPR) at Salzburg in April 1984. More long-term, the idea for the workshop originated in the approach being developed for my own work on Italy and in an interest in testing this cross-nationally. The detailed framework included as an appendix to the first chapter specifies the various concepts and hypotheses that have influenced this approach; and it is the seven dimensions itemised in this framework that have acted as guidelines in revising the contributions to this book.

In carrying through this project, the principal intention has not been to present only another study of coalitions in Western Europe but rather to attempt something more ambitious by taking a fresh look at coalition theory in the light of coalition experience, and using this multi-dimensional framework as applied to the West European area for interpreting the dynamics of coalitional behaviour as a whole. Inevitably, in view of the – now more recognised – complexities of the subject, such an approach has to be inductive in its methodological design. While traditional coalition theories, first and foremost deductive or formal in style, have been important in pioneering work in this field and are still relevant, particularly in evaluating motivation in coalition formation, they have increasingly been found insufficient for handling these complexities. The main problem therefore has been to incorporate into coalition studies other important determinants or variables of coalitional behaviour that have rarely or not at all been considered previously, while at the same time structuring this broader view of the subject in a reasonably coherent way. Our theoretical framework seeks to accommodate these different aspects of coalitional behaviour more or less comprehensively, allowing comparative lessons to be derived systematically from country case-studies. Its point of departure is to acknowledge that the subject is inherently a complex one, and that above all it must be regarded as a continuous process and not one confined to selected points of time. We have attempted in short to relate theoretical approaches to the reality of coalition politics, and in doing so to avoid the pure abstraction of the formal theories on the one hand and the over-descriptiveness of some of the empirical work on the other.

An overriding requirement in coalition studies has been to overcome their relative isolation from other fields of political science and most notably comparative government. It goes without saying that coalition politics is central to many standard problems of comparative government, such as the nature of political authority and the power configuration, decision-making, ideology and even the stability of systems ultimately in some cases. There have in fact been signs, though only recently, of fresh thinking along these lines – and this is reviewed in the first chapter of the present book – especially when interest has focussed on the need for taking into consideration contextual factors in coalitional behaviour. But progress has been slow, not least because work on this subject has encountered the absence in the past of much fruitful co-operation between systems analysis broadly speaking, mathematical modelling and empirical or specialist research on coalition politics.

However, if the answer is for more elaborate and systematic inductive theorising about coalitional behaviour, it cannot pass without mention that this method has so far been marked by analytical weaknesses and in particular by looseness of construction. In this present study, the multi-dimensional frame-work adopted has deliberately concentrated on the role of political parties as coalition actors within the wider context of the party systems in which they operate, seeing that parties are individually and collectively the central intermediary channel between state and society in the kind of liberal democracies we are examining. It follows from this line of enquiry that advantage should be taken of insights and lessons from work on West European party systems, thereby helping to close the gap between this area which has progressed significantly in recent times and coalition studies which have not essentially kept pace with this development. Furthermore, given the various pitfalls of comparative politics as we know it, this project has opted for an area study frame of reference with Western Europe and its equivalent cross-national political patterns offering manageable scope for dealing with the complexities of coalitional behaviour. This work has been exploratory and does not claim to be definitive. Nevertheless, we hope to broaden and deepen coalition studies and to promote a new direction in current and future research. For this reason, this volume also includes two research notes at the end by way of drawing attention to ongoing theoretical work on the subject by participants in the original workshop.

The structure of this book is straightforward, consisting of some theoretical or comparative chapters with the large part being devoted to national case-studies.

The first chapter argues and elaborates the inductive theoretical framework, while the second chapter examines in broad terms the merits and demerits of the standing formal coalition theories. Subsequent chapters apply the multi-dimensional framework, which was revised in the light of the workshop proceedings, allowing for flexibility in treating country-specific conditions. Historically, this project has given prior consideration to developments in coalitional behaviour since the later 1960s in line with our interest in relating these to important changes in West European party systems in the period up to the present time, while not losing sight of how these developments compare with earlier post-war patterns of coalition politics in the countries in question.

This volume draws on new material and sources in the various chapters, several utilising survey findings, others elite interviews, while generally benefiting from historical and journalistic accounts. Where relevant, too, the chapters take note of the state of literature on coalitional behaviour in the given country and what interpretative lines this has presented. This volume also broaches the virtually unexplored comparative field of local coalitional behaviour and includes neglected country studies like Spain, France and Italy. Some of the contributors – namely, Michael Laver and Eric C. Browne – have been long involved in work on coalition theory, while virtually all of them have been engaged in research on their countries' party systems or coalition politics independently of this project. The workshop at Salzburg also benefited from the participation of others – Ian Budge, Luigi Graziano and Hans van Mierlo – whose contributions on this subject have been published elsewhere.

Geoffrey Pridham
Bristol, May 1985

I   An inductive theoretical framework for coalitional behaviour: political parties in multi-dimensional perspective in Western Europe

(a) The importance of multi-dimensional approaches in coalition analysis

Coalition studies are strongly in need of rethinking in terms of theoretical approaches, particularly with respect to contextual factors which influence behaviour. This is a very basic need because of the long neglect of such factors in empirical research on this subject despite their obvious importance in political reality. The pioneering theoretical frameworks for the analysis of coalition formation developed in the 1960s and early 1970s, while certainly still useful in pointing directions in coalition studies, have increasingly been found inadequate for handling the complexities of this subject. These were based on simple and direct applications of mathematical models of n-person game theory. Already, some attempt has recently been made to satisfy the demand for new and systematic knowledge, especially on Western Europe, such as by the welcome volumes edited by Eric C. Browne and John Dreijmanis and by Vernon Bogdanor.[1] Although these tend to question the applicability of the formal coalition theories, they do not really seek to think anew theoretical approaches in any comprehensive way.

This deficiency is not for lack of any indications about how to pursue such an endeavour, as discussed below in the relevant literature on political parties. From this it emerges that any reworking of coalition theory should be multi-dimensional in approach, and that it should in particular focus on linkages between coalition politics and theories of party systems, seeing that political parties have always been acknowledged by coalition theorists as the central actors in the game. Apart from some specific examples, this general question of linkages – of seeing coalitional behaviour in its broader context, as it were – has not been really explored by the body of theory on the subject. It is, indeed, the intention of this present volume to develop such an interpretative approach on an inductive basis. In doing so, we acknowledge and draw on the results of previous formal or deductive theories of coalition formation, but attempt to broaden and deepen the scope of coalition analysis, taking account of important variables not considered by previous theories. In short, our aim is to develop a framework that catches the dynamics of coalitional behaviour as a whole, and indeed to promote coalition studies in this direction rather than merely by way of further refinements of the lines so far developed by the formal theories.

While these formal theories have had the merit of focussing on certain obviously key components of coalition politics and have been ambitious in their theoretical exercise of testing assumptions against a wide selection of cross-national data, achieving some level of predictive success, it is evident that they fail to take account of a range of variables or determinants of coalitional behaviour highlighted by studies of party systems, where these have pointed towards the problems of decision-making processes in political parties. These include questions of a structural and societal nature, a recognition of the influence of party development or history as well as of internal party relationships on political behaviour and, particularly, a greater appreciation of the effect of different forms of motivation and ideology. The principal problem with the original coalition theories has been that they are too formalistic and too limiting in their conceptual handling of political processes, deriving expectations related to the allocation of payoffs and the composition of cabinets. Moreover, they are too static in their analytical approach, paying little attention to developments within inter-electoral periods. In other words, the formal theories have tended to be essentially uni-dimensional. This is true especially of the original mathematical modelling which gave birth to coalition theorising, with the size factor in coalitions as their point of departure. At best, they have been bi-dimensional since some of the policy-based theories have combined size with ideology. The formal theories have also tended to be predominantly if not exclusively predictive in their purpose, so that perhaps inevitably simplistic and also unrealistic concepts about political parties have habitually influenced their analysis. This is less likely to occur in a multi-dimensional approach based on an inductive mode of reasoning extrapolated from the functioning of party systems, where one salient and really crucial consideration, for instance, must be variation in types of parties.

Altogether, it may be said that, while the study of party systems and of individual political parties has advanced significantly as a central area in the growth of professional political science since the 1960s, coalition studies have not essentially kept pace with this development. This is not least because they have remained strictly outside the scope of the analysis of party systems, with its general concern with the dynamics of party development and system stability and change, precise testing of new typologies and insights from research findings on mass attitudes and other behavioural problems. What is particularly surprising is the minimal treatment, if not virtual neglect, of questions of coalition politics, alliance strategy and inter-party relationships altogether in comparative politics texts, not to mention those specifically devoted to party systems.[2] This is despite the fact that coalitional behaviour is central to so many basic concerns of comparative government, such as the organisation of political authority, decision-making, ideology, the power configuration and even the stability of systems as such.

Only recently, this isolation of coalition studies and their particular deficiencies of approach have been identified more as an imperative concern. This is an outcome of a late revival of interest in coalitional studies, but also of some new thinking about problems of change in West European party systems. Klaus von Beyme (1983) has emphasised that 'research on coalitions on the basis of game theory has not come to grips with the peculiarities of European party systems, since it has started out from American assumptions of a system where all the relevant groups are seen to have "allgemeine Koalitionsfähigkeit" and to calculate in a rational way the advantages of forming coalitions'.[3] More generally, Lawrence Dodd has argued in a collection of new approaches to the study of cabinet coalitions (1984) that the increasing effort to 'focus on the real politics that underlie cabinet behaviour' is useful and long overdue, and that it is necessary to integrate coalition theory and the analysis of party systems 'with a broader and deeper understanding of cabinet politics'.[4] Influences from the relatively new area of policy studies also seem to have contributed to this recent awareness of the need for a fresh approach to coalition research. Above all, policy studies are relevant here as they have emphasised the dynamics of the political system in different decision situations and furthermore the importance of the environment as a source of constraints on decision-makers as well as for examining the interaction between structural variables and the political process. Notably, there has been much debate in the literature on policy studies about the relative impact of structural features (socio-economic variables) as against political variables or day-to-day dynamic processes on policy outcomes.[5]

The overriding need, therefore, is for a dynamic framework in which to analyse coalitional behaviour, given that the formal theories have been static in their outlook (on this, see the following chapter by Laver). It is also important, consequently, that coalition formation and coalition maintenance should above all be seen together as one continuous process. It is only in the past few years that attention in the subject has begun to shift away from the traditional and somewhat exclusive interest in coalition formation to coalition duration or durability,[6] with some attempt to readjust coalition theories to this change. The volume on new approaches on this subject edited by Lijphart centred attention on the question of cabinet durability, though primarily at the level of parliamentary politics.[7] Similarly, Browne and Gleiber have begun to develop an 'events' approach to the problem of cabinet stability, using a stochastic model for assessing coalition persistence, performance and dissolution. Their research programme is described in the second research note at the end of this book, while their own case-study here of one coalition government in the French Fourth Republic applies this approach. This 'events' approach is an important undertaking in the direction of relating both formation and maintenance, by placing the question of cabinet stability within the larger context of conditions which lead to the achievement of stability for democratic regimes, and by recognising here the influence of socio-cultural factors as well as balancing environmental demands with government responses.[8] This programme does, nevertheless, entail a monumental task in the collection of 'events' data (on which see research note at the end).

This requirement for assessing coalitional behaviour as a continuous process makes the deliberate inclusion of time as an essential variable quite compelling. Such reasoning has begun to appear in the discussion of coalition theories, and is of course crucial in steering coalition research away from the static approach of the formal theories. There is also the special historical aspect of the time variable, whereby past coalitional experiences or more generally the prior state of inter-party relationships may be said to weigh in the balance of coalitional decisions. An interesting development of this perspective is the familiarity and inertia index advanced by Franklin and Mackie.[9] They suggest that successive formation outcomes in a given country may not, in reality, be totally independent events in which size and ideology have the opportunity of acting *de novo*; rather they should be viewed as part of an historical sequence, and that ideological affinity may be perceived in the light of past government co-operation. In other words, ideological similarities might be contaminated by familiarity through parties building up experience of governing in different combinations with each other. (The concept of inertia follows from this as it tends to favour continuity, for once a coalitional option is established it may require considerable effort to change it.) Overall, this historical angle on coalitional behaviour is considered of sufficient importance to incorporate it as one of the seven dimensions discussed in this book.

(b)   Coalitional behaviour dynamics and the study of party systems: establishing contextual linkages

The multi-dimensional framework adopted by this book has been constructed around the hypothesis of political parties as the central dynamic actors in coalition politics as follows (this is set out at the end of this chapter; see 'The multi-dimensional framework: political parties and coalitional behaviour in Western Europe: guidelines based on workshop proceedings'): historical, institutional, motivational, horizontal/vertical, internal party, socio-political and environmental/external. Since the need, as already noted, is to explore and analyse the dynamics of coalition politics as a continuous process, the role of political parties is seen as providing the key to this approach. Such an hypothesis is in line with previous coalition theories, whether formal or inductive, as well as consistent with the nature of the political systems in Western Europe as forms of 'party government'. Bearing in mind, furthermore, that it is essential for any new approach in coalition theory to consider contextual influences on coalitional behaviour, it follows that political parties should be viewed not merely as individual actors here but as actors operating within given party systems, and for that matter wider environments. In other words, seeing that parties are the primary linkage between the political system and society in liberal democracies in addition to being the political base and reference point of decision-makers, it becomes unavoidable for any analysis of coalitional dynamics not to assess this within the context of party systems as a whole. Admittedly, party systems invariably do not transmit let alone account for all the external demands or influences which impinge on decision-makers in coalition politics – take, for instance, those deriving from the social, economic or international environment – but they do provide the most viable starting-point and basis for constructing the necessary comparative framework. This multi-dimensional framework is discussed directly in the next section, but first of all we present the reasoning behind it.

Since formal theories are largely static and focus on only certain, albeit important, features of coalition politics, such a multi-dimensional approach needs to be inductive. While the formal theories have given most attention to office-holding, they have, however, been particularly fruitful in identifying and predicting problems of policy distance between coalition or coalescent partners. Additionally, as Laver argues in the following chapter, there are various generalisable phenomena that might be brought within the scope of formal theories, such as a more flexible definition of working majorities to include, for example, minority governments, the trade-off between office-seeking and policy-seeking, and the effects of electoral feedback (notably through opinion polls) on bargaining power. But there is a whole range of dynamic factors in coalitional behaviour – seen in reality as it were – which relates to what Ian Budge has called 'the richness and complexity of decisions made by leaders at crucial historical junctures',[10] or for that matter too on more routine occasions. To mention only some, apart from those just indicated: the very dynamics of coalition relations as a continuous process within the life of a given cabinet, namely accumulated experience; the impact of policy decisions during the same time period and the need to differentiate more between various policy areas rather than talking blandly about 'policy distance'; changing issue priorities and, more broadly, changing party strategic goals during a legislative period; the dynamics of internal relationships within individual parties, such as the changing positions of leaders and changing balance between factions; and, generally, the dynamics of party development, notably the rising and declining fortunes of parties within party systems and changes in their constituencies. While there is clearly room for national and even individual party variation on such questions, these various dynamics factors broadly confirm the essential role of political parties in studying coalitional behaviour.

An inductive theory should therefore have the merit of offering substantially more scope than the formal theories in dealing with the complexities of our subject. The potential weakness, however, of inductive theorising is that, compared with the formal theories, they may lack scientific rigour; and this is broadly true of inductive theorising on coalitions up to the present time (some of these are discussed below in this chapter). At the same time, given growing scepticism about the scientific value of much traditional comparative work, in particular over its inadequate conceptualisation, problems of equivalent hard information between different countries, analytical flaccidity, deficiencies of contextual awareness in dealing with a wide range of background variables and, generally, the looseness of wide-ranging cross-national approaches, there is a strong case here for adopting the area studies method. Macridis and Cox have pointed out that 'one approach to the study of comparative politics is the more systematic and precise use of the area concept', provided that 'if the concept of an area is to be operationally meaningful for the purpose of comparison, it should correspond to some uniform political patterns against which differences may be studied comparatively and explained'.[11] In short, Western Europe provides exactly such an area study framework because of the various similarities of the liberal democracies within it. Furthermore, with reference to our subject, so much of the empirical work carried out so far has in any case concentrated on the West European area because of the multiplicity of examples there.[12]

For our purposes here, West European democracies are seen as essentially party-orientated and party-motivated. The description of these systems as cases of 'party government' or even as 'party democracies' comes from the decisive role played by parties in formulating and deciding policy as well as in mobilising popular support for their proposals and actions, thereby acting implicitly or explicitly as crucial agents of system stability. Clearly, this working hypothesis has to be modified for those systems in Western Europe which are semi-presidential, such as France, Finland and post-revolution Portugal. All the same, in the national case-studies examined in this volume some account is taken where applicable of the possibility of influence over coalition politics of agents other than political parties, such as Ursula Hoffmann-Lange's inclusion of 'non-political' elites in her analysis of changing coalitional preferences in the Federal Republic of Germany. In general, such other elites (especially economic ones) are seen as enjoying influence via political elites rather than exercising power, so that neo-corporatist tendencies are really indirect as a factor in coalition politics. There is also the special case of local politics, which as a comparative area is completely new in coalition studies. Some modification to this hypothesis about the centrality of parties in the coalition game has to be made for this level of politics, a problem discussed by Mellors and Brearey with regard to degrees of politicisation and partisanship locally. More generally, the debate in recent times about a trend towards mass disaffection from parties in Western Europe might at first appear to call into question this hypothesis: however, in fact, actual evidence for such a basic change has been found at best unclear.[13]

Turning, therefore, to the study of party systems in Western Europe, what are the main lessons or relevant insights to be drawn for elaborating an inductive framework for coalitional behaviour? Taking comparative work as a whole, certain important but really obvious points quickly come to mind: that political parties tend intrinsically to be complex entities, hence multi-faceted requiring multi-dimensional treatment; the need for differentiation between types of political parties, ideologically, organisationally and sociologically; and, that political parties are more than just institution-bound actors, and in particular must be considered also as socio-political forces. This already questions in a basic way the rather simplistic concepts of 'political party' adopted by the formal theories. For these theories, parties have often been considered merely a feature of the size factor so that attention has dwelt on such matters as whether certain parties should be excluded from theory testing on grounds of smallness. It follows that the primary question of what constitutes a 'political party' for the purpose of coalition studies should be viewed and approached more comprehensively.

Referring to older comparative studies of party systems, these constructed grand-scale models which attempted to explain the dynamics of party development. The traditional numerical approaches, with their dichotomising between two-party and multi-party systems, had not really provided this for they tended themselves to be static, although Sartori's thesis of polarised pluralism and subsequent work[14] did draw attention to the dynamics of ideological divides. Conventional comparative texts emphasised the variety of functions performed by parties and sought to categorise these, e.g. leadership recruitment, policy generation, control of government organs and societal integration. Their conclusion, implicit or explicitly developed, was that these various functions evidently interacted. For instance, Apter (1963), in a text summarising work on party systems up to that time, identified three main relationships followed by parties: with the state, with society and those between parties themselves.[15] The last of these relationships included such components as party competition, the management of conflict by leaders, ideological compatibility and polarisation, but clearly these could well affect variables relating to the other two relationships, such as social cleavages and the setting and attaining of goals in government. More interestingly, Easton's analysis of political systems looking at interrelated components and processes (inputs or demands and support, aggregation and regulation, outputs) was useful in attempting a more systematic explanation of the relationship between state and society, with parties seen as the crucial 'gatekeepers' in liberal democracies. In particular, he underlined the importance of environment or 'the obvious fact that a system does not exist in a vacuum'.[16]

Thus, even from examining traditional comparative work on party systems, the deficiencies of the formal coalition theories become highlighted.

If this is so, what then does the more sophisticated work since the 1960s on party systems in Western Europe offer specifically? Somewhat in contrast with the fifties and sixties when European party systems had been viewed as inherently stable,[17] the main overarching theme since then has been change in these systems; and hence research has attempted more directly than before to investigate the intricacies of party system dynamics. The literature on party politics in contemporary Europe has, however, while recognising basic changes, failed to form a clear consensus on its exact nature and significance. Some have simply emphasised a 'de-freezing' of traditional cleavages; others have assessed more comprehensively the possibilities of party system transformation; while still others have talked about a challenge to parties *per se*.[18] Although important work has been carried out on particular aspects of party systems – above all, on voting behaviour and societal change, but also on ideology and spatial models of party competition as well as to some extent on party identification – more comprehensive work on party system dynamics has really been lacking. As Pedersen has noted, 'it is hard to come to grips with static as well as dynamic relationships in party systems; conceptual frameworks, classifications and typologies abound; so do configurative studies; but what it is that makes party systems "tick" still largely belongs to the unchartered part of the political science field'.[19] In encouraging a dynamic model of party system change, he comments that

> there exists a complex and intricate relationship between the various dimensions of the party system format. The format contains not only mechanical predispositions in Sartorian terms, but an internal mechanic as well. However, this mechanic is not very well understood, at least not in multi-party systems. But change in the party system cannot and should not be understood only in terms of these factors. After all, change in real-life electoral politics is made by individuals who change their behaviour.[20]

If this difficulty continues to face the broader area of the study of party systems, it should be no great surprise that wider considerations of party system dynamics, particularly of the multi-party version, have hardly influenced coalition studies if they have been acknowledged at all.[21] Accordingly, such basic changes as have occurred in West European party systems since the 1960s have not really entered the domain of coalition theory, e.g. the effects of economic recession and government overload, territorial change, crises of participation, challenges to party dominance and the emergence of new parties as well as questions relating to system stability. Only Dodd (1976) has really attempted to introduce problems like cleavage conflict as affecting cabinet stability into coalition studies (discussed below in the third section).

Equally, few attempts to theorise about these new perspectives of party systems have weighed their possible relevance to coalition politics. Only recently, Panebianco's *Modelli di Partito* (1982), aiming at reviving organisational approaches to party development – which he sees as not having progressed much since Michels and Duverger – argued that this should proceed by focussing on the interaction between internal party dynamics and the environment.[22] Only too aware of the complexities of party behaviour and concerned to emphasise the reality rather than formality of party structures, Panebianco among other things related the politics of alliances specifically to internal party dynamics (organisational stability, the 'exchange relationship' between leaders and followers and party identity), as well as to more recognised determinants such as electoral competition.[23] He pointed out that coalitional relationships may have destabilising effects on party organisation in addition to the latter exerting possible constraints on the former. In other words, there is a two-way relationship of inter-party/intra-party determinants which is worth exploring in theoretical and empirical research on coalition politics. Panebianco argued furthermore that paradoxically the more stable alliances are likely to occur between opponents (those who are ideologically distant) rather than competitors (ideologically close and rivals for the same constituency).[24] Developed from his organisational perspective, this is at a general level a debatable point subject of course to empirical testing, though it usefully throws sceptical light on traditional coalition theorists' use of the ideological proximity model. But most important of all, Panebianco was rightly concerned with analysing the politics of alliances within the wider environment.

The view in this present study is that important changes in West European party systems since the 1960s themselves may be incorporated with no great difficulty in an inductive framework drawing on the analysis of party systems. For instance, the increase in electoral volatility, the greater challenge to established parties in this time of economic recession and reduced governmental performance each hold important implications for coalitional behaviour; and it is relevant to consider how far they may enter the calculations of coalition actors. It is also reasonable to assume that such changes in party systems – whether involving a trend away from political parties as such or not – may well emphasise the need for these actors to look beyond 'winning' the 'present game'. On a separate point, they have also been useful in drawing attention to the possibility of constraints on decision-makers in coalition politics, for the formal theories have always been implicitly if not unequivocally elitist in their assumptions (implicitly so at least in their acceptance of parties as unitary actors). Important changes like these in West European party systems have of course reduced further the general relevance of the formal coalition theories. In the view, again, of Klaus von Beyme in his analysis of governments, parliaments and the structure of power in political parties in Western Europe, 'recent changes in the party systems, the rise of new parties and the development of new patterns of oppositional behaviour have weakened the ability of formal coalition theories to predict outcomes successfully'. This is because in his view polarisation of the major components of some party systems in Western Europe 'makes most of the theoretically possible coalitions – which according to coalition theory increase with the number of parties – politically impossible', where 'even coalitions that are considered as politically possible by the elites sometimes are resisted from the grass-roots'.[25] Such broader or environmental considerations are included in the approach of this book, and are highlighted for instance in those chapters dealing with the impact of the changing cleavage structure on coalition politics in Belgium, of depillarisation on the pivotal role of the Christian Democrats in the Netherlands and also of recent public disillusionment with the established parties in Italy.

Finally, in identifying relevant contextual linkages for an inductive approach to coalitional behaviour, what specialist expertise can be utilised from recent research on West European political parties? Generally speaking, the main developments in the study of party systems have derived from the field of political sociology. Indeed, 'change' has been construed as first and foremost electoral change. However, despite the study of electoral data achieving much methodological sophistication, there has been virtually no attempt to assimilate insights or knowledge from this into coalition research.[26] This may well be a consequence of psephology being an autonomous sub-field of political science, thus confirming the separateness noted earlier between comparative politics and coalition theory, the latter having subsumed elections or rather simply their results as part of majority-building resources. Yet in reality, it really goes without saying, electoral considerations are usually a prime consideration among political elites in liberal democracies – sometimes intermittently, but usually as a regular concern. As Laver notes in the next chapter, the effect of electoral feedback may be incorporated comfortably in any dynamic theory of coalitional behaviour. Seeing, however, that actual or prospective electoral behaviour can interact with other possible determinants of coalition politics (e.g. perceived policy impact, internal party morale and the current standing of party leaders), it follows that an inductive framework is the most viable method for handling the complexity of such situations.

An important feature of this problem of electoral dynamics on which some work has now been carried out in the form of spatial models is party competition. These offer a healthy antidote to the static assumptions about policy distance of the formal theories. As Budge has commented about the left–right continuum with regard to Western Europe: 'Usually these assumed orderings are taken as fixed over the whole postwar period, a heroic but unrealistic assumption given the vast political changes since 1945.'[27] But research on competitive behaviour between parties was altogether slow in developing,[28] so that the possible influence of such work on parties for coalition studies has only recently begun to be explored. And, for that matter, there are still aspects of party competition as such hardly investigated, notably the relationship between political agenda setting (as in coalition politics) and the dynamics of party competition.[29] The research project on party manifestos (see Research Note by Michael Laver at the end of this volume) is, therefore, an important attempt to measure systematically policy closeness as independent from coalition policy within multi-dimensional spaces (often left–right but also religious, urban/rural and others more complex), and in doing so to chart changing policy distances between parties over time.

Following directly from this is the basic problem of ideology which has been insufficiently developed as a variable in coalition studies. Or rather, definitions of it have hardly moved beyond bland generalisations so that benefit could clearly be drawn here from systematic work on party systems. The latter has admittedly encountered its own difficulties of definition, and consequently much confusion has remained over the concept of ideology. In applying lessons to coalitional behaviour, the relationship between ideology and policy-making is most relevant, especially with work focussing on the frameworks used for defining problems as well as solving them.[30] There has, in fact, been some fresh thinking about this complex problem with direct reference to coalitional behaviour. Recognising the need for a more subtle handling of this question, Boute's subjective policy distance approach argues that De Swaan's policy distance theory based on the proximity between the issue preferences of adjacent coalescent partners is very restrictive because of its assumption that every actor has the same subjectivity (objective ordering). According to Boute, 'to describe a real world political situation using only the actors' weight and their position on a unidimensional ordinal scale is, at best, a very rough representation of reality'. He therefore suggests a model of subjective policy distance based on 'distance' as being very relative and assuming that different actors do not necessarily have the same perception of parties' (and coalitions') relative positions on an ordinal policy scale. This also takes account of the fact that the positions of some coalitions are left indeterminate.[31] In a review of the main findings of studies on West European parties, Ian Budge has proposed a comparative framework for explaining party behaviour in government to 'capture at least some of the complexities of actual decisions', adopting as central postulate the pursuit of specific policy objectives by politicians in place of starting with 'over-sophisticated notions of space and policy-distance'.[32] At a more concrete level, Panebianco stresses the importance of measuring the effective impact of ideology in relation to other factors given its determining influence on party organisational development, notably in furnishing the symbolic resources of party identity and in shaping the external image of a party – a point that might well be taken over by coalition research. Overall, the main lesson from the study of party systems concerning ideology is that it is essential for this to be handled differentiatedly in its effect on both coalition formation *and* maintenance.

Theoretical work on party structures and internal party processes is, by comparison, much less advanced, although some insights are available for coalition studies, especially from current research.[33] So far as theorising has offered any advantage for examining this dimension of coalitional behaviour, it has been over the question of leadership and specifically of elite control.

Leadership has been to the forefront of the theories about consociational democracy which have concentrated on the question of elite control against the background of cleavage bridging. Such theories have of late been taken to task in the light of cleavage change in party systems since the 1960s, but also because they have been posited on a somewhat one-way view of elite dominance.[34] Nevertheless, for constructing an inductive approach to coalitional behaviour they have demonstrated the need to consider the quality itself of leadership, vertical links in leader–follower relationships and also leadership in relation to societal factors. As Pappalardo has written, in a review of consociational democracy theories, cleavage change and the de-stabilisation this may bring have given rise to the situation where 'the process of coalition formation between the developing and declining alignments has become very slow and cumbersome', so that laboriously constructed multi-party cabinets may well have a short duration and fail to secure elite co-operation.[35] In his recent book on models of political parties, Panebianco has attempted to develop organisational studies beyond Michels' rather simplistic theory of oligarchy, and in doing so has presented a more sceptical view of leadership.[36] He prefers the term 'dominant coalitions' to 'leadership', allowing for internal differences as well as the likelihood that leaders operate under some form of constraints and do not necessarily possess liberty of action. In particular, Panebianco talks about 'zones of uncertainty', notably in the environment, which are not automatically subject to control by elites.

Certain particular lessons emerge from this for coalition studies, such as variations in leadership control between parties, the rapidity or otherwise of party decision processes and, above all, the influence of factors other than formal structural procedures. For instance, the role of parliamentary parties in relation to party structures is one rather neglected in party research, but with important implications for leadership and indirectly for executive/legislative relations as well as for the question of political parties as unitary actors, which has been one of the main *a priori* assumptions of the formal coalition theories. While Duverger originally touched somewhat one-dimensionally on the relationship between parliamentary parties and their extra-parliamentary structures (whether the former predominated over the latter), Klaus von Beyme has argued that this relationship is more complex than commonly assumed.[37] He talks of a variety of factors affecting this power relationship, written party rules often being a misleading indicator here, and of the possibility of a shifting power balance within parties, drawing attention to the time dimension. Contrary to Duverger, he continues, the relationship between parliamentary party groups and their own structures 'is not a one-way road'; and there are even certain factors overarching this rather dichotomous relationship within parties and strengthening both sides simultaneously (such as the professionalisation of political elites, and also the increase in prime-ministerial power). Von Beyme concludes on this 'complicated network of influences' in the relationship:

> The distribution of power within the different bodies of the parties and its impact on parliament and government is an intervening variable, dependent on the type of party (bourgeois or socialist), on the party system (degree of fragmentation), on institutional

variables (such as the power of the head of state, parliamentary rules, party laws, incompatibility rules) and the relations between parties and pressure groups.[38]

We have here an acknowledgement both that any variable examination of executive/legislative relations may involve going beyond the parliamentary arena, and also that the question of leadership cannot be viewed too one-dimensionally.

Such structural problems have been something of a forgotten consideration too in coalition theory, though they must be seen as important variables for inclusion in any dynamic theory. Important new insights may also be drawn from the Mannheim project on middle-level elites in parties, based on cross-national survey data on attitudes among delegates to party congresses. Already, this has emphasised their conditional support for leadership (e.g. changes in alliance strategy may be perceived by them as threatening their positions and prospects), that leaders depend on middle-level elites for mobilisation and that the former have constantly to bear in mind their parties' relations with the overall political system.[39] Some of these ideas from the Mannheim project have been directly applied by Niedermeyer with respect to the West German case of coalitional change, where the top leaderships usually calculate about the relationship between parliamentary power and different levels within their own party structures. He emphasises the middle-level elites in the latter as an important intermediary channel affecting the ability of the leadership group to carry their party as a whole along strategic paths.[40] More comprehensive systematic work on decision-making within parties remains a relatively unresearched field, for aspects like membership participation and policy involvement[41] and other complexities of internal organisational life are potentially relevant for understanding coalitional behaviour.

In trying to relate party structures and internal party processes to coalition studies, the enduring question of parties as unitary actors cannot be avoided. Some reassessment of this is long overdue if only because it is one area where reality is seen to clash visibly with the formal theories, particularly if we analyse party structures in terms of different hierarchical divisions (on which see the chapter by Laver). As Daalder has commented, it is politically relevant to regard a party as a unitary actor under certain circumstances (e.g. presenting an election programme, deciding to enter a coalition following a decision to commit the entire party). However, he points out:

> in the actual world of politics it is hardly defensible to regard a party as a unitary actor ... even in the examples just given, there is bound to be disagreement, before the actual decision is taken, as well as on its later application in practice ... a decision on the investiture of a new coalition cabinet does not preempt a need for continuous decision-making on concrete decisions to follow.[42]

In similar vein, Budge has argued that most parties have clearly defined positions on which most of their members at least temporarily agree, as during coalition formations, but that in dealing with the functioning of governments over a full legislative period internal party differences or factions emerge whose existence affects the policies governments make.[43] Although faction politics usually does not push demands to the extent of ultimately jeopardising party unity, the individual policy preferences of factions are one interesting area for investigating coalitional behaviour, especially where they represent different interests and evaluate divergently coalition relationships with other parties. There is even a branch of empirical literature on party factionalism, some of which has related this in specialist work to alliance politics.[44] This has at least had the merit of underlining the existence where applicable of multiple and rival leadership groups with internal organised support.

From the foregoing discussion, it has become evident that the study of West European party systems – its various deficiencies notwithstanding – offers a range of different lessons and insights that promises to enrich the quality of coalition studies significantly. Altogether, this simply begs for the cross-fertilisation of approaches and methods between these two previously separate areas of research in political science, or at least for the direct application of results from work on political parties to that concerned with coalitional behaviour. Some progress has, as noted, recently been made in this fashion over specific aspects of coalition research, and there are signs of a new and general trend in this direction. It is perhaps no surprise that similar problems as in coalition studies of marrying theory with practice have also been present up till now in the study of party systems. Discussing the constant appearance of highly detailed studies of parties in different West European countries against the need for a theory which summarises their major findings, Ian Budge comes to the following conclusion:

> that a general theory of democratic party government is applicable to Western Europe and that the descriptive–institutional and formal theorising traditions are by no means opposed. Separate development has impoverished both. Theories have been too abstract to integrate detailed evidence satisfactorily, while descriptive research has lacked a broad framework within which to locate its findings.[45]

The same consideration should apply to new approaches in coalition theory.

(c)   An inductive theoretical framework for the analysis of coalitional behaviour

It follows from the hypothesis of political parties as the central dynamic actors in coalition politics and from the need to investigate their role here in terms of contextual linkages that an inductive theoretical framework is required. Indeed, it is imperative for handling the complexity of this subject in a viable and comprehensive way. Furthermore, seeing that it is crucial to construct such a framework around the dynamics of coalitional behaviour as a whole, this has above all to approach coalition politics as a continuous process (the time dimension) as well as focus on relevant contextual linkages. Obviously, the scope of this kind of inductive theorising is potentially very broad, for we are verging on the analysis of political systems as a whole albeit confined intentionally as here to liberal democracies in Western Europe. The decision has therefore been to formulate this inductive framework multi-dimensionally, revolving strictly around the role of political parties as coalition actors within the context of their party systems.

How do we arrive at the actual selection of the seven dimensions in this present study (see accompanying appendix at the end of this chapter)? Clearly, directions and insights from the preceding survey of analyses or theories of party systems are considered or incorporated in our framework, e.g. that parties are multi-faceted, performing a variety of different though often interrelated functions; that parties should be viewed as socio-political forces as well as institutional actors; and, above all, that coalition politics and inter-party relationships generally may well involve the role of parties as a whole, or at least it cannot be *assumed* at the outset that they do not. Such lessons are of course palpable to any student of party systems, although for that very reason it is compelling that they should be integrated into coalition theory. But there are various conceptual or definitional problems which require some clarification in presenting this inductive framework.

One straightforward hypothesis, which initially influenced this inductive approach in an attempt to relate theory and practice, emphasised that arithmetical considerations (the starting-point for so many formal theories) cannot be treated in isolation. That is, placing together the literature on party systems and previous coalition theory, it could be postulated that there is, broadly speaking, an interplay between this arithmetical variable and a series of political dimensions in coalitional behaviour, with the dynamics of this interplay in Western Europe revolving around the role of parties. While these arithmetical considerations refer simply to respective parties' strengths in a given legislature (usually the official point of departure for coalition negotiations), the political dimensions encompass a variety of determinants which may or may not be located within the institutional arena. In fact, several important ones are not. What is interesting in practice is the actual relationship between these arithmetical and political dimensions, for the distinction between the two can rarely be clear-cut. For instance, election results create arithmetical possibilities in the game of coalition options, but they may also be said to pronounce on the credibility of coalitional alternatives, depending presumably on the extent to which party leaders have stated any prior commitments or preferences. In short, political determinants can influence the arithmetical determinant, or be assumed to have done so; just as the arithmetical consideration might also create its own political pressures, forcing reluctant politicians into coalitions or allowing them to rationalise any new coalition positions they may adopt. It may be hypothesised, therefore, that what may be arithmetically possible is not necessarily politically feasible; equally, what may be politically desirable – on the part of intending coalition partners – may not always be arithmetically possible. On a specific point here, it is assumed there is a substantial and qualitative difference between party strategies on the one hand and actual coalitional behaviour on the other, with a variety of intervening variables, both arithmetical and political.

In addition, there is the definitional problem of what a 'coalition' is. This requires some elucidation because one particular consequence of looking at coalitional behaviour within the (complex) context of party systems is to induce some scepticism on this point, mainly since this cannot be divorced from the conceptual problem of what 'power' is. Somewhat in contrast with the formal coalition theories, which have concentrated on cabinet office-holding or on 'bargaining power' in coalition formation (particularly the 'resources' of parliamentary strength), the analysis of party systems warns us against employing 'power' as an unspecified umbrella term and calls attention to constraints on its use by politicians. One possibility is to adopt the familiar distinction between 'power' and 'influence'. But whatever the definition of the former, it is necessary to assess the exercise of power in the sense of policy formulation and policy-making on a continuous basis; and this involves political relationships more broadly than just those conducted within executive or legislative institutions. As Dahl has argued, power may be exercised in an implicit as well as direct way, through conviction as well as coercion.[46]

Formal coalition theories have taken account only of coalitions which are literally formal or 'governing'; i.e. cabinet membership being the exclusive criterion for the role of coalition actor. But 'informal' coalition or alliance arrangements have been sufficiently common, and in some countries increasingly so, for them to be deserving of inclusion. In Italy, variations of such 'informal' arrangements have been an intermittent practice in the whole post-war period, while in Scandinavia there has been a strong informal pattern in coalition-building drawing on behavioural norms, traditions of consensualism and a regular habit of issue-based alliances. Furthermore, in several countries examined in this book an anti-(formal) coalition outlook has been present in some parties, such as in Ireland, Scandinavia and to some extent Italy, which, as Fitzmaurice notes, is perverse from the point of view of traditional coalition theory. In Jordi Capo's detailed analysis of post-Franco Spain, we have a 'convergence' between parties expressed through the method of cross-party pacts during the constituent period and beyond in the interest of consolidating the new democracy there. While this may or may not in the course of Spanish democratic politics be seen as an exceptional period, this particular example was historic in its importance as an informal coalitional arrangement.

In general, behind such informal versions of coalitional behaviour there might be present a variety of motives, including a desire to influence cabinet policy without taking full or overt responsibility for it (for electoral or other reasons), an attempt to bridge ideological differences (notably in Italy), the determining influence of party history or ideology (as with the Labour parties in the UK and

Ireland), simply a calculated refusal to share power (Fianna Fail in Ireland), or the mutual recognition of an overriding national interest as in Spain. In the view of Lijphart, such informal arrangements make for an ambivalent meaning of coalition membership, entailing not only a definitional problem but also one with theoretical implications for the policy-based theories.[47] One usual answer has been to distinguish between 'exclusive coalitions' (i.e. formal ones) and 'legislative coalitions'; and a refinement of this is Laver's identification in the following chapter of 'stable voting coalitions' as against 'unstable voting coalitions', thus drawing attention to the quality of the informal arrangement in question. Altogether, it seems certain criteria have to be followed when assessing 'informal' coalitions, and these must relate to their policy effects. This is particularly as some of them have had a binding character, even though invariably less comprehensive than in the case of formal coalitions. To state the obvious, political parties are still the central actors in the former instance with many of the same factors relevant in these 'informal' versions of coalitional behaviour. Admittedly, some specific motives are perhaps peculiar to them, but in fact these only underline additionally the need to consider linkages between coalition politics and party systems as a whole.

There are two related aspects of 'informal' coalitions which have been given some thought in coalition theory, though only fairly recently. Firstly, minority governments clearly do not accord with the size criterion of coalition formation but, as Strom has argued, they need to be incorporated as something more than aberrations within a rational choice paradigm.[48] That is, contrary to conventional explanations, they may well be rational solutions under specified conditions (such as those mentioned in the previous paragraph), requiring therefore some modification to theories of government or coalition formation. Secondly, the role of support parties does of course ride roughshod over the *a priori* assumption that parties are essentially interested in acquiring a share in cabinet power, leaving us with the policy influence motive as uppermost. Support parties have surfaced in earlier literature; indeed, De Swann favoured viewing them as coalition members. But they have not really been built into the body of coalition theory as such, and the real world of coalition politics requires that they should be.

Finally, what inductive theoretical work has previously given thought to this kind of multi-dimensional framework based on linkages between coalitional behaviour and party systems? Three inductive theoretical approaches have helped in its elaboration here. They are also worth some detailed mention, seeing that so far they have hardly been applied in developing a comprehensive inductive theory of coalition behaviour, despite their usefulness in identifying linkages with party systems. These three publications are: Maurice Duverger, *Political Parties: their organisation and activity in the modern state*, 3rd edition (Methuen, 1964); Lawrence C. Dodd, *Coalitions in Parliamentary Government* (Princeton University Press, 1976); and Sven Groennings, E. W. Kelley and Michael Leiserson (eds.), *The Study of Coalitional Behavior: theoretical perspectives and cases from four continents* (Holt, Rinehart and Winston, 1970).

Duverger, in fact, devotes only a short section to party alliances in his standard work, looking historically at various categories and considering, though briefly, the impact of party structures and ideologies. Various points are relevant to our study: that a distinction may be made between governmental, parliamentary and electoral alliances with complex relations between them (e.g. 'the absence of solidarity at the electoral level diminishes solidarity in parliament and government'); concerning the stability of alliances, many different factors are involved, such as party structure, the social basis of parties, historical traditions and the ways in which opinion is formed; and, that there is an ambiguity or flexibility in alliance behaviour which may or may not be helped by the internal structure of parties. Duverger argues that all alliances are unequal, and that the degree of inequality depends on the parties' respective strengths, their 'position on the political chessboard' and their internal structure (i.e. in helping to determine ideological firmness), implying inherent, regular and possibly continuous conflict in all such relationships between parties.[49] If there is one dominant theme in Duverger's overview of coalition politics, it is that political parties are complex entities, and that it is important to view them both horizontally in relation to each other and vertically in terms of their own relationships with their bases, whether electoral or activist.

Lawrence Dodd, arguing for a differentiated approach to coalitional behaviour, starts with the hypothesis that 'the impact of party systems on cabinet durability is a much more complex and multivariate process' than previously supposed, and concludes that there are three party-system variables which play a determining role in affecting coalition formation and maintenance: cleavage conflict, fractionalisation and stability. He also provides an explanation for oversized cabinets, as most likely to emerge from unstable and hyper-fractionalised parliamentary party systems. On the question of cleavages, Dodd discusses their effect on the willingness of parties to coalesce on the grounds that parties need to act in a manner that advances their constituencies. According to Dodd, therefore, parties may gain cabinet status, but at the high risk of electoral defeat in the next election at the hands of their disappointed cleavage constituencies, although much depends on the nature of cleavages in party systems (i.e. the general level of conflict or polarisation). He pursues this line of reasoning by arguing that the coalitional status of cabinets is at least partially a function of the party system via the parliamentary parties; that cabinet durability is a function of cabinet coalitional status; and hence cabinet durability is indirectly affected by cleavages.[50] Dodd's theoretical approach, therefore, has the merit of placing the question of political distance between coalition actors in a deeper setting, and altogether it reveals a greater concern for the environment in which coalitions are formed than previous coalition theories.

Sven Groennings looks in some detail at different party-political determinants in an approach to coalition formation and maintenance, outlined in his 'Notes towards theories of coalition behaviour in multi-party systems: formation and maintenance' (chapter 23 of his edited volume). Emphasising the need for a more comprehensive approach in assessing party-political variables, he sees this as the key to interpreting coalitional behaviour on a continuing basis. Groennings provides a schema for coalition maintenance as well as formation, both predicated on the firm view that coalitional behaviour is a dynamic process. Four sets of variables are presented as common to both formation and maintenance: situational (e.g. external pressures like public opinion, constitutional variables such as election laws, the stability of the situation), compatibility (ideology, social base, policy goals, structure, leadership, prior party relationships), motivational (e.g. rewards, identity preservation) and strategic or interaction variables (influence and bargaining, size and resources, position in the political spectrum, etc.). For coalition maintenance, he adds one further set of variables under the rubric of apparatus, namely cabinet positions as the basis for influencing particular policies and other mechanisms whereby the coalition relationship and its decision-making are institutionalised ('the decision-making structure is more than a cabinet; it is also a system of making decisions . . . dissent is bound to occur in any coalition; the significant question is how it should be handled').[51] Groennings is particularly insistent that ideology must be subjected to closer and more differentiated scrutiny and more precise definition, so far as both coalition formation and maintenance are concerned.

Groennings' approach provides many pointers for formulating a comprehensive comparative framework or inductive theory for coalitional behaviour. It does, however, require further elaboration and refinement and to be made generally more systematic. The multi-dimensional approach of this book is therefore to some extent a matter of going beyond that of Groennings. For instance, motivation has been amplified, compatibility has been divided between various dimensions, while environmental factors have been given their own salience in one special dimension.

To summarise, the seven dimensions listed and detailed below at the end of this chapter are the outcome of the overall reasoning developed in this chapter, based on the need for establishing contextual linkages to coalitional behaviour and thereby relating coalition studies to the study of party systems. That is, they draw most of all on the focal points of, as well as insights from, the recent study of such systems in Western Europe, while taking account of the range of general dynamic factors in coalitional behaviour as identified earlier in this Introduction. They also benefit from the inductive theoretical approaches just outlined in addition to other coalition theory of the formal school; at the same time, exploring areas so far untrodden by them since none of these have been both comprehensive and systematic concurrently. Furthermore, seeing that one basic lesson of studying political parties is that their various functions invariably interact, the course chosen here is to break down this framework of looking at coalitional behaviour within the context of party systems into its key component elements and examine them in turn. This is seen as the most effective way of dealing with the complexity of this subject. While the variables selected and detailed under each of the seven dimensions are largely self-explanatory, some final comment is necessary regarding the categorisation behind these dimensions.

Firstly, the historical dimension draws attention at the beginning of the framework to the time dimension of coalition politics, particularly with respect to the role of parties as coalition actors. The obvious assumption based on reality is that parties accumulate experience during a coalition relationship with other parties but also have experience resulting from previous such relationships. Namely, the dynamics of coalitional behaviour are not only a matter of the current relationship seen as a *continuous* process, but may also be affected by previous patterns of co-operation (e.g. the former might in part be justified by negative experiences of other coalitions in the past). There is, furthermore, room here for variations in national patterns, such as whether coalitions are required to be strictly formal ones (as in West Germany) or if informal versions have become something of a convention (as in Italy). This consideration of the impact of historical influences and generally of the time dimension leads directly to further dimensions.

The next two dimensions encompass the main directions developed so far by the formal theories. The second or institutional dimension is based on the hypothesis that the formal structure of the political system includes both constraints and opportunities for decision-makers in their initiation and pursuit of coalitional relationships. That is, institutional regulations in these liberal democracies are aimed at providing checks on executive power for those to whom it is granted. Behind this may lie the basic question of the relationship between the state and the political parties, of how far the latter dominate the functioning of the former and 'populate' it (e.g. how much coalition politics enters the area of patronage and bureaucracy). But most of all the focus here is on the dynamics of legislative decision-making and generally of the policy-making process. Again, there is much scope on this point for national variation on such matters as the nature of the government/opposition divide, the form of electoral systems (as particularly important in determining the arithmetical strength of different parties) and overall political structures. Some modification has to be made under this dimension for local politics, where as Mellors and Brearey show, we have the special problem that in some countries there is difficulty in locating 'executive power', if not the absence of an executive as such.

Thirdly, the most difficult dimension to evaluate is that of motivation. This is because it contains a collection of forms of motivation which in practice usually interact, some of which are generalisable while others must be treated in an *ad hoc* fashion. Several of these are familiar in studies of coalition politics, such as questions of policy closeness and the trade-off between office-seeking and policy-seeking as well as the much employed left–right continuum. Dynamic factors worth highlighting are changes in the weights of individual parties and in their policy preferences or expectations in addition to changing issue priorities and the tensions that develop within coalitions, all of which may be drawn from the observation of coalition politics in reality. One particular point of interest is how far party leaders become 'prisoners' of their parties' strategies as previously developed, but this takes us to the next two dimensions.

Dimensions four and five turn attention more to 'vertical' linkages in addition to those just discussed focussing on 'horizontal' ones, i.e. those concerned with essentially the national–political level. The fourth or horizontal/vertical dimension may be presented briefly, as this simply looks at the nature of the political systems in terms of centre–periphery relations, where there is quite some variation across Western Europe. It concentrates on a two-way problem: how much do national leaders or party strategists control sub-national coalitional behaviour (vertical–downwards), and what effect do developments in the latter have on the former (vertical–upwards)? Because of the importance of this so far unresearched area, a special chapter in this volume looks comparatively at coalitional behaviour in local politics. Fifthly, internal party considerations constitute a special dimension because these are very relevant to the problem of elite control or, alternatively, of constraints on elites as well as throwing significant light on the elementary assumption of the formal theories – now contested – about parties as unitary actors. Moreover, the study of party systems has drawn attention to the need for handling differentiatedly the question of leadership, not to mention the importance of the reality and not just the formality of party structures. The solution must be, therefore, to focus on the dynamics of internal party processes, and specifically on such variables as the changing position of leaders within their own parties and the changing balance of internal party factions. The main hypothesis here is that of an interaction usually developing between inter-party and intra-party relationships.

The last two dimensions carry the analysis of coalitional behaviour into wider or deeper areas of party systems, and for this reason they are more difficult to measure. They are distinctly beyond the scope of formal coalition theories and their methodology, but they are prime cases for inclusion in an inductive theoretical framework for testing some important assumptions against national variation. The sixth or socio-political dimension includes a range of different variables, but there are certain main themes. In particular, the most familiar is that of electoral politics which definitely has to be built into any dynamic approach in order to take account of such real pressures as the effects of oncoming elections on a given coalition, the changing demands and preferences of electorates and how these may affect the relative popularity of coalition partners, and generally the dynamics of overall party development, including the changing fortunes of different political parties. We are, in effect, considering the problem of polarisation at a deeper level, not just in the parliamentary arena, particularly in relation to the intensity of cleavages and their influence on the stability of coalitional relationships. The seventh or environmental/external dimension simply involves a series of wider considerations in coalitional behaviour, notably the impact of developments often beyond the direct control of coalition actors as well as the role of other possible actors which may indirectly influence coalition politics, like the media and the actions of foreign governments. If there is a leitmotiv to these different themes, it is that coalition actors operate in a world of uncertainty in which events occur that might constrain their behaviour or affect their own relationships in some unexpected way. So far, this leitmotiv has been hardly visible to more conventional studies of coalition politics.

One important advantage of this multi-dimensional framework is that being inductive in its theoretical approach, generalising especially with respect to the real world of politics, it allows for flexibility in its application to country case-studies, which form the greater part of this volume. That is, this framework has deliberately sought to glean lessons from the empirical as well as theoretical study of party systems which – to state the obvious – are nationally embedded. To take an important example, the fundamental problem of change which has been the principal focus of recent research on political parties has to be interpreted to a significant extent by country-specific factors, although leaving much scope for cross-national comparisons. At the same time, while this present study has also drawn on previous coalition theory, it should be pointed out that the latter also encountered from the beginning much national variation in the testing of hypotheses. This has continued to mark theoretical work on coalitional behaviour up to the present time. For instance, Schofield and Laver (1985) have recently found significant differences between countries in their application of different theories of coalition payoffs for West European systems for the whole of the post-war period.[52] And, as Browne and Gleiber point out in their Research Note at the end of this book, there are distinct cross-national differences as to the rate at which cabinets are expected to fall according to their 'events' conceptualisation of cabinet stability.

Differences between national political systems are thus vital in the study of coalition politics, and they consequently have to be built into any new theoretical approach. Since national differences are the common concern of both the traditional formal coalition theories as well as obviously of empirical research on this subject, it would appear there is some basis for establishing an interpretative bridge between these two previously rather separate schools of political analysis, or, to put it more grandly, between theory and practice. In other words, whereas macro-level analysis and empirical research on micro-level processes have tended to follow separate investigative paths, there is every reason to marry these two approaches if we avoid the pure abstraction of the formal theories on the one hand and the over-descriptiveness of some of the empirical work on the other. This is most likely to be found in developing an inductive theoretical framework for the analysis of coalitional behaviour, as argued and developed in this introductory chapter.

While the national case-studies which follow in this book generally illustrate and confirm national variation in patterns of coalitional behaviour and, in particular, the regular incidence of country-specific factors, it also emerges from the application to these case-studies of the seven dimensions that there is indeed significant mileage here for systematic cross-national comparisons. The proceedings of the workshop at Salzburg indicated that useful generalisations could be derived from this kind of framework, and the rethinking involved in the revision of the papers further underlined its validity, given that the intention of the project was exploratory and not to expect categorical answers. There are, for instance, similarities in the problems of pivotal or centre parties in harmonising inter-party with intra-party relationships. Generally the experience of these different West European countries tends to argue against considering political parties as unitary coalition actors at least automatically; several of them demonstrate the relevance of examining coalitional behaviour in the light of changing cleavage structures, while the fundamental but complex question of motivation is highlighted as requiring careful handling and as really multi-dimensional in itself. But it is otherwise left to the reader to follow the exact degree of applicability of the various dimensions in each country. This may be done straightforwardly, since the chapter subdivisions follow flexibly the sequence of the multi-dimensional framework.

Bearing in mind increasing doubts expressed about the comparative approach or the way this has been utilised so far in political science, as noted earlier, it is very tenable that the various difficulties here are significantly reduced by concentrating on a given type of political system or a certain recognised area of the world. That is the starting-point for this inductive theory, seeing that Western Europe is such an area and also one which comprises exclusively liberal democracies. Hopefully, this helps to offset, though it cannot rival, the scientific rigour of the formal coalition theories. In other words, since the compelling need is for a more comprehensive analysis of coalitional behaviour than so far offered by other theories, this multi-dimensional framework trades off the advantages of depth and greater scope for handling the complexity of this subject within an area with equivalent political patterns against the breadth and abstract appeal of other theories. Whether such a theoretical framework is viable for other areas of the world remains to be seen, but then coalition politics of the kind examined in this book is essentially a preserve of the liberal democratic form of political system, wherever it may be found.

Appendix. The multi-dimensional framework: political parties and coalitional behaviour in Western Europe

Guidelines based on workshop proceedings

1. Hypotheses

In most formal approaches the party is retained as a unitary actor. This is acceptable in a theoretical model. It is also politically relevant whenever a party does act as one actor; e.g. when it presents an election programme, or decides to enter a cabinet on the basis of a decision that commits the entire party ... However, in the actual world of politics, it is hardly defensible to regard a party as a unitary actor ... Even in the examples just given – presenting an election programme, or deciding on a coalition – there is bound to be disagreement before the actual decision is taken, as well as on its later application in practice ... a decision on the investiture of a new coalition cabinet does not pre-empt a need for continuous decision-making on concrete decisions to follow ... Clearly, then, the study of both party and party systems must enter into the internal structural and policy-making processes of parties.

Recent changes in the party systems, the rise of new parties and the development of new patterns of oppositional behaviour have weakened the ability of formal coalition theories to predict outcomes successfully ... even coalitions that are considered as politically possible by the elites sometimes are resisted from the grass-roots; the individual voters in most multi-party systems lack the rational character that underlies the assumptions of formal coalition theories in so far as these look upon parties and voters as similarly rational beings, maximising the benefits of their political group ... most of the specific propositions of coalition theories do not work under the conditions of the European multi-party systems; research on coalitions on the basis of game theory has not come to grips with the peculiarities of European party systems, since it has started out from American assumptions of a system where all the relevant groups are seen to have *allgemeine Koalitionsfähigkeit* and to calculate in a rational way the advantages of forming coalitions.

(Hans Daalder and Peter Mair (eds.), *Western European Party Systems: continuity and change* (Sage, 1983), pp. 21, 342–5)

Several recurring themes in the workshop are specified or alluded to here:

- that political parties cannot essentially or automatically be considered as unitary actors in the coalition game
- the importance of taking into account a variety of informal determinants of coalitional behaviour
- that it is imperative to consider the coalitional relationship as a continuing process, encompassing both formation and maintenance
- that coalitional behaviour has to be assessed within a wider political framework than just the institutional context
- that political parties are obviously the key or central actors in the coalitional game, though not to the exclusion of other possible actors
- that qualitative changes in West European party systems since the 1960s reinforce the need for a different approach to coalitional behaviour along these lines
- that coalitional politics is an inherently complex and often 'messy' affair, where expectations of rational behaviour may well be unrealistic.

It follows that the starting-point and follow-through in any modified or new approach in coalition studies should be to focus on political parties in the full sense, and that this is surely the best way of trying to meet the difficult task of marrying theory and practice here. In doing so, it is hypothesised that traditional coalition theories may still offer interpretative mileage – according to the case in question – but that seen critically they tend to be too simplistic, rather too abstract or at best too one-dimensional, e.g. in focussing simply on coalition formation as an exclusive exercise or on policy distance alone.

2. Defining a new approach to coalitional behaviour

Basically, the need is for an overarching framework to cover this relationship between political parties in the full sense and coalitional behaviour – which should be neither too abstract (raising interesting but not always applicable ideas) nor too descriptive (with a low explanatory value). Seeing that generally Western European states are to some degree or other party democracies, any such approach has to revolve around the linkage between coalitional behaviour in particular and party systems in general; or, put more grandly, what relationship we might be seeking to establish between coalition theory and any relevant theories of party systems.

This has been the major gap in both theoretical and empirical coalition studies, and in a way a surprising gap in view of the prominence of party studies on Western Europe. Some arguments in favour of this approach are:

- it provides a more comprehensive and differentiated basis for analysing this complex subject than those previous approaches which have been postulated on the assumption, explicit or implicit, of parties as unitary actors
- it covers different forms of party alliances and not merely those involving formal coalitions, e.g. electoral, oppositional (with a prospect of becoming governmental) or parliamentary, and thus governmental alliances of less formal kinds
- it draws attention to constraints on political elites in their coalitional relationships deriving from a variety of party pressures (thus giving consideration to changes in party systems, including participatory demands, increasing issue consciousness, and hence a more critical awareness of government performance)
- it offers a method of continuity in evaluating the subject (coalitional relationships as a continuing process).

In defining such an approach, we have little assistance from previous coalition theories so far as this relationship between coalitional behaviour and party systems is concerned. As noted in the original synopsis for the workshop, Duverger, Dodd and especially Groennings* provide some angles, but with the possible exception of the last of these they do not offer any comprehensive framework. While Groennings influenced several of the workshop papers, it was recognised that his approach needed to be reordered and made more systematic.

The following is an integration of the original workshop synopsis, the approach of Groennings, the suggestions made at the final session of the workshop on the revision of papers for publication and the approach presented in the paper on Italy.

3.   Components of a multi-dimensional approach to coalitional behaviour

(i)   Historical dimension

Time span – 'Events' approach
Historical developments relevant to coalitional politics, e.g. cleavages in party systems
Party history, development of party support over time
Traditions of party co-operation with other parties, cross-party leadership co-operation and experience: precedents as positive or negative, as possible conditioning factor on further coalitional relationships – such experience and its conditioning effects on party activist bases.

---

*The works referred to are: Maurice Duverger, *Political Parties* (Methuen, 1964), section on party alliances; Lawrence C. Dodd, *Coalitions in Parliamentary Government* (Princeton University Press, 1976); and Sven Groennings, E. W. Kelley and Michael Leiserson (eds.), *The Study of Coalition Behavior* (Holt, Rinehart and Winston, 1970), ch. 23.

(ii) Institutional dimension

Institutional regulations – rules of the game – constitutional constraints or opportunities, electoral systems

The arithmetical determinant – respective party strengths in legislatures as starting-point for coalitional relationships

Styles of bargaining

Identification of coalition actors – political elites first and foremost – other elites, e.g. economic, media?

Patronage factor in coalitional behaviour

Nature of government/opposition divide – related to whether coalitions are purely formal ones or include informal alliances

Oversized coalitions, minority governments

Effect of bureaucracies on policy formulation

(iii) Motivational dimension

Obvious and main question of power vs. policy motivation – but what does this exactly mean? Can the two be so strictly separated?

Is 'power' to be seen just narrowly as office-holding?

Policy goals – policy demands – consistent or changing policy priorites

Policy distance between individual parties, but not to be seen statically – convergence or conflict in, degree of overlap in, broader question of ideological compatibility – party identity

Party positions in the ideological spectrum of left/right

Input in ideology – manner of transmission – its relationship with other motivations

Party strategy – different party strategies – short-term and/or long-term considerations of

Dictates of multi-party systems – individual parties ultimately dependent on each other in order to translate their strategies into action

Relationship between party strategies in general (the 'theory') and actual coalitional behaviour (the 'practice') – movement or direction in individual party strategies

Electoral movement - effect on policy demands/demands for cabinet posts

Categorisation between leading parties/pivotal parties/smaller parties – role of centre parties

Relationship between arithmetical (see above) and political variables (as encompassing policy and other ones)

(iv)   Horizontal/vertical dimension

The relationship between these two levels:

Horizontal = first and foremost inter-party relations at national institutional
  level, also including national party leaders acting as extra-cabinet wirepullers

Vertical = two parallel forms of centre-periphery relations:
  - parties operating downwards through the state structure – nature of the
    state structure/degree of power devolution to sub-national levels –
    coalitions in regional and local politics – questions of sub-national party
    autonomy from national leaderships (vertical–downwards)
  - effects of sub-national coalitions on national coalitional behaviour
    (vertical–upwards)
  - regional and local politics as possible 'laboratory' for alliance
    experimentation

(v)   Internal party dimension

Party structures – variation between different parties

Levels of party centralisation, e.g. Groennings: 'It is easier for a party with loose
  central control to coalesce with another party of the same character than one
  with tight discipline, because a highly centralised party can present a threat to a
  loosely structured party.'

Question of elite control over followers vs. pressure from/influence of latter on
  leaderships
  - need (or degree of) for leaders to carry followers on strategic paths
  - levels of participation within parties – deference, passivity or activism –
    activist involvement in policy formulation
  - link again with ideology, activists as carriers of

Internal divisions over party strategy - at leadership level, etc.

Party factions – as factor determining party strategy and coalitional options

Question of political roles (e.g. going into government) as affecting balance in
  relationship between leaders and followers
  - possible need for party to adapt its internal decision-making and
    communication process

(vi)   Socio-political dimension

Development and stability of norms guiding/affecting coalitional behaviour –
  public views on – how much pressure from
  - aspects of political culture, e.g. anti-coalition norms

Relationship between parties and their social bases – variety of forms
  - need for social consensus as factor conditioning coalition politics
  - problems of bridging social fragmentation
    i.e. vertical relations in a wider and deeper context

Prominent feature: parties and their electorates – central to the weight of individual coalition actors

Cleavage conflict (cf. Dodd) – effects on potential co-operation across party barriers

Control over social bases as crucial in creating social consensus behind coalitional relationships, *or*: how much do 'social forces' help to determine the coalitional behaviour of elites?

Parties' links with interest groups – form of – degree of institutionalisation in relationship parties/their social bases

(vii)   Environmental/external dimension

Generally, the impact of events ('events' environment – interplay of action and reaction)

International influences – political and diplomatic

International economy – as constraint on or stimulus to party alliances

Role of the media

Possible question of system stability - effect on inter-party relations – theories of consociational democracy

The intimacy of small-country politics

Notes

I should like to thank Michael Laver and Paul Whiteley for their helpful comments on an earlier version of this chapter.

1. Eric C. Browne and John Dreijmanis (eds.), *Government Coalitions in Western Democracies* (Longman, 1982); Vernon Bogdanor (ed.), *Coalition Government in Western Europe* (Heinemann, 1983).

2. Exceptions to this neglect are Arend Lijphart, *Democracies: patterns of majoritarian and consensus government in twenty-one countries* (Yale University Press, 1984), esp. ch. 4, although the author is himself a noted coalition theorist; Maurice Duverger, *Political Parties* (Methuen, 1964); and Angelo Panebianco, *Modelli di Partito* (Il Mulino, 1982). The last two are discussed in this present chapter, while note is taken of passing reference to coalition politics in Hans Daalder and Peter Mair (eds.), *Western European Party Systems: continuity and change* (Sage, 1983). Reasons for this neglect seem, among other things, to lie in the fact that this subject has at the theoretical level fallen between the two analytical stools of mathematical modelling on the one hand and the conventional mould of much comparative government on the other.

3. Klaus von Beyme, 'Governments, parliaments and the structure of power in political parties' in Daalder and Mair, *Western European Party Systems*, p. 342.

4. Lawrence C. Dodd, 'The study of cabinet durability' in Arend Lijphart (ed.), *New Approaches to the Study of Cabinet Coalitions*, special issue of *Comparative Political Studies*, July 1984, pp. 155–61.

5. See J. Steiner, 'Decision process and policy outcome: an attempt to conceptualise the problem at the cross-national level', *European Journal of Political Research*, vol. 11, September 1983, p. 313.

6. E.g. M. Laver, 'Dynamic factors in government coalition formation', *European Journal of Political Research*, 1974, pp. 259–70; Lawrence C. Dodd, *Coalitions in Parliamentary Governments* (Princeton University Press, 1976); and P. Warwick, 'The durability of coalition governments in parliamentary democracies', *Comparative Political Studies*, vol. 11, 1979, pp. 465–98.

7. See note 4.

8. See Eric C. Browne *et al.* 'An "events" approach to the problem of cabinet stability' in Lijphart, *New Approaches to the Study of Cabinet Coalitions*, p. 170.

9. Mark N. Franklin and Thomas T. Mackie, 'Familiarity and inertia in the formation of governing coalitions in parliamentary democracies', *British Journal of Political Science*, vol. 13, July 1983, p. 284.

10. Ian Budge, 'Parties and democratic government: a framework for comparative explanation', *West European Politics*, January 1984, p. 95.

11. R. C. Macridis and R. Cox, 'Area study and comparative politics' in R. C. Macridis and B. Brown (eds.), *Comparative Politics: notes and readings* (Dorset Press, 1964), pp. 102–3.

12. E.g. Abram De Swaan, *Coalition Theories and Cabinet Formations: a study of formal theories of coalition formation applied to nine European parliaments after 1918* (Elsevier, 1973); and Dodd, *Coalitions in Parliamentary Government*.

13. E.g. see Peter Mair, 'Adaptation and control: towards an understanding of party and party system change' in Daalder and Mair, *Western European Party Systems*, pp. 405–29.

14. See Giovanni Sartori, 'European political parties: the case of polarised pluralism' in J. LaPalombara and M. Weiner (eds.), *Political Parties and Political Development* (Princeton University Press, 1966), pp. 137–76, and also his *Parties and Party Systems: a framework for analysis* (Cambridge University Press 1976).

15. David Apter, introduction to Part V on political parties in Harry Eckstein and David E. Apter (eds.), *Comparative Politics: a reader* (The Free Press, 1963), pp. 327–32.

16. David Easton, 'The analysis of political systems' in Macridis and Brown, *Comparative Politics*, p. 91. See also his *A Systems Analysis of Political Life* (Wiley, 1965).

17. Most notably, S. M. Lipset and Stein Rokkan (eds.), *Party Systems and Voter Alignments: cross-national perspectives* (Free Press, 1967).

18. See Peter Mair, 'Party politics in contemporary Europe: a challenge to party?' in Stefano Bartolini and Peter Mair (eds.), *Party Politics in Contemporary Western Europe*, special issue of *West European Politics*, October 1984, pp. 170–84.

19. Mogens N. Pedersen, 'Changing patterns of electoral volatility in European party systems, 1948–1977: explorations in explanation' in Daalder and Mair, *Western European Party Systems*, p. 29.

20. *Ibid.*, pp. 64–5.

21. See the useful chapter by F. van Winden, 'Towards a dynamic theory of cabinet formation' in Manfred J. Holler (ed.), *Coalitions and Collective Action* (Physica-Verlag, 1984), pp. 145–59, where he argues that 'how to explain and predict these coalitions is a central problem for the study of multi-party systems'.

22. Panebianco, *Modelli di Partito*.

23. *Ibid.*, esp. pp. 406–10.

24. *Ibid.*, pp. 406–7.

25. Von Beyme, 'Governments, parliaments and the structure of power in political parties', p. 342.

26. See van Winden, 'Towards a dynamic theory of cabinet formation', p. 145.

27. Budge, 'Parties and democratic governments', p. 99.

28. David Robertson, 'Dimensional analysis and the study of party competition', paper at Political Studies Association (British) conference, 1971: 'as a topic of research the behaviour of political parties in relation to their rivals is not, however, at all well worn; with the exception of ad hoc works like the Nuffield election studies and the more esoteric investigations of coalition behaviour by the mathematically inclined, we are left with a literature that covers almost every aspect of party behaviour but that of competition and strategy'.

29. David Robertson, *A Theory of Party Competition* (Wiley, 1976), p. 191.

30. E.g. papers for the ECPR workshop on 'Ideology after the End of Ideology Debate: recent theorising and empirical applications', Freiburg, 1983, see report in *ECPR News Circular*, June 1983, pp. 25–7.

31. S. Boute, 'Subjective policy distance theory' in Holler, *Coalitions and Collective Action*, pp. 113–26; also his 'On De Swaan's policy distance coalition theory', *European Journal of Political Research*, vol. 10, September 1982, pp. 313–20.

32. Budge, 'Parties and democratic government', p. 100.

33. On this point and generally on the development of studies on West European party systems, see Hans Daalder, 'The comparative study of European parties and party systems: an overview' in Daalder and Mair, *Western European Party Systems*, pp. 1–27.

34. See the useful critique of theories of consociational democracy by Adriano Pappalardo, 'The conditions for consociational democracy: a logical and empirical critique', *European Journal of Political Research*, vol. 9, December 1981, pp. 365–90.
35. *Ibid.*, p. 373.
36. Panebianco, *Modelli di Partito*.
37. Von Beyme, 'Governments, parliaments and the structure of power in political parties', pp. 341–67.
38. *Ibid.*, pp. 366–7.
39. Karlheinz Reif, 'Some notes on the role of middle-level party elites', paper for 4th annual meeting of the International Society of Political Psychology, 1981.
40. Oskar Neidermayer, 'Möglichkeiten des Koalitionswechsels: zur parteiinternen Verankerung der bestehenden Koalitionsstruktur im Parteiensystem der Bundesrepublik Deutschland', *Zeitschrift für Parlamentsfragen*, 1982, pp. 85–110.
41. See Stefano Bartolini, 'The membership of mass parties: the Social Democratic experience, 1889–1978' in Daalder and Mair, *Western European Party Systems*, pp. 139–75.
42. Daalder, 'The comparative study of European parties and party systems', p. 21.
43. Budge, 'Parties and democratic government', p. 101.
44. E.g. see F. Belloni and D. Beller (eds.), *Faction Politics: political parties and factionalism in comparative perspectives* (ABC-Clio, 1978); David Hine, 'Factionalism in West European parties: a framework for analysis', *West European Politics*, January 1982, pp. 36–53; also papers of the ECPR workshop on 'Factionalism in the Political Parties of Western Europe', Florence, 1980 (see report in *ECPR News Circular*, June 1980, pp. 13–18). On Italy, see Alan Zuckerman, *Political Clienteles in Power: party factions and cabinet coalitions in Italy* (Sage, 1975), and his *The Politics of Faction: Christian Democratic rule in Italy* (Yale University Press, 1979); as well as Grand Amyot, *The Italian Communist Party: the crisis of the Popular Front strategy* (Croom Helm, 1981).
45. Budge, 'Parties and democratic government', p. 117.
46. R. Dahl, 'The concept of power', *Behavioural Science*, 1957, pp. 201–15.
47. Lijphart, *Democracies*, ch. 4, pp. 53–4.
48. See the useful discussion of minority governments in Kaare Strom, 'Minority governments in parliamentary democracies: the rationality of non-winning cabinet solutions' in Lijphart, *New Approaches to the Study of Cabinet Coalitions*, pp. 199–227.
49. Duverger, *Political Parties*, p. 344.
50. Dodd, *Coalitions in Parliamentary Government*, ch. 8.
51. Groennings in *The Study of Coalition Behavior*, pp. 461–2.
52. Norman Schofield and Michael Laver, 'Bargaining theory and portfolio payoffs in European coalition governments, 1945–83', *British Journal of Political Science*, vol. 15, April 1985, pp. 143–64.

2 Between theoretical elegance and political reality: deductive models and cabinet coalitions in Europe

Theories of government coalition formation tend to have one of two academic pedigrees. On the one hand, there are theorists who set out to understand the workings of coalition government. Usually, their theories are *inductive* in methodological style, being based on generalisations from the real world of politics to the more abstract world of political theory.

On the other hand, there are formal theorists, usually with a background in rational-choice theory, who tend to regard actual government coalitions as data on which to test essentially *deductive* analyses. These are based upon *a priori* assumptions, of varying plausibility, about the motivations of the actors. Many of the deductive theories were originally tested using the time-honoured technique of paying graduate students money to play a rather formalised and artificial game. The view of 'coalitions' that evolves through this process, not surprisingly, is one of coalitions of individuals, each attempting to capture some clearly specified prize.

It would be remarkable if such different pedigrees did not result in quite different offspring. An appreciation of this confrontation between inductive and deductive styles of reasoning is essential to an understanding of the purpose of this book. Deductive theories of coalition formation have had a good run for their money, so far. They have achieved levels of predictive success much higher than those usually encountered in the social sciences. Indeed, in a footnote to one of the several articles on the testing of the theories of coalition portfolio *payoffs*, the authors note that their findings, with an r^2 of 0.86, pass the interocular trauma test (they hit you between the eyes).[1] Similarly, good results were derived in the early tests of formal predictions of coalition *membership* if, of course, we ignore the fact that coalition theories do not predict minority governments, and that minority governments are really rather common.[2]

It must be noted that there is some methodological debate over what, precisely, constitutes a statistically significant result in the testing of a deductive coalition theory but, by any standards, inductive theorising has been significantly less successful.[3] It has yet to gel into a coherent body of theory and, probably as a consequence, has yet to pull off any predictive coups. The trouble with formal theories, therefore, is not so much that they are bad at what they set out to do; they are not. The problem is that they do not set out to do much that is interesting. They don't explain 'coalition behaviour' in any real sense, because coalition behaviour comprises a whole bundle of phenomena, most of which formal theories are ill-equipped to address.

Since the purpose of this book is neither to reject formal theories out of hand, nor to engage in a new wave of inductive theorising *ab initio*, rather building on what we already have and exploring areas thus far untrodden by the formal theories, it is important to assess in general terms the interpretative mileage offered by these theories.

One of the more interesting general conclusions that can be drawn from existing empirical tests of formal theories is that the results are highly country-sensitive. This was found, one way or another, in each of the early tests of *formation* theories.[4] Country-specific results have also been found recently in tests of portfolio payoff theories. Schofield and Laver found that, in explaining the distribution of portfolios to coalition members, *either one theory or another* was overwhelmingly superior in eleven of the twelve countries for which they had data. In other words, they found that coalition systems could be classified according to the type of distributional process that appeared to be at work.[5]

Differences *between* countries, therefore, are critical for the analysis of coalitions. Such differences, relating for example to institutional, cultural and social factors, comprise one of many sets of variables that cannot easily be built into most current formal theories. At this stage in our understanding of the coalitional process, to conduct anything other than a country-specific analysis of the phenomena involved is to do great violence to reality. Each of the remaining chapters in this book, therefore, comprises a single-country analysis, organised around a broadly inductive set of themes.

Before moving to these, however, it is worth taking a little time to map out the broad areas of coalition behaviour covered by the formal theorising to which this whole enterprise is a response.

(a) The static nature of most formal theories

Most formal theories of coalition formation are essentially *static*. They set out to explain static aspects of the coalition game in a given system, including the party membership of the coalition cabinet on formation, the distribution of cabinet portfolios between members' parties, and the agreed policy package that results from formation negotiations. These properties of the coalition *on its formation* are explained in terms of a series of static variables. These include, notably, the distribution of seats between parties in the legislature, the policy packages advanced by parties at election time, and the size of the legislative majority needed in order to control the government.

Each inter-electoral period tends to be taken on its own as a discrete object of analysis, so that the *history* of coalition in any given system has no place in the model. Very few of the theories say much about what goes on *within* an inter-electoral period. Most of the predictions they make cannot change until a new election produces a new set of parameters.

Many of the more interesting aspects of coalition politics tend, of course, to concern *dynamic* aspects of the situation. These include the collapse of existing coalitions, the tensions that develop within a coalition cabinet, the effect of an approaching election on relations between the government parties, the develop-ment of personal or ideological links between coalition partners, and so on. While there have been some attempts to build a historical dimension into formal theories, the results have generally done little to add any real richness to formal analyses of coalition politics.[6] The lack of any genuinely dynamic element in the formal theories must be seen as one of their least attractive features.

(b)   The general assumption of rationality

Formal theories of coalition behaviour operate on the basis of a general *a priori* assumption of rational decision-making by the relevant actors. Actually, rational-choice *coalition* theories are rather more defensible than rational-choice theories of most other aspects of the political process, those of mass voting behaviour, for example. The assumption that the leaders of major political parties bargain in a hard-headed fashion about who is to form a government, about who is to be Prime Minister or Foreign Secretary, and about what is to go into a coalition budget seems really rather plausible. Indeed, if rational-choice theories cannot work reasonably well in the field of coalition politics, it is difficult to see where they can work well at all.

The general assumption of rationality tends to be operationalised in a number of more specific forms when it is applied by particular coalition theories. As I have indicated, these tend to have a pedigree in the game theoretical literature. The specific *a priori* assumptions used are often implicit, but can broadly be stated as follows:

(1)   The 'actors' in the coalition game are unified parties, each of which can be treated as a single bargaining entity.

(2)   Coalition governments must command majority support in the legislature.

(3)   Parties are motivated by either or both of two objectives. The first is to get into government. The second is to fulfil fundamental policy objectives. The first may of course be a precondition for the second.

(4)   All winning combinations of parties represent possible coalition govern-ments. Some may be more probable than others.

More detailed specifications of these assumptions characterise different theories. Nevertheless, the four core characteristics outlined above are properties of nearly all formal theories of coalition politics. In practice, of course, each is an approximation, and much of what follows in this book can be interpreted as an attempt to spell out quite how much of an approximation is involved in each country. Some general points can, however, be made about each assumption.

(c) Four main a priori assumptions examined

Assumption 1: 'The actors in the coalition game are unified parties, each of which can be treated as a single bargaining entity.'

This assumption, of course, is *never* wholly fulfilled. What we must consider, therefore, is whether it is *so* completely unrealistic as to be worse than useless. Parties can clearly fragment at random, or on the basis of any number of criteria. For the sake of simplicity, however, we can easily identify six basic levels within many political parties. These define a set of hierarchical divisions, and the actors to be found at each level of the hierarchy may well have different objectives in relation to the outcome of coalition negotiations. The levels are:

(a) the party leader
(b) the front bench (those who are, or who have realistic aspirations to be, in the cabinet)
(c) the back benchers (those whose votes are required to sustain a government in office, and whose seats are at risk in the next election)
(d) national executive
(e) the party workers
(f) the party supporters.

It is obvious that deep differences of opinion about the relative costs and benefits of any potential coalition may arise between any of these levels in the party hierarchy. A particular option, for example, may attract the party leader and those who get seats at the cabinet table. It may repel disappointed candidates for portfolios (particularly if these reckon that the prospects of a ministerial motor car are better in an alternative coalition). Some back benchers may favour coalition because they estimate that the party's participation in government will be an electoral bonus. Party activists, concerned above all with party policy, may deplore the policy concessions made in order to join the coalition, while some party voters may favour, and some may oppose, the coalition.

The different objectives that may motivate different sections of a party highlight two important aspects of the relationship between *intra*-party politics and *inter*-party politics. In the first place, the prospect of coalition may pull a party apart. This opens up the possibilities of quite the opposite tendency to that which is accepted as the received wisdom for one-party governments. In Britain and the United States at least, it tends to be assumed that parties will unite when in government, but divide in opposition. In coalition systems, on the other hand, the prospect of government participation seems likely to be a divisive issue. The concessions that must inevitably be made exercise some sections more than others, while the real benefits of office are clearly *very* unevenly distributed within the party. The key distinction between one-party and coalition governments in this respect, of course, is that coalition parties *choose* to participate in government, and it is the process of choosing that is likely to be divisive. Single-party majority governments, in contrast, have power thrust upon them, and have nothing to decide.

In the second place, the precise *hierarchical structure* of a given party will play a big part in determining the effects on it of the prospect of participation in a coalition. A party with a relatively autocratic hierarchical structure, for example, may tend much more to behave *as if* it were a unitary actor. Decisions on coalition membership may be in the hands of the leader, advised by a few cronies, so that one person can in fact speak for the party. A quite different situation arises in a party with an institutionalised system of decision-making by delegates or representatives. As we shall see in the case of Ireland, two parties (Fianna Fail and Fine Gael) can be taken into coalition effectively by their respective leaders while the third (Labour) can only go in subject to ratification by a special delegate conference in which anti-coalition activists are well represented.

Thus an important empirical concern should be to identify the relevant actors *within* the parties in a coalition system, and to evaluate the effect of the institutional structure of party decision-making. When parties do *not* function *as if* they were unitary actors, coalition will obviously have a significant effect on intra-party politics. This, indeed, is one of the most interesting aspects of coalition politics, yet one that cannot easily be considered by formal theories.

Assumption 2: 'Coalition governments must command majority support in the legislature.'

Minority situations often result in minority governments, which may or may not be coalitions. For the period covered by the Taylor and Laver tests of coalition theories, only 87 out of the 132 governments formed in minority situations controlled a legislative majority. Herman and Pope, using a different time scale and set of countries, found 126 governments with majorities out of 200 minority situations,[7] while Strom recently found that 35 per cent of all governments studied did not command a majority. While the frequency of minority governments is often acknowledged, the full implications for coalition bargaining of the possibility of a minority administration have yet to be properly explored.

The reality, of course, is that governments must be able to secure voting majorities in the legislature, but that they do not need to do this solely on the basis of the votes of members of government parties. Non-government parties may support the government, according to one of two basic models.

(a) *Stable voting coalitions.*[8] A particular non-government party or parties may provide long-term support for the government. This is done without taking any cabinet seats, but often on the basis of discussions over government policy that result in major concessions to the supporting parties. This is the type of agreement that led to the Lib/Lab pact that maintained the 1974/9 British Labour government in office, but it is capable of sustaining governments that formally control far less than a majority of the legislature, as is sometimes the case in Denmark. In such circumstances, the question really concerns whether it is the majority-winning criterion or the very definition of a coalition that needs changing. On balance, it seems worth retaining the definition of a coalition in terms of cabinet membership, and allowing a quite separate role for stable support parties. These, after all, are not part of the *government*.

The role of support parties, however, does highlight the need to distinguish very clearly between *legislative* coalitions and *executive* coalitions, a distinction that can easily be blurred in practical discussions.

(b) *Unstable voting coalitions.* When a government controls just less than a majority, it can sometimes depend on a less formal and more unstable set of legislative coalitions in order to stay in power. Issues can be taken in an *ad hoc* manner and individual arrangements worked out over each, to enable the government to win key votes. The 1982 Haughey administration in Ireland was an example of this, as was the short period of legislative chaos that followed the failure of the British Lib/Lab pact. Such possibilities tend to influence coalition negotiations in situations where one party is close to a majority, and when the possibility of 'going it alone' is clearly on the cards. In general, the prospect should serve to enhance the bargaining position of parties that are already close to a majority.

The crucial point, however, is that the effective 'winning' criterion *can* be significantly less than control over a bare majority of seats in the legislature. Formal coalition theories find this possibility difficult to deal with, since it leaves open the practical prospect, not to mention the theoretical certainty, that a number of coalitions will *simultaneously* satisfy the winning criterion. Further constraints must therefore be employed before any theory may proceed further on this basis.

Some of these constraints are discussed in the sections that follow. The role of party ideology, however, imposes a further constraint that may enable minority governments to be relatively secure. A condition that coalition members should be *relatively* close to one another in policy terms can lead a minority coalition of one or more parties to be effectively 'winning' in the sense that there is no alternative coalition of parties that can agree to replace it. This can create a form of ideological *immobilisme*, and the position of the Christian Democrats in Italy springs immediately to mind.

For the sake of clarity, however, consider a hypothetical example in which five parties are ranged on an ideological left–right scale as follows:

	Left				Right
Party	A	B	C	D	E
% Seats	30	5	30	5	30

Coalition BCD, controlling 40 per cent of seats, may be effectively winning in the sense that only a voting coalition of A and E can defeat it. In practical terms the distance between A and E might be so great that there would never be an issue on which they would agree to combine forces and bring down the minority BCD administration.

This is a perfectly generalisable phenomenon that can be expressed quite clearly in 'rational-choice' terms, yet it does not seem to have found its ways into game-theory inspired approaches, for which the mathematics of the majority criterion provide theoretical elegance at the cost of political realism.[9] On this basis, in a one-dimension policy space, the winning criterion for coalitions of the centre could go down as low as $\frac{1}{3}$ + 1 of legislative seats before problems arise. For coalitions at the extremes, of course, the winning criterion would remain at a bare majority, since the prospect of voting coalitions to defeat these would be much more real.

This produces the awkward conclusion that different winning criteria apply for different coalitions. It also highlights one of the ways in which the nature of the policy space of a coalition system can condition the likely outcomes. The awkward possibility that a given configuration of policy positions and seat distributions can enable the formation of undefeatable minority governments is difficult to reconcile with existing coalition theory. But it is no less relevant, nonetheless.

Rather easier to handle within formal theories is the situation in which the winning criterion is significantly *greater* than a bare majority. This situation may arise, among other reasons, because constitutional amendments requiring a qualified majority are on the policy agenda, or because party discipline is poor and solid party votes in the legislature cannot be guaranteed, even on crucial issues. Here we are dealing with the familiar concept of the necessary 'working majority' for a government. The effective size of this will obviously vary widely between states with different cultural, institutional and ideological traditions as well as varying from time to time *within* states, depending on the current issue agenda. Thus in Ireland, a party government system *par excellence* with rigid party discipline on most matters, three-seat government majorities have seemed quite secure, even luxurious. In the French Fourth Republic, when even the concept of 'party' was often far from clear, constitutional problems arose in part because effective working majorities were in practice unattainably large, creating the classic version of *immobilisme*.

There is no problem in principle that prevents formal coalition theories from specifying larger-than-minimal majorities. In practice, a rather messy methodological problem arises; this concerns the need to specify precisely *what* the working majority in a given situation might be. This must obviously be done *independently of which coalitions actually form*. If it cannot be done, then deductive formation theories based on varying winning criteria cannot be tested.

In general terms, however, the problem of minority governments is the more pressing for formal coalition theories, since minority governments are clearly so common in practice. There are two general ways forward. The first is to work with the quite separate concepts of a cabinet coalition and of a (stable or unstable) legislative coalition. The second is to modify the concept of winning to produce an 'effectively winning' criterion that may, in particular circumstances, be considerably greater or less than 50 per cent of legislative seats.

Either way, a trade-off between rigour and realism must be made when it comes to testing deductive theories. However, inductive generalisation from historical experience in the specific country studies that follow is as good a method as any to set this process in motion.

Assumption 3: 'Parties are motivated by the desire to get into government and/or enact certain policies.'

While there are exceptions to the first part of this assumption, it seems on balance to be the least controversial of those underlying coalition theory. Even those parties that are very reluctant to go into *coalition* with others are rarely reluctant to go into *government* if they can do so on their own terms.

The question that arises, therefore, concerns the willingness of parties to trade off their basic objectives in exchange for a share of the rewards of office. One set of objectives, about which it is hard to generalise, concerns personalities. Certain high-profile personalities can be reluctant to sit beside one another at the cabinet table, a factor that can act as an important *ad hoc* constraint on coalition bargaining. A more general constraint of the same general type concerns the unwillingness of certain parties to share power *with anyone*. This appears as a hostility to coalition *per se*, and has been an important constraint on minority situations in Britain, for example, since the experience of the coalition governments of the thirties. Indeed, it appears to be part of the British political culture that the two main parties prefer to have all of the power for some of the time, rather than some of the power for most of the time. This attitude, of course, tends to be more prevalent in parties that do have a realistic chance of at least sometimes commanding a legislative majority.

The major set of objectives that must often be compromised in order to achieve office, however, concerns policy. It is part at least of the mythology of representative government that political parties are in business to promote certain policy positions. There may be two underlying reasons for this, each of which has rather different implications for the process of coalition government.

The first possible role for policy is that politicians seek office and that in order to gain office they must put forward policies that will generate popular support. This is very much the Downsian view, and leads to the conclusion that politicians will modify policies in order to maximise support.[10] If we adopt this 'cynical' version of the assumption, coalition bargaining is constrained by the *longer-term* effects on electoral prospects of *short-term* involvement in coalition. Politicians may be unwilling to make policy compromises to go into government if they fear subsequent electoral retaliation. The policy preferences of the *electorate* thereby act as a constraint on bargaining over coalition formation.

The other, less cynical, version of the assumption regards politicians as valuing policies *for their own sake*. Policy concessions thereby involve a *direct* cost denominated in terms of a fundamental objective. It may be that politicians value office solely for the ability that it gives them to influence policy, or it may be that the rewards of both office and policy outputs are valued independently. This is likely to vary from culture to culture and from party to party; the precise trade-off between office-seeking and policy-seeking motivations is something that needs to be subjected to empirical investigation. Specifically, there is a need to elaborate, for each party that is considered, whether office-holding is valued as a means to achieve policy objectives, whether policy promises are used as a means to achieve office, or whether there is a trade-off between the two.

The effects of various types of possible interaction between office-seeking and policy-seeking motivations are rarely reflected in formal theories. In fact, while some theories do consider party policy as an element in the formation process, the search for ideologically compact coalitions is usually seen as a way of minimising bargaining costs rather than of maximising some intrinsic policy payoff. If a trade-off between policy payoffs and the payoffs of office does take place, a specification of the trade-off function used by any given party demands difficult empirical work. Such functions could, of course, be set by assumption, and some indication of the likely practical effect of different trade-off functions could thereby be derived.

Within the more instrumental view of the role of party policy in the process of coalition formation, some empirical purchase can be gained from information that is already available. This concerns the impact of electoral feedback on a party's bargaining position, and the relevant information can be found in public opinion polls.

Most coalition systems have regular opinion polls, and most of these include questions tapping the level of satisfaction with the current government. These results are typically broken down by the voting behaviour or preferences of the respondents. It is thus possible both for politicians and for researchers to gauge the popularity, among potential supporters, of each of the government parties' current participation in coalition. This is a matter that must surely feed back into the politics of coalition and is clearly an issue that is relevant to the development of *dynamic* coalition theories. Changing anticipations of the electoral response, reflected in movements in the polls, may well change the government parties' attitudes to coalition quite dramatically during the life of a coalition. They may well, for example, affect *de facto* bargaining power. Parties that face electoral disaster may be reluctant to exercise any threat to bring down the government. Yet it is on this very threat that their bargaining power is based. Conversely, government parties that expect to make electoral progress when the government falls may be quite keen to flex their muscles. They may derive considerable *de facto* bargaining power from opinion poll feedback.

With relatively few exceptions,[11] current formal coalition theories are based on an office-seeking hypothesis. The full implications of the truly variable-sum games generated by policy-seeking motivations have yet to be systematically incorporated into the approach. Party policy has tended to be bolted on to the theories as something of an afterthought, a phenomenon that owes a lot to the immense influence of Riker's early work on coalitions, which viewed the process as an essentially zero-sum game. The full impact of incorporating policy motivations unequivocally into formal theories is far from clear, but an empirical review of the scale of the problem is clearly a useful starting point.

Assumption 4: 'All winning combinations of parties represent possible coalition governments.'

This statement is as much a consequence of the preceding three assumptions as it is an independent assumption in its own right. Having considered the empirical relevance of the three assumptions discussed above, it is clear that all winning combinations of parties do not represent possible coalition governments. This may be because of personality clashes between leaders, because some parties simply refuse to go into coalition, because there are fundamental incompatibilities in the policy stances of certain parties, and it may be for one of many other reasons. The elimination of certain potential combinations of parties from the game, however, has a fundamental impact on coalition bargaining.

The bargaining power of a party is affected by the number of threats that it can make. In this context, a threat concerns the possibility of joining an alternative coalition, or of leaving an existing coalition and bringing it down. (The latter, of course, amounts to the same thing, since it involves joining a winning *voting* coalition in order to defeat the government.) When one or more coalitions are removed from the list of theoretical possibilities, the threats associated with it are also removed. Unless the missing coalition is the grand coalition of all parties, there is obviously a redistribution of bargaining power, since some parties lose threats and others do not. This may even produce a situation in which a party may look quite powerful on paper, belonging to a range of mathematically plausible coalitions, yet be powerless in practice if each of these is ruled out on one *ad hoc* bargaining criterion or another.

Elegant mathematical formulations of bargaining power do not respond well to the *ad hoc* deletion of certain coalitions from the universe. The imposition of side constraints upon the set of winning coalitions in a given situation can have unexpected and paradoxical effects on such models. Yet the fact remains in practice, of course, that certain potential coalitions *can* be effectively written off as serious prospects, for reasons that even the dogs in the street appreciate. An approach that insists upon retaining these as members of a prediction set, in the name of theoretical elegance, is unlikely to command much respect.

In short, it is clear that some of the mathematical possibilities in a coalition situation are, quite simply, political impossibilities for one reason or another. No *a priori* model can handle such matters, for obvious reasons, and this provides a further dimension that can be added to coalition studies by country-specific empirical analyses.

(d)   Conclusions

There are many points in the process of studying real-world coalitions at which a choice must be made between making the theory more realistic and preserving its elegance. The advantages of realism often seem overwhelming. It would be most unwise, however, to disregard entirely the advantages of elegance. Formal theories derive from a rational-choice paradigm that is by now well developed and widely accepted. They thus have considerable intellectual resources upon which to draw. Every practical modification made to the theories in the name of realism distances them a little more from that paradigm, with the attendant danger that they become mere rationalisations of choice rather than rational-choice theories.

In fact, the issues that have been raised can be divided into those that demand *ad hoc* assumptions based on specific circumstances, and those that reflect generalisable phenomena that might be incorporated into formal theories.

Internal party politics, for example, does have general features, such as the institutional structure of the party. The effect of these, however, is likely to vary on a basis that is very specific to individual parties. It is unlikely, therefore, to be capable of integration into a formal theory. Intra-party politics may help us to explain deviant cases, of course, but is unlikely to do so in a manner that will yield significant development of general theories.

The matter of what constitutes a working majority, however, does have some aspects that cannot be generalised, but others which can be integrated into a general theory. Thus the impact of the ideological configuration of parties on the effective majority needed to hold on to government can, in principle, be built into an algorithm for identifying 'winning' coalitions. This would have the major advantage of bringing at least some minority administrations within the scope of formal theories. Matters relating to party discipline, however, will almost inevitably need to be treated on an *ad hoc* basis. The trade-off between office-seeking and policy-seeking can readily be formalised. The problem with this is to assemble relevant data. The effect of electoral feedback on bargaining power also seems a prime candidate for inclusion in any dynamic theory.

The reader is urged, therefore, when going through the various country-specific chapters in this book, to bear this general distinction in mind. In that way we may be able to begin the development of a constructive critique of coalition theory, with some hope of being able to develop revised, and more realistic, models. It would be no trouble at all, of course, to construct a long list of the many ways in which formal theories do not apply to Party X in Country Y at Time Z. Such a list can be constructed for any general theory. The only intellectually satisfactory way to replace an inferior theory, however, is to replace it with something demonstrably superior. Typically, this is the result of a systematic analysis of the empirical failings of the current approach, an endeavour to which the rest of this book is effectively dedicated.

Notes

1. These results can be found in Browne and Franklin (1973), p. 460.
2. See especially Taylor and Laver (1973), De Swaan (1973). For good discussions of minority governments, see Herman and Pope (1973) and Strom (1984).
3. For a good review of these methodological issues, see De Swaan and Mokken (1980).
4. See Axelrod (1970), Leiserson (1966), Dodd (1976), Taylor and Laver (1973) and De Swaan (1973).
5. See Schofield and Laver (1985).
6. See, for example, Laver (1974), Laver and Underhill (1982) and Franklin and Mackie (1983).
7. See Taylor and Laver (1973), p. 223, Herman and Pope (1973) and Strom (1984), p. 194.
8. Herman and Pope use the terms 'supported' and 'unsupported' minority governments to refer to broadly the same distinction as is made here between stable and unstable voting coalitions.
9. The real reason for this may be that such a criterion would be messy to build into one of the existing computer algorithms for identifying the set of winning coalitions. It cannot be impossible do this, however, since the problem is determinate. A solution would, of course, depend on including data on party policy positions as well as on seat distribution in the calculation of the 'winning' set.
10. This version of the assumption needs to be modified in a world of perfect information. Many changes in legislative representation do not affect the chances of power. A party that already controls a majority needs no more legislative support, while many minority configurations, such as a three-way split, are such that major changes in legislative support do not affect coalition prospects (see Laver 1981: 147–53 for a fuller discussion of this). If we assume, however, that information on likely election results is poor, then politicians will always be forced to maximise their voting support. This will never do them any harm and it may do them some good.
11. For one theoretical treatment of policy-seeking coalition formation, see Budge (1985).

References

Axelrod, R. 1970. *Conflict of Interest*. Chicago: Markham

Browne, E. and Franklin, M. 1973. Aspects of coalition payoffs in European parliamentary democracies. *American Political Science Review, 67*: 453–69

Budge, I. 1985. Beyond office-seeking: a pure policy-pursuing theory of parties in government. Unpublished paper, University of Essex

Budge, I., Robertson, D. and Hearl, D. (eds.) 1986. *Party Strategy*. Cambridge University Press

De Swaan, A. 1973. *Coalition Theories and Cabinet Formations*. Amsterdam: Elsevier

De Swaan, A. and Mokken, R. 1980. Testing coalition theories: the combined evidence. In L. Lewin and E. Verdung (eds.), *Politics as Rational Action*. Dordrecht: Reidel

Dodd, L. 1976. *Coalitions in Parliamentary Government*. Princeton University Press

Franklin, M. and Mackie, T. 1983. Familiarity and inertia in the formation of governing coalitions in parliamentary democracies. *British Journal of Political Science, 13:* 284

Gamson, W. 1961. A theory of coalition formation. *American Sociological Review, 26:* 373–82

Herman, V. and Pope, J. 1973. Minority governments in Western democracies. *British Journal of Political Science, 3:* 191–212

Laver, M. 1974. Dynamic factors in government coalition formation, *European Journal of Political Research, 2:* 259–70

1981. *The Politics of Private Desires*. Harmondsworth: Penguin Books

Laver, M. and Underhill, J. 1982. The bargaining advantages of combining with others. *British Journal of Political Science, 12:* 75–90

Leiserson, M. 1966. Coalitions in Politics, unpublished PhD dissertation, Yale University

Schofield, N. and Laver, M. 1985. Bargaining theory and portfolio pay-offs in European coalition governments 1948–1983. *British Journal of Political Science, 15:* 51–72

Strom, K. 1984. Minority governments in parliamentary democracies. *Comparative Political Studies, 16:* 199–227

Taylor, M. and Laver, M. 1973. Government coalitions in Western Europe, *European Journal of Political Research, 1:* 205–48

Warwick, P. 1979. The durability of coalition governments in parliamentary democracies, *Comparative Political Studies, 2:* 465–98

3   *Changing coalitional preferences among West German parties*

(a) *Introduction*

In 1949, deputies of ten parties and three independents were elected into the first Bundestag (federal legislature) of the Federal Republic. At that time, it was by no means clear whether the high fractionalisation that had been characteristic of the Weimar Reichstag would continue in the new legislature. However, Adenauer was able to form a government coalition including only three parties which disposed of 52 per cent majority of the seats.[1] Throughout the fifties, a process of concentration among the political parties represented in the Bundestag took place, which reduced the number to four in 1957 and to three in 1961. It is only since 1983 that, with the newly founded Green party (*Die Grünen*), a fourth party came again into the game. Nevertheless, only once, in 1957, did the Christian Democrats win an absolute majority in the Bundestag, and coalition governments have been the rule.

In this chapter, I shall limit myself to studying the coalitional behaviour of the political parties in the period between 1968 and 1982, when only three parties played a significant role in West Germany, i.e. the Christian Democratic party (CDU/CSU), the Social Democratic party (SPD) and the liberal Free Democratic party (FDP). Under the conditions of this party system, aside from the possibility of an all-party coalition which was never formed, three coalitions of two parties are possible and have in fact come into existence. In the language of formal coalition theory, all three are *minimal winning coalitions*, while only the Social-Liberal coalition governments of 1969, 1976 and 1980 were also *smallest-size coalitions*.

Coalition theory offers two possible explanations for the fact that the Grand Coalition[2] of the two big parties CDU/CSU and SPD lasted for only three years, while coalitions of one of the big parties with the much smaller liberal party have prevailed.[3] The first considers only payoffs in terms of portfolios which will be larger under the latter condition. The second explanation has to do with the programmatic distances between the parties. Under the assumption of a single left-right policy continuum on which the FDP as the *centre party* is located somewhere between the CDU/CSU on the right and the SPD on the left, a grand coalition does not fulfil the criterion of a *minimum-connected winning coalition* which predicts that coalitions will be formed between ideologically adjacent parties. While the assumption that the FDP is located in the centre of the party space has been questioned by some authors, e.g. by Grofman (1982), it will be shown in a later section that it is indeed correct in many respects.[4]

Thus, the smallest size as well as the minimum-connected winning criterion both grant a pivotal role to the FDP in the West German party system. This is manifested in the formation of governments as well as during their existence. The FDP decides whether a Christian Democrat or a Social Democrat is elected as Chancellor. All major changes in government have been initiated by the FDP. Its withdrawal from the long-standing Christian-Liberal coalition with the Christian Democrats in 1966 paved the way for the Grand Coalition and later for the formation of the first federal government without the CDU/CSU, i.e. the Social–Liberal coalition which took over in 1969. In 1982 its renewed turn towards the Christian Democrats restored the former configuration. Thus, changes in federal government have to date always been brought about by decisions of the party elites and particularly by the FDP leadership rather than by the voters whose voting behaviour is remarkably stable and shows no major shifts from one election to the next (Gibowski 1981; Troitzsch 1980: 225ff).

The pivotal role of the FDP is also borne out by the fact that it has achieved a higher participation rate in state and federal governments than any other party. On the federal level, it was a member of 70 per cent of the federal governments that have been formed thus far (14 out of 19). In terms of the duration of its participation in governments, this rate is even somewhat higher: it has participated in the federal government for 311 out of the 424 months from September 1949 until the end of 1984 (73.3 per cent) (cf. Haungs 1983).

Two more characteristics of West German coalitional behaviour are worth noting. The first is that not all coalitions are equally likely at a certain point in time, even if they are all possible in principle (*allgemeine Koalitionsfähigkeit*). Secondly, coalitions are rarely formed as a result of post-electoral negotiations among the parties. Instead, the intention to form a certain coalition is usually stated before an election takes place, and the public is aware beforehand of which government will be formed under which electoral conditions.[5]

In the light of the remarkable stability of coalition governments in the Federal Republic, it seems particularly interesting to study the reasons for the rarely occurring changes in coalition. Four factors seem of relevance in this respect. The first and most obvious reason is *growing policy differences* between the partners of a governing coalition. Partial disagreements are, of course, normal in any co-operation of two distinct parties. As long as the current priorities allow the execution of policies in which the common goals outweigh the programmatic differences, disagreement in less relevant policy areas can be played down by neglecting them, i.e. avoiding decision-making matters on which agreement cannot be achieved (Norpoth 1982: 17). During the Grand Coalition, this strategy was explicitly followed and denominated as the *Ausklammern* ('discarding') of controversial issues.[6]

However, once the commonalities are exhausted and priorities change, either by internal developments of the parties or enforced by events beyond the control of the party elites (e.g. the oil shock or rising unemployment rates), the strain within a governing coalition can become unbearable and make its dissolution mandatory.

A second factor is changes in *the degree of sympathy or dislike between the parties*. While this will normally be highly interrelated with ideological distance, it nevertheless constitutes a dimension of its own. This becomes clear when we consider the inevitable frustrations arising from the continuous necessity to reach compromises in a coalition, or the often highly polemic style of the political debate between government and opposition. Both may lead to a higher degree of dislike between parties than might be expected from policy distances alone. In contrast, during the formation of a new coalition and during the first time of its existence, sympathy and goodwill among the parties involved will be greater and may help to bridge policy disagreements. In West Germany, the expression *Koalitionsklima* ('coalitional climate') has become a widely used label for the degree of strain in intra-coalitional co-operation.

In countries, however, where all parties are oriented towards participation in government, as is the case in West Germany (Smith 1979: 137), a coalition will normally not be dissolved before the opportunity to form an alternative coalition is available. The contours of this new coalition should already be distinguishable in a rapprochement between the new partners in policy positions as well as in mutual sympathy. This is also favoured by the constitutional requirement for a 'constructive vote of no confidence'.

Thirdly, one can assume that the decision for coalitional change will also depend on considerations of electoral success, and this tends to caution against such a change being rapid. An *erosion in public support* for the governing parties may contribute to the dissolution of a governing coalition. Conversely, the decision to form a new coalition will only be made if its partners expect that they have a realistic chance to win the next election. In that respect, voter attitudes are an important factor in coalitional behaviour. Competence ratings of the different parties, coalitional preferences and the evaluations of the present government will be taken into account by the party leaders, even if they can expect that a certain part of their supporters will vote for them regardless of their coalitional behaviour.

Finally, the immediate social environment of the party leaders should not be neglected. They do not operate in a social vacuum and their behaviour is not only influenced by their own goals and expectations of electoral success, but also by the policy and coalition preferences of important reference groups such as party activists and party members, as well as interest groups and those parts of the mass media which normally support them. Thus, even if a government still enjoys a high amount of public support, a *loss in support among elites* may contribute to its dissolution.

This chapter will try to determine how far these factors have played a role in the formation and dissolution of the Social–Liberal coalition between 1968 and 1982. Apart from references to generally available evidence, the analysis will be primarily based on survey data of elites and voters gathered since 1968. In order to study the dynamic relations between the different factors in detail and to determine their relative importance, time series data would, of course, be needed. In particular, the question of how policy disagreements are related to the decline in mutual sympathy between the partners of a coalition and whether these two, in turn, are the cause or rather consequence of a withdrawal of public support is beyond the scope of our data. By looking at the positions of different groups of elites and voters at different points in time, it is, however, possible to identify those groups which were ahead of others in their evaluations of parties and coalitions in 1968/9 and in 1981/2, i.e. opinion leaders who played an important role in the opinion formation during both periods of coalitional change.

(b)   Data base

Three national elite surveys carried out in 1968, 1972 and 1981 constitute the major data base for a systematic analysis of the changes in the coalitional preferences of elites. It would go too far in the present context to describe the sampling design of the studies in detail.[7] Suffice it to note that the positional approach was used to identify elites, and that political as well as non-political elites were included in the studies.

The *political elites* include the members of federal and state governments as well as the leaders of political parties and parliamentary parties (*Fraktionen*) on federal and state level. Among the *non-political elites*, holders of leadership positions in other sectors were interviewed, i.e. in civil service, business, trade unions, mass media, etc. Although small in size and of little numerical relevance as voters, the non-political elites nevertheless serve as important reference groups for political leaders. Their attitudes are, therefore, relevant for political decision-making.

In the context of the intended analysis, information on voter attitudes is relevant for two reasons. As was mentioned before, voter attitudes are taken into account by the political elites. Secondly, a joint analysis of elite and voter attitudes is necessary in order to study the dynamics of public opinion formation.

Table 3.1 *Surveys used for the analysis*

Name of survey	n	Time of survey
Elite survey, 1968	808	Jan.–May 1968
Pre-election study, 1969, population 21 years and over	1,158	Sept. 1969
Elite survey, 1972	1,825	Feb.–July 1972
Pre-election study, 1972, population 18 years and over	2,052	Sept.–Oct. 1972
Elite survey, 1981	1,744	Mar.–July 1981
Population survey, 1982, population 16 years and over	2,006	Jan.–Feb. 1982

It may help to answer the question as to which groups among elites and voters changed their coalitional preferences earlier than others. For that purpose, an attempt was made to find general population surveys carried out at about the same time as the elite surveys. For 1969 and 1972 the pre-election surveys of the German Electoral Data project[8] could be used. Unfortunately, the 1969 survey took place more than a year after the first elite survey. By that time it was already clear, at least to a considerable part of the West German public, that the FDP had moved towards the SPD, whereas this was much less obvious in 1968. The third general population survey used for the analysis was part of the West German elite study of 1981. It was, however, carried out only at the beginning of 1982 for technical reasons. Table 3.1 gives some basic information about the six surveys used for analysis.

(c) Coalitional preferences of voters

Tables 3.2, 3.3 and 3.4 show the distributions of coalitional preferences of elites and voters in 1968/9, 1972 and 1981/2. The number of response categories differed somewhat between the studies, but each included the following five categories:

- government by the SPD alone
- government by the CDU/CSU alone
- Social–Liberal coalition, SPD–FDP
- Christian–Liberal coalition, CDU/CSU–FDP
- Grand Coalition, CDU/CSU–SPD.

The missing value categories (others, NA) were omitted from the computations. This seems justified since normally only about 10 per cent of the respondents fell into one of these categories.[9] For the purpose of these analyses, elites and voters were broken down by vote intention, which can be assumed to have a decisive influence on which government one prefers.

Apart from their descriptive value, the survey data on the development of coalitional preferences of elites and voters are particularly suited to studying the sequence of opinion formation. They can help to explore the degree of latitude party leaders enjoy with regard to their coalitional behaviour. Some authors have claimed that this latitude is less pronounced in West Germany than in other countries because strong normative expectations have developed, restricting the coalitional options available to party leaders. In discussing coalitional behaviour in the Federal Republic, Smith concludes that 'new rules of coalitions' have been established in 1969 which not only oblige party leaders to declare their coalitional intentions before an election takes place, but also to treat them as binding commitments for the whole legislative term (Smith 1979: 141). If this is true, voter reactions to changing coalitional arrangements should be particularly strong and put severe limits on the latitude of party leaders. It does not, however, preclude coalitional changes being initiated by party leaders as long as these norms are not violated.

The empirical results can shed some light on these processes by showing under what conditions voters are willing to follow the coalitional decisions taken by party elites. Survey data analysed by Norpoth indicate that the coalitional preferences of the voters of all parties change in accordance with the coalitional decisions made by the party leadership. Between 1965 and 1969, preference for the Grand Coalition increased among Christian Democratic voters from 37 per cent to 83 per cent.

SPD voters had favoured this coalition already in 1965 by a margin of 70 per cent, which remained constant until the 1969 election (Norpoth 1980: 429). After the formation of the Social–Liberal coalition, however, SPD voters reversed their preference ratio for the Social–Liberal vs. the Grand Coalition (Norpoth 1980: 431f).

No comparable change could be found among Christian Democratic and Liberal voters. Whereas the former clung to their previous choices, a majority of the latter had already been in favour of the new coalition before the election (Norpoth 1980: 432). Changes among the FDP voters had, thus, already occurred before the 1969 election. Support for the Christian–Liberal coalition dropped to a bare 23 per cent in 1969, while preference for the Social-Liberal coalition increased from 22 per cent to 56 per cent.

In counting these margins, Norpoth had to disregard, however, the considerable number of voters of the two big parties favouring a single-party government. Thus, for 30 per cent of the CDU/CSU and for 41 per cent of the SPD voters, preference for either of the coalitional constellations is not known. Nevertheless, the presumption that voter preferences follow elite decisions is further supported by the sympathy ratings for the different parties. In 1969, the average rating of Christian Democratic voters for the SPD was higher (+ 1.6) than that for the FDP (+ 0.4). Before the formation of the Grand Coalition, instead, both parties had got the same average score: SPD + 0.4 and FDP + 0.2.

Conversely, SPD voters in 1969 preferred the CDU/CSU (+ 1.7) to the FDP (+ 0.7). Notwithstanding this, the FDP scored higher among SPD voters in 1969 than during the years before. While its average sympathy score had always been

Table 3.2 *Coalition preferences of elites and voters, 1968/9*
Percentages based on respondents with preference for one of the
governments listed below

	n	SPD alone n (%)	CDU/CSU alone n (%)	SPD–FDP Social– Liberal coalition n (%)	CDU/CSU –FDP Christian– Liberal coalition n (%)	CDU/CSU –SPD Grand Coalition n (%)
Political elite						
SPD	50	41 (82.0)	2 (4.0)	3 (6.0)	0 (0.0)	4 (8.0)
CDU/CSU	52	0 (0.0)	44 (84.6)	0 (0.0)	5 (9.6)	3 (5.8)
FDP	18	0 (0.0)	0 (0.0)	11 (61.1)	6 (33.3)	1 (5.6)
Non-political elites						
SPD supporters	223	126 (57.0)	14 (6.3)	30 (13.6)	1 (0.5)	50 (22.6)
CDU/CSU supporters	324	4 (1.3)	172 (53.8)	5 (1.6)	48 (15.0)	91 (28.4)
FDP supporters	97	7 (7.4)	6 (6.4)	37 (39.4)	31 (33.0)	13 (13.8)
All non-political elites	688	138 (20.8)	204 (30.7)	74 (11.1)	82 (12.3)	167 (25.1)
Population						
SPD voters	451	174 (41.2)	3 (0.7)	80 (19.0)	1 (0.2)	164 (38.9)
CDU/CSU voters	438	6 (1.5)	122 (30.0)	5 (1.2)	39 (9.6)	234 (57.6)
FDP voters	44	2 (5.0)	0 (0.0)	21 (52.5)	9 (22.5)	8 (20.0)
Population total	1,158	193 (19.5)	141 (14.2)	116 (11.7)	57 (5.8)	483 (48.8)

negative until the presidential election in March 1969, where the FDP deputies had voted for the SPD candidate Heinemann, it became positive for the first time after that event (+0.2). The increase for the CDU/CSU was, however, more pronounced: in October 1966, shortly before the formation of the Grand Coalition, it had still been as low as −0.3 (figures reported in Klingemann and Pappi 1970: 129). Among FDP voters, the CDU/CSU had a slight lead over the SPD in 1966, which was reversed for the first time after the Heinemann election. In the pre-election study of 1969, they ranked the SPD (+1.9) better than the Christian Democrats (+1.6).

In 1972, after three years of Social–Liberal coalition, preference for the Grand Coalition option had gone down to only 20 per cent among SPD voters. The majority of SPD and FDP voters supported the governing Social–Liberal coalition, while 58 per cent of the Christian Democratic voters preferred the SPD to the FDP and only 39 per cent the other way round (Norpoth 1980: 429).[10] These figures remained remarkably constant until the beginning of 1982 (cf. Tables 3.3 and 3.4).

With regard to FDP voters, we are in the unique position that in addition to survey results their actual voting behaviour also gives clues about coalitional preferences. In federal elections FDP voters, to a much higher degree than voters of the big parties, make use of split-ticket voting. While casting their second, decisive vote for the FDP list, many of them use the opportunity to give their first vote to the candidate of another party.[11] Split-ticket voting was particularly frequent in 1972, 1980 and 1983: in these elections more than half of the voters with a second vote for the FDP gave their first vote to the candidate of another party. In 1972 and 1980, the vast majority of these first votes was cast for the SPD candidate, while in 1983 nearly 83 per cent of them went to the Christian Democratic candidate (Berger *et al.* 1983: 558; Schultze 1983: 70).

At first glance this may look like an impressive shift of FDP voters towards the newly-installed Christian–Liberal coalition. It is, however, often maintained that these split-ticket voters are not genuine FDP voters, but rather supporters of either SPD or CDU/CSU who want the FDP to surmount the 5 per cent quorum needed to enter the Bundestag in order to save the existing government (so-called *Leihstimmen*). This interpretation is fostered by the fact that journalists as well as politicians have indeed sometimes recommended using that strategy.

Naturally, the ballot itself does not allow us to distinguish between these interpretations. But the observed shifts in split-ticket voting should alert us to a major problem involved in studying electoral support for the parties over time, namely that a high amount of individual-level change in voting behaviour might be involved. Panel studies have regularly shown that even relatively stable aggregate results disguise considerable shifts on the individual level. It cannot be ruled out, particularly for a small party like the FDP, that changes in coalitional preferences and split-ticket voting are primarily caused by an exchange of voters. Data on individual-level change are therefore needed in order to substantiate the presumption that voters change their coalitional preferences rather than their voting behaviour in reaction to the changing coalitional behaviour of party leaders.

In analysing the pre- and post-election panel study of 1969 and the recall question for the 1965 election, Norpoth was able to show that this was indeed the case for most of the voters of the two big parties. They accepted the coalitional strategies of their party leaders, and did not sanction them by withdrawing voting support or by means of lower sympathy ratings (Norpoth 1980: 434). In contrast to SPD and CDU/CSU voters, however, Norpoth found more serious fluctuations among FDP voters in reaction to coalitional changes of the FDP. 'Only 40% of the previous (1965) FDP voters indicate a vote intention or decision for the party in 1969. It comes as no surprise that the FDP came perilously close

Table 3.3 *Coalition preferences of elites and voters, 1972*
Percentages based on respondents with preference for one of the governments listed below

	n	SPD alone n (%)	CDU/CSU alone n (%)	SPD–FDP Social–Liberal coalition n (%)	CDU/CSU –FDP Christian– Liberal coalition n (%)	CDU/CSU –SPD Grand Coalition n (%)
Political elite						
SPD	110	78 (72.2)	0 (0.0)	28 (25.9)	2 (1.9)	0 (0.0)
CDU/CSU	128	1 (0.8)	110 (88.0)	0 (0.0)	7 (5.6)	7 (5.6)
FDP	47	0 (0.0)	0 (0.0)	46 (100.0)	0 (0.0)	0 (0.0)
Non-political elites						
SPD supporters	456	206 (47.1)	4 (0.9)	182 (41.6)	4 (0.9)	41 (9.4)
CDU/CSU supporters	806	4 (0.5)	301 (40.9)	9 (1.2)	228 (31.0)	194 (26.4)
FDP supporters	203	2 (1.1)	1 (0.5)	130 (71.4)	34 (18.7)	15 (8.2)
All non-political elites	1,540	214 (15.3)	318 (22.8)	325 (23.3)	277 (19.9)	261 (18.7)
Non-political elites: selected reference groups						
Media elite, SPD supporters	119	45 (39.1)	1 (0.9)	55 (47.8)	1 (0.9)	13 (11.3)
Media elite, CDU/CSU supporters	107	0 (0.0)	40 (40.8)	2 (2.0)	22 (22.4)	34 (34.7)
Media elite, FDP supporters	42	1 (2.7)	0 (0.0)	28 (75.7)	6 (16.2)	2 (5.4)
Business elite, CDU/CSU supporters	320	2 (0.7)	102 (34.7)	1 (0.3)	124 (42.2)	65 (22.1)
Business elite, FDP supporters	59	0 (0.0)	0 (0.0)	29 (55.8)	18 (34.6)	5 (9.6)
Trade union elite, SPD supporters	42	33 (80.5)	0 (0.0)	8 (19.5)	0 (0.0)	0 (0.0)
Population						
SPD voters	942	303 (33.6)	9 (1.0)	456 (50.6)	16 (1.8)	117 (13.0)
CDU/CSU voters	666	8 (1.3)	350 (55.7)	9 (1.4)	107 (17.0)	154 (24.5)
FDP voters	122	8 (6.9)	4 (3.4)	69 (59.5)	26 (22.4)	9 (7.8)
Population total	2,052	349 (18.7)	422 (22.7)	582 (31.3)	173 (9.3)	336 (18.0)

to extinction in that election, barely exceeding the 5% minimum of the total vote' (Norpoth 1980: 435).

Zülch estimates that even less than 25 per cent of its voters of 1965 voted for the FDP in 1969 (1972: 87f). The assumption of an exchange of FDP voters in reaction to the formation of the Social–Liberal coalition in 1969 is further confirmed by studies showing that the FDP electorate has undergone consider- able changes in its social composition. It lost support among the self-employed old middle class that constituted its traditional voter base (Klingemann and Pappi 1970: 124ff; Pappi 1973: 200; Zülch 1972: 97). Although the FDP still draws a good deal of its voters from this class, the majority of them come from the new middle class whose members generally show much less stable party affiliations (Pappi 1973: 210f). This means that the FDP does not command a stable, socio-economically defined voter basis, as the two big parties do, which can rely on majority support among Catholics (CDU/CSU) or trade union members (SPD) (Fliszar and Gibowski 1984: 70; Kaack 1980: 40ff). This makes the party dependent on floating voters who cast their votes according to issue considerations rather than traditional loyalties or stable party identification.

Altogether, the empirical results show that norms regulating the coalitional behaviour of the parties coexist with a high degree of latitude for party elites to pursue their coalitional strategies. While Christian Democratic and Social Democratic voters are willing to accept the coalitional policies their parties adopt and change their coalitional preferences in accordance with those policies, voters of the Free Democrats are extremely sensitive to the coalitional behaviour of the FDP leadership. This was demonstrated in 1969, and it presumably happened again in 1982. The FDP losses after the formation of the Christian–Liberal coalition in 1982 were even more severe than those in the aftermath of 1969. Even when the party managed to return to the Bundestag in 1983 with 7 per cent of the votes, it failed to surmount the 5 per cent barrier in no less than six out of eight state elections from autumn 1982.[12] Whether the strong reactions were a consequence of the violation of the coalitional commitment made by the FDP leadership before the 1980 election, namely to support Helmut Schmidt's government for the whole legislative term, is not known. The earlier losses in the 1969 election, where the coalitional change had taken place while the FDP was in opposition, indicate, however, that the very decision to form a new coalition was a more important factor than the violation of the norms of 'fair' coalitional behaviour.

It seems as if the FDP suffers foremost from its genuinely ambivalent position in the West German cleavage system, which results in a politically heterogeneous voter basis. It constantly has to accommodate an economically conservative wing with a reform-oriented Social–Liberal wing (Broughton and Kirchner, this volume). Any coalition it enters signifies a change in balance between these wings, and results in a loss of the dedicated voters of the 'losing' wing.

The survey data also give some empirical foundation to the normative discussion of whether the formation of specific coalitions is in accordance with 'voter wishes'. We can realistically assume that the voters of the two big parties wish foremost that their party participate in the government. They give the party leadership the leeway to form whatever coalition it considers necessary to pursue this goal. The same, however, is not true for FDP voters. With regard to 1969, it was heavily disputed whether the FDP had stated its intention to form the Social–Liberal coalition clearly enough before the election. While Gringmuth (1984: 39f), Veen (1976: 12) and Zülch (1972: 78) maintain that the party had left the coalition question open during the campaign, other authors claim that it was not only stated in advance but also that this message had reached the FDP voters (Kaase 1970: 48; Smith 1979: 140). Our data as well as those used by Kaase and Zülch (1972: 109) show that a majority of the FDP voters in 1969 indeed favoured the new Social–Liberal coalition.

In 1982 the situation was different. Our survey data show that a majority of 63.4 per cent of the FDP voters still supported the Social–Liberal coalition. Thus, while the exchange of voters in 1969 had taken place before the formation of the new coalition, it occurred only after the toppling of Helmut Schmidt's government in 1982. But again, FDP voters were prompt to react to this move of the FDP leadership.

(d) Coalitional preferences of elites

The results show clearly that the elites in 1968 and 1981 were well ahead of the voters with regard to their coalitional preferences. Whereas in 1968 only one-quarter of the non-political elites were still in favour of the then governing Grand Coalition, the same was true of nearly half of the population. This is even more astonishing given the fact that the population survey took place more than one year later.

One must, however, not forget that the population is in general more in favour of coalition governments than the elites. Whereas in 1968/9 more than 70 per cent of the political elites and more than 50 per cent of the non-political elites preferred a single-party government, only 34 per cent of the population did so. Thus, the smaller numbers for the Grand Coalition among the elites may be at least partly a result of this fact. In order to control for this systematic difference between elites and voters, the sympathy ratings for the different parties were used to ascertain the numbers of the SPD elites who preferred the CDU to the FDP or, rather, the other way round. According to these, 70.8 per cent of the SPD politicians and 55.9 per cent of the SPD supporters[13] in the elites preferred the FDP to the CDU, whereas more than one year later nearly 40 per cent of the SPD voters were still in favour of the Grand Coalition.

In contrast to the results for the SPD, the Christian Democratic politicians and elite supporters were split in their second choice: 59.6 per cent of the former and 64.8 per cent of the latter preferred the SPD to the FDP, and can therefore be classified as favouring the then existing coalition.

Thus, already in 1968 a clear majority of the politicians of the Social–Liberal

Table 3.4 *Coalition preferences of elites and voters, 1981/2*
Percentages based on respondents with preference for one of the governments listed below

	n	SPD alone n (%)	CDU/CSU alone n (%)	SPD–FDP Social-Liberal coalition n (%)	CDU/CSU–FDP Christian-Liberal coalition n (%)	CDU/CSU–SPD Grand Coalition n (%)
Political elite						
SPD	124	70 (58.8)	0 (0.0)	43 (36.1)	0 (0.0)	6 (5.0)
CDU/CSU	125	0 (0.0)	79 (64.2)	0 (0.0)	39 (31.7)	5 (4.1)
FDP	25	0 (0.0)	0 (0.0)	20 (80.0)	5 (20.0)	0 (0.0)
Non-political elites						
SPD voters	355	98 (29.9)	0 (0.0)	199 (60.7)	3 (0.9)	28 (8.5)
CDU/CSU voters	647	0 (0.0)	159 (25.4)	8 (1.3)	403 (64.3)	57 (9.1)
FDP voters	283	0 (0.0)	3 (1.2)	108 (41.7)	129 (49.8)	19 (7.3)
All non-political elites	1,470	114 (8.4)	181 (13.4)	353 (26.1)	585 (43.2)	121 (8.9)
Non-political elites: selected reference groups						
Media elite, SPD voters	56	9 (17.6)	0 (0.0)	41 (80.4)	0 (0.0)	1 (2.0)
Media elite, CDU/CSU voters	92	0 (0.0)	19 (20.7)	4 (4.3)	59 (64.1)	10 (10.9)
Media elite, FDP voters	52	0 (0.0)	0 (0.0)	20 (42.6)	23 (48.9)	4 (8.5)
Business elite, CDU/CSU voters	302	0 (0.0)	68 (23.3)	1 (0.3)	196 (67.1)	27 (9.2)
Business elite, FDP voters	84	0 (0.0)	1 (1.4)	13 (17.6)	54 (73.0)	6 (8.1)
Trade union elite, SPD voters	69	38 (56.7)	0 (0.0)	22 (32.8)	1 (1.5)	6 (9.0)
Population						
SPD voters	528	153 (32.3)	3 (0.6)	271 (57.3)	4 (0.8)	42 (8.9)
CDU/CSU voters	714	6 (0.9)	409 (63.6)	8 (1.2)	176 (27.4)	44 (6.8)
FDP voters	236	3 (1.5)	10 (5.2)	123 (63.4)	46 (23.7)	12 (6.2)
Population total	2,206	187 (12.3)	467 (30.7)	456 (30.0)	272 (17.9)	137 (9.0)

parties and the elite supporters of the SPD wished the new coalition. The FDP supporters in the non-political elites were, however, less clear-cut in their preferences. Their answers were much more dispersed over the whole range of alternatives and only about 40 per cent advocated a Social–Liberal coalition. Noticeably, a sizeable minority of about one-third among FDP leaders and elite supporters alike preferred a return to the old Christian–Liberal coalition.

In 1972, the Social–Liberal coalition enjoyed nearly unanimous support among the politicians and elite supporters of the SPD and FDP alike. Even among FDP supporters, preference for a Christian–Liberal coalition had decreased to only 18.7 per cent. Social Democratic support for the coalition with the FDP again becomes clearer when we take the party rank orders into account. Ninety-eight per cent of the Social Democratic politicians and 87 per cent of their elite supporters preferred the FDP to the Christian Democrats.

For the latter, the situation was much less comfortable. Given the consolidation of the Social–Liberal government, there was little hope of forming a coalition with either of the other parties (Pridham 1982: 149). This is reflected in the rather high number of Christian Democratic politicians who preferred a single-party government by the CDU/CSU. In the light of these figures, the failed attempt to topple the government by co-operating with conservative FDP deputies seems to have been the only realistic way to get back into office.

The high number of respondents in the elite surveys of 1972 and 1981 as compared to 1968 allows a further subdivision of the supporters of the different parties according to their sector location. Thereby, it is possible to study the coalitional preferences of groups which can be assumed to be of particular importance to the party leaders, namely the representatives of those interest groups which traditionally have been closely affiliated with one of the political parties. These are the business leaders who mainly support the CDU/CSU (1981: 65.8 per cent), but also the FDP (18.3 per cent), and the trade union leaders who are predominantly affiliated with the SPD (79.3 per cent). Additionally, the supporters of the three parties in the media elite have been analysed separately. Their coalitional preferences seem particularly important since they have the unique opportunity to communicate them to a larger public.[14]

Two results in Table 3.3 deserve special mention. Among the business leaders with an FDP preference, only a slight majority of 55.8 per cent supported the Social–Liberal coalition in 1972, whereas a sizeable minority of 34.6 per cent still advocated a Christian–Liberal coalition. Equally remarkable is that also 42.2 per cent of the CDU/CSU supporters in the business elite favoured this coalition. Thus, the business elite continued to be a stronghold of advocates of a Christian–Liberal coalition even at a time when the formation of such a coalition was extremely unlikely.

The second interesting result concerns the trade union leaders. They overwhelmingly favoured a single-party government by the SPD. While this was never a realistic possibility, their preference nevertheless reflects the big distance between trade unions and the FDP, which posed a serious problem for the SPD leadership, who had to deal with both groups.

In 1981, a clear majority of Christian Democrats in the non-political elites favoured the formation of a Christian–Liberal coalition. On the other hand, more than 60 per cent of the CDU/CSU leaders and voters advocated a single-party government by the CDU/CSU. If we again take the party rank orders into account, it becomes, however, quite clear that the FDP was predominantly preferred over the Social Democrats.

Among the Free Democrats, the elite supporters already showed a slight plurality (49.8 per cent) in favour of a coalition with the CDU/CSU. This majority is particularly high among the FDP supporters in the business elite (73.0 per cent). In contrast, 80 per cent of the FDP politicians interviewed and 63.4 per cent of the voters of that party still clung to the Social–Liberal coalition.

With regard to the FDP politicians, the possibility cannot be ruled out that those who pursued the coalitional change most actively were less willing to be interviewed. But even if we assume that all 15 FDP leaders who were in the original sample but refused to be interviewed were in favour of a coalitional change, it would only indicate an equal split among the FDP leadership in 1981. Instead, it seems more realistic that the actual relation was about 65 per cent to 35 per cent in favour of the Social–Liberal coalition. The fact that the change could be effected already slightly more than a year later should remind us of two basic reservations to be made when predicting political decisions from survey data. The first is that there exist considerable differences of power even among top elites which cannot be accounted for in looking only at the distribution of attitudes. The second is the fact that political processes can develop considerable dynamics which cannot be studied by survey methodology.

The data also give some support for the assumption that FDP leaders perceived the coalition question as a matter of tactics rather than conviction. While 80 per cent of them indicated a preference for the Social–Liberal coalition, the party rank orders show that only 32 per cent of them preferred the SPD over the CDU. Forty-four per cent instead preferred the CDU and 24 per cent gave equal ratings for both big parties. The respective proportions among the FDP supporters in the non-political elites are the following: 33.6 per cent for the SPD, 50.5 per cent for the CDU, and 15.9 per cent equal ratings.

The vast majority of the Social Democratic elites, finally, were still in favour of the Social–Liberal coalition. What seems, however, more important with regard to the SPD is that the number of supporters of a single-party government has declined since 1972. One explanation of this rather unexpected result could be that the confidence in the SPD's capability of solving the pending economic problems had decreased at the beginning of the 1980s even among SPD leaders and supporters. Another possibility which cannot be ruled out is that a number of conservative Social Democrats in the elites, with regard to the more radical wing in their own party, appreciated the retarding role of the FDP more than they could admit in public.

(e) Party support and the choice of coalitional strategies

It was said before that the perceived chances of winning electoral support influence the strategies followed by the political elites. Even when it could be shown that voters by and large approve of the coalitional decisions taken by the political leaders by changing their coalitional preferences accordingly, there are limits to elite manipulation of public opinion. This is not only true for FDP voters who are particularly prone to reacting to party decisions not in accord with what they consider adequate, but also for the loyal followers of the big parties, though to a lesser degree.

While voter attitudes give only scarce information on what parties and governments should do in a certain situation, dissatisfaction with political outputs will inevitably lead to a withdrawal of support. Thus, voter attitudes serve as restrictions rather than as guidelines for elite behaviour. Accordingly, elites assess the current mood among the voters and calculate voter reactions to their own behaviour. They also have more or less accurate hypotheses as to what decisions will or will not be accepted.

In this vein, voter evaluations of government performance are particularly relevant for coalitional behaviour, since the partners of a governing coalition are not normally held equally responsible for it. It seems therefore natural that each party tries to claim responsibility for successful actions while blaming failures on the other party or parties. In the case of a continuous failure of a government to cope with pending problems, such a disposition of a governmental party will, however, become impossible in the long run. When this becomes apparent, the dissolution of the existing coalition may be considered as a reasonable strategy for party survival.

This was obviously the case in the FDP leadership in the mid-sixties as well as in the early eighties. At both times, the FDP feared that a continuation of the existing coalition would lead to its electoral defeat in the next election. Zülch reports that in 1966 the crisis of the Christian–Liberal coalition was triggered by severe losses of the FDP in two state elections and its following attempt to regain a more independent profile (1972: 24; cf. also Gringmuth 1984: 31ff).

Voter dissatisfaction did not, however, play any role in the dissolution of the Grand Coalition in 1969. Not only did nearly 80 per cent of the respondents declare in the 1969 pre-election survey that the Grand Coalition had been successful, but nearly 58 per cent wished its continuation after the election. The main reason lay, instead, entirely on the elite level. In a study carried out by Engelmann in 1969 in which parliamentarians, party activists and voters were interviewed, the author found that an overwhelming majority of 70 per cent of the elite respondents thought that the Grand Coalition was bad for democracy, whereas this was only true for 26 per cent of the mass sample (Engelmann 1972: 35ff). The data of our 1968 elite study confirm this. While 82 per cent of the elites said that the formation of the Grand Coalition had been justified under the political conditions of 1966, 64.9 per cent claimed that its continuation would be of disadvantage to democracy. The most frequent arguments brought forward in an open-ended question were the lack of opposition (31.9 per cent) and the blurring of party differences (14.2 per cent).

In contrast to this, survey data for the early eighties[15] show that voter dissatisfaction again played an important role for the fate of the Social–Liberal government. Satisfaction with the government as measured on a scale ranging from $+5$ to -5 declined from a comfortable $+1.2$ in January 1981 to an unprecedented low of -0.4 in August 1982 (Berger *et al.* 1983: 563f). This was particularly marked among FDP voters (decline from $+1.8$ to $+0.4$), whereas SPD voters showed not only much more satisfaction with the government at both points in time, but also a smaller decline from $+2.9$ to $+2.1$.

Similarly, if we turn to the ratings of the individual parties, it can be seen that the SPD suffered a continuous decrease in popular sympathy after the 1980 election. At the turn of 1981/2 its values had dropped below $+1.0$. The FDP curve is of similar shape but the FDP values were nearly uniformly higher than those of the SPD. At the same time the values for the CDU fluctuated around $+1.3$ and showed a slight increase after April 1982 (Berger *et al.* 1983: 562).

The most important indicator of electoral support and the most relevant in terms of votes is, of course, the vote intention of the respondents. Repeated surveys show that the percentage of respondents expressing a vote intention for the SPD declined rapidly in the first half of 1982, while the FDP support remained rather stable.

The FDP leaders were well aware of the fact that the various indicators of support for the government and the governing parties pointed downwards. It was therefore rational on their side to assume that the decline would continue and that the FDP, too, would be affected by it sooner or later. Thus, the conclusion to leave the governmnent seems well justified.

A survey carried out on behalf of the FDP leadership in June/July 1981, which was designed to probe for the potential reactions of FDP voters to a coalitional change, demonstrates that the party leaders pursued exactly the same kind of reasoning. With an internal paper of the FDP, which was published by the *Frankfurter Rundschau* on 22 August, the development of government and party popularity was analysed, followed by a report on the results of the study. These results also constitute the data base of a more scholarly analysis by Gibowski (1981). They show that a majority (52 per cent) of the FDP voters advocated the general norm that a coalition should not be dissolved during a legislative term. Seventy-seven per cent of them wished the continuation of the Social–Liberal coalition until 1984. Asked for their coalitional preference, 56 per cent favoured the Social–Liberal government, and 27 per cent a Christian–Liberal one (cf. the slightly different values of Table 3.4).

The survey also included several questions probing for voter reactions under different political scenarios, assuming increasing difficulties in co-operation between the FDP and the SPD. The most pertinent question, however, concerned the hypothetical vote intention in the event of the FDP declaring before the next election its intention to form a new coalition with the Christian Democrats. It resulted in an overall loss of about 10 per cent of the FDP voters, resulting from net losses of one-third and net gains of one-quarter. The title of the analysis indicates that this was deemed to be the central result of the survey: 'A coalitional statement [*Koalitionsaussage*] in favour of the Christian Democrats would not be fatal' (*Frankfurter Rundschau*). Even when Gibowski assumes that the prediction of losses is more realistic than that of potential gains (1981: 13f), the margin of FDP votes for the hypothetical question comes very close to the electoral return of the FDP in the 1983 Bundestag elections.

Thus, the FDP leadership was prepared to suffer again a considerable exchange in voters when it left the Schmidt government in September 1982. This was, by the way, shortly after the opinion poll in August 1982 which had yielded the above-mentioned most negative rating ever measured for a federal government (−0.4), and showed that the vote intention for the Christian Democrats had gone up to more than 50 per cent. The chance of an absolute majority of the CDU/CSU represented a particular danger for the FDP, since this would have deprived it of its pivotal role in the West German party system.

The FDP's expectation, however, that its stable voter basis exceeded the 5 per cent level was overly optimistic. Opinion polls after the formation of the Christian–Liberal government showed the FDP so far below the 5 per cent barrier that its return to the next Bundestag seemed doubtful (Berger *et al.* 1983: 574). This was mainly due to the way in which the old government had been toppled, which was criticised by 60 per cent of the voters (Berger *et al.* 1983: 567). It was only in January 1983 that the party regained the strength needed to secure its legislative survival.

The data in Table 3.5 show that among the non-political elites support for the parties of the Social–Liberal coalition was already rather low in spring 1981. This becomes particularly evident if we compare the elites to the general public at the same time. The much lower ratings of the elites, though partly due to the fact that the SPD generally enjoys much less support among the non-political elites than among voters,[16] remain even when we control for vote intention. This corroborates the presumption that political developments show themselves earlier in elite than in voter opinions (Wildenmann 1975: 278ff). Wildenmann concluded from these results as early as March 1982 that 'The elites wish the change' ('Die Elite wünscht den Wechsel').

(f)   The change in 'coalitional climate' between 1972 and 1981/2

Changing mutual sympathy ratings of the political parties can serve as an indicator of changes in the relations between the parties. Unfortunately, no such question had been included in the 1968 elite study, which limits the analysis to the years between 1972 and 1981. Above, the sympathy ratings have already been

Table 3.5 *Mean sympathy ratings for*
SPD, CDU and FDP in the early eighties

	SPD	CDU	FDP
Population[a]			
September 1980	+2.0	+1.1	+1.2
May 1981			
All respondents	+1.3	+1.3	+1.3
SPD voters	+3.5	−0.1	+1.7
CDU/CSU voters	−0.6	+3.4	+0.7
FDP voters	+1.6	+0.5	+3.7
April 1982	+0.6	+1.1	+0.9
August 1982	+0.3	+1.4	+0.2
October 1982	+1.2	+1.3	−0.8
March 1983	+1.2	+1.9	−0.2
Non-political elites, 1981			
All non-political elites	+0.1	+1.5	+0.7
SPD supporters	+2.8	−0.7	+0.3
CDU/CSU supporters	−1.5	+3.0	+0.1
FDP supporters	+0.2	+1.2	+2.7

[a] These survey results were made available by the
Forschungsgruppe Wahlen, Mannheim.

used as a supplementary measure of coalitional preferences for those elite
respondents who had indicated a preference for a single-party government. In
this section, however, the metric information yielded by the ratings will be used
rather than the ordinal one.

Most authors describe the co-operation during the first years of the Social–
Liberal government as harmonious (Gringmuth 1984: 9f; Haungs 1983: 102;
Smith 1979: 145). This is also reflected in our data. The mutual ratings of SPD
and FDP politicians are rather positive. At the same time, a high degree of
polarisation between coalition and opposition parties can be seen.

During the second half of the 1970s, however, the co-operation in government
became increasingly difficult. The replacement of the founders of the coalition,
Willy Brandt and Walter Scheel, in the offices of Chancellor and Vice-Chancellor
by Helmut Schmidt and Hans-Dietrich Genscher was presumably of more than
just symbolic significance. Verheugen calls it the 'turning-point' (*Zäsur*) dividing
two periods of Social–Liberal government (1984: 59). 'The above-mentioned
personal turnover symbolized at the same time a change in coalitional climate: the
vigorous spirit [*Aufbruchsstimmung*] of 1969 was superseded by a persistent
disenchantment, a concentration on matters which seemed imperative in the light
of the deteriorating economic conditions' (Haungs 1983: 102).

The sympathy ratings of the party leaders in 1981 reflect this change rather
clearly. The SPD and FDP have drifted apart, while the CDU and FDP have
moved closer. The FDP politicians give nearly equal ratings for SPD and CDU,

Table 3.6 *Mean sympathy ratings for the political parties, 1972 and 1981/2*

	Sympathy ratings for:			
	CDU	SPD	CSU	FDP
1972				
SPD politicians	− 1.6	+ 3.7	− 3.6	+ 2.4
CDU politicians	+ 3.1	− 1.4	+ 1.7	− 2.0
CSU politicians	+ 2.4	− 2.0	+ 2.6	− 1.7
FDP politicians	− 1.9	+ 1.6	− 3.6	+ 4.1
Non-political elites				
SPD supporters	− 1.0	+ 2.7	− 3.3	+ 1.9
CDU/CSU supporters	+ 2.3	− 0.6	+ 0.9	− 0.6
FDP supporters	− 0.1	+ 1.1	− 2.4	+ 3.0
Population				
SPD voters	− 0.8	+ 4.0	− 1.8	+ 1.8
CDU/CSU voters	+ 3.2	− 0.2	+ 2.6	− 0.3
FDP voters	+ 0.6	+ 2.4	− 0.9	+ 3.2
1981/2				
SPD politicians	− 1.1	+ 3.3	− 3.0	+ 0.8
CDU politicians	+ 4.2	− 2.2	+ 3.1	− 0.7
CSU politicians	+ 3.8	− 3.1	+ 4.5	− 1.6
FDP politicians	+ 0.5	+ 0.4	− 2.1	+ 4.2
Non-political elites				
SPD voters	− 0.7	+ 2.8	− 2.8	+ 0.3
CDU/CSU voters	+ 3.0	− 1.5	+ 1.5	+ 0.1
FDP voters	+ 1.2	+ 0.2	− 1.1	+ 2.7
Population				
SPD voters	− 0.7	+ 3.3	− 2.0	− 0.4
CDU/CSU voters	+ 3.4	− 1.3	+ 2.2	+ 1.1
FDP voters	+ 0.1	+ 1.2	− 1.5	+ 2.7

though both are only slightly positive. Among the FDP supporters in the non-political elites, the CDU has even passed the SPD. CDU leaders and elite supporters rate the FDP less negatively than in 1972, though not (yet) positively. Remarkably enough, almost no rapprochement between the FDP and CSU has taken place: their mutual ratings are still far in the negative range. This hostility indicates the endemic conflict between these parties in the new government.

The results can be traced back to the avowedly strained climate within the Social–Liberal coalition in the summer of 1981. Already they show a trend among the FDP towards the Christian Democrats which was even more marked among the FDP elite supporters than among the FDP leaders themselves.

Dalton and Hildebrandt (1983), in analysing the development of distances between the voters of the three parties from 1961 to 1980, stress as a major result that the perceived polarisation between the SPD and Christian Democrats has increased considerably, whereas the distance between the SPD and the FDP has decreased during this time. Our data supplement their analysis in an important way by allowing us to compare voter ratings to those of the elites. The average scores in Table 3.6 show clearly that the mutual evaluations among Christian Democrats on one side and Social Democrats on the other are more negative and, thus, more polarised among political elites than among party supporters in the non-political elites who, in turn, show more polarisation than the voters.

The growing polarisation found by Dalton and Hildebrandt can, therefore, also be interpreted as a reaction of the voters to the much higher degree of polarisation in the elites during the seventies. This possibility is, in fact, explicitly mentioned by the authors. Even more interesting, however, is their presumption that the polarisation among the voters may escape elite control and that elites cannot just switch it off whenever it becomes inconvenient (1983: 79).

This optimistic assumption may, however, overrate voters' abilities to form political attitudes independently from elite opinion leadership. Our analysis of the development of coalitional preferences supports instead the expectation that voters will again follow the elites' decisions. Only with regard to the FDP voters does the assumption seem justified that voter attitudes are more resistant to the moves of their party. In accord with their prevailing coalitional preference, they still rated the SPD higher than the CDU in 1982. But the FDP leadership tries to overcome this resistance by deliberately taking the risk of losing a part of its voters each time it changes sides, and so far its calculations have been fair enough to ensure its survival.

(g) Policy positions

The literature on political parties and coalitions differs with regard to the importance which is attributed to substantive policy positions as compared to the striving for power positions (Max Weber: *Ämterpatronage*) as a motive in politics. Notably, representatives of the economic theory of politics (Downs, etc.) have assumed that the latter is the primary goal of parties whereas the substantive policy positions are no more than a by-product of it.

The FDP has often been accused of being in the first instance oriented towards participation in government regardless of its programmatic profile. If this were true, policy agreements or differences should not play any role in its coalitional behaviour. Our data can show whether the shifting coalitional preferences of the FDP leaders and FDP supporters in the elites were also accompanied by increasing differences over policies in the recent Social–Liberal coalition.

The analysis will be limited to a comparison of the issue positions of elites between 1972 and 1981. The index scores in Table 3.7 were computed from a number of issue statements which the respondents had to rate according to their degree of approval/disapproval. The indices tap three distinct issue areas which have emerged as the main domains of political conflict between the parties in 1972: social policy, foreign policy and economic policy (Hoffmann-Lange *et al.*

Table 3.7 *Issue positions of elites in three issue areas, 1972 and 1981*

Political elite	n	1972 Social policy	1972 Foreign policy	1972 Economic policy
Political elite				
SPD	110	5.0	3.8	4.1
CDU/CSU	128	3.6	2.3	2.8
FDP	47	5.0	3.7	3.3
Non-political elites				
SPD supporters	456	4.9	3.9	3.9
CDU/CSU supporters	800	3.7	2.6	2.6
FDP supporters	203	4.4	3.4	3.1
		1981	1981	1981
Political elite				
SPD	124	5.3	4.3	4.6
CDU/CSU	125	2.8	2.7	2.4
FDP	25	4.7	3.6	2.5
Non-political elites				
SPD supporters	318	4.8	4.2	4.2
CDU/CSU supporters	670	2.9	2.9	2.4
FDP supporters	214	3.7	3.6	2.6

1980: 55ff). Although the individual statements differed somewhat between 1972 and 1981, the indices should allow comparisons over time as long as the results are interpreted cautiously (cf. Hoffmann-Lange 1986).

In 1972, the elite attitudes showed clearly that the common basis of the Social–Liberal coalition lay in the fields of foreign policy (détente policy; Ostpolitik) and social policy (e.g. liberalisation of criminal law, introduction of comprehensive schools). In economic policy matters the FDP was instead somewhat closer to the Christian Democrats.

The basic pattern has not changed much in 1981, but some noticeable shifts have occurred. The FDP has moved even closer to the Christian Democrats in economic policy. The politicians of both parties occupy practically identical positions, while at the same time the polarisation between them and the Social Democrats has increased. In foreign policy, the FDP has moved into a position between the two big parties. By looking at the individual issue statements plus an additional question concerning a general evaluation of détente policy, one can characterise the FDP position as at the same time pro-American and in favour of détente policy. The Christian Democrats, instead, combine a pro-American stance with a more traditional anti-communism, while the Social Democrats favour détente policy and advocate somewhat more independence from US foreign policy. In social policy, finally, the FDP is still closer to the SPD in 1981.

These results correspond to those Niedermayer has found for party delegates, namely that there are two basic cleavage lines deeply rooted in the value orientations and organisational affiliations of FDP politicians (1982: 90ff). The social reformism axis divides in our data, as well as in his, persons with and without religious affiliations and also corresponds closely to the number of postmaterialists. The economic conflict divides trade union members from non-members. Foreign policy attitudes constitute a third dimension which is, however, not rooted as deeply and handled more pragmatically.

Verheugen, as well as Norpoth (1982), gives similar characterisations of the basic cleavage structure in West Germany. Verheugen claims that agreement in economic and foreign policy constituted the basis of the Christian–Liberal coalition already from the beginning of the Federal Republic, whereas the FDP always had more in common with the SPD in the fields of interior, judicial and educational policy (1984: 29). This pattern changed during the second half of the sixties when the FDP started to advocate a more active policy towards Eastern Europe, which became the common basis of the Ostpolitik initiated together with the SPD.

Compared to our data, however, Norpoth (1982: 15f) tends to locate the FDP position too far to the right on economic policy and too far to the left on the dimension he labels 'Religion and Culture'. While this may be true for some issues on which the FDP takes particularly pronounced positions (e.g. welfare policy, immigration policy), it does not seem justified for the overall position of this party. Our data instead support the notion of the FDP as a centre party in all three issue areas, whose position oscillates between those of the two big parties. This is further confirmed by the self-placement of the respondents on the left–right scale. The FDP leaders place themselves right in the centre of the 10-point scale (5.3), whereas the SPD leaders have an average score of 3.8, and the CDU/CSU leaders 6.1.

The data on the issue positions of the party leaders show that the distance between the SPD and FDP increased between 1972 and 1981 in all three issue areas, but most markedly in questions of economic policy. On the other hand, the CDU/CSU–FDP distance diminished in economic and foreign policy, while it remained constant in the field of social policy.

Our data confirm therefore that an increased conflict over economic policy divided the parties of the Social–Liberal coalition in 1981. This conflict was also the main reason for the definite end of the coalition in 1982. Given the high salience attributed to economic matters at the beginning of the 1980s as compared to social policy and foreign policy, the coalitional change was justified on grounds of substantial policy differences.

This can be further substantiated by looking at the policy priorities of the respondents. The answers given to an open-ended question concerning the most important problems of the Federal Republic show that the high salience attributed to Ostpolitik and to educational policy in 1972 had given way to concerns about security policy, energy policy and employment policy in 1981 (cf. Hoffmann-Lange 1986).

Table 3.8 *Issue positions of FDP politicians and FDP supporters among non-political elites according to second rank in party rank order, 1981*

	For comparison: SPD politicians	First rank: FDP Second rank: SPD	Second rank: CDU	For comparison: CDU/CSU politicians
Social policy	5.3	4.5	3.5	2.8
Foreign policy	4.3	4.0	3.4	2.7
Economic policy	4.6	3.0	2.3	2.4

The role policy questions played in the final stage of the Social–Liberal government can also be explored by looking for systematic policy differences within the FDP. This was done by breaking FDP respondents down by the party they had ranked second in sympathy. Since the number of FDP leaders interviewed ($n = 25$) was too small to allow a further subdivision, they were analysed together with the FDP supporters in the non-political elites. The analysis revealed clear differences in the expected direction as the values in Table 3.8 show. These results again closely parallel those of Niedermayer, who found similar differences (1982: 109).

(h) Conclusion

The analysis has shown that coalitional decisions are mainly elite decisions. The results indicate that voters only react to these decisions, either by changing their opinions in the same direction or by deserting the party. Whereas the first reaction is more typical for the voters of the Social Democrats and Christian Democrats, the latter is more frequent among FDP voters.

The fact that party supporters in the non-political elites have been found to be more in agreement with the party leaders than voters can be traced back to two different reasons. The first is that they are more aware of the political changes going on within the political parties, and therefore react earlier to them than ordinary voters. Another and more likely explanation is that they are themselves involved in the opinion formation process which precedes the decision-making of the political parties. This should be particularly true for the media elites and the big pressure groups. These groups did not, however, differ much from the other party supporters in the non-political elites in their coalitional preferences, and are, hence, not ahead of the other elites. One important exception has to be noted, however. The supporters of the FDP in the business elite have never favoured the Social–Liberal coalition to the same extent as the other FDP supporters, let alone the FDP leaders themselves. In 1982, they were the most active promoters of the formation of the current Christian–Liberal government. Attempts to influence the intra-party balance by giving financial support to members of the (economically) conservative party wing are particularly noticeable in this respect (Verheugen 1984: 131). Some of the details of this practice were revealed during the continuing investigations concerning illegal donations to the parties by business corporations and individual businessmen (*Parteispendenaffäre*).

The change in coalition was accompanied, in 1969 as well as in 1982, by changes in the sympathy ratings for the parties by elites and voters. In 1981/2 the same was true for issue attitudes. Given the centre position of the FDP, which on one of the major cleavage lines, i.e. social policy, is closer to the SPD while it is closer to the CDU/CSU in economic policy, it seems natural that a change in coalition reflects more a change in policy priorities than in substantive policy positions. But the data revealed that shifts in the latter have taken place, too, thus driving the FDP nearer to the Christian Democrats for two reasons.

While the results have shown that elites take a more active part in coalition formation than voters, this does not mean that they are unresponsive to public demands. The FDP reactions to the decline in support for the Social–Liberal coalition in 1982 have demonstrated this rather forcefully.

Notes

1. There are formally two independent Christian Democratic parties, the CDU and its Bavarian 'sister party', the CSU (Christian Social Union). Though both differ somewhat in organisational structure and ideological appeal, it seems justified to treat them as a single party, particularly since they do not compete for votes. The CSU is limited to Bavaria where the CDU, in turn, has no regional party organisation.
2. The Grand Coalition between CDU/CSU and SPD is sometimes called Great Coalition, e.g. by Engelmann (1972) and Merkl (1970), but the term Grand Coalition is more common and will therefore be used here.
3. There is agreement in the literature to regard the time of the Grand Coalition as a transitional period ('interlude') between the Christian–Liberal and the Social–Liberal period. Cf. Haungs 1983: 99f; Norpoth 1982: 13.
4. Norpoth (1982: 13ff) distinguishes four independent though related issue dimensions on which the FDP assumes different positions *vis-à-vis* the two bigger parties. Though not implausible in many respects, his analytic approach is highly impressionistic.
5. Thus, the question of which government coalition will be formed does not normally play a role in coalition negotiations. Instead, these are mainly concerned with policy questions (*Regierungsprogramm*) and the distribution of portfolios among the parties. Cf. Smith 1979; Norpoth 1982: 19.
6. Even if we assume that co-operation and not confrontation prevails in a government coalition, policy differences continue to exist, and can be traced back to different programmatic outlooks. In a Christian–Liberal coalition, the FDP assumes the role of a 'liberal corrective' (*liberales Korrektiv*) with regard to the law and order policy advocated by the Christian Democrats, while it plays a retarding role (*Bremser*) with regard to Social Democratic state interventionist policies in a Social–Liberal coalition. Cf. Norpoth 1982: 13; Smith 1979: 145.
7. The studies were conducted by research teams at the University of Mannheim. Principal investigator was Rudolf Wildenmann (1972, together with Werner Kaltefleiter, University of Kiel, and 1981, together with Max Kaase, University of Mannheim).
   Machine-readable codebooks which also include an outline of the study designs are available at the Zentralarchiv für empirische Sozialforschung, Cologne. Elite Survey 1968, ZA No. 1138; Elite Survey 1972, ZA No. 0796; Elite Survey 1981, ZA No. 1139.
8. These studies are also documented in machine-readable codebooks: Pre-election study 1969, ZA No. 0426; Pre-election study 1972, ZA No. 0635.

9. One exception is the general population survey, 1982, where more than 30% of the respondents
   did not indicate a preference for one of the coalitions on the list. The main reason for this may be
   that this study was carried out at a time when no election was imminent: hence, it also had a much
   higher number of respondents (26.3%) who did not even indicate a vote intention. An additional
   6.7% wanted to vote for the Greens or other parties instead of the three 'established' parties. Of
   these, altogether 728 respondents, only 28.7%, indicated a preference for one of the coalitions on
   the list.
10. In the 1972 pre-election study respondents with a preference for a single-party government (cf.
    Table 3.3) were further probed to indicate their coalitional preference if such a government
    should not be feasible. Norpoth reports the distribution for the latter question.
11. According to the West German electoral law each voter has two votes. The second one is cast for a
    party list while the first one is for the constituency candidate. With the first votes, candidates are
    elected directly by simple plurality rule. These direct seats won by a party are, however,
    subtracted from the overall number of seats this party has won in terms of second votes: i.e. the
    distribution of seats in the Bundestag is ultimately determined by the second votes. Records
    about split-ticket voting are part of the representative voting statistics of the Federal Bureau of
    Census (Statistisches Bundesamt) which collects information about voting behaviour according to
    age cohorts and gender in a representative sample of constituencies.
12. This is, however, at least partly also the result of a secular decline of the FDP in state elections
    since the 1970s for which no convincing explanation has so far been brought forward.
13. In the elite surveys of 1968 and 1972, respondents were not asked for their vote intention. Party
    support was instead measured as the first rank in a rank order of the parties according to
    sympathy.
14. I am well aware of the fact that the attitudes of the media elites are not an adequate indicator of
    mass media coverage, which would have required content analyses. But, nevertheless, the
    changes which occurred among the media elites should at least partly reflect what was going on at
    the mass media level.
15. Source: regular surveys of the Forschungsgruppe Wahlen, Mannheim. I am greatly indebted to
    Wolfgang G. Gibowski for having made unpublished figures available.
16. In all three elite surveys, no more than one-third of the non-political elites indicated a preference
    for the Social Democratic party, though with marked differences between elite sectors. Social
    Democrats are particularly weak among business elites and particularly strong among trade
    union elites.

References

Berger, Manfred, Gibowski, Wolfgang G., Roth, Dieter and Schulte, Wolfgang 1983.
Regierungswechsel und politische Einstellungen. Eine Analyse der Bundestagswahl
1983. *Zeitschrift für Parlamentsfragen, 14*: 556–82
Bohnsack, Klaus 1983. Die Koalitionskrise 1981/82 und der Regierungswechsel 1982.
Zeitschrift für Parlamentsfragen, 14: 5–32
Dalton, Russell J. and Hildebrandt, Kai 1983. Konflikte und Koalitionen im
Parteiensystem. In Max Kaase and Hans-Dieter Klingemann (eds.), *Wahlen und
politisches System. Analysen aus Anlaß der Bundestagswahl 1980*. Opladen:
Westdeutscher Verlag, pp. 58–80
Dodd, Lawrence C. 1976. *Coalitions in Parliamentary Government*. Princeton University
Press
Engelmann, Frederick C. 1972. Perceptions of the Great Coalition in West Germany.
Canadian Journal of Political Science, 5: 28–54
Fliszar, Fritz and Gibowski, Wolfgang G. 1984. Die Wähler der Parteien. *liberal, 26*: 67–
78
Gibowski, Wolfgang G. 1981. Koalitionsstrukturen in der Bundesrepublik Deutschland.

Paper presented at the meeting of the Working Group 'Parteien – Parlamente – Wahlen' of the Deutsche Vereinigung für Politische Wissenschaft, Mannheim

Gringmuth, Hans F. W. 1984. *Der Handlungsspielraum der Freien Demokratischen Partei als Artikulationspartei.* Frankfurt: Peter Lang

Grofman, Bernard 1982. A dynamic model of proto-coalition formation in ideological N-space. *Behavioral Science, 27:* 77–90

Haungs, Peter 1983. Koalitionen und Koalitionsstrategien in der Bundesrepublik. In Hans-Georg Wehling (ed.), *Westeuropas Parteiensysteme im Wandel.* Stuttgart: Kohlhammer, pp. 95–112

Hoffmann-Lange, Ursula 1986 (forthcoming). Eliten zwischen Alter und Neuer Politik. Konstanz und Wandel der Konfliktlinien in den Eliten der Bundesrepublik. In Hans-Dieter Klingemann and Max Kaase (eds.), *Wahlen und politischer Prozeß. Analysen aus Anlaß der Bundestagswahl 1983.* Opladen: Westdeutscher Verlag

Hoffmann-Lange, Ursula, Neumann, Helga and Steinkemper, Bärbel 1980. *Konsens und Konflikt zwischen Führungsgruppen in der Bundesrepublik Deutschland.* Frankfurt: Lang. An abridged English version, 'Conflict and consensus among elites in the Federal Republic of Germany', appears in Gwen Moore (ed.), *Research in Politics and Society. Vol. 1: Studies of the Structure of National Elite Groups.* Greenwich, Conn.: JAI Press, 1985, pp. 243–83.

Kaack, Heino 1978. *Die F.D.P.,* 2nd edn, Meisenheim: Anton Hain

1980. Das Volksparteiensystem der Bundesrepublik Deutschland und die Situation der FDP. In Lothar Albertin (ed.), *Politischer Liberalismus in der Bundesrepublik.* Göttingen: Vandenhoeck and Ruprecht, pp. 32–47

Kaase, Max 1970. Determinanten des Wahlverhaltens bei der Bundestagswahl 1969. *Politische Vierteljahresschrift, 11:* 46–110

Klingemann, Hans D. and Pappi, Franz Urban 1970. Die Wählerbewegungen bei der Bundestagswahl am 28. September 1969. *Politische Vierteljahresschrift, 11:* 111–38

Merkl, Peter H. 1970. Coalition politics in West Germany. In Sven Groennings, E. W. Kelley and Michael Leiserson (eds.), *The Study of Coalition Behavior: theoretical perspectives and cases from four continents.* New York: Holt, Rinehart and Winston, pp. 13–42

Niedermayer, Oskar 1982. Möglichkeiten des Koalitionswechsels. Zur parteiinternen Verankerung der bestehenden Koalitionsstruktur im Parteiensystem der Bundesrepublik Deutschland. *Zeitschrift für Parlamentsfragen, 13:* 85–110

Norpoth, Helmut 1980. Choosing a coalition partner. Mass preferences and elite decisions in West Germany. *Comparative Political Studies, 12:* 424–40

1982. The German Federal Republic: coalition government at the brink of majority rule. In Eric C. Browne and John Dreijmanis (eds.), *Government Coalitions in Western Democracies.* New York: Longman, pp. 7–32

Pappi, Franz Urban 1973. Parteiensystem und Sozialstruktur in der Bundesrepublik. *Politische Vierteljahresschrift, 14:* 191–213

Pridham, Geoffrey 1982. The government/opposition dimension and the development of the party system in the 1970s: the reappearance of conflictual politics. In Herbert Döring and Gordon Smith (eds.), *Party Government and Political Culture in Western Germany.* London: Macmillan, pp. 130–53

Schultze, Rainer-Olaf 1983. Regierungswechsel bestätigt. Eine Analyse der

Bundestagswahl vom 6. März 1983. In Hans-Georg Wehling (ed.), *Westeuropas Parteiensysteme im Wandel*. Stuttgart: Kohlhammer, pp. 45–82

Smith, Gordon 1979. *Democracy in Western Germany*. London: Heinemann

Troitzsch, Klaus G. 1980. Grenzen der Stabilität des etablierten Parteiensystems: Wähler, Wahlverhalten und politische Einstellungen. In Heino Kaack and Reinhold Roth (eds.), *Handbuch des deutschen Parteiensystems*. Opladen: Leske and Budrich, vol. 1, pp. 225–59

Veen, Hans-Joachim 1976. *Opposition im Bundestag*. Bonn: Eichholz Verlag

Verheugen, Günter 1984. *Der Ausverkauf. Macht und Verfall der FDP*. Reinbek: Rowohlt

Wildenmann, Rudolf 1975. Towards a sociopolitical model of the German Federal Republic. In Rudolf Wildenmann (ed.), *Sozialwissenschaftliches Jahrbuch für Politik*. Munich: Olzog, vol. 4, pp. 273–301

  1982. Die Elite wünscht den Wechsel. *Die Zeit, 11*: 6–7

Zülch, Rüdiger 1972. *Von der FDP zur F.D.P. Die dritte Kraft im deutschen Parteiensystem*. Bonn: Eichholz Verlag

4 The FDP and coalitional behaviour in the Federal Republic of Germany: multi-dimensional perspectives on the role of a pivotal party*

(a) Introduction

Given that every elected national government in the 35-year history of the Federal Republic of Germany has been a coalition of varying political complexions and that the creation of an economically successful and stable social structure is often assumed to have resulted from the constant necessity for compromise by the participating parties, it might be expected that numerous studies of coalitional behaviour in the post-war Republic would now exist.

Whilst many aspects of the country's development have been studied in detail and several excellent and wide-ranging books written as a result (Baker *et al.* 1981; Conradt 1982; Döring and Smith 1982), both the formation and the maintenance of federal coalitions have been neglected as topics worthy of analysis by social scientists. Mass electoral behaviour, the establishment of a new 'political culture' and the policy outputs of the party system have all received greater attention, as have the roles and functions of the major political parties since 1949, the SPD (Social Democrats) and the CDU/CSU (Christian Democrats).

The third party in the system for most of the post-war period, the FDP (Free Democrats), has only rarely been investigated in any depth, although some aspects of its behaviour were highlighted in the different chapters of the book edited by Albertin (1980).[1] Recent work on coalitions in the Federal Republic (Norpoth 1982; Schmidt 1983; von Beyme 1983) has looked more closely at the role of the FDP, but these analyses did not consider the party in terms of a

* This is a revised version of a paper originally presented at the ECPR Joint Sessions of Workshops, Salzburg, April 1984. We would like to thank Geoffrey Pridham, Geoffrey Roberts and Ursula Hoffmann-Lange as well as the other participants in the workshop for their helpful comments.

coherent framework which emphasises the impact of 'party factors' in coalitional behaviour.

Consequently, they did not concentrate on such questions as changing party identity over time or socio-political constraints as factors which colour specific options for the FDP within the overall process of coalition government formation. We intend to focus principally on the behaviour of the FDP with reference to the roles the different dimensions have played in influencing the party's decisions over its available coalition possibilities at any one time.

The relationship between the national FDP leadership and each of the separate *Land* parties, for example, has been important in the degree to which each state party has been able to assert its local autonomy in relation to the formation of coalitions which are different in political complexion to the one prevailing in Bonn at the same time. We will look at the importance of this particular factor when we examine the horizontal/vertical dimension below.

We must also consider the political context which the FDP has to take into account as it makes its decisions over participation in particular governments. Important amongst these 'contextual factors' are the 5 per cent electoral exclusion barrier, the personal relationships between different party leaders, attitudes towards minority governments and the divide between governing and opposition parties. All of these factors are relevant to any consideration of the second dimension of our framework which encompasses the institutional 'rules of the game' and the established norms and practices pertaining to coalition behaviour.

Previous studies have not attempted to analyse or emphasise the importance of internal party procedures or relationships (the internal party dimension) with regard to coalitional behaviour, although the assumption that parties can automatically be regarded as 'unitary actors' appears increasingly untenable. In the same vein, concentration on the social bases of parties, the institutionalisation of cleavage conflicts and electoral changes within multi-party systems have sometimes served to obscure questions about 'ideological input' (the motivational dimension) in coalition decision-making processes.

Nevertheless, all the above-mentioned factors are topics of importance to any study of the FDP, given its geographically and ideologically divided party structure and its need to maintain a credible electoral appeal as an independent party with a unique profile.

We need to analyse the FDP's coalitional behaviour using a more complex, multi-dimensional approach which considers all these different influences if we want to shed more light on the party's behaviour in the processes of government formation and maintenance. Although previous research in the field of coalition politics has tended to concentrate on ideas such as ideological distance between parties and criteria relating to size and coalition durability, we intend to look in more detail at specific 'party aspects' as they relate to and influence the coalitional behaviour of the FDP.

The initial task in this regard must be to set out the party's role within the post-war German political system as a backdrop to our consideration of the seven dimensions which make up our framework of analysis.

(b)   The political background

The gradual creation of a newly democratic and stable political structure in the post-war Federal Republic of Germany, after the Weimar years of social fragmentation and the brutality of the Nazi dictatorship, has to be regarded as a remarkable achievement. Memories of the immediate past, however, inevitably came to profoundly affect the main political elements of the country's *Grundgesetz* ('Basic Law') as well as the pronouncements of leading politicians on the most important issues of the day.

For the first time, political parties were given key roles to play in the formation and representation of public opinion. Emphasis on the value of a broad, social consensus, conciliation and moderation all helped to integrate the people of the Federal Republic behind an approach to politics which provided the continuity necessary to fully exploit the potential of the *Wirtschaftswunder* ('economic miracle') of the 1950s.

Whilst the country's post-war political culture can be criticised as being overly legalistic and too cautious in outlook, the widespread popular attitude of protecting the considerable benefits produced by the present system rather than taking any risks on an unpredictable future is easily comprehensible in view of the turbulence and disruption which preceded the Second World War.

The FDP, like the two major parties, clearly had to take such developments into account as it formulated its political strategy, and the party managed to maintain an independent existence and profile whilst other small parties were succumbing to the imperatives of political integration and Adenauer's tactics of absorption and amalgamation. It did so by stressing the importance of the party's role as a 'corrective' partner to one of the main parties as a guarantee of 'balance' in the conduct of government as well as the FDP's function as a *Mehrheitsbeschaffer* or 'pivot' in the process of coalition formation (Rémy 1975). In this way, the party has been able to exploit its 'hinge' position between two much larger parties so that it can usually determine the political complexion of the federal government as well as ensure that it is almost permanently included in such a government with one or other of the main parties.

Being a party of crucial importance when it comes to the question of government formation has conferred considerable opportunities on the FDP to exert substantial influence on the running of the country despite an often slender support base within the electorate at large. It has, for instance, always managed to extract a disproportionate number of cabinet portfolios from its major coalition partner of the time relative to the number of Bundestag seats which it holds. The FDP has often controlled such important ministries as Justice or the Interior, Finance or Economic Affairs, Foreign Affairs and sometimes Agriculture (Schmidt 1983: 44, 46).

Given the FDP's size, it is clearly not in a position to initiate the process of coalition negotiations or to offer inducements to the other parties. As a party with different options available, it is able to wait for the SPD or the CDU/CSU to make the first move. However, by highlighting its position as a free agent able to coalesce with either depending on the advantages for the FDP in doing so, the party had to tolerate disputes and dissension from within its own ranks concerning the strategy it should pursue. It was nevertheless essential that the FDP retained its ability to form coalitions with either major party as a credible option if it was to maintain its influence within the government as well as its electoral appeal to 'coalition voters' willing to support the party by 'ticket splitting'.

Whilst it is clearly advantageous for the FDP to participate in government for the opportunities such involvement allows to project the party to the electorate and to highlight the competence of its leaders in office, internal party pressures and conflicts as well as the ever present need to tend the party's shallow electoral roots often serve to complicate its coalitional options. The specific factors which together determine the FDP's behaviour will be set out below as we examine each of our seven dimensions in turn. The first dimension details historical developments as the FDP has attempted to secure its own long-term niche in the political landscape of the post-war Federal Republic.

(c)   The historical dimension

Since the FDP managed to secure its position as a 'pivot' within the German party system, the Free Democrats have developed a strong tradition as 'coalitional actors' in the sense that the party's identity appears very closely linked to its decisions regarding government participation with one of the major parties. This situation clearly presents the party with a number of recurring problems concerning its autonomy of action and the nature of its electoral appeal, but, before 1966, the FDP was simultaneously able to set itself apart from the Christian Democrats with regard to foreign policy whilst credibly claiming some of the credit for the sustained economic success of the immediate post-war period. In this way, the FDP maintained an independent party profile as well as sustaining its attraction to voters as a 'brake' and a guarantor of the fruits of the country's socio-economic reconstruction.

The sudden economic problems of the mid-1960s forced the Free Democrats to reconsider their position. Erhard's plans for tax increases caused severe conflict within the ruling federal coalition to such an extent that the FDP went into opposition, making way for the Grand Coalition between the Christian Democrats and the Social Democrats. The impotence of the Free Democrats outside government was a main cause of the heated debate within the party about the need to pursue a strategy in relation to the major parties which would allow the FDP to form coalitions with either if necessary.

In theory, the FDP could have exploited its 'pivotal' position by forming a coalition with the Social Democrats after 1966, but such a government would only have had a majority of six in the Bundestag. In addition, major doubts about the feasibility of a coalition between parties with markedly different views on economic questions of central importance as well as widespread uncertainty about the then unproven competence of the Social Democrats in federal office ensured that such an option was not taken up.

However, it became ever clearer between 1966 and 1969 that the FDP could achieve little in opposition given its size and lack of resources. Denied the chance to exploit its usually crucial position within the party system, the Free Democrats were increasingly forced to develop an alternative strategy which included the possibility of forming a federal coalition with the SPD as a serious option. The additional fear that any continuation of the Grand Coalition after 1969 could bring about major changes such as the introduction of 'majoritarian voting' strengthened the hand of the 'social reformers' within the FDP who could also point to the threat to the Free Democrats posed by the neo-Nazi NPD, particularly at state level.[2]

Nevertheless, any attempt at rapprochement with the SPD needed to overcome the resistance of the 'economic liberal' wing of the FDP, which had dominated the party's outlook since 1945 by promoting the virtues of the free market when the need to rebuild the German economy was clearly paramount. Even so, if the Free Democrats wanted to escape from a position of only being able to go into federal government with the Christian Democrats and to widen their coalitional options so as to fulfil a 'pivotal' role with either major party, they could not afford to ignore the lessons of the period between 1966 and 1969.

A clear sign that the Social Democrats were no longer to be regarded as inevitable opponents came in early 1969 when the FDP parliamentary party voted for the SPD's candidate for the federal presidency, Gustav Heinemann. Another important factor on the road towards the formation of a federal coalition between the SPD and the FDP after the 1969 election was the development of a close personal relationship between Willy Brandt, the SPD's Chancellor candidate, and Walter Scheel, the FDP leader.

This was very much in line with the tradition in the Federal Republic of regular contacts between the leadership elites in different parties. In this way, views, perceptions and changes of mood are quickly disseminated and friendships can be used to sort out political problems with regard to either coalition formation or maintenance.

The relationship between Helmut Kohl and Hans-Dietrich Genscher was also significant in the coalition switch of 1982, as was the deterioration in the partnership between Helmut Schmidt and Genscher within the SPD–FDP coalition after the 1980 federal election.[3]

After 1969, the FDP had clearly reasserted its role as an indispensable political force in the process of federal government formation and, with that, its options were greater than before. Such success did not, however, directly increase the party's autonomy of action or strengthen its electoral appeal since the FDP was still regarded as a 'coalitional party' playing an essentially functional role. The development of an *allgemeine Koalitionsfähigkeit* ('ability to form coalitions with all the other parties') by the Free Democrats after 1969 also has to be seen in relation to the component elements of our second dimension, if we want to understand better the continuing constraints which the party had to face up to even after that date.

(d) The institutional dimension

The lessons of the Weimar Republic are clear to see in terms of the political 'rules of the game' practised in the Federal Republic and whilst, as with the general political developments mentioned above, all parties have had to take note, a number of the factors which can be subsumed within our institutional dimension have had a particular significance for the FDP and its coalitional behaviour since 1949.

Firstly, and most obviously, there is the 5 per cent electoral barrier, below which no party is represented in the Bundestag, a measure designed as one means of preventing party system fragmentation. This provision made it difficult for small parties to survive, so much so that there were only three parties represented in the lower chamber (CDU–CSU counting as one party) after the 1961 federal election. In 1949, there had been ten parties.

This means that the FDP has constantly to keep its electoral appeal in mind and to ensure that the party is attractive to enough voters to enable it to survive in the parliamentary arena. Evidence suggests that FDP 'loyalist voters', the party's *Stammwählerschaft*, are very thin on the ground (some assess this group as being as few as 2 per cent of the total electorate),[4] and thus the necessity of attracting support from 'coalition voters' is clear and, consequently, an ever present concern of the FDP national party leadership.

Secondly, there remains a strong prejudice, within the political elite as well as the mass electorate, against minority governments. Majority coalitions have been widely accepted as the post-war norm, an attempt to avoid the chaos of the Weimar years when numerous, short-lived administrations proved incapable of coming to terms with increasingly desperate socio-economic problems.

In this sense, coalitions in the Federal Republic are formal rather than informal, with the FDP benefiting as a result, since, if its support is needed to create a majority (almost always the case), it will be taken into government and allotted its share of the spoils in the way of portfolios, patronage and policy influence. Even when the CDU/CSU won an absolute majority of the votes in 1957 (50.2 per cent) for the first and only time in the post-war period, it still chose to form a coalition with a minor party, the DP (Deutsche Partei).

When the SPD–FDP coalition broke up in the autumn of 1982, the idea of the Free Democrats tolerating an SPD minority government from outside until new elections could be called was one obvious possibility. Predictably, that idea came to nothing, with the formation of a CDU/CSU–FDP *majority* coalition, hardly a surprising outcome in a country where minority administrations are still equated in the national psyche with inefficiency and instability, a feeling which the FDP has cleverly exploited in its propaganda and its electoral appeal.

Thirdly, there still lingers in the Federal Republic a widespread view that opposition parties should not oppose too hard and that they should not engender 'unnecessary' conflict in a supposedly consensual society.[5] Elections are decided more by perceptions of the government's overall performance than by appreciation of the 'alternative' critique provided by the opposition, and since the FDP is almost always in government, it can do a lot to ensure its own parliamentary survival by promoting the view as widely as possible that the government of which it is a member has 'succeeded' and that the party deserves to be given enough support to enable it to continue the 'good' work.

The government/opposition divide is perhaps loaded even more in favour of the government as a result of this situation (the *Amtsbonus*) than in other countries, and this is something which the FDP has been particularly adept at exploiting for its own benefit.

These three factors have been important in setting the parameters within which the Free Democrats have had to operate. However, a question of crucial significance to the way in which the party has chosen to define its role within the political system concerns the reasons for its participation in government. To what extent is the FDP trying to ensure the implementation of 'liberal' principles and precepts by the coalitions of which it is a member, or is the party more interested in government participation on the basis of power rather than policy?

(e)   The motivational dimension

As the FDP managed to repeat its initial electoral successes by stressing its 'functional' role as a 'coalitional party', the question of the nature of its own identity and policy preferences became increasingly subsumed beneath considerations of how its position and influence could best be secured and strengthened, despite the party's roots in liberal traditions dating back to Weimar.

Dual emphasis on both the party's functional role as a 'corrective' and its 'ideological input' in terms of coalition decision-making was not necessarily incompatible. However, the FDP's electoral success on the basis of its 'corrective' role and its constant need to sustain its potential voting support meant that the effect of the 'ideological input' was often difficult to discern, even though the party made frequent references to liberalism as its guiding principle.

The concentration on developing an image and role for the party which stressed its utility as a 'brake' on one of the major parties was reinforced by opinion-poll evidence which suggested that ordinary electors found it difficult to think of positive (or even negative) things to say about the FDP which clearly relate to either the party's principles or policies. More often, responses to such questions refer to the role of the Free Democrats in preventing absolute majorities for either main party in the Bundestag and approval of the FDP's 'function' within the system.[6]

However, if the FDP was intent on broadening its coalition options by proving that it could be a partner for either the SPD or the CDU/CSU but a mere appendage of neither, it made sense to try to develop a more detailed image in terms of the principles which informed the party's policy stands. Such an approach also had the advantage of allowing party activists a greater say in the way in which the FDP was to be perceived by the mass electorate, and it also permitted the party leadership to hold the party together within a federal coalition with the Social Democrats more easily by shifting the emphasis of debates within the party away from coalitional strategy to the nature and practical application of liberalism.

One of the problems inherent in such a move stems from the fact that liberal principles tend to produce general defences of such things as the free market economy and the prevailing constitutional order rather than specific policies and, in addition, such ideas were generally accepted as being 'good', a situation unlikely to win potential supporters over to the FDP or to galvanise party members towards greater efforts. It also meant that the FDP was unable to profile itself clearly on such matters or to claim issue positions where a consensus between all the main parties already existed. In this way, the FDP was inevitably forced to retreat from specific to general criticism of the 'excesses' of the major parties in order to demonstrate its 'usefulness'.

Since the ordinary voters seemed to perceive the FDP without substantive reference to the party's ideas, the electoral appeal of the Free Democrats could continue to be based on 'functional' attributes rather than a specific policy platform. In this sense, there might appear to be no necessary conflict between the two, with activists formulating ideas for consideration as coalition policy whilst the national leadership continued to stress the party's qualities as a 'protector' of the status quo.

However, the development of a unique profile for the FDP in the early 1970s saw the ascendancy of the 'social reformers' within the party who articulated the desire to enact reforms in such areas as employment and education rather than a ritual adherence to orthodox financial policies. Nevertheless, even the 'social liberals' were unable to ignore the requirements of ensuring the party's parliamentary survival. Given the size of the FDP's support base, its ability to continue to play a 'pivotal' role is largely dependent on the 'success' (usually measured in terms of economic performance and perceptions of general competence) of the governments in which it participates. Any reforms could possibly endanger this imperative, in addition to the difficulties involved in implementing new ideas in a political system where legitimacy is achieved more through stability and continuity than innovation and change, and where vote maximisation is invariably achieved by playing down specific proposals in favour of generalities.

This conflict between the need to ensure a broad electoral appeal and the desire to implement specific policy preferences is unlikely to disappear in an age of continuing economic stringency, when hard choices have to be made and clear winners and losers decided upon. The hegemony of the 'economic liberals' within the FDP was firmly re-established after the switch in coalition partners from the SPD to the CDU/CSU on 1 October 1982, with the result that all policy options are now subject to economic considerations based on the requirements for sustaining growth.

The FDP had been content to support the general line of the Social Democrats, firstly under Willy Brandt and then under Helmut Schmidt, as long as the reasons which had first brought the two parties together in 1969 gave rise to realisable policy aims. Foreign policy agreement in general and Ostpolitik in particular enabled the SPD–FDP coalition to survive, despite increasing evidence throughout the 1970s of divergent priorities with regard to social spending between the two parties in the wake of external pressures exerted by oil crises and world recession.[7]

Such pressures eventually came to undermine the *raison d'être* of the SPD–FDP coalition, with the difficulties of taking Ostpolitik any further after the initial treaties had been signed and the necessity of constraining social reforms in the light of economic uncertainty combining to sever the central strand of agreement joining the two parties together.

The disputes within the FDP between the 'social' and the 'economic' liberals reflect different interpretations of the essential elements of the party's identity as well as its coalitional strategy. The 'conservative' liberals continue to emphasise the need to project an image to the electorate based on an orthodox approach to the economy and the value of the FDP as a 'corrective'. This involves the placing of a 'functional' electoral appeal as a key plank in the party's strategy at the expense of detailed 'ideological baggage'. Whilst the 'social reformers' within the FDP recognise the impossibility of ignoring the imperatives of electoral survival, they tend to see the party's current difficulties as a result of its inability to define itself as anything other than an appendage of the CDU.

This viewpoint has gained greater currency with the rise of the Green party, particularly at state level, where the position of the Free Democrats as the third party within the system is under serious threat. The seemingly desperate search by the FDP national leadership for novel policy positions on such issues as controls on nuclear power stations and the rights of *Gastarbeiter* families to enter the Federal Republic might appear to represent agreement with the view of the 'social' wing of the party, but the already apparent ability of the Greens to outflank the FDP in terms of 'owning' issues presents a highly potent danger in electoral terms as well.

Indeed, the whole role that the Free Democrats have played in the post-war

Table 4.1 *The participation of the FDP in federal coalitions, 1949–85*

Date	Chancellor	Parties in government
20 Sept. 1949	Adenauer (CDU)	CDU/CSU–FDP–DP
20 Oct. 1953	Adenauer II	CDU/CSU–FDP–DP–BHE
24 Oct. 1957	Adenauer III	CDU/CSU–DP
14 Nov. 1961	Adenauer IV	CDU/CSU–FDP
17 Oct. 1963	Erhard (CDU)	CDU/CSU–FDP
26 Oct. 1965	Erhard II	CDU/CSU–FDP
1 Dec. 1966	Kiesinger (CDU)	CDU/CSU–SPD
21 Oct. 1969	Brandt (SPD)	SPD–FDP
15 Dec. 1972	Brandt II	SPD–FDP
16 May 1974	Schmidt (SPD)	SPD–FDP
15 Dec. 1976	Schmidt II	SPD–FDP
5 Nov. 1980	Schmidt III	SPD–FDP
1 Oct. 1982	Kohl (CDU)	CDU/CSU–FDP
6 Mar. 1983	Kohl II	CDU/CSU–FDP

DP = German party; BHE = Refugee party.
Source: Abridged from von Beyme (1983: 18).

political system of Germany could be taken over by the Greens if the latter continue to attract votes as at present. If the FDP cannot play the role of an essential party in the process of majority government formation at federal level, the whole future of the party would be in severe doubt. The party's very strong 'government orientation' is hardly surprising given its size, lack of resources and its strategic position within the political system, with the party not being included in the national government for only seven years since 1949 (see Table 4.1).

Debates over the relative importance of the FDP's role in power and its 'ideological input' will be largely academic if the party is unable to continue to play a 'pivotal' role after the next federal election. In that sense, it is difficult to separate out questions of the party's identity from other relevant factors such as electoral appeal. The rise of the Green party at *Land* level has had the effect of re-emphasising the divisions within the FDP about the party's identity and its desire for office, but it has also highlighted the nature of the relationship between the national leadership and the individual state parties which together make up the party. We will look next at the question of centre-periphery relations within the FDP with the aim of establishing the importance of state coalitions for overall party strategy.

(f) The horizontal/vertical dimension

The national FDP is made up of the eleven state parties (including West Berlin) which correspond with the federal division of the country as a whole, and these territorial divides continue to reflect the different emphases between 'social' and 'economic' liberals mentioned before. As a result, the political complexion of

Table 4.2 *The participation of the FDP in coalitions at state level, 1945–85*

	Date	Partners	Present government (Feb. 1986)
Baden-Württemberg	4/52– 9/53	SPD	
	10/53–6/60	All parties	
	6/60–6/64	CDU + BHE	CDU
	6/64–12/66	CDU	
Bavaria	12/54–10/57	SPD + BP + BHE	CSU
	10/57–12/62	CSU + BHE	
Bremen	12/51–12/59	SPD + CDU	SPD
	12/59–12/71	SPD	
Hamburg	8/45–9/46	CDU + SPD	
	11/46–2/50	SPD	
	12/53–11/57	CDU + DP	SPD
	12/57–4/66	SPD	
	4/70–6/78	SPD	
Hesse	12/70–10/82	SPD	SPD
Lower Saxony	5/55–11/57	CDU + DP + BHE	
	5/59–6/63	SPD + BHE	
	6/63–5/65	SPD	CDU
	6/74–12/75	SPD	
	1/76–5/78	CDU	
North Rhine-	8/46–12/46	SPD + Z + KPD	
Westphalia	12/46–4/47	CDU + SPD + Z	
	7/54–2/56	CDU	SPD
	2/56–3/58	SPD + Z	
	7/62–12/66	CDU	
	12/66–6/80	SPD	
Rhineland-Palatinate	6/51–5/71	CDU	CDU
Saarland	1/61–7/65	CDU	
	7/65–7/70	CDU	SPD
	4/77–12/82	CDU	
Schleswig-Holstein	9/50–6/51	CDU + BHE + DP	
	6/51–7/51	CDU	CDU
	7/51–1/63	CDU + BHE	
	1/63–5/71	CDU	

BHE = Refugee party; BP = Bavarian party; DP = German party; KPD = Communist party; Z = Centre (Catholic) party.
Source: Adapted and updated from Schmidt (1983: 42–3).

coalitions at state level in which the FDP has participated has varied considerably, both between different *Länder* and over time (see Table 4.2).

Whilst, in theory, fundamental political and organisational decisions within the FDP are supposed to be taken at national level, in reality the party's participation or not in state governments with the Social Democrats or the Christian Democrats or sometimes both is a matter for each *Landesverband*. This is not to deny that the federal party leadership can make its views known or that it can attempt to cajole or persuade errant state parties back into line. However, the fact remains that there have virtually always been contrary coalitions formed at either federal or state level, an indication that the national FDP leadership has simply not been able to summon up sufficient authority to force recalcitrant state parties to keep in step.

This situation of different coalitions at different levels of the political system can be a useful card for the FDP leaders to hold, since it makes clear that alternative coalition options are available and, on that basis, the FDP has more room to manoeuvre. It is also perhaps able to exert more influence at national level as a result, since inevitably any change in a coalition at *Land* level sparks off rumours of a possible change in the federal government by making it apparent that the FDP does not automatically see itself as a member of a particular political 'block' and that the 'Bonn model' is not one that has to be rigidly adhered to.

The FDP has usually tried to keep its options open at state level by not becoming too closely identified with either major party. During the mid-1970s, it attempted to go into government with the CDU in such states as Lower Saxony and Baden-Württemberg in order to 'balance' the federal position of the party as a partner of the SPD.

State elections can be regarded as important 'barometers' of public opinion at a particular time and state governments as 'laboratories' for alternative coalition formations in Bonn. In a political system without by-elections, *Land* elections are ascribed considerable significance with regard to the popularity of the federal government of the moment, something which is reinforced by the involvement of national political figures in state election campaigns and the general emphasis on non-local issues and themes. Whilst there have certainly been exceptions to this, such as the controversy over the extension of Frankfurt airport and the question of the waste disposal plant at Gorleben in Lower Saxony, the interpretation of election results at state level is normally based on the 'message' they are sending to the federal government in Bonn.

The FDP's electoral base at state level is as unstable and variable as at national level, and thus the party's very survival is open to doubt if it becomes 'contaminated' by the unpopularity of its major coalition partner of the time, over and above predictable vote losses as a result of an 'opposition effect' in state elections against the parties forming the federal government.

The evidence that disaffection with the SPD was also rubbing off on the FDP throughout 1981/2 brought this danger into sharp focus, and the electoral decline of the Free Democrats at state level is likely to have been a major factor in the eventual decision to switch federal coalition partners to the Christian Democrats.

Electoral longevity is as vital a concern to the FDP at state level as at national level, since the 5 per cent electoral barrier is also in operation in *Land* elections. However, as the party also tries to secure and exploit a pivotal role at state level, it has to change its tactics somewhat since it cannot appeal for voters to 'split their tickets' when most electors have only one vote. Although this fact forces the FDP to give a new slant to its state election campaigns, its overall emphasis on the value of the party as a 'corrective' or 'brake' is undiminished.

Nevertheless, the collapse of the SPD–FDP national coalition in 1982 amidst accusations of 'regicide' by the Free Democrats has worsened the chances of the party being able to fulfil such a role. With each elector having only one vote at state level, if the FDP is successful in winning over CDU sympathisers, this might well mean that any proposed CDU–FDP coalition does not have majority support if direct vote transfers between the two parties take place (the last two state elections in Hesse have illustrated this possibility).

The rapid decline of the FDP at state level since 1982 (the party is now represented in only five of the eleven *Landtage*) cannot simply be explained by the problems involved in ensuring government participation. The challenge of the Greens poses an immediate threat to the ability of the FDP to continue to play a pivotal role at the sub-national level. Whilst it appears that the Greens are capable of attracting protest votes from all parties, the nature and size of the FDP's electoral base mean that it is in particular danger if the Greens can capture its potential supporters amongst the young, the well-educated and urban dwellers. Such a development might well force the FDP back on to its 'loyalist voters', but this group is simply not large enough for the party to be sure of surmounting the 5 per cent barrier.

The current parlous state of the FDP at state level has added to the tensions within the party as a whole, with traditional disputes over policy intensifying the desire of several state parties not to subordinate their prerogatives and views to the wishes of a national leadership perceived as demoralised and incapable of giving the party any new sense of direction.

The importance of state coalitions for overall party strategy is therefore variable. Whilst *Land* governments can clearly be used as test beds for potential coalition changes at federal level, particularly in terms of establishing the FDP as an indispensable political force in the process of government formation, the likely electoral consequences of carrying through such a change have meant that the relationship between the different state parties and the national leadership has sometimes been strained and lacking in co-ordination.

Another important factor in this regard has been the lack of emphasis by the FDP over the years on developing an integrated party machinery and organisation which would permit the constituent organs a more formal say in the way the party is run. We now want to consider the impact of the internal party dimension as it affects the FDP's coalitional options and strategy.

(g)   The internal party dimension

The question of how far the FDP can be regarded as a 'unitary actor' in coalition politics is clearly of central importance to this particular dimension. On the face of it, the divisions within the party are obvious. The party was originally formed from a variety of separate groups which had sustained the liberal tradition during the Weimar Republic. Whilst unity within one party was essential if the perpetual splits of the previous Republic were to be avoided, it did mean that the party was made up of a number of distinct groupings which ensured that the possibility of regular clashes over the party's federal coalition options has always existed.

In the light of this, running the FDP as a loose federation with a high degree of regional rather than national decision-making made sense. Since each of the party's constituent organs was determined to hold on to its independence, the development of defined methods of national deliberation and policy formulation was surrounded by ambiguity and uncertainty, even though the party established the usual panoply of committees and congresses. It also meant that the bigger *Land* parties were, in effect, able to dominate the federal party's course, since the number of delegates each state party is entitled to send to the annual party congress (nominally the *oberste Organ* of the party) is decided on the basis of the membership figures in each *Land* as well as the last federal election result in each one. As a result, North Rhine-Westphalia emerges as the *Land* party with by far the most potential influence within the party, whereas Bremen, at least formally, is unable to bring much weight to bear.

There is clearly an overlap here between internal party procedures developed within the FDP and the centre–periphery relationships dealt with in the last section, something which is perhaps inevitable given the main structuring of the party according to the *Länder* and the coincidence between the territorial and ideological divides. These divisions place increased responsibility upon the national leadership elite to keep the party united and, in general, they have been successful in this, although there have been a number of stormy party congresses, particularly in the late 1960s when the option of forming a federal coalition with the SPD first became a possibility and then a probability.

This display of unity might also be a sign of a lack of alternatives for much of the FDP membership rather than widespread agreement about the party's role. However, as Barton and Schmitt (1980) point out, there is a high degree of social homogeneity inside the FDP, with party members coming almost exclusively from upper- and middle-class backgrounds. Furthermore, the necessary weakness of the *Parteiapparat* at the centre of the party structure as a result of the state power bases leaves a gap which could be filled by *Vereinigungen* ('incorporated groups or associations') with a consequent threat of factionalism or 'organised dissensus'.

However, the lack of authority of the national party organisation allied with the similar social status of much of the membership have ensured that the FDP is divided neither in terms of 'social-structural' nor 'party-functional' variables. The possibility of the party being divided by factions grouped around different leaders has also been avoided, although the existence of different 'tendencies' with divergent priorities and emphases continues to provide a major potential source of internal party conflict.

The absence of any clearly defined chain of responsibility for national decision-making within the FDP has permitted the national leadership to take the final decisions about coalition formation at federal level. This situation is reinforced by the 'cadre' nature of the FDP's development and by the fact that it is by far the smallest party in terms of members in the Federal Republic. At the end of 1981, the Free Democrats had 86,747 members, whereas the CSU alone had more than 175,000.[8]

There also appears to be a tendency amongst the ordinary FDP membership to leave the party rather than stay and fight when a coalition decision is taken with which they disagree. It is estimated that 29,000 members left between 1969 and 1970 after the change to the SPD and roughly 8,000–9,000 left soon after the switch back to the Christian Democrats in 1982.[9] A fluctuating and uninvolved membership seems likely to ensure ever greater influence for the national party leadership.

Years spent conducting coalition negotiations in secret have fostered a strong tendency within the national FDP leadership to take decisions and then to present them to the party as a whole only for rubber-stamping, not for discussion. It was alleged at the time that the party's Präsidium never formally debated the change in coalition partners to the CDU/CSU in 1982 and that the leadership effectively neutralised known opponents of the move within both the Präsidium and the party executive.[10] A similarly swift decision-making technique was apparent in the speed with which Martin Bangemann was chosen to succeed Otto von Lambsdorff as federal Economics Minister in the summer of 1984.

The answer to the question we posed at the start of this section must therefore be that the FDP cannot be regarded as a unitary actor, but that this doesn't really affect to any degree the coalitional strategy of the party. The disregard by the national party leadership of opposing views and their reliance on achieving legitimacy for decisions *after* they have been implemented rather than before strongly suggests elite control of vital federal decisions more than respect for the need to develop an integrated and coherent party machinery.

One factor which the leadership elite has constantly to keep in mind is the need to preserve and strengthen the party's electoral base and hence its parliamentary survival. The risk of alienating some of the party's 'coalitional voters' by changing partners at federal level is clearly very serious if other potential sympathisers cannot be won over to the party's cause as a result. We now want to look at the elements of a dimension which we have already mentioned in passing in other sections – the socio-political dimension and its influence on the FDP's coalitional behaviour.

(h) The socio-political dimension

The FDP's electoral base has traditionally been heterogeneous, comprising both 'social' and 'national/economic' liberals at the same time, as well as 'coalitional' voters who approved of the party's strategy at a particular juncture. Given the requirement of surmounting the 5 per cent barrier, the party has always had to be very careful about any action which could estrange any section of its potential voting support.

In this sense, the change to the Social Democrats in 1969 was a gamble which very nearly failed, when the FDP won only 5.8 per cent of the second (list) votes cast, its lowest share ever. In the early 1970s, the Free Democrats were able to gain the backing of SPD sympathisers for their role in the federal coalition of the time, almost in 'exchange' for the votes of Christian Democratic sympathisers dismayed at the FDP's decision to switch sides. The fear that a change back to the Christian Democrats in 1982 might not produce enough votes at the subsequent federal election was an important factor in the hesitancy of the FDP to make such a move. In addition, there were obvious problems in legitimating such a change against a widely respected and popular Chancellor amidst charges of opportunism and placing self-preservation before loyalty to the re-elected coalition.

The change of 1982 continues to rankle with many Social Democrats and the way in which it was carried out remains sufficient to reinforce the present animosities that exist between the SPD and the FDP, the degree of which makes any coalition between the two in the immediate future highly unlikely. The danger for the FDP and its continuing ability to act as a 'pivot' within the political system emanates from the possibility that the Greens will evolve into a sufficiently homogeneous grouping to assume the role of 'kingmakers' with the SPD, although this is at present unpredictable, given the inability of the Greens to decide on tactics or whether they want to be an orthodox political party or an altogether broader movement.

Both the coalition changes in 1969 and 1982 were made after a long assessment of the risks for the FDP in doing so. Clearly, the imperative of sustaining an electoral base of sufficient strength to clamber over the exclusion barrier acts as a constant and constraining element in the strategic thinking of the FDP leadership. Whilst, as we mentioned before, there is a widespread expectation that coalitions in the Federal Republic will be formal, the recent experiment in Hesse where the Greens supported a minority SPD administration from outside the government suggests that the role which the FDP has fulfilled over the post-war period is no longer accepted as being automatically essential. Even though the agreement between the Social Democrats and the Greens in Wiesbaden broke down relatively quickly, the fact that it was done at all opens up the possibility of new forms of coalition creation in the future. Late in 1985, a formal coalition between the SPD and the Greens was agreed in that state.

Even though the FDP has to take account of the likely reaction of its potential supporters when it is considering a coalition change, it also has to consider the preferences of its financial backers and contributors to its funds. The FDP does, in fact, receive a high proportion of its money from the state in the form of reimbursement of election expenses, but even so it is still heavily in debt after the 1983 federal election.[11] In contrast to the SPD and the CDU/CSU, the Free Democrats do not receive much support from groups such as industrial trade unions or the churches, although they do receive some help from several white-collar unions. The party does, however, receive cash from industrial conglomerates such as the Horten group and, even though all contributions to political parties may be in doubt in the light of the outcome of the Flick scandal, the FDP is simply not rich or robust enough to ignore the political preferences of willing and able industrial supporters.

Even given the party's persistently weak financial situation, the FDP will not fail to survive purely for lack of funds. The main threat to the party's ability to continue to play a 'corrective' role clearly stems from the rise of the Green party outside the system of broad consensus which the three main parties slowly built up after the war. The Greens are clearly less likely to go along with the traditional, institutionalised method of cleavage conflict and management, and they are also unlikely to be willingly drawn into the system of close personal co-operation across party barriers. They are more a force for change and unpredictability than moderation and if they prove capable of attracting sustained electoral support on that basis, the FDP is in danger of losing its long-term role as an indispensable party in the process of coalition government formation at federal level.

Nevertheless, it remains perfectly possible that the FDP will be able to reassert its position within the party structure by stressing its ability to 'protect' the system against the 'threat' posed by the Greens. The cautious nature of the German electorate will certainly aid the FDP in this task, as will other factors pertinent to the environment/external dimension.

(i)   The environment/external dimension

When the FDP decided to change coalition partners to the Christian Democrats in 1982, they fully realised that their electoral fate would largely depend on the economic success of the newly formed coalition. Whilst reaffirming its commitment to financial orthodoxy inevitably reduced the party's scope for establishing and maintaining more than a superficially independent profile, such a move was very much in line with a long-standing obsession with the health of the German economy which all the traditional parties share.

Such an attitude is not difficult to understand when one takes account of the Weimar years, but the continuing nervousness about even the slightest short-term problem is sometimes difficult to comprehend when the basic structure of the economy appears to be in good shape. The concern of the political elite about the country's socio-economic well-being has been widely communicated to the bulk of the German electorate and, as such, the FDP's emphasis on its value as a 'protector' and a 'guarantor' of economic stability is likely to continue to find a widespread resonance amongst ordinary voters.

The Free Democrats are often supported in this by their treatment in the mass media, where they are routinely accepted as 'coalitional actors' fulfilling an important role in terms of system stability. Whilst this kind of interpretation helps in legitimating the party's actions and attitudes, it does mean that the FDP is unable to stress its autonomy and independence of action, though, as we have seen, this does not present an immediate problem in terms of the party's electoral appeal.

The development of a legalistic and cautious political culture in the Federal Republic has also aided the Free Democrats in their position as a 'brake' on one of the other major parties. Reliance on the norms of the *Rechtsstaat* found much support within German society at large, as did the FDP's backing for attempts to 'normalise' relations with the DDR and the other countries of Eastern Europe. The entrenched position of the Federal Republic as a key member of NATO and the EEC means that there is little room for originality in the field of foreign affairs any more, although Ostpolitik provided an important bond within the SPD–FDP coalition after 1969.

All the political parties have to take account of the external pressures on them within the present-day political culture of the Federal Republic. The FDP is clearly positioned on the side of caution and slow-moving reform if and when economic conditions permit. In this way, it reflects the general mood of many of the ordinary voters towards protection of present benefits rather than taking risks on an inevitably uncertain future.

(j) Conclusion

By developing and applying a multi-dimensional approach to the study of the FDP's coalitional behaviour in the Federal Republic of Germany since 1949, we have taken a broader view of the constraints and the imperatives which have set the parameters for the party's decisions in this area. This is not to deny the value of other ways of analysing coalition politics such as ideological distance between parties or the significance of size, but merely to indicate that concentration on such aspects to the exclusion of such things as contextual factors and internal party procedures and relationships will probably leave much of the story untold.

Of the seven dimensions established earlier in the book that together make up our framework, it seems clear that all have some relevance for the FDP in terms of the processes of coalition formation, maintenance and change. Many of the component elements of the dimensions relate directly to the role of the Free Democrats as government 'kingmakers' for much of the post-war period and the party's ability to effectively decide the political complexion of administrations at both national and state level.

The whole basis of the FDP's electoral appeal, for example, is directed towards stressing the utility of the party as a 'pivot' positioned between two much larger parties and its functional role as a 'corrective'.[12] In this, the Free Democrats are able to exploit the more cautious instincts built into the reconstructed political culture of the Federal Republic for their own benefit by seeking to emphasise the need to protect the benefits produced by the present system rather than taking risks implementing a policy of reform.

Whilst the FDP has been able to win electoral support by fulfilling the role of a 'brake', it has always had to be careful about instigating conflict with either the SPD or the CDU/CSU through its efforts at maintaining an independent profile within the governing coalition. Nevertheless, the latter has been essential to the aim of keeping alternative coalition options open in the future as well as exerting immediate influence on policy. In this sense, the years between 1969 and 1982 can be regarded as the FDP's most 'successful' period since the war in that the party could simultaneously 'moderate' the intentions of the Social Democrats in the federal government, whilst retaining in the background the possibility of changing partners to the Christian Democrats as a credible alternative.

The disputes within the FDP about the need for greater 'ideological input' by the party rather than seemingly total reliance upon the exerting of a purely functional role within the system are clearly important to a better understanding of the party's behaviour. Whilst questions of motivation go to the very heart of any party's thinking over coalition participation, in the case of the FDP the coincidence of different attitudes on this matter with extant ideological and territorial divides within the party has given the disagreements over strategy a much reinforced significance, both in the way in which internal conflicts are expressed and how vital decisions affecting the whole party are taken.

We have considered many of the factors which have influenced the coalitional behaviour of the FDP and in the process highlighted the importance of the motivational dimension, internal party structure and decision-making and the ever present constraints of the socio-political reality which the party has always to take into account, none of which have been examined before using a coherent framework of analysis.

Focussing on the immediate electoral problems for the FDP posed by the Green party is clearly important, but a fuller explanation of the party's coalitional decisions requires consideration of the 'party aspects' we have dealt with here. The role which the FDP has played in the political system of the Federal Republic necessitates the use of a multi-dimensional approach if we want to delve deeper into the mysteries of coalitional politics.

Notes

1. Several of the chapters in the book edited by Lothar Albertin are relevant to any study of the FDP. In particular, the pieces by Karsten Schröder and Wolfgang Vonhausen, 'Die Behandlung der Koalitionsfrage auf den Bundesparteitagen der F.D.P. von 1967 bis 1969', pp. 195–210, and by Albertin himself, 'Die koalitionspolitische Umorientierung der F.D.P., 1966–1969. Fall oder Model?', pp. 211–21, are especially relevant. Another piece by Oskar Niedermayer, entitled 'Möglichkeiten des Koalitionwechsels: zur parteiinternen Verankerung der bestehenden Koalitionsstruktur im Parteiensystem der Bundesrepublik Deutschland', *Zeitschrift für Parlamentsfragen*, 1982, pp. 85–110, is also useful.

   There is not much material on the FDP available in English other than the articles and papers cited in our references. We have written two pieces on the party, entitled 'The F.D.P. in

Transition – Again?', a shortened version of which was published in *Parliamentary Affairs*, vol. 37, no. 2, Spring 1984, pp. 183–98. The complete version is available as paper no. 7 in the series Essex Papers in Politics and Government (Department of Government, University of Essex). We also wrote an earlier version of this paper for the ECPR Joint Sessions of Workshops in Salzburg, April 1984, entitled 'The F.D.P. and Coalition Formation in the Federal Republic of Germany: "Ideological Input", Party Structure and Party Strategy'.

2. Although the NPD made a strong showing in several state elections between 1966 and 1969, they polled only 4.3% at the 1969 federal election and thus the party was not represented in the Bundestag.

3. The state of the relationship between Schmidt and Genscher is documented in the book by Klaus Bölling, *Die letzten 30 Tage des Kanzlers Helmut Schmidt: ein Tagebuch* (Rowohlt Taschenbuch, Hamburg, 1982).

4. At the 1983 federal election in Schleswig-Holstein, the FDP received 6.3% of the votes cast. A week later, in a state election there, the party received only 2.2%.

5. In a survey carried out in 1982, more than 60% of the respondents agreed to some degree with the statement that it was the job of the opposition to support the government in its work and not to criticise it. *General Social Survey (ALLBUS 1982)*, Zentralarchiv der Universität zu Köln, Study no. 1160.

6. In an Allensbach Institute poll of July 1956, even amongst people who had previously stated that the FDP came nearest to their own views, 11% did not know why they liked the FDP, 17% gave replies which were coded 'other' and 14% of the responses dealt with the FDP being a 'good' party with the 'right' programme. Peter and Elisabeth Noelle-Neumann (eds.), *The Germans. Public Opinion Polls, 1947–1966* (Verlag für Demoskopie, Allensbach, 1967), p. 428.

   In the 1980 *Wahlstudie*, 24 different responses were given to the question 'Why did the FDP win votes?' at the 1980 federal election. None had much to do with 'liberal' ideas. Zentralarchiv der Universität zu Köln, Study no. 1053.

   There is also an interesting article by Hans D. Klingemann on this theme in Albertin (1980) entitled 'Der Wandel des Bildes der F.D.P. in der Bevölkerung. Das Image der Freien Demokratischen Partei in der Bevölkerung der Bundesrepublik Deutschland vor den Bundestagswahlen 1972 und 1976', pp. 125–50.

7. The SPD–FDP federal coalition had always been 'open' with regard to economic affairs (Norpoth 1982), but the two parties could be placed next to one another on issues such as cultural and foreign policy. This is not to play down the importance of economic disagreements between the SPD and the FDP, the significance of which became ever clearer after 1980. A good discussion of policy distance can be found in Schmidt (1983: 44–56).

8. FDP figures supplied by the Bundesgeschäftesstelle in Bonn; CSU figures – *Süddeutsche Zeitung*, 21 March 1983, p. 10.

9. Figures for 1969–70 – Henning (1982: 47); 1982 estimate – *Frankfurter Allgemeine Zeitung*, 21 March 1983, p. 10.

10. *Der Spiegel*, 4 October 1982, p. 23.

11. In order to finance the 1983 federal election campaign, the FDP ran up debts of around 10 million DM, whereas contributions only amounted to about 4 million DM. *Der Spiegel*, 30 January, 1984, p. 34.

12. The idea of 'balance' and stress on 'reasonableness' are apparent in much of the FDP's propaganda and election material. For example, the party's slogan at the 1972 federal election was 'Vorfahrt für Vernunft' ('campaign for reasonableness and common sense'), and such expressions and concepts have virtually always characterised the party's attempt to strengthen its appeal to the German electorate.

References

Albertin, Lothar (ed.) 1980. *Politscher Liberalismus in der Bundesrepublik*. Göttingen: Vandenhoek and Ruprecht

Baker, Kendall L., Dalton, Russell J. and Hildebrandt, Kai 1981. *Germany Transformed: political culture and the new politics*. Cambridge, Mass.: Harvard University Press

Barton, Terry and Schmitt, Hermann 1980. Silent factionalism: concealed cleavages in West German political party organisations. Paper prepared for workshop on 'Factionalism in the Political Parties of Western Europe', ECPR Joint Sessions of Workshops, Florence

Bickerich, Wolfram (ed.) 1982. *Die 13 Jahre. Bilanz der sozialliberalen Koalition.* Hamburg: Rowohlt

Conradt, David P. 1982. *The German Polity*, 2nd edn. London: Longman

Dalton, Russell J., and Hildebrandt, Kai 1983. Konflikte und Koalitionen im Parteiensystem. In Max Kaase and Hans-Dieter Klingemann (eds.), *Wahlen und politisches System. Analysen aus Anlass der Bundestagswahl 1980.* Opladen: Westdeutscher Verlag, pp. 58–80

Döring, Herbert and Smith, Gordon (eds.) 1982. *Party Government and Political Culture in Western Germany.* London: Macmillan

Engelmann, F. C. Perceptions of the great coalition in West Germany, 1966–69. *Canadian Journal of Political Science, 5*(1): 28–54

Henning, Friedrich 1982. *F.D.P. Die Liberalen. Porträt einer Partei,* vol. 218, Geschichte und Staat. Munich: Günter Olzog

Kaack, Heino 1974. Die Liberalen. Die F.D.P. im Parteiensystem der Bundesrepublik. In Richard Löwenthal and Hans-Peter Schwarz (eds.), *Die zweite Republik. 25 Jahre Bundesrepublik Deutschland – eine Bilanz.* Stuttgart: Seewald Verlag, pp. 408–32
(ed.) 1979. *Die F.D.P. Grundriss und Materialien zu Geschichte, Struktur und Programmatik,* 3rd edn. Meisenheim am Glan: Anton Hain

Merkl, Peter H. 1970. Coalition politics in West Germany. In Sven Groennings, E. W. Kelly and Michael Leiserson (eds.), *The Study of Coalition Behavior: theoretical perspectives and cases from four continents.* New York: Holt, Rinehart and Winston, pp. 13–42

Norpoth, Helmut 1982. The German Federal Republic: coalition government at the brink of majority rule. In Eric C. Browne and John Dreijmanis (eds.), *Government Coalitions in Western Democracies.* London: Longman, pp. 7–32

Pulzer, Peter 1978. Responsible party government and stable coalition: the case of the German Federal Republic, *Political Studies, 26*(2), June: 181–208

Rémy, Dominique 1975. The pivotal party: definition and measurement. *European Journal of Political Research, 3*(3), September: 293–301

Roberts, Geoffrey 1978. Organisation, identity and survival: the Free Democratic Party in West Germany. Paper prepared for workshop on 'Mass Political Organisations', ECPR Joint Sessions of Workshops, Grenoble

Schmidt, Manfred G. 1978. The politics of domestic reform in the Federal Republic of Germany. *Politics and Society, 8*(2): 165–200
1983. Two logics of coalition policy: the West German case. In Vernon Bogdanor (ed.), *Coalition Government in Western Europe.* London: Heinemann, pp. 38–58

Schuchardt, Helga and Verheugen, Günter (eds.), 1982. *Das liberale Gewissen.* Hamburg: Rowohlt Taschenbuch

Verheugen, Günter 1982. Sozialer Liberalismus. *liberal, 24*(4): 261–72

von Beyme, Klaus 1983. Coalition government in Western Germany. In Vernon Bogdanor (ed.), *Coalition Government in Western Europe.* London: Heinemann, pp. 16–37

Zülch, Rüdiger 1972. *Von der FDP zur F.D.P. Die dritte Kraft im deutschen Parteiensystem.* Bonn: Eichholz Verlag

5   *Cabinet stability in the*
     French Fourth Republic:
     the Ramadier coalition government
     of 1947

In keeping with the overall aim of this volume to expand enquiry on the general subject of coalition behaviour, our intention in this is to explicate some of the conditions we expect to be associated with an acceptable theory of cabinet stability in parliamentary democracies, and, in an initial appraisal, discuss some implications of such factors in the setting of politics in the French Fourth Republic. In so doing, we seek to build on earlier work which has developed the outline of an 'events' approach to the problem (Browne, Frendreis and Gleiber 1984). The tradition of prior research has conceived cabinet stability as an attribute of cabinets which is operationalised in units of time and conditioned by configurations of other attributes characteristic of cabinets. Thus, cabinet stability is conceived as variable longevity (duration) dependent upon the variable values of salient cabinet attributes.

From a theoretical standpoint, identified attributes are expected to supply cabinets with a quality of 'inherent stability', which acts so as to protect or shield them from disturbances occurring in the environment. Regression analyses have given an indication of the ability of such attributes to condition duration, but the observed coefficients of determination have been so modest as to cast doubt on the ability of such models to achieve an acceptable empirical level of explanation.

An events perspective departs significantly from the standard attributes approach by identifying environmental events and conditions, arriving in the decision space of cabinet decision-makers, as the central theoretical element involved in an explanation of cabinet stability. Yet, systematic investigation of such events and conditions, and cabinet decisional responses to them, has gone almost completely unnoticed and unexplored. It is our goal to develop an events-based model of cabinet stability, ultimately capable of accounting for the persistence and demise of cabinet governments.

(a) Political events and cabinet stability

An events approach to the problem of cabinet stability focusses attention on a specification of the political context within which cabinet decision-making occurs. In so far as stability may be taken to be a function of a cabinet's persistence over some interval of time, we may treat that interval as constituting a series of decision points where the existence of a cabinet is continuously reaffirmed until at some point the decision is made to dissolve the cabinet. Since stability is seen as the outcome of a decision process, its explanation depends on our ability to specify the components of that process.

As we have stated, the standard attributes approach to the problem has attempted to explain cabinet duration as being a function of selected attributes of cabinet actors and the decision-making setting. Thus, researchers have identified such things as the ideological affinity of actors, whether the cabinet is majority or minority, single-party or coalition status, the number of cabinet members, and other similar measures as important determinants of cabinet longevity. Collectively, these attributes are implicitly expected to weaken or strengthen the ability of cabinet decision-makers to resist the effects of destabilising occurrences in the political environment. For example, a cabinet which is, say, ideologically conflicted is presumed less capable of successfully deflecting, accommodating or resolving demands from the environment than is one which is not so conflicted. This is the quality of cabinets we have named 'inherent stability', and the research findings relating such stability-inducing attributes with cabinet duration have shown a modest relationship of approximately $R^2 = .20$ over several samples of cabinets in Western European parliamentary democracies (Dodd 1976; Sanders and Herman 1977; Taylor and Herman 1971).

Given that environmental intrusions on decision-makers are implicit in attributes models of cabinet stability, a focus on events seeks an explicit specification of such elements with respect to their timing, magnitude and intensity, and their relationship to the decisional process occurring during the tenure of cabinets. Verbally, we expect the persistence of a cabinet to depend upon the willingness or ability of cabinet actors (either singly or collectively) to continue support for the cabinet's existence. This support is 'tested' continuously in the presence of events arising in the environment and impacting on the governmental decision-making arena (normally, cabinet and parliamentary decision-making). Presumably, the event environment is configured in such a way that cabinet decision-makers experience (at various times) both support for their continued participation in government and demands for their withdrawal.

In considering the events environment, we can immediately appreciate that many relevant events originate with cabinet actors themselves. By initiating policies, these actors attempt to structure the environment to suit their own purposes; that is, to create benefits and channel them in ways which are intended to reinforce their own parliamentary standing. Additionally, cabinet actors introduce events into the environment by reacting to demands which arise in conjunction with the aspirations and grievances of extraparliamentary actors (e.g. citizens and interest groups, allies and enemies). Thus, the events environment is characterised by an interplay of action and reaction, with events initiated sometimes by cabinet actors and sometimes by other actors operating in other decisional systems, both domestically and internationally.

Given the expectation that an events flow characterises the environment of cabinet actors, it is important that some means of classifying events be identified so as to assess the significance of various events and events clusters as they arrive in the decisional space of cabinet actors. In so far as events constitute 'natural' phenomena, they may be considered to possess a unique 'history'; that is to say, a given event may inaugurate a process which cumulates by generating subsequent events over time. We might expect that the clustering of events is an important source of the intensity with which demands are made on cabinet decision-makers. Alternatively, some events may be seen as 'isolated' in time and/or space, and may, for that reason, be diffuse in their impact, despite apparent magnitude or intensity.

Another important consideration in the classification of events is the policy domain to which they belong. While events classifications of this sort are likely to be at least somewhat arbitrary and may be expected to vary in content across countries, they should accurately portray the complexity of the issue environment generating events and allow assessments of differential scope, rates and intensity.

Political issues are either substantive or normative, where substantive issues concern allocations of resources and policy and normative issues deal with redefinitions of rules of decision-making. They may be seen to condition one another in a reciprocal (non-recursive) fashion. For example, it is commonly held that domestic political issues are of far greater salience to both citizens and governmental decision-makers than are events generated beyond the borders of the nation. These issues acquire their importance from the fact that they describe conditions which are directly experienced by citizens in terms of their impact on daily living and represent domains of interest over which the political system may be said to have direct control. Prototypical of such an issue area is the domestic economy, the operation of which allocates opportunities and wealth among the population and the performance of which is capable of producing satisfaction or dissatisfaction within the population. Additionally, issues involving religious difference are commonly found to be of significance in European parliamentary democracies, most especially as concerns the propriety of state sponsorship of ecclesiastical interests. Finally, issues relating to the legitimacy of the constitutional order occasionally arise in the domestic political environments of parliamentary democracies, and are capable of placing great strain on the ability of governments to function.

In addition to political events which are generated within the issue domains of domestic politics, the international political arena is also a source of events capable of having a destabilising impact on cabinet governments. For Western parliamentary democracies, these have, since the Second World War, arisen in two issue domains; encompassing what have been styled East–West issues and North–South issues. The former involve events arising out of a concern for the provision of national security against external threats, most prominently associated with foreign policy initiatives of the Soviet Union and the Warsaw Pact countries. While the issues in this domain are primarily military, associated with them have been policy questions relating to the development of a European economy, most especially with respect to the receipt and allocation of Marshall Aid, and, later, the creation of the European Economic Community. North–South issues involve the relations of economically developed Western democracies with the nations of the so-called Third World. Currently, some of the activity on this dimension centres on initiatives pursued through the agencies of the United Nations and the EEC, but bilateral aid and development projects, particularly centred on former colonial dependencies, are common. Additionally, the demand of developed economies for increased energy supplies has (at least temporarily) increased the scope of the North–South issue domain and the generation of events within it. However, the most significant set of events in this issue domain is, by now, largely historical and emanates from the experiences former colonial powers had with the demands of their dependencies for national independence. While decolonisation had a demonstrable impact on the stability of governments in all former colonial powers, it was particularly acute in France, where it eventually led to the downfall of the Fourth Republic.

(b)   An events conceptualisation of cabinet stability

Having given a general description of the issue domains we expect to characterise the generation of destabilising events for cabinets, we may proceed with a conceptualisation of cabinet stability from an events perspective. As we have argued, the stability of cabinets is conceived as a decision process which is temporarily defined (it has a beginning in investiture and an ending in dissolution). As a decision process, political actors possess proximate control over the continuation or termination of the cabinet. The termination of a cabinet may be effected by a variety of means, and these may be summarised initially as either the result of some positive act to end the cabinet's existence or as the consequence of the intrusion of some event from the environment, sufficient of itself to terminate the cabinet without the positive act of political actors. The first of these termination processes implies a failure of governance in that some member (or members) of the cabinet withdraws voluntarily from further participation. Alternatively, the resignation of the government may be forced by the withdrawal of confidence by parliamentary voting. It is the circumstances surrounding terminations of this kind that have excited the greatest theoretical interest.

The second type of cabinet termination is not occasioned by political conflict, but rather presents actors with a politically 'neutral' demand from the environment that cannot be legitimately ignored. These terminations are prototypically associated with the expiration of the parliamentary term and the constitutional requirement that elections be held so that citizens may exercise their sovereignty over the institutions of government. From the standpoint of cabinet stability, the necessity of renewing parliament within a specified period stands, as it were, as a marker in time and constitutes an event from the environment which cannot be overcome by political actors. Additionally, a special case of this type of event is the death in office of the head of government, which is typically accompanied by a resignation of the cabinet. Thus, inasmuch as the passage of time is an important component of the idea of cabinet stability, it is seen that all cabinets are prone to dissolution and, by implication, instability (all have a bounded life expectancy). Cabinets may succumb shortly after taking office or may enjoy an extended tenure, depending upon their ability to continue benefiting from office, upon their ability to avoid loss of confidence, the length of time remaining until the parliament must be renewed, and the occurrence of randomly timed events, like the death of prime ministers.

From the previous discussion, we claim that cabinets terminate their existence as a result of events which either originate within the environment provided by the political institutions of a nation, or originate in the larger domestic or international environment and are transferred, as a result of their salience, to the governmental decision-making environment. Events originating from within the governmental decision-making environment are either policy initiatives designed to structure the particular issue domains to which they are relevant in ways which are believed beneficial to those controlling the decision-making process, or they are reactive policies, or responses, to events and conditions which arise or obtain in the various issue domains of the external or governmental decision-making environments. Events arising in the external environment are either reactive to governmental policy initiatives, or represent initiatives by non-governmental actors intended to alter or preserve the status quo. Thus, events activities may be seen as occurring within two, analytically distinct, environments, the one being the larger social system (including both domestic and international venues), and the other the political decisional system (including both parliament and the cabinet, and their respective subsystems − i.e. committees and ministerial departments).

As the focal point of governmental decision-making, the cabinet assumes responsibility for the stewardship of the nation. This role is legitimised by virtue of the requirement that its activities retain the confidence of the elected representatives of the people. This is expected to be assured as a result of the formation of cabinets which enjoy majority support in parliament. Typically, cabinets are composed of party elites who, collectively, determine policy and submit their proposals to the parliament for approval. When the party composition of the cabinet reflects a majority in parliament, it is expected that the cabinet will continue to enjoy parliamentary confidence. When, as is sometimes the case, the party composition of the cabinet reflects a parliamentary minority, the continuation of parliamentary confidence requires that cabinet initiatives be supported by votes formally identified with parties that have not accepted responsibility for governing. Thus, cabinets may terminate as a result of the defection of parliamentary members associated with parties represented in the cabinet (parliamentary party indiscipline), or as a result of the defection of non-cabinet actors who had been supporting cabinet initiatives on parliamentary votes.

In addition to the problem cabinets have in maintaining parliamentary support for their policies, cabinets also confront the difficulty of maintaining internal cohesion over time. Strains within cabinets are occasioned by conflicts or disagreements which may develop across actors (typically, factions in single-party cabinets or separate parties in coalition cabinets). The result of such conflict is likely to vary considerably across cases encompassing anything from resolution on the basis of compromise or ignoring the issue to the withdrawal of one (or all) parties from further participation in the cabinet.

Moving outside of the governmental decision-making environment, the most proximate actors to it are the various political party organisations. These organisations are responsible for preserving the ideological basis (if any) of the parliamentary parties and organising the electorate in support of their candidates for office. While there appears to be a great deal of variation across parties and countries in the degree to which parliamentary parties are subject to the influence of party organisations, the decisions of these organisations, in conference particularly, may be expected to condition the flexibility of the parliamentary party in its behaviour towards other actors in the governmental decision-making environment.

Often a significant presence in both party organisations and governmental office are representatives of established interest groups. As such, they constitute an important source of events through their sponsorship of actions and activities by their memberships, and they may be influential in the transmission of such demands to the governmental decision-making environment. The most obvious of such groups are labour and employer organisations, but also influential are more specialised interests like producers' groups and foreign-policy lobbies.

To this point we have sketched the environmental context within which we expect events to be generated. In general, we have identified two environments, the external social system and the governmental decision-making system, as constituting primary locations for the articulation of demands and the receipt of inputs from actors. Within these environments, we have indicated the major actors associated with the generation of events. What remains in our description is to distinguish from this context the nature of the *setting* which defines the operating conditions (or the general status quo) that conditions the experiences of the actors.

Whereas we have described the events context as being comprised of international and domestic issue domains and actors, we conceive the setting confronted by actors as a set of currently existing conditions defining prominent characteristics of political and social life, encountered by actors as they engage in decision-making behaviour. In general, the values taken by these conditions describe various 'system states' over time, and may be taken to impose 'boundary conditions', or limits, on the social, economic and political activities which are likely to be undertaken by actors. It should be apparent that the relationship between a description of system states and the occurrence of events is reciprocal, in that the values taken by the various indicators of setting variables are likely to be conditioned by the events which have preceded them (and vice versa).

As a first appraisal, we conceive three aspects of the events setting to be especially relevant to our concern with cabinet stability. First, there is the nature of the fiscal and monetary setting within which actors operate. Perhaps the most important elements in this area are inflation and unemployment, changing rates of which are liable to give impetus to feelings of satisfaction or dissatisfaction among the population. Also important in this area is the size of the money supply, the various discount rates, the level of foreign and domestic debt, the terms and volume of trade, and the availability of scarce resources. Second, all democratic societies have incurred international obligations which commit the resources of the nation and which create the basis for the intrusion of events from outside its borders. Finally, the scope of the public sector in the domestic economy is likely to condition the volume of events which are manifested in the governmental decision-making environment. This is especially the case where the government stands in the economy as a major employer or consumer.

In summary, the stability of cabinets is seen as a function of the occurrence of events in the environments of cabinet decision-makers. These may originate in their immediate environment as policy initiatives or reactions of cabinet or parliamentary actors, or they may come from the larger social environment within which the government operates. Events arise as demands on, or supports for, government activity pertinent to the particular issue. Response to these events may result in increasing the level of satisfaction among concerned individuals and groups, may produce no change in satisfaction levels, or they may induce dissatisfaction. Hence, events may arise and have a short life-span, petering out rather rapidly, or they may engage increased attention and spread beyond their point of origin, both spatially and temporarily, gathering intensity. Finally, the probability of events arising in an environment is also most likely a function of changes occurring in the various conditions described above as setting variables. Thus, increasing rates of inflation unindexed in any reasonably precise way by wage levels are likely to increase the probability of events generation in the economic issue domain, most likely in the form of strike activity.

(c)   Events in the French Fourth Republic: the Ramadier government

It will be immediately apparent that the application of an events perspective to assess the problem of cabinet stability in particular countries imposes data collection requirements of vast proportions. We have elected to begin a detailed investigation with a consideration of the experiences of cabinets in the French Fourth Republic. While our work is not yet far advanced, even with respect to this limited research site, we have been able to sketch the outline of major issue domains, to identify significant actors, and compile a reasonably complete events chronology for the year 1947, encompassing the entirety of the cabinet headed by Paul Ramadier. Naturally, this chronology will be extended through time and across countries as resources permit.

While our discussion is presently confined to a very limited case-study, we feel there are certain advantages which attach to the particular case we have selected. First, coalition research on France has been singularly lacking in the literature, even though the Fourth Republic presents a very rich example of such subject matter. Second, during the months the Ramadier government held office (January–November 1947) the production of events across the issue domains we identified earlier was considerable. While not exactly a microcosm of Fourth Republic events, our research on this period allows us an opportunity to fix the issue context of the Fourth Republic reasonably well, and to observe some of the dynamics of events flows. Third, the availability of events data in English is not uniform across all countries which have experience with cabinet government. However, the problem this poses is minimised in the French case, since reporting services have traditionally concentrated effort on the larger European democracies, allowing access to rather detailed accounts of French events. Finally, though beyond the scope of the present effort, the Fourth Republic, because the regime itself succumbed in the end to the flow of events, allows us the opportunity to observe a completed process; that is, to study the relationship between cabinet stability and regime stability. This is, itself, an important and not well-understood research area.

(d)   Events and the stability of the Ramadier government

In the traditional literature, a variety of explanations have been put forth to account for the instability of French cabinets in the Fourth Republic (see Leites 1959; MacRae 1967; Werth 1956; Williams 1954). One of the most prominent of these has been the claim that the presence of anti-system parties (notably the Gaullist RPF and the PCF) put pressure on an ideologically conflicted group of moderate (system-defending) parties, resulting in their inability to sustain the necessary parliamentary majority for government programmes given the presence of a large permanent opposition. Other studies have pointed to the self-interested proclivities of *ministrables*, who are presumed willing to bring down a cabinet in hopes of either gaining (regaining) ministerial office or acquiring more desirable portfolios. Still others seek explanations in the instability of parties in and out of parliament; the first in terms of voting indiscipline, the second in terms of schism or faction. While all these explanations have yielded valuable insights and considerable investigation, none has commanded the consensus of the scholarly community as constituting a fully persuasive accounting of the phenomenon of French cabinet instability.

Since at this point in its development our analysis is descriptive, we begin by considering what has been called the 'durability' of French cabinets. As noted above, the contemporary approach to an understanding of cabinet stability has been to relate the presence (absence) of identified stability-inducing attributes to the duration of cabinets. The most successful of these attempts (Warwick 1979) identified four independent attributes as especially important factors in accounting for cabinet longevity. These include: (1) whether a cabinet spans cleavage dimensions; (2) whether a cabinet is majority or minority; (3) the number of parties represented in the cabinet; and (4) whether the cabinet enjoys 'minimum winning status'. For the cabinets of the Fourth Republic, these factors are capable of explaining only 13 per cent of the variance in cabinet duration (in months), a value that is somewhat less than we have observed in replications of Warwick's analysis on much larger samples of cabinets (Browne *et al.* 1982). We have argued that attributes such as these furnish a quality of inherent stability to cabinets, which may be interpreted as their relative vulnerability to disrupting intrusions from the environment. The very low value of the multiple coefficient of determination for the French case indicates that these attributes insulate cabinets only weakly if at all from such intrusions.

Inasmuch as attributes fail to provide much in the way of inherent stability to French cabinets generally, we expect the analysis of the events history of the Fourth Republic to hold particular promise for this research site. As stated earlier, at present we possess reasonably complete events data for only the Ramadier government. However, the period this covers is particularly rich with respect to the variety of events which were produced, and they are likely to give an indication of the ways in which events from various domains intrude upon the decisions politicians make with respect to the continuation or dissolution of their governments.

(e) A short history of the Ramadier government

Paul Ramadier (SFIO) was invested as Premier of the first majority cabinet of the Fourth Republic on 21 January 1947, with an investiture vote of 549–0–65 (with 35 PRL and 15 Independent Republicans included among those abstaining under the last figure). His government lasted for a relatively long time by Fourth Republic standards, resigning on 19 November 1947 in the midst of widespread and escalating strike activity and civil violence. It fell to the successor Schuman (MRP) government to end these disturbances, which was accomplished with reasonable dispatch, largely through the heavy-handed methods of the Interior Minister, Jules Moch (SFIO).

Ramadier's cabinet was the final expression of what is known as *tripartisme*, the joint responsibility for national affairs shared among the major political forces emerging from the wartime resistance: the Communists (PCF), Socialists (SFIO) and the Popular Republicans (MRP). In constructing his government, Ramadier sought to give it as broad a parliamentary base as possible, the ensuing cabinet containing ministers from the Radical Socialists, UDSR and Independent Republicans as well as the SFIO, PCF and MRP. An indication of difficulties to come was observed in the negotiations leading to the presentation of the cabinet, when the MRP objected to the distribution of the National Defence Ministry to the PCF, a post long coveted by that party. Here, Ramadier effected a compromise which allowed the PCF the Defence Ministry while diluting its functions by creating ministries for War, Navy and Air and distributing them to other parties.

During the tenure of Ramadier's government, two major crises were confronted and, at least in the short term, overcome. The first of these was the expulsion of four of the five Communist ministers by governmental decree on 2 May, after the ministers in question voted against a confidence motion on the government's wage-freezing policy. With their expulsion, the fifth PCF minister resigned voluntarily, and the PCF went into opposition, ending the period of *tripartisme*. The second major crisis occurred when the October municipal elections recorded a 40 per cent vote for Gaullist candidates who stood with the General against the 'regime of parties'. Three days after the voting, on 22 October, the cabinet resigned en masse, leaving Ramadier (still Premier) to regroup. In the ensuing reorganisation, the number of ministries was reduced from 26 to 13, and UDSR lost its representation at this level. In presenting his new cabinet on the 23rd, Ramadier announced that there would be no change in the cabinet's policy or programme. A week later, the reorganised cabinet received a vote of confidence (300–280) in the National Assembly.

While neither of these events proved sufficient to terminate the government, it is readily seen in the confidence vote of 30 October that its ability to govern effectively had become precarious. At one level, this was obviously due to the atrophy of party support for the government in parliament. However, it is at other levels that we can most clearly see the crumbling of governmental effectiveness. We may begin to appreciate this process by first looking at the events surrounding the expulsion of the PCF from the cabinet.

Pivotal in the process is the position of the SFIO. Internally, the party was divided with respect to the attitude it should take towards the PCF as a coalition partner. This division, which became sharper with time, arrayed the supporters of Mollet against those of Blum and Ramadier. For Mollet, a left-dominated government was crucial for the success of socialist goals, and this would be best realised by close co-operation with the PCF in cabinet. Blum, on the other hand, was deeply suspicious of the intentions of the Communists and favoured the development of close contact with the United States in the face of the rapidly developing enmity of the United States and the Soviet Union.

The event which most probably had the greatest effect on the crystallisation of this division was the announcement of the so-called Truman Doctrine on 12 March. By declaring its intention to support the 'free peoples of the world' in their efforts to resist armed minorities aided by outside interests, the United States identified the Soviet Union (and by extension, what were viewed as its foreign counterparts, e.g. the PCF) as a threat to peace and freedom, and called upon its allies to join up with America to combat the Soviet danger. Thus, the presence of the PCF in the French cabinet became something of an embarrass-ment when the government was confronted with the necessity of dealing with the United States over matters pertaining to the disbursement of desperately needed economic assistance. In the end, the issuing of the decree removing the Communist ministers from the cabinet precipitated a crisis within the SFIO, with the Mollet faction arguing before the National Council that the SFIO should resign from the government and the Blum/Ramadier forces arguing the necessity of remaining in office so as to combat the threat de Gaulle had recently posed to the legitimacy of the regime. The decision of the SFIO National Council on 6 May was to carry on in government, by a vote of 2,529–2,115.

If the SFIO was willing to abandon the solidarity of the left, most commentators agree that the position of the PCF in government was tenuous at best from the very start. The major events leading to the isolation of the PCF in government, and its eventual expulsion in May 1947, span several issue domains. First, the Ramadier cabinet inherited from previous governments a fluid and volatile situation in Indo-China. Here the French were pursuing a *de facto* policy of colonial reconquest against the independence aspirations of the Vietminh, aided by much of the army general staff in the area, the colonial service and leading elements of the MRP.

The principal events in this issue domain occurred prior to the investiture of Ramadier in November and December of 1946. These were the shelling of the Vietnamese quarter of Haiphong by the French cruiser *Suffern* (killing 6,000), and the so-called 'Hanoi massacres', where 40 French were killed and 200 taken hostage. By January 1947, civil war had spread throughout Indo-China, with the Vietminh active in the countryside, especially in Annam and Tongking, and the French garrisons consolidating and expanding their perimeters. During January and February, the French reinforced their garrisons and began taking the offensive. During the period December 1946 to March 1947 there was much confusion in Paris over exactly what was transpiring in Indo-China. Admiral d'Argenlieu, acting as the top civilian administrator in the area and leader of the Indo-China colonial lobby, made the case for the re-establishment of French control in the area, arguing that the several proposals for negotiation issued by Ho Chi Minh were disingenuous.

In March 1947 the National Assembly debated Indo-China policy. On the 11th, PCF and MRP deputies came to blows, and on the 14th, after it was asserted that the Indo-China revolt was fomented by Communists, a Radical Socialist deputy accused the PCF of supporting France's enemies. With this, the PCF walked out of the session, only to return later to engage in verbal insults. Thereafter, the PCF began to abstain on votes of government policy affecting Indo-China, even though the party was committed to it by virtue of its cabinet membership. On 22 March, Ramadier threatened to resign the government if the PCF would not stop abstaining. A compromise was struck whereby PCF deputies would be allowed to abstain so long as the Communist ministers supported government policy. Later the failure of PCF ministers to support a government policy in another issue domain furnished the reason for the expulsion from government.

No sooner had this uproar over Indo-China subsided than a rebellion against French authority broke out in Madagascar on 29 March. The fighting was rather quickly contained, and airborne reinforcements were dispatched on 4 April. Implicated in the revolt were some of the deputies and senators from Madagascar, some of whom were arrested in Paris. On 16 April, the PCF, in protest over this action, precipitated a row in the cabinet. Later, on 7 May during the debate in the National Assembly over the Madagascar situation, the PCF introduced a motion to establish a commission of enquiry to investigate the causes of the revolt. This was defeated (probably because the commission would have witnessed excessive reprisals by the French military) and the cabinet was voted confidence (9 May). In any event, by 7 May the PCF was in opposition and freed from the necessity of supporting cabinet policies.

If the PCF was estranged from other members of the cabinet on issues pertaining to colonial policy (the PCF was most forthright about support for independence movements), it was also a liability to the government in its relations with the United States. There is some evidence to indicate that as early as May 1946 the United States had urged French leaders (Blum in particular) to prevent the PCF from participating in the government. The SFIO resisted this pressure, as indicated above, in view of the sizeable electoral popularity of the Communists and because of their predominant position in France's largest trade union organisation, the CGT. The announcement of the Truman Doctrine at the time of the opening of the Moscow Conference served both to solidify the division of positions on the future of Europe between the United States and the Soviet Union and served notice to America's allies in Europe that they should align their policy with that of the United States to stop the threat of Soviet expansionism. The continuing presence of Communist parties in the governments of allied powers was seen in America as inimical to its efforts to underwrite and maintain the security of the area. With the Moscow Conference ending in failure (24 April) and the Soviet Union isolated from the allied powers, the governing Communist parties in Belgium and Italy had gone into opposition. Still the PCF hung on in France.

The putative cause of the expulsion of the PCF from the cabinet occurred as a result of an event arising in the economic issue domain. At the Renault works in Paris on 25 April there was an unofficial strike by metal workers, who demanded an hourly wage increase of 10 francs. The wage demands of the Renault workers were the result of general economic conditions which were increasingly working to their economic disadvantage. The French economy had been experiencing both severe inflation and critical shortages of necessary commodities, especially food and energy supplies. To cope with the inflation, the first government of the Fourth Republic promulgated a policy known, after the Premier, as the 'Blum experiment'. The object of this policy was to stabilise economic conditions by controlling both prices and wages. A number of decrees were published during the first ten days in January 1947, cutting prices on a large range of commodities and setting new controls on various bank rates. It is generally acknowledged that compliance with the policy was at best sporadic, and it proved a boon to black-market profiteers.

On 5 February, the Communist-dominated CGT demanded the institution of a national minimum wage after perceiving that the Blum experiment was not proving effective. All cabinet parties except the PCF opposed this demand on the ground that wages could not be allowed to rise until the cost of living had stabilised. This led to token strikes in the public service industries and among newspaper workers. On 24 April (the day before the Renault strike) the cabinet held an emergency meeting to deal with the deteriorating food situation, particularly with respect to the availability of wheat, and issued a decree reducing the bread ration and regulating the use of flour.

On 30 April, the cabinet met again to deal with the demands of the Renault workers. Excepting the PCF, the government parties agreed that giving in to the wage demands at Renault would trigger a wave of similar demands across the economy, and thus destroy its wage stabilisation policy. Opportunistically, the Socialist and MRP press had been supporting the claims of the strikers, while at the same time their ministers had been taking a hard line in cabinet. In this setting, the PCF walked out of the 30 April cabinet meeting dealing with the Renault strike, while those remaining supported a policy of denying the workers' wage claims. On 2 May, Ramadier asked for a vote of confidence on his wage-freezing policy, and, when it came up on 4 May, four of the PCF ministers voted against the government. A decree was immediately issued removing the offending ministers from the government.

There is little doubt that the departure of the PCF from the cabinet seriously weakened its ability to govern. Not only was its majority diminished by the loss of more than 160 votes (which were more or less continuously cast against the government from that point onward) but, freed from the responsibilities of governing, the PCF could pursue its ideological interests by initiating direct action in the economy by virtue of its control over the CGT. From this point on, the government was forced to respond to a rising tide of wage demands, which undermined and then killed its economic stabilisation policy, and it also found it necessary to turn and face a new threat to its existence, one posed by the hero of the Republic, General de Gaulle.

De Gaulle emerged from political retirement on 27 February 1947 when he spoke at a military ceremony at Bruneval. He used the occasion to attack the constitution of the Fourth Republic and otherwise express his dissatisfaction with the regime of parties. On 7 April, he again spoke at Strasbourg, and on that occasion called upon the French people to unite in a nation-wide movement of national union. Shortly thereafter, the Rally of the French people was officially formed to give substance to the General's disgust with French political institutions. Beginning in June, de Gaulle embarked on a schedule of speaking engagements castigating the Communists as puppets of the Soviet Union and as a Fifth Column bent on the enslavement of France. He also indicated a deep distrust of Germany and the necessity of joining with America as the best defence against a resurgence of German militarism. With municipal elections scheduled for October, the RPF announced on 20 August that it would run candidate lists nation-wide. At the same time, a new parliamentary group was formed in support of (though not formally associated with) de Gaulle and the RPF.

While de Gaulle was busily blasting away at the Communists and the ineffectualness of the institutions of the Fourth Republic, the government was facing a crisis in the economy. In reaction to the food shortage (occasioned both by the failure of the wheat crop and the willingness of the peasantry to hold food off the market so as to enjoy higher prices), food riots broke out in Dijon and Lyons on 19 May, and similar incidents were recorded in several other cities over the next few days. Also on the 19th, 40,000 people with small and medium-sized businesses met in Paris to call a strike for 10 June in protest at the regulation of prices. On 20 May, 80,000 dock workers struck and workers in the gas and electrical utilities threatened to go out. Then on 5 June a strike beginning in a Paris locomotive depot spread rapidly, shutting down the entire rail system. In the ensuing negotiations with the government, the strikers won significant concessions. Under pressure from the unions, D. Mayer (Minister of Labour and Social Security) announced a new cabinet policy on 15 June permitting direct labour/management negotiations over bonus payments so long as such agreements did not initiate price rises. This represented a significant departure from the wage-freezing policy the government had to this point been trying to enforce.

Immediately thereafter, the CGT withdrew support for the government's anti-inflation policy and demanded sliding-scale wage adjustments pegged to the cost of living and an increase in the minimum wage. On the 17th, the National Assembly passed a bill to increase the wages of civil servants in the face of a threatened nation-wide strike. Then on 20 June, Robert Schuman (Minister of

Finance) presented the National Assembly with a financial retrenchment plan designed to deal with the growing budget deficit. At the heart of the bill was a proposal to raise the price of certain controlled goods and services (e.g. tobacco, rail fares, postal charges) and to abolish subsidies across the board except for the coal industry. The plan was denounced by the PCF and the unions as inflationary in view of anticipated price rises with the abolition of subsidies. On the 21st, the Assembly Finance Committee rejected the proposal, but reversed itself the next day. On the 24th, the bill passed in the National Assembly, 302–241–59, with abstentions coming from the centre of the political spectrum. Public reaction was a wave of strikes, the most serious being in the coalfields where, over a two-day period, 250,000 miners went out. On the 28th, the coal strike was settled when the Minister of Industrial Production agreed to wage increases and production quota bonuses.

The enactment of the Finance bill on 24 June marked the final collapse of the Blum experiment as an operative economic policy for the government. From this point onward, the Ramadier government struggled to defend its budget against a torrent of expenditure claims (mostly for wages and salaries) spurred on by an inflation it was unable to control. On 4 July, the government received a vote of confidence on its economic policy (331–247–30). In his speech to parliament, Ramadier attempted to infuse optimism into an objectively bleak economic picture by pointing to the help France could expect from receipt of Marshall Aid, promised by the American Secretary of State in June 1947. On 7 July, the SFIO National Council considered the issue of the party's continuation in the government. After criticism of its policies was aired, the party endorsed continuation 2,576–2,058–127.

During July, the government apparently struck a deal with the CGT over civil service salaries, heading off a nation-wide strike of 1.2 million employees called for the 15th, and on 17 July passed a bill in the National Assembly granting pay rises. Later in August, the National Assembly voted for a reduction in the civil service work force of 300,000 employees, granting severance pay. Then on 1 August the CGT and the Conseil National du Patronat reached an agreement (known as the Palais Royale Agreement) which called for an 11 per cent rise in wages, decontrol of prices of non-essential commodities, and the gradual decontrol of other goods as demand and production reached equilibrium. The cabinet response to this initiative was swift and negative, fearful of the effect a general price rise would have on the economy.

At this point, Mollet seems to have wrested control of the SFIO from the cautious Ramadier. At its conference in Lyons on 14–17 August, Ramadier sought to defend his government from Mollet's charge that it had abandoned Socialist principles for the sake of maintaining office. He cited the need to retain power in order to combat the danger posed to the Republic by de Gaulle (now vigorously attacking its institutions and performance) and by the PCF (which had recently appealed for reinstatement to the cabinet to fight Gaullism).

However, in response to Mollet's motion that the party should pursue its principles in power if possible and out of power if necessary, the conference supported this view 2,443–2,002. It then proceeded to present a policy document dealing with economic policy and elect a substantial Mollet majority to the party's Directing Committee.

By the end of the month, the government had capitulated on the economy, issuing a decree on the 22nd allowing an 11 per cent wage rise and decreeing on the 31st the deregulation of prices called for by the Palais Royale Agreement. Additionally, the food crisis grew worse owing to further failure in the harvest, such that between 27 and 29 August the cabinet issued a series of decrees reducing further the bread ration and restricting the sale of meat. Finally, a decree was issued banning imports from the United States (excepting essential items) due to a severe dollar shortage. The immediate response to this was a wave of strikes across the country for improved food supplies and wages (29 August to 1 September).

On 29 August, the Ramadier government, to offset rising production costs, presented a subsidy bill for the coal and steel industries to the National Assembly. This was a severe test for the government, which was proposing large expenditures that, at least in the short term, would do nothing to alleviate the crisis being experienced at a personal level by the bulk of the French working population (one estimate had the average French worker spending three-quarters of his or her wages on food). On 2 September, the Assembly Finance Committee rejected the subsidy bill by 12–6 (PCF)–3 (SFIO). The next day, Ramadier uncoupled coal and steel in the bill, staking confidence in his government on passage of the subsidy for coal production. Confidence was voted on 5 September, 292–243–54. The vote precipitated a crisis in the government because confidence was only obtained as a result of the abstention of right-wing deputies outside the governing majority. Voting against the government were many who were formally committed to it, including large defections from the Rassemblement des Gauches and the SFIO. Ramadier expressed to President Auriol his desire to resign the government in face of the loss of its majority in the National Assembly, but Auriol dissuaded him from doing so. For its part, the SFIO Executive Committee, now controlled by the Mollet faction, met on 6 September and agreed to hold a 'trial' of Ramadier in December to ascertain why his government was not pursuing the Socialist policies put to the government in its August directive.

During the rest of September, the cabinet set up a commission to suggest ways of dealing with rising prices and inflation and, on the 26th, issued a decree requiring increased planting of certain cereals. Sporadic strikes broke out at the ports and utilities, some of which escalated to violent confrontations with the police. On 9 October, just ten days from the holding of municipal elections, the government announced a major economy measure designed to deal with the deficit, including budget and tax reform and cutbacks on expenditures for government building programmes and capital equipment purchases. Blunting any effect this initiative might have had on the outcome of elections, however, was the outbreak of a strike of the Paris Métro workers on 11 October which was quickly generalised to include CGT-organised transport workers. The effect of the strike was to paralyse the Paris Métro until the 21st, two days after the elections.

The municipal elections were a tremendous victory for Gaullist candidates all over France, who came to control the city councils and mayors' offices in a substantial majority of large and medium-sized cities. This result precipitated the resignation of all of Ramadier's cabinet ministers in view of the apparent repudiation of the government parties by the electorate. Rather than resign his government, however, Ramadier decided on a reorganisation, and the new cabinet was announced the next day along with a statement which promised there would be no change in cabinet policy or programme. Crucial to this decision, it appears, was the perception that a resignation of the government would lend legitimacy to de Gaulle's accusations against the Republic, and this the government would not allow. In fact, in statements issued on 27 October and 12 November, de Gaulle called for the National Assembly to be dissolved and for the holding of new parliamentary elections, since the recent election had, to his mind, clearly repudiated the regime of parties. In the end, Ramadier's reorganised cabinet was presented to parliament for a vote of confidence on 30 October, which it obtained by 300–280.

While the government was stiffening to defend the Republic, conditions in the economy were rapidly deteriorating. November began with a series of strikes by Paris civil service employees which were brought to an end on 9 November with a government promise of amnesty and pay adjustments. Then on 12 November, riots and strikes broke out in Marseilles, where violence appears to have been directed against the RPF taking over the city government. On 12–13 November, the CGT met to discuss strategy with the aim of compelling the government to discuss a 'vital minimum' wage for workers and other economic and financial problems. The Communist majority favoured a nation-wide campaign of agitation in order to confront directly the government's wage policy, while the Socialist minority argued that a general strike, since it is a revolutionary instrument, would be ineffective as an instrument for bargaining. This disagreement set the stage for the subsequent split in the CGT and the formation of a Socialist-dominated organisation, the FO. In the end, with violence occurring in Marseilles and the port facilities being shut down, the government dispatched troops to restore order and get the ports open again. At this point, the MRP tabled an interpellation, which Ramadier managed to postpone until 18 November. Events in the south deteriorated rapidly with ports all over the Mediterranean being closed down. On the 16th, the strikes spread to Paris with bus and tram workers going out and, on the 17th, coal miners in the Nord struck along with oil refinery workers at Sete. In Le Havre and Toulon, the

Communists staged demonstrations. In the face of growing labour unrest, Ramadier submitted the resignation of his government on 19 November without an adverse vote in the Assembly being taken.

(f) Interpretation and conclusion

What explanation of the fall of the Ramadier government shall we give? Was it the result of the militant demands of an organised and mobilised working class placing incessant demands on the government for higher wages? Was it a strategy of the French Communist Party which, after its unceremonious expulsion from the government, bent its efforts to the destruction of the government? Was it the failure of Ramadier to maintain control of the SFIO, or was it the Truman Doctrine which narrowed the flexibility of the government to manoeuvre confidently and successfully in the parliamentary arena of French politics? Was it the threat de Gaulle posed to the Fourth Republic or the success of the RPF in the municipal elections? Perhaps the explanation is found in the critical shortages of food and raw materials or in the severe inflation experienced during the period. Or perhaps it was all of these things, and more.

Any and all of the events and conditions just enumerated may reasonably be held to be contributing factors in the occurrence of the downfall of the Ramadier government. However, their identification does not by itself constitute a basis upon which a scientific explanation can be confidently built. Part of the reason why this is so resides in the inherent limitations of the study of individual cases. Since we have observed only one instance of cabinet downfall, we have no obvious way to generalise about its occurrence with respect to conditions observed in its environment, since the particular confluence of factors present may be idiosyncratically related to the phenomenon of interest. Thus, whatever it is that determines the stability of cabinets is not validly inferred from the observation of this particular case. However, it is possible to draw some provisional conclusions about the effect of events from the experience of this government.

In considering the experience of the Ramadier government, it appears, as we suggested earlier, that domestic events assume a greater importance for the stability of government than do events arising beyond the domestic environment. This, of course, is not to claim that extranational events do not kill cabinets or contribute heavily to their downfall. Rather, it would appear that it is necessary for such events to be *experienced* domestically for them to achieve much political impact. For example, the events in Indo-China and Madagascar described above appear to have threatened the stability of the government only inasmuch as they were intruded into the governmental decision-making environment by the behaviour of the PCF. Once the PCF was expelled from the cabinet, Indo-China policy appears to have enjoyed at least a grudging consensus in cabinet and excited little response from the general public. Interestingly, it would seem that extradomestic events are, in terms of cabinet stability, less important in their intrinsic manifestation that they are for their indirect effects. Thus, as the Indo-China war wore on into the 1950s, the commitment to policy objectives necessitated allocations of resources which affected adversely the ability of succeeding governments to meet their domestic commitments and expectations. In dealing with these, successive governments came more and more to rely on US military aid to continue the Indo-China policy, eventually affecting both its content and the ability of French governments to influence policy in other domains (particularly, European security policy).

With respect to domestic events observed during the Ramadier government, the pre-eminence of economic affairs in the period stands out. It is likely that this is largely a function of extraordinary conditions associated with such structural problems as inadequate energy, labour and food supplies, giving rise to widespread dissatisfaction, particularly among those whose wages and salaries were controlled directly by the government. However, the volume of strikes occurring in the period may as well be related to the predominance of the Communists in the unions, and their willingness to use the strike weapon as an instrument of the class struggle as much as for the purpose of increasing the economic well-being of the membership. This is suggested by the apparent willingness of the industrial working class to curtail strike activities during the period when the PCF was in the cabinet and to accelerate such activities thereafter.

At bottom, however, it is the tenacity with which the government held on to office that is most remarkable. Not only did the government survive two major threats to its continuation, the departure of the Communists and the Gaullist victory in the municipal elections, but it also withstood several other crises as well, including a serious policy difference within the SFIO, the loss of its positive parliamentary majority on the coal subsidy, and the failure of its major economic policy. In spite of these events, the government soldiered on. And when it died, it was less the result of an execution than of exhaustion.

If we are able to characterise the downfall of a government in terms of the specific events which precipitate it or as an inability to continue, it is perhaps more pertinent to enquire as to why the government failed to fall before it did. The analysis problem with which we are confronted is that our observations of cabinet stability are dichotomous: that cabinets live until they die. What is needed is some way to assess the ability of cabinets to withstand the occurrence of disrupting events as the tenure of a cabinet progresses through time.

While current attributes studies posit such a quality for cabinets, what we have called its inherent stability, it is conceived in these studies as invariant over time, being a constant function of attribute values present at the time of cabinet formation. We believe that it will be theoretically fruitful to conceive a cabinet as it tracks through time as being more or less vulnerable to the impact of disrupting events which are generated in its various environments and issue domains. If cabinets exhibit variable degrees of vulnerability over time, this indicates that expectations of their longevity are similarly variable, depending both upon the level of vulnerability at successive points in time and the corresponding magnitude and intensity of events appearing in the environment of cabinet actors successively over time. In this conception, unlike the earlier attributes research on cabinet stability, time becomes a dimension on which events are ordered and cabinet vulnerability is charted, and not the dependent phenomenon of interest.

The overall focus of this chapter has been on the factors contributing to the stability of cabinets. By the identification of issue domains and actors in the environment of cabinets, our treatment coincides with the general concern of this volume with an assessment of the influence of systemic factors on coalitional processes. For the Ramadier government, the international factor is evident in the attempt by the United States to influence decisions in Paris against inclusion of the PCF in government; the internal party dimension is exposed by divisions between the leadership of various parties and also by intra-party leadership disputes and voting indiscipline in parliament; and, of course, the stability issue itself is centred upon the institutional dimension, involving the decision of cabinet actors to respond to events as they intrude into its arena from the other dimensions. The suggestion which emerges is that the specification of important coalitional processes is an exacting and complex problem, pointing to the need for greater refinement of measures and a heightened sensitivity to behavioural influences operating at several analysis levels.

Appendix 1. Glossary of political parties and groups

French name	English equivalent	Short name
Confédération générale du travail	General Confederation of Workers	CGT
Conseil national du patronat français	French National Council of Employers	CNPF
Force ouvrière	Workers' Force	FO
Mouvement républicain populaire	People's Republican Movement	MRP
Parti communiste français	French Communist party	PCF
Parti républicain de la liberté	Republican party for Freedom	PRL
Parti républicain radical et radical-socialiste	Radical party	Rad Soc
Rassemblement du peuple française	Rally of the French People	RPF
Rassemblement des gauches républicaines	Rally of the Republican Left	RGR
Républicains Indépendants	Independent Republicans	Ind Rep
Section française de l'internationale ouvrière	Socialist party	SFIO
Union démocratique et socialiste de la Résistance	Democratic and Socialist Union of the Resistance	UDSR

Appendix 2. The Ramadier coalition cabinet of 1947

The Ramadier government was invested on 21 January 1947 and fell on 19 November of the same year. During its tenure, it first lost its Communist ministers through their expulsion, and on 22 October all of Ramadier's ministers resigned, leaving him to effect a major reorganisation. The composition of the cabinet is listed below.

Original cabinet		Reorganised cabinet	
Ramadier (SFIO)	Prime Minister	Ramadier (SFIO)	Prime Minister, France d'Outre Mer
Thorez (PCF)	Vice-Premier, Minister of State		
Teitgen (MRP)	Vice-Premier, Minister of State		
Delbos (Rad Soc)	Minister of State	Delbos (Rad Soc)	Minister of State
Roclore (Ind Rep)	Minister of State	Bidault (MRP)	Foreign Affairs
Gouin (SFIO)	Minister of State, and President of Planning Commission	Depreux (SFIO)	Interior
		Marie (Rad Soc)	Justice
Bidault (MRP)	Foreign Affairs	Teitgen (MRP)	Armed Forces
Tanguy-Prigent (MRP)	Agriculture	Schuman (MRP)	Finance
Depreux (SFIO)	Interior	Moch (SFIO)	Economic Affairs, Public Works, Transport, Reconstruction and Planning
Schuman (MRP)	Finance		

Name	Portfolio
Philip (SFIO)	National Economy
Billoux (PCF)	National Defence
Coste-Floret (MRP)	War
Jacquinot (Ind Rep)	Navy
Maroselli (Rad Soc)	Air
Marie (Rad Soc)	Justice
Moch (SFIO)	Public Works and Transport
Tillon (PCF)	Reconstruction
Letourneau (MRP)	Commerce
Lacoste (SFIO)	Industrial Production
Croziat (PCF)	Labour and Social Security
Maranne (PCF)	Public Health and Population
Moutet (SFIO)	France d'Outre Mer
Naegalen (SFIO)	Education
Mitterrand (UDSR)	War Veterans and War Victims
Bourdan (UDSR)	Youth, Arts and Letters
Roclore (Ind Rep)	Agriculture
Lacoste (SFIO)	Industry and Commerce
D. Mayer (SFIO)	Social Affairs
Naegalen (SFIO)	Education
Bechard (SFIO)	Secretary of State to President of the Council of the Republic

Note: On 2 May 1947 the five Communist ministers left the government and were replaced by Delbos (Rad Soc) to Defence, Lacoste (SFIO) to Minister of State for Labour and Social Security, and Moch (SFIO) to Industrial Production and Reconstruction. On 9 May, the following appointments were made: D. Mayer (SFIO) to Labour and Social Security, Thomas (SFIO) to Posts and Telegraphs, R. Prigent (MRP) to Health and Population, Bechard (SFIO) to Secretary to the President of the Council of the Republic, and Letourneau (MRP) to Reconstruction.

References

Bogdanor, V. 1983. *Coalition Government in Western Europe*. London: Heinemann

Browne, E. and Dreijmanis, J. (eds.) 1982. *Government Coalitions in Western Democracies*. New York: Longman

Browne, E., Frendreis, J. and Gleiber, D. 1982. Cabinet stability as a Poisson process. Mimeo.

  1984. An 'events' approach to the problem of cabinet stability. *Comparative Political Studies*, *17*: 167–97

De Swaan, A. 1973. *Coalition Theories and Cabinet Formations*. Amsterdam: Elsevier

Dodd, L. 1976. *Coalitions in Parliamentary Government*. Princeton: University Press

Facts on File: 1947

Keesings Contemporary Archives: 1946–1948

Leites, N. 1959. *On the Game of Politics in France*. Stanford University Press

MacRae, D. 1967. *Parliament, Parties, and Society in France 1946–1958*. New York: St Martin's Press

Riker, W. 1962. *The Theory of Political Coalitions*. New Haven: Yale University Press

Sanders, D., and Herman, V. 1977. The stability and survival of governments in western democracies. *Acta Politica*, *26*: 346–77

Taylor, M., and Herman, V. 1971. Party systems and governmental stability. *American Political Science Review*, *65*: 28–37

Warwick, Paul 1979. The durability of coalition governments in parliamentary democracies. *Comparative Political Studies*, *11*: 465–98

Werth, A. 1956. *France: 1940–1955*. London: Robert Hale

Williams, P. 1954. *Politics in Post-war France: Parties and the Constitution of the Fourth Republic*. London: Longmans, Green

CHRIS RUDD*

6   Coalition formation and maintenance in Belgium: a case-study of elite behaviour and changing cleavage structure, 1965–1981

(a) Introduction

The formation and maintenance of government coalitions in Belgium have attracted little scholarly research. In English, there have been chapters in the collection of country-specific studies edited by Bogdanor (1983) and by Browne and Dreijmanis (1982). Elsewhere, studies have primarily been historical-descriptive accounts (Höjer 1969; Lemaître 1982; Luykx 1978) with a tendency to concentrate upon the constitutional procedures of coalition formation (Delpérée 1983). This dearth of literature is surprising, considering that coalitions have been the predominant form of government in Belgium since the introduction of universal male suffrage in 1919. There were merely nine days of single-party government between the wars and since 1946 there have been only two cases of single-party government – the Christian-Social majority governments of 1950-4 and the Christian-Social minority government of June–November 1958.

Even if traditional coalition theorists were to focus their research upon Belgium, they would be confronted with a number of serious difficulties. Traditional coalition theory, focussing on policy distance and/or ideological similarities between potential coalition partners, rests upon two basic assumptions: (a) that parties are monolithic actors; and (b) that payoffs are discernible prior to coalition negotiations (Axelrod 1970; De Swaan 1973). Both these assumptions, as we shall see later, are violated in the case of Belgium. Belgium presents a further problem in that the country now has three relatively

*I am grateful to David Broughton, Derek Hearl and Geoffrey Pridham for their useful comments on earlier drafts of this chapter.

autonomous party subsystems – one in Vlaanderen (Flanders), one in Wallonie and one in Brussels. The political conflict between the regions is not new, but the situation became much more acute during the 1960s and 1970s with the appearance of the community parties as significant political actors and the splitting of the three traditional parties into separate linguistic wings (this latter point emphasising the question-mark against treating the parties before they split as unitary actors). Thus, we are dealing not only with different parties in different regional party systems where the policy distance between parties within the *same* ideological family can be greater than the distance between parties of *different* ideological families, but also, at the level of the electorate, the salient social cleavages are not necessarily the same in each region (see Frognier 1973; 1978).

None of this is to say that it is either unproductive or impossible to adopt a policy-distance approach to Belgian coalition formation (for example, see Budge, Robertson and Hearl, forthcoming). It does, however, suggest that it might be fruitful to examine coalition formation using an analytical framework which contains a number of variables or dimensions in addition to that of policy distance. It is just such an alternative framework as set out in the introductory chapter that we shall seek to apply to the Belgian case.

It would of course be possible to relate all the dimensions to coalition formation in Belgium. Space forces us, however, to select only certain aspects of those dimensions considered to have particular importance for Belgium. For this reason, the environmental/external dimension will not be discussed directly. Belgium does not play any major role in either the East–West or North–South dialogue. The siting of American missiles in Western Europe has not, at least until very recently, been a major political issue as it has in the Netherlands and the Federal Republic of Germany.

As regards the vertical dimension, that is, the relationship between national and local/regional politics, this too has had little significance for national coalition formation. This is largely due to the unitary nature of the Belgian political system. Following the constitutional reforms of 1981 which decentralised the political decision-making process to the regions and communities, it could be that the vertical dimension has come to assume more importance. As yet it is still too early to tell and the full process of devolution will not be completed until after the next general election.

(b)   Historical influences

As pointed out above, coalition governments are the norm in Belgium. Furthermore, minority coalitions are rare, the only two post-war examples being the Tindemans I and IV coalitions (see Table 6.1). Tindemans I was intended simply as a basis for an enlarged coalition which would include the community parties. Tindemans IV was merely a caretaker government until fresh elections could be held.

Table 6.1 *Belgian governments 1947–85*

Name	Duration	Composition	Requisite[a] majorities (1972 onwards)	General remarks
Spaak II	March 1947–June 1949	S + C		
Eyskens I	August 1949–June 1950	C + L		⎫ Christian-Social single party
Duvieusart	June 1950–August 1950	C		⎪ majority governments
Pholien	August 1950–January 1952	C		⎬ Anticlerical coalition
Van Houtte	January 1952–April 1954	C		⎪ Minority single-party government
Van Acker IV	April 1954–June 1958	S + L		⎭
Eyskens II	June 1958–November 1958	C		
Eyskens III	November 1958–March 1961	C + L		
Lefevre	April 1961–May 1965	C + S		
Harmel	July 1965–February 1966	C + S		
Vanden Boeynants I	March 1966–February 1968	C + L		
Eyskens IV	June 1968–November 1971	C + S		
Eyskens V	January 1972–November 1972	C + S	No	
Leburton	January 1973–January 1974	C + S + L	Yes	Grand coalition
Tindemans I	April 1974–June 1974	C + L	No	Transitional minority coalition
Tindemans II	June 1974–December 1976	C + L + RW	No	
Tindemans III	December 1976–March 1977	C + L + RW	No	
Tindemans IV	March 1977–April 1977	C + L	No	Minority caretaker coalition
Tindemans V	June 1977–October 1978	C + S + FDF + VU	Yes	
Vanden Boeynants II	October 1978–December 1978	C + S + FDF + VU	Yes	
Martens I	April 1979–January 1980	C + S + FDF	Yes	
Martens II	January 1980–April 1980	C + S	No	
Martens III	May 1980–October 1980	C + S + L	Yes	Grand coalition
Martens IV	October 1980–April 1981	C + S	No	
M. Eyskens	April 1981–November 1981	C + S	No	
Martens V	December 1981–October 1985	C + L	No	

Key: C = Christian-Social parties   FDF = Front Démocratique des Francophones
     S = Socialist parties   RW = Rassemblement Wallon
     L = Liberal parties   VU = Volksunie

[a] Two-thirds majorities plus majorities in each linguistic region.

Another prominent characteristic of post-war Belgian coalitions has been the presence of the Christian-Socials since 1947 in every government except one. This immediately raises the questions as to whether this makes the Christian-Social party a 'pivotal' party. To answer this we need now to turn our attention to the cleavage structure underlying the party system.

An understanding of (and the changes in) the cleavage structure are essential to any explanation of the types of coalitions formed and their stability. It has often been stated that, from the First World War until the early 1960s, the religious and socio-economic cleavages were the main determinants of mass and elite political behaviour in Belgium (see Hill 1974; Lorwin 1966). In the absence of any major nationwide surveys before 1968, it is hard to confirm or disconfirm this supposition as regards mass behaviour. However, as regards elite party political behaviour, there is little evidence to back up the view that religion has played an important role in coalition formation. If religion had been of some importance, we would have expected to find anticlerical/clerical coalitions being formed and the existence of religious issues as the basis for the formation and collapse of coalitions. Little or no such evidence exists. There has only ever been one anticlerical coalition formed between the Socialist and Liberal parties (1954–8) and, with the exception of this coalition, religious issues have never been a principal reason for the formation or resignation of coalition governments.[1]

It was, therefore, the position of the three main parties along the socio-economic dimension that was crucial. In respect of this left–right dimension the Christian-Social party was a centre party with a powerful labourist wing pulling it towards coalition with the Socialist party and a bourgeois wing favouring an alliance with the Liberals (for further details on party factions see below). Since the Socialist and Liberal parties were far apart on economic issues and because anticlericalism was never, except in 1954, a sufficiently salient political issue for the parties to be able to ignore their economic differences, the Christian-Socials became almost by default coalition 'king-makers'. No viable majority coalition was possible which did not include the Christian-Socials.

This situation did not basically change after the 1950s. It merely became increasingly complex. The political expression of the linguistic cleavage had successfully been contained within the established party system until then. But between the 1958 and 1965 elections, the party system began to undergo a fundamental change. The conflict between Flemish and French speakers became such that not only do we witness the rise of the community parties, but the established parties themselves began to experience tensions between their two linguistic wings. The Christian-Socials formally separated into two linguistic parties in 1968 to be followed by the Liberals in 1972 and the Socialists in 1978. Therefore, the number of significant political party actors increased from three (Christian-Social, Socialist, Liberal) in 1958 to nine (two Christian-Social parties, two Socialist parties, two Liberal parties and three community parties) in 1978.

The implications of this for coalition making were far-reaching. The whole process of coalition negotiation, formation and maintenance was now much more complex. New issues relating to the communal conflict were on the negotiating table. The number of potential coalition formations was greatly increased. Parties within the same ideological family often found themselves opposed on linguistic issues but allied on economic questions. An added complication was created by the attempts made to find a constitutional solution to the linguistic problem, as constitutional changes require parliamentary approval of two-thirds majorities. This constitutional factor will be more fully explored later. First, we need to consider one final historical characteristic that may have a bearing on the behaviour of Belgian parties towards each other.

'Belgium', according to Lijphart, 'can legitimately claim to be the most thorough example of consociational democracy' (Lijphart 1980: 1). Lijphart used the term 'consociational democracy' to refer to those regimes where majority rule is restrained by certain institutional features which instead facilitate power sharing.

> In contrast with the tendency of majoritarian democracy to concentrate executive power in one-party and bare-majority cabinets, the consociational principle is to share executive power in broad coalition. Such a coalition does not necessarily comprise all the political parties; the crucial characteristic . . . is that power is shared among representatives of the different *communities* into which the society is divided.
>
> (1980: 4–5)

This reinforces the earlier observation that minority, single-party and anticlerical coalitions are rare in Belgium. Some have also argued that the entry into coalitions by the community parties – Rassemblement Wallon (RW) in 1974, Front Démocratique des Francophones (FDF) and Volksunie (VU) in 1977 – were the result of a desire by the established elites to accommodate community demands (see Rudolph 1976/7; Zolberg 1977). Any policy that aimed to resolve the community issue could not be formulated without the formal participation of those parties whose support in the two communities was well demonstrated at the polling booth. We should question, however, whether the sole motive behind the established parties' acceptance of the community parties as government partners was based on a commitment to consociationalism. Mughan has argued with some conviction that the established elites adopted a coalition strategy deliberately designed to 'undermine the new leaders' [of the community parties] bases of support' (Mughan 1983: 436). If this was indeed the case, it was a highly successful strategy against the FDF and RW but less so against the VU.

Such an argument tends to confuse the issue. There is no evidence of a conscious conspiracy amongst the established elites to destroy the new parties any more than there is evidence they wanted to destroy each other. Neither would elite behaviour during negotiations suggest a commitment to seeking any kind of social consensus over the community problem. What is clear, however, is that the need for constitutional revision imposed on the parties the need for coalitions with two-thirds majorities. Unless a grand coalition of the three traditional political families was possible, arithmetic made it necessary to consider the community parties. This is certainly a more convincing explanation of the community parties' involvement in national coalitions than the conspiracy theory.

(c) Institutional constraints

By the mid-1960s it had come to be widely recognised by the political elite that the growing conflict over the community issue – which had led to street violence in a number of Belgian towns – could only be dealt with by some form of constitutional revision. At the dissolution of parliament in 1965, a 'Declaration of Intent to Revise' was made, making the next parliament a constituent assembly. No revisions were actually achieved during the 1965–8 parliamentary session and another 'Declaration of Intent' was made prior to the dissolution in 1968. During the 1968–71 constituent assembly, a number of constitutional amendments were passed and three articles in particular demand our attention. Article 86-B stated that 'with the possible exception of the Prime Minister, the cabinet comprises an equal number of French speaking and Dutch speaking ministers' (Senelle 1980). Although, formally, this prevents the formation of a purely Flemish or Walloon national government, in practice it is unlikely that such a coalition could ever be contemplated in the first place as it would mean one of the linguistic wings of at least two of the three traditional families entering a government without its sister party. Article 86-B does, however, force the Prime Minister when distributing cabinet portfolios to take account not just of the electoral weight of each coalition party but also of which linguistic community they represent.

Of more importance were articles 107-D and 59-B. Article 107-D set down that Belgium was to comprise three regions (Brussels, Wallonie and Vlaanderen) and two communities (Flemish and Francophone). Article 59-B stipulated that legislation concerning the composition and competences of the community and regional bodies 'must be passed with a majority vote within each linguistic group of both Houses, providing the majority of the members of each group are present and on condition that the total votes in favour in the two linguistic groups attain two-thirds of the votes cast'. There are two conditions here: a two-thirds majority in the whole parliament *and* a simple majority in each linguistic group. These constitutional conditions established certain parameters for the formation of governments throughout the 1970s. The actual changes to the constitution made in 1971 had not presented major problems for coalition formation at the time because all the parties, the community parties included, were more or less in agreement on the general principle of Belgium being comprised of three regions and two communities. However, the detailed implementation of the constitutional provisions concerning the organisation, functioning and competence of the new community and regional bodies was to provoke divisive and acrimonious debate between the parties.

Table 6.2 *Seat distribution: national, 1946–81*

Election year	Christian-Social	Liberal	Socialist	Communist	Volksunie	FDF–RW	Others	Total
1946	92	17	69	23	—	—	1	202
1949	105	29	66	12	—	—	—	212
1950	108	20	77	7	—	—	—	212
1954	96	25	86	4	1	—	—	212
1958	104	21	84	2	1	—	—	212
1961	96	20	84	5	5	—	2	212
1965	77	48	64	6	12	5	—	212
1968	69	47	59	5	20	12	—	212
1971	67	34	61	5	21	24	—	212
1974	72	33	59	4	22	22	—	212
1977	80	33	62	2	20	15	—	212
1978	82	36	59	4	14	15	2	212
1981	61	52	61	2	20	8	8	212

Source: Ministry of Interior.

The problem facing the political leaders, therefore, was how to bring together a coalition with a two-thirds overall majority and a majority in each linguistic group. Two broad alternatives were available: a three-party (or 'grand') coalition of the traditional parties or a coalition of two traditional parties and one or more of the community parties. As any coalition without the Christian-Social parties would not have attained, given the distribution of seats (see Tables 6.2 and 6.3), a two-thirds majority, there were only two options within this second alternative: Christian-Social + Liberal + Community party(ies) or Christian-Social + Socialist + Community party(ies). The Tindemans I, II and III governments were attempts at the former, Tindemans V and Martens I at the latter.

The Leburton coalition of 1973–4 was an effort at the grand coalition alternative – Christian-Social + Socialist + Liberal. This was in fact the first grand coalition since 1945. This in itself reflects the urgency with which the established parties viewed achieving a solution to the Flemish–Francophone conflict, particularly as it was felt that the two-thirds majority held by the three parties might be lost at the next election and that this would be the 'last chance' to complete the constitutional reforms approved in 1970–1 (Luykx 1978: 628). Yet the rarity of grand coalitions also indicates the difficulties of holding such coalitions together given the disparity of views on economic issues held by the Socialist and Liberal parties. What made co-operation even more difficult in the Leburton government was the hostility between the unitarist Liberal Francophone party (PLP) and the more federalist-inclined Flemish Christian-Social party (CVP).[2] It is revealing to note that at the CVP, PLP and Socialist party congresses held to approve the involvement of their parties in government, the vote in each was less than 2:1 in favour (Lemaître 1982: 111). Given such lukewarm support by over half the coalition partners plus the disagreement over economic policy at a time of the unfolding energy crisis, it is little surprise the coalition was short-lived.

Table 6.3 *Seat distribution across three regions, 1946–81*

Election Year	Christian-Social			Liberal			Socialist			Communist			Flemish Nationalist			Francophone Nationalist		
	V	W	B	V	W	B	V	W	B	V	W	B	V	W	B	V	W	B
1946	58	23	11	8	5	4	27	32	10	3	15	5	—	—	—	—	—	—
1949	64	29	12	12	9	8	27	30	9	1	8	3	—	—	—	—	—	—
1950	68	27	13	7	7	6	28	47	12	—	6	1	—	—	—	—	—	—
1954	60	25	10	11	8	6	32	40	14	—	3	1	1	—	—	—	—	—
1958	62	29	13	10	5	6	31	40	13	—	2	—	1	—	—	—	—	—
1961	60	26	10	8	6	6	32	39	13	—	4	1	4	—	1	—	—	—
1965	51	18	8	18	19	11	27	28	9	—	5	1	11	—	1	—	2	3
1968	45	14	10	17	22	8	27	25	7	—	4	1	18	—	2	—	7	5
1971	42	16	9	18	11	5	28	27	6	—	4	1	19	—	2	—	14	10
1974	45	18	9	19	9	2	25	27	7	—	3	1	19	—	3	—	13	12
1977	50	20	10	15	14	4	26	30	6	—	1	1	17	—	3	—	5	10
1978	51	21	10	20	14	2	24	28	6	—	3	1	12	—	2	—	4	11
1981	36	18	7	20	24	8	20	35	6	—	2	—	17	—	3	—	2	6

Key: V = Vlaanderen
           W = Wallonie
           B = Brussels

Source: 1946–77: Luykx (1978).
1978 and 1981: Ministry of Interior.

With the Socialists against any further coalition which included the Liberals, this left Tindemans, whose personal preference was a coalition with the Liberals rather than the Socialists, to attempt to form a coalition between the Christian-Socials and Liberals. This would then form a basis to which would be added one or more of the community parties in order to give the coalition its two-thirds majorities. Tindemans failed in this strategy. Although he was able to widen his coalition to include the RW he was unable to incorporate either the FDF or VU. Tindemans then turned to the second option – a coalition of Christian-Socials, Socialist and community parties. In this he was more successful, forming a Christian-Social + Socialist + FDF + VU government in June 1977. This coalition had the requisite majorities but was unable to achieve any positive policy decisions because of the conflict, primarily between the CVP and FDF but also between the CVP and the Francophone Christian-Social Party (PSC), over the status to be assigned to the Brussels region.

The failure to achieve anything worthwhile by coalitions of two established parties and the community parties focussed attention once more upon the feasibility of a grand coalition. This, as we have seen, had failed in 1973–4. The situation had changed somewhat since then. To start with, alternatives to the grand coalition had been tried and found wanting. Secondly, the monopolisation of government resources in seeking solutions to the regional question had led to a neglect of basic economic policy at a time of severe crises in the Belgian economy – falling production and investment and rising unemployment. This, coupled with the electoral losses of the community parties, was sufficient to bring the traditional parties together in a coalition under Martens. The success of this coalition in producing a package of proposals, which included a further revision of certain constitutional articles as well as setting the composition and competence of the new regionalised bodies, was based upon two implicit compromises between the coalition parties. First, it was agreed to defer the intractable issue of the status of the Brussels region to a later date. Second, no major economic initiatives would be debated or undertaken until after the community legislation had been approved. After such a time, the Liberals and Socialists reserved the right to evaluate the government's proposed economic and financial plans. Following the approval of the constitutional legislation in August 1980, debate began over economic policy. When it became clear that the proposed economic and financial measures proposed by Martens lacked 'rigour', the Liberals promptly left the government. By this time, however, the success of the grand coalition had removed the 'constitutional constraint'. Subsequent coalitions have not needed the two-thirds majorities and have been of the simple bipartite type: Christian-Social + Socialist (Martens IV and M. Eyskens I) or Christian-Social + Liberal (Martens V) with economic rather than community criteria being the basis for their formation.

This discussion of the Belgian constitution raises an interesting question regarding traditional coalition theories. Why should a minimum winning coalition be equated with an absolute majority when, as in the case of Belgium in the 1970s, it was a two-thirds majority that was considered 'minimum winning'? Belgium is not alone in requiring special majorities to change its constitution. But in no other country have proposed constitutional changes dominated the formation of governments for such a lengthy period – over ten years, during which there were a dozen governments and five national elections. The Finnish case is similar in some respects. The Finnish constitution states that a two-thirds majority is required for tax increases designed to be in force for longer than a year. The extent to which this influences coalition formation has yet to be fully explored. The fact remains, however, that of the 20 majority governments in Finland since 1945, over half have held at least two-thirds of the seats in the Eduskunta (De Swaan 1973; Nyholm 1982).

A second related point concerns the situation of having a minimum winning coalition for constitutional issues, while at the same time an oversized coalition on economic issues. A grand coalition of Christian-Socials, Socialists and Liberals could impose a constitutional solution upon the community parties, yet such a coalition was difficult to form and maintain due to the mutual antagonism between the Liberals and the Socialists over economic policy, and could be sustained only when economic policy initiatives were 'frozen'. This, as we have seen, compounded the instability during the 1970s because the alternative to the grand coalition was a coalition of two traditional parties and one or more of the community parties which were just as difficult to form and hold together as the grand coalition.

Before ending this section on the institutional dimension, some consideration must be given to the effect of election results on coalition formation. There are two aspects to election results. First, elections determine the absolute number of seats held by each of the parties. This in turn affects the possible combinations of parties holding absolute or two-thirds majorities. For example, between 1946 and 1965, any Christian-Social + Socialist coalition would have held at least a two-thirds majority. The electoral successes of the community parties from 1965 onwards robbed such a coalition of this two-thirds majority. A potential Christian-Social + Liberal coalition even lost its absolute majority of seats between 1971 and 1977 (see Table 6.4). Hence, the likelihood, given the constitutional constraint, of grand coalitions or the inclusion of the community parties in national governments.

Second, electoral gains and losses also have an effect on party behaviour other than the determination of the number of seats they hold (see Table 6.5). Looking first at the community parties, their electoral success in the 1965, 1968 and 1971 elections made them less willing to risk losing their untainted image by becoming involved in any coalition government. The small electoral reversals for the VU and RW in 1974 made them more receptive to the overtures from Tindemans. But the RW's experience of government office not only split the party but led to a halving of its vote. This clearly contributed to the RW's refusal to consider further government participation. Having not apparently learnt the lessons from the experience of the RW, the VU entered in June 1977 the Tindemans V coalition and subsequently lost nearly one-third of its vote in the 1978 election. The VU leadership viewed this as a censure of its involvement in government and refused to consider rejoining a reconstructed Tindemans cabinet. There were recriminations within the party and Hugo Schiltz, who had been one of the main proponents of coalition participation, was forced to resign the VU party chairmanship in 1979.

The Christian-Social parties' secular decline in electoral support appears to have been of little consequence for their coalition behaviour until the heavy electoral defeat in 1981. Even then, only the PSC seriously questioned further government participation. Undoubtedly, the Christian-Social parties view themselves as natural parties of government and as such do not consider their electoral 'defeats' as necessitating a movement into opposition.

Again, as for the Socialist and Liberal parties, electoral gains and losses during the late 1960s and 1970s have had little influence on their willingness or unwillingness to join coalitions. The 1981 election was an exception once more, when the large Liberal gains made them the outright 'psychological' winners of the election. They were then able to bargain from a position of strength in the subsequent coalition negotiations.

Finally, it should be pointed out that Belgium is not unique in respect of election results not always having a decisive importance for coalition formation. There are no 'rules of the game' that force parties suffering electoral decline – such as the Christian Democratic parties in Italy and the Netherlands – to leave government, nor for parties experiencing major electoral successes – for example the Italian Communists – to enter government.

(d) Intra-party and intra-family relationships

In most polities, the party dimension would involve looking at the relationship between parties (inter-party) and the relationship between factions within the parties (intra-party). In the case of Belgium, such analyses have been complicated by the splitting of each of the three traditional parties representing the three ideological families into two linguistic wings. This presents us with four levels of relational analyses: *inter-family* – the relationship between the ideological families; *intra-family* – the relationship between the linguistic wings of the same ideological family; *inter-party* – the relationship between the linguistic wings of different families; *intra-party* – the relationship between factions of the same party.

In this section we shall restrict our attention to the intra-family and intra-party relationships, saving the other two levels of relationships until the following section. Although it is possible to distinguish between the intra-party and intra-family relationships analytically, it is often difficult to disentangle the two with

Table 6.4 *Votes for Chamber of Representatives 1946–81*

Party (or 'family' of parties)	1946	1949	1950	1954	1958	1961	1965	1968	1971	1974	1977	1978	1981
1. Christian-Socials (CVP + PSC)	42.5	43.6	47.7	41.1	46.5	41.5	34.4	31.7	30.0	32.3	35.9	36.2	26.4
2. Socialists (SP + PS)	32.6	29.8	35.6	38.6	37.1	36.7	28.3	28.0	27.3	26.7	26.8	25.4	25.1
3. Liberals (PVV + PLP)	9.5	15.3	12.0	13.0	11.8	12.3	21.6	20.9	16.4	15.2	15.6	16.4	21.5
4. Flemish Federalists (VU)	—	2.1	—	2.0	2.0	3.5	6.7	9.8	11.1	10.2	9.8	7.0	9.8
5. Flemish Separatists (VB)	—	—	—	—	—	—	—	—	—	—	—	1.4	1.1
6. Francophone Federalists (FDF + RW)	—	—	—	—	—	—	2.3	5.9	11.3	10.9	7.3	7.1	4.2
7. Ecologists (AGALEV + ECOLO etc.)	—	—	—	—	—	—	—	—	—	—	—	0.9	4.8
8. Anti-tax (RAD/UDRT)	—	—	—	—	—	—	—	—	—	—	—	0.9	2.7
9. Communists (KPB/PCB)	12.6	7.5	4.7	3.6	1.9	3.1	4.6	3.3	3.1	3.2	2.7	3.3	2.3
10. Others	2.8	1.7	—	1.7	0.7	2.9	2.1	0.4	0.8	1.5	1.9	1.4	2.1
Total	100	100	100	100	100	100	100	100	100	100	100	100	100

Source: Adapted from Hearl and Rudd 1982.

Table 6.5 *Electoral gains and losses, 1958–81*[a]

Election	Christian–Social parties		Socialist parties		Liberal parties		Community parties		
	CVP	PSC	SP	PS	PVV	PLP	FDF	RW	VU
1958–61	−5.6	−4.1	+1.9	+0.3	+1.8	+1.3	—	—	+2.6
1961–5	−7.1	−6.8	−5.0	−11.4	+5.0	+14.0	—	—	+5.6
1965–8	−4.8	−3.0	+1.3	−0.6	−0.4	+0.7	+8.6	+7.3	+5.3
1968–71	−1.2	−0.2	−1.6	−0.1	+0.2	−9.2	+15.9	+10.6	+1.9
1971–4	+1.1	+2.1	−1.9	+2.4	+0.9	−2.3	+5.1	−2.4	−2.0
1974–7	+5.0	+3.0	−0.1	+1.6	−2.9	+3.8	−4.7	−9.8	−0.2
1977–8	−0.1	+1.7	−1.0	−2.3	+2.8	−2.1	+0.5	+0.3	−4.9
1978–81	−11.8	−7.3	−0.8	−0.4	+3.9	+5.1	−12.8	−3.8	+4.5

[a] Electoral gains and losses in the Brussels region have not been included for the parties of the three traditional families or the VU. The RW does not in fact stand candidates in the Brussels region whilst the FDF is an exclusively Brussels party.

any precision. Changes in the factional balance of power or the policies pursued by the factions will almost inevitably have consequences for the intra-family relationship. We shall, therefore, first examine the three political families separately, looking at the nature of party factions where they exist as well as the relationship between each family's linguistic wings. This will be followed by a number of concrete examples to demonstrate the interaction between the intra-party and intra-family relationships.

That parties cannot be treated as unitary actors is underlined in the example of the Christian-Social parties. Looking first at the CVP, we can identify three main organised factions of workers (Christelijk Werkersverbond – ACW), farmers (Boerenbond – BB) and the small and medium-sized businesses (Nationaal Christelijk Middenstand Verbond – NCMV). There is little doubt that the ACW constitutes a major source of support for the CVP – at least in terms of the voters it can mobilise behind the party at election time. With the main affiliated organisation of the ACW being the Flemish Christian Trade Union Movement (ACV) and with the majority of CVP voters identifying with the working class (Malderghem 1981), the ACW has had some success in orientating the CVP towards centre-left coalitions with the Socialists.

While the ACW's attitude towards the CVP has at times been highly critical, the Boerenbond has shown unwavering support for the party considered to be the most vigorous defender of agricultural interests. Smits (1982) suggests that this unconditional support is due not only to a coincidence of interests but also to the significant representation of Boerenbond men on the party's electoral list. Furthermore, the Agriculture Minister is nearly always a Boerenbond 'appointee'.

The NCMV, established in 1948, has, like the Boerenbond, given the CVP consistent support over the post-war period. Without a mass membership, the

Table 6.6 *Standen affiliation of CVP MPs*

	1964	1965	1974	1977	1978	1981
ACW	42 (35%)	40 (37.1%)	47 (48%)	51 (49%)	52 (48%)	41 (50%)
BB	25 (20.8%)	24 (22.2%)	15 (15%)	18 (17%)	18 (17%)	15 (18%)
NCMV	32 (26.7%)	28 (25.9%)	21 (22%)	21 (20%)	23 (21%)	15 (18%)
BB + NCMV			5 (5%)	5 (5%)	6 (6%)	6 (7%)
Independent	21 (17.5%)	16 (14.8%)	10 (10%)	10 (9%)	9 (8%)	6 (7%)
	120	108	98	105	108	83

Source: Debuyst (1967) and Smits (1982).

Table 6.7 *Standen affiliation of PSC MPs*

	1964	1965	1974	1977	1978	1981
MOC/DC	16 (27.6%)	15 (33.3%)	15 (38%)	18 (40%)	17 (36%)	11 (32%)
AA	5 (8.6%)	5 (11.1%)	—	—	—	—
CEPIC	26 (44.8%)	17 (37.8%)	8 (20%)	10 (22%)	11 (23%)	7 (21%)
Independent	11 (19.0%)	8 (17.8%)	17 (42%)	17 (38%)	19 (41%)	16 (47%)
	58	45	40	45	47	34

Source: Debuyst (1967) and Smits (1982).

NCMV is still able to exercise considerable influence on the party through its political committee which groups together all NCMV-sponsored MPs (see table 6.6).

Unlike the CVP, there are only two significant factions within the PSC.[3] There is essentially a left-right division between a Labour Movement (Mouvement Ouvrier Chrétien – MOC) and a middle-class or non-manual Federation (Mouvement Chrétien des Indépendants et des Cadres – MIC). The MOC has always had a strained relationship with the PSC – more so than its Flemish counterpart, the ACW, has had with the CVP. There was a feeling within MOC that the PSC had always been run in the interests of the conservative Federation and that MOC had never received its fair share of favourable positions on the party's electoral lists or on its National Committee and National Bureau (Debuyst 1967). Despite an improvement in MOC's representation during the 1960s (see Table 6.7) this failed to satisfy the MOC leaders, who still felt the party too right-wing orientated. They, therefore, sought to group together all progressive forces both inside and outside the party and what emerged in 1972 was a new movement, Démocratie Chrétienne (DC), whose adherents came not just from the PSC but also from the RW and the FDF.

Numerically, MIC was much smaller than both MOC (with its affiliated Christian Walloon Trade Union Movement – CSC) and its Flemish counterpart, the NCMV. This belied, however, the significant influence which MIC exerted through its support amongst members of the PSC leadership. In the 1960s MIC had felt that the party was becoming increasingly influenced by MOC and the establishment of DC in 1972 convinced MIC of the need to counterorganise – which it did with the formation of CEPIC (Centre Politique des Indépendents et Cadres Chrétiens). CEPIC's attacks on the trade unions met with considerable sympathy in many quarters of the party. By the end of the 1970s, two-thirds of PSC ministers were CEPIC members. Following the poor showing by the PSC in the 1981 election and fresh scandals concerning CEPIC's connections with right-wing extremist organisations, the party leaders decided to distance the party from CEPIC. PSC MPs were asked to leave CEPIC – which they did only to re-form, with five unaffiliated MPs, a new grouping called the Rassemblement du Centre (RDC). The RDC now holds a plurality of PSC MPs.

At the intra-family level, there has always been tension between the Flemish and Francophone wings of the Christian-Social family. A formal split did not take place, however, until 1968, when the Flemish demand that the French-speaking faculties of Leuven University be transferred from that Flemish city to Wallonie was supported by the CVP and opposed by the PSC. From 1968 onwards, two separate parties existed. There is little doubt that the CVP dominates its Francophone sister party. The CVP has always been the leading party in Vlaanderen, while the PSC has at best only been the second party in Wallonie; in 1965, 1968 and 1981 it fell to third place behind the Liberals. So whilst the CVP can with some validity claim to speak for Vlaanderen and the Flemish movement, the PSC can make no parallel claims for Wallonie.

Turning now to the Socialist family, it is unrealistic to talk of organised factions within the Francophone Socialist (PS) and Flemish Socialist (SP) parties in the same way we did for the CVP and PSC. Left and right *tendances* exist as they do in most political parties. But because the Socialist parties prohibit factionalism as such, these *tendances* are not so formally structured as in the case of the Christian-Social parties by an extra-party body like the ACW/MOC or NCMV/CEPIC. Formal links, however, do exist between the Socialist parties and trade unions, although collective trade union affiliation to the parties ended in 1945.

Since the early 1960s, the Walloon Socialist Trade Unions (FGTB) have attempted to force the PS into a stronger defence of the declining Walloon economy. During the wave of national strikes of 1960–1, the PS had given unenthusiastic backing to the FGTB's participation. This caused a cooling of the PS–FGTB relationship and many Socialist trade unionists looked to the RW as an alternative political outlet for their discontent. By the mid-1970s the PS realised the danger of being outflanked by the RW on economic issues. The Francophone Socialists also saw the potential of becoming the dominant political force in a Walloon region, free from a central government dominated by Christian-Socials. The PS has subsequently taken a much more hard-line stance in defence of Walloon economic interests.

The Flemish Socialist Trade Union Movement (ABVV) has adopted a more moderate position than the FGTB towards economic issues, which reflects the healthier economic situation that exists in Vlaanderen in comparison to Wallonie. The ABVV, therefore, has been less willing to become involved in strikes against government economic policy and has been more favourable to the idea of SP participation in government with the Christian-Socials (and Liberals) than the FGTB has with respect to PS involvement in such coalitions.

The linguistic wings of the Socialist family split only as recently as October 1978. But co-operation between the wings had already become difficult in the early 1970s with the suspicion on both sides that linguistic solidarity was being placed above social solidarity (Ceuleers 1980). The PS, as the largest party in Wallonie, has tended to dominate the SP but never to the same degree as the CVP *vis-à-vis* the PSC. Certainly there is little objective reason for the SP to feel inferior, receiving as it does a larger percentage of the *national* electorate than the PS. It would appear, however, that being the majority party in a region endows a kind of 'psychological superiority'.

Even more than with the Socialist parties, there is little point in talking about organised factions within the Liberal parties. There are certain white-collar/professional trade unions which lean towards the Liberal parties, but none has a large membership, nor do they have any significant voice within the parties as such. The relatively small size of the Flemish (PVV) and Francophone (PLP) Liberal parties in terms of membership may work against the development of organised factions. The parties tend to be pragmatic rather than ideological in their approach to political power and, although *tendances* do exist, they focus more on personalities – De Clerq in the PVV, Damseaux and Gol in the PLP – than on policies.

As regards relationships between the Liberal parties, after a few turbulent years in the early 1970s the two parties have avoided open conflict on the community issue, a compromise being easier to achieve once it was agreed to defer a decision on the Brussels problem. On economic policy there are a few major differences, both being committed to the free market economy with the PLP taking perhaps a stronger Friedmanite position than the PVV.

There have been a number of occasions when the operation of these intra-party and intra-family relationships has had an effect on coalitional behaviour. During the Leburton grand coalition, the PS had been under increasing pressure from the FGTB to pull out of the coalition, as the trade unions felt that the decline in the Walloon economy could not be reversed whilst the PS was part of a Flemish-dominated national government. Furthermore, the PS itself feared that its association with the Christian-Social parties in government had enabled the RW to assume the mantle of the only true defender of Walloon interests. To prevent this 'policy outflanking' the PS would have to free itself from the constraints of government and adopt a more radical stance over the community issue. This aggravated the PS relationship with the Flemish Socialists who, situated in the half of the country experiencing greater economic growth, took a more pragmatic and moderate attitude towards participation in the national government.

During this same Leburton coalition, the CVP was divided between two factions, one supporting future coalitions with just the Liberals and the other backing coalition with just the Socialists. The former, led by Tindemans with the backing of the CVP Youth, Boerenbond and NCMV, gained ascendancy over the latter (mainly the ACW with Martens as their spokesman) once it became apparent that the PS was hesitant about entering into fresh coalition negotiations following the collapse of the Leburton government in January 1974.

The ACW's dissatisfaction over the coalition with the Liberals continued throughout the first four Tindemans governments. In June 1977, the Socialists replaced the Liberals in government, but Tindemans remained as Prime Minister. After the 1981 election, the possibility of a Christian-Social + Liberal coalition arose once more and, although the ACW was unable to prevent the formation of such a coalition, it did succeed in ensuring that Martens rather than Tindemans became Prime Minister.

It was also during the late 1970s that the latent mistrust between the CVP and PSC turned into a more manifest mutual hostility. The intra-family relationship was severely strained during the protracted negotiations over the community problems. While the CVP appeared on the one hand to renege on earlier concessions made to the Francophones, the PSC's involvement in the Front des Partis Francophones (see below) only reinforced the CVP's intransigence. The CVP was not, however, internally united on the community issue. As Lemaître (1982: 231) points out, there were three identifiable groupings in the CVP: the conservative unitarists opposed to any kind of regionalisation; the hard-line *flamignants* who viewed any compromise as a concession to the Francophones; a group of waverers who felt that a minimum of concessions should be made if this would elicit Francophone support for a compromise formula. The Egmont Pact, the outcome of negotiations between the government parties over the community problem, was effectively undermined by these divisions within the CVP. There was, ironically, an alliance between the conservative unitarists and *flamignants*, the former opposed to the Egmont Pact *per se*, the latter objecting to what they perceived to be unacceptable concessions to the Francophones.

Events in the early 1980s saw further interesting developments within the PS. At the 1980 PS congress, the party chairman, André Cools, had been criticised for accepting the Martens government policy of income restraint and for his personal role in the merging of the two Walloon steel firms, Cockerill and Sambre-Meuse (Deweerdt 1981). Cools was forced to stand down in 1981 and was replaced by Guy Spitaels who, conceding to rank-and-file discontent, took a hard-line stand over issues such as the indexing of wages and state subsidies to Walloon industries. It was this hard-line policy which directly brought down the Mark Eyskens government. It almost appears as if the PS were prepared to go into opposition in order to leave its hands free to become the leading political force in

Wallonie. The PS did in fact gain the presidency of the Francophone Community Executive and alternated the presidency of the Walloon Regional Executive with the PLP. This withdrawal by the PS into regional politics may not last should devolved power from the centre prove to be less than expected.

One final point on the intra-party dimension needs to be made. We have mentioned on more than one occasion that party participation in government coalitions has been subjected to party congress for approval. This in theory should assign considerable control to party members over party leaders. In reality, the party leaders' control of the party apparatus is such that party congresses primarily play a legitimising function. On only one occasion since 1945 has a party congress rejected its leadership recommendation to participate in a proposed coalition (this was the congress of the Brussels Liberal party in 1974 with respect to the Tindemans I coalition) (De Winter 1981). In the wider context, this underlines the domination of the top decision-making bodies of the parties within the whole coalition process, from the initial negotiations to the actual distribution of ministerial portfolios.

From this discussion of the interaction between the intra-party and intra-family relationships with respect to the effect it has had on party coalitional behaviour, a number of general points can be made regarding the Christian-Social and Socialist parties. For the former, party factional conflict has primarily revolved around the question of whether to coalesce with the Socialists – favoured by the left-wing factions – or the Liberals – favoured by the bourgeois factions. The left–right factional split in the CVP is fairly even. In the PSC, the right often has the upper hand given the relative weakness of the Christian trade unions in the Walloon industrial heartlands. The PSC instead draws the bulk of its support from non-manual employees and on economic issues, therefore, favours alliances with the Liberals. This has at times brought it into conflict with the CVP, not just because of the strong trade union representation in the CVP, but also because of the distrust by the federalists in the CVP of the Liberal parties' commitment to federalism.

A similar situation exists for the Socialist parties. The Walloon Socialist trade unions have always been opposed to any PS participation in a coalition that included the Liberals. By the end of the 1970s, the unions even began to question a PS coalition with the Christian-Socials. Instead, the unions pressed the PS to call for the decentralisation of economic powers and the implementation of Socialist economic policies in Wallonie. The Flemish Socialist trade unions, however, situated in a more prosperous economic climate, were more predisposed towards SP coalitions with either the Christian-Socials or Christian-Socials and Liberals. This produced a conflict between the SP and PS over joint coalition strategy, the SP reluctantly having to follow the PS line given that an end to the alliance between the two Socialist parties would harm the SP more than the PS. The SP, unlike the PS, would be unable to compensate for the loss of potential influence at the national level by playing a role in regional government given the dominance of the Flemish region by the CVP.

It can be seen, therefore, that it is the CVP and PS that often take the initiative in coalition negotiations and that developments within these parties are very influential factors in the coalition formation process.

(e) Motivation and maintenance

An attempt will be made here to try to unravel the thorny problem of whether Belgian political parties in their coalition behaviour have been motivated purely by power or by policy or by some combination of the two. What we shall do is draw out some general themes running through the various dimensions already discussed and, in conjunction with the inter-family and inter-party relationship, try to relate them to the maintenance of coalitions in Belgium during the 1970s.

As regards ideological compatibility, the Socialist and Liberal parties have never sat easily together in coalition as a result of their disagreement over financial and economic policy. Only the necessity of resolving the community crisis has had enough importance to bring the two parties together in the same coalition. Otherwise the Socialists have opted for 'cures of opposition', as in 1974 and 1981, or vetoed Liberal participation, as in 1977. This illustrates the difficult alternatives that both the Liberals and the Socialists have had to face at one time or another in either compromising their economic policy goals and entering a grand coalition or taking a more inflexible stand even at the sacrifice of government office (the Liberal exit from Martens III was an example of just such a sacrifice).

This willingness, at times, of both the Liberal and Socialist parties to put principles of policy before the exercise of government power belies the end-of-ideology thesis that posits the subordination of a party's programmatic function to that of the party's governing function (Epstein 1980). This finding is perhaps more surprising for the Liberal parties, as parties on the right of the political spectrum are usually regarded as being more pragmatic and power-oriented than parties of the left. Certainly the behaviour of the Belgian Liberal parties can be contrasted with that of the West German FDP, which has been willing to change its policy priorities and emphases to enable changes in coalition partners to take place. However, such a comparison must take into account the different party system position occupied by the respective parties. The FDP, as a centre party, is subject to alliance pressures from the Social Democrats on the left and the Christian Democrats on the right. The Belgian Liberal parties, situated to the right of both the Socialist and Christian-Social parties, do not face such alliance pressures from two sides – which, incidentally, reinforces the internal cohesion of the Liberal parties noted in the previous section.

In Belgium, it is the Christian-Social parties which occupy the centre or pivotal position in the party system. The strategic position of the Christian-Socials, plus their combined electoral strength which prevents single-party majority governments by either the Socialists or the Liberals, has enabled them to participate in nearly every government since 1919. Thus, the Christian-Social parties have come to see themselves as natural – if not indispensable – parties of government. Only once, in 1981, did either of the two parties seriously consider moving into opposition. (This was the PSC – or, more precisely, the DC faction within the PSC.) As such it is unrealistic to examine the behaviour of either the CVP or PSC with respect to their position on a power–policy continuum. Yet while coalition participation in itself is not open to debate for these parties, *who* to participate with is a major issue and it is over the question of coalition partners that policy conflicts and policy compromises occur. One could argue that a 'rational' strategy for the Christian-Social parties to pursue in order to maximise policy goals would be to play off the Socialists and the Liberals against each other by forming coalitions first with one, then with the other. This would assume, however, a unity of action within the Christian-Social family and this, as we have seen, is not a tenable assumption. There are the factional conflicts within each party, primarily of a left–right nature, but there also exists the unitarist–federalist divide which is most acute within the CVP. At the intra-family level, the Christian-Social family has always endured conflicts between its Flemish and Francophone wings and the formation of separate parties in 1968 has simply institutionalised this conflict. Thus, as a centre party, the alliance pressures from both the left and right, Flemish and Francophone, aggravate the factional and party relationships within the Christian-Social family.

Undoubtedly the dominant political issue in Belgian politics from the mid-1960s onwards was the conflict between the Francophone and Flemish communities. The conflict contained a number of highly complex, divisive and emotive issues, such as the drawing of a constitutional boundary between the two communities, the reallocation of parliamentary seats between the regions, the status to be assigned to Brussels, the question of special facilities for linguistic minorities and the composition and competences of the new sub-national bodies. A partial coincidence of the economic and community cleavages further complicated the situation, for example the use of central government subsidies for declining Walloon industries and the uneven distribution in favour of Flemish enterprises of government investment. It has to be emphasised that many of these issues were new, new in a sense that political parties had never before been forced to state their position on them clearly.

At first, the established parties had rejected any idea of the federalisation of Belgium. By 1981, all were responsible for approving the constitutional changes which achieved just that. In the intervening years the parties had often been uncertain of which way to move, of the reaction of their electorates and of the behaviour of each other. On economic and social issues they were more certain of what their own and other parties' positions were. Trade-offs over policy goals on these issues were, thus, easier to discern, compromises easier to make and negotiations easier to conduct. The emergence of a new political cleavage changed all this. It introduced into the coalition formation process the uncertainty element – uncertainty of one's own position and uncertainty of other actors' positions. To make matters worse, there were now more actors to take into account.

Of considerable importance was the fear felt by the established parties of being outflanked by the community parties. This was of particular relevance for the PS *vis-à-vis* the RW, and the CVP *vis-à-vis* the VU. As we have seen, the PS was at first lukewarm about the idea of economic decentralisation. But the RW expounded this view as being the only way in which Wallonie could solve its economic problems. As these problems mounted and the RW's electoral successes continued, the PS was forced to rethink its strategy. An analogous situation existed between the CVP and VU. The CVP was gradually forced into a more and more federalist stance in order to combat its loss of support to the VU. The CVP thus became more intransigent in coalition negotiations towards the Francophone parties, particularly the FDF, and effectively torpedoed the early government formation attempts of Tindemans.

We should note that the linguistic conflict also provoked inter-party alliances, that is alliances between parties belonging to the same linguistic community but a different ideological family. The most concrete example of such an alliance was between the Francophone parties during the latter half of the 1970s. In November 1978, the PS, PSC and FDF had made a common declaration in defence of Walloon and Brussels interests. On the eve of the December 1978 elections, these same parties formed a common Front des Partis Francophones which, although not a formal electoral alliance, was intended as a demonstration of linguistic solidarity. Under the new governments of Martens 1 (CVP/PSC–SP/PS–FDF) a commission was established to consider the powers and organisation of the proposed regional councils. Following the commission's recommendations made in November 1979, the Francophone parties in the government – PS, PSC, FDF – felt that it had not been made sufficiently clear by the commission that the Walloon and Brussels regional councils would have the right to block any legislation considered to be against Francophone interests and that the Brussels region would have equal status with the Flemish and Walloon ones. The three parties signed a pact in January 1980 stipulating their common position on the above issues.

This alliance amongst the Francophone parties, however informal, produced angry responses from the Flemish parties, especially the CVP and SP. The CVP and SP felt that the other three government parties had, in fact, formed a coalition within a coalition, thus undermining the authority of the (Flemish) Prime Minister and his government. A government crisis developed which was resolved only when a compromise solution made by Martens was accepted by both the PSC and the PS. This compromise, however, involved delaying a decision over the Brussels question and as such was unacceptable to the FDF. But the FDF, without the support of the other Francophone parties, was isolated and it was subsequently left no alternative but to leave the government. It should be recalled that the FDF's entry into government in the first place had only been possible with the support of the PS. The PS had been motivated to do this because it viewed the FDF as a useful ally against the CVP and not because the PS was particularly sympathetic to the FDF's defence of middle-class Francophones in Brussels. Once Walloon and Brussels interests became separated, this effectively ended the unity of action between the Francophone parties.

The discussion can be linked to the question of coalition maintenance – or perhaps more accurately the lack of maintenance. Between 1971 and 1981, the average government duration was less than one year compared to an average of $2\frac{1}{2}$ years in the 1960s and $1\frac{1}{2}$ years in the 1950s. How can we account for this increase in coalition instability? From what has already been said, the fundamental reason concerned the placement on the political agenda of a set of new policy problems along with a new set of political actors sitting around the bargaining table. This produced uncertainty and the problems that this usually causes for coalition formation and maintenance. All the parties were in a sense jockeying for a specific position along the new community cleavage, trying to create a policy image for themselves. It would be no exaggeration to say that the parties were going through identity crises during this period. A final element adding to the general atmosphere of uncertainty was the ambiguous position of the electorate over the community issue. Had the electorate expressed a clear preference either for the retention of the unitary state or its federalisation, the traditional parties in particular would have had a better idea of what a likely vote-maximising position would have been. Yet a survey as late as 1979 showed that 34.2 per cent of respondents considered themselves as unitarists, 25.2 per cent as federalist, 13.2 per cent somewhere in between the two and 27.3 per cent held no view or failed to give any response (Delruelle *et al.* 1982; for earlier surveys see Delruelle *et al.* 1966 and 1970; De Ridder 1978). Given such results, it was never going to be very easy to plan future party strategy.

As a consequence of all this uncertainty, coalition negotiations were protracted and often chaotic with frequent interruptions caused by the withdrawal of one group or another from the proceedings (Obler *et al.* 1977: 39). Even after a coalition was formed, the difficulties did not end because policy formation is obviously a continuous process and having once formed a coalition with a general commitment to resolving the linguistic conflict, policy details had to be worked out and legislation implemented. It was then that policy differences became more apparent. To make matters worse, party positions on policies changed over the period, as did the issues themselves. In the early 1970s, the status of Brussels was the most contentious issue. By the late 1970s, the competence of the regional bodies attracted the parties' main attention in this regard. Over the same period, the Liberal parties went from being unitarists to conditional federalists with similar policy shifts being made by the other traditional parties.

(f) Conclusion

The party systems of Western Europe have been analysed as configurations of politically salient social cleavages (Lipset and Rokkan 1967). As such, it is no surprise that a change, therefore, in the cleavage configuration will change the relationship between the parties in the system. If a new (or old) social cleavage has become politicised we can, also, expect the emergence of new political parties. This is precisely what occurred in Belgium after 1961. In such a situation, it then requires the parties to work out a new *modus vivendi* in this changed political environment. The effect on coalition behaviour is likely to be both direct and long-term, as the whole process of coalition-making is concerned with the nature of the relationships between parties. If a new cleavage produces new issues and new parties, this destabilises existing party relationships. Parties can adapt to changed conditions but often need time to do so. In this respect, the coalition game in Belgium in the 1970s was being played between new actors with a new set of rules.

Dodd, in his *Coalitions in Parliamentary Government* (1976), tried to deal with the question of cleavage saliency and its impact on coalition status and cabinet durability. Strangely, although Dodd explicitly contrasted the inter-war and post-war party system in terms of salient cleavages, he failed to identify the change in cleavage saliency that was occurring in Belgium from the 1960s onwards. This is unfortunate because, as this chapter has shown, the crucial development affecting Belgian coalition formation in the 1970s was just such a change in the hierarchy of salient cleavages. The durability of coalitions was affected as well as the criterion for assessing the status of a coalition – a minimum winning coalition no longer being one that just had a simple majority of seats. With hindsight it would be tempting to use Dodd's approach to reanalyse the Belgian case. There would, however, be a number of difficulties with this. First, precisely because of the newness of the situation and the constantly changing policy agenda, it is difficult to be sure of the relative positions of the parties with regard to the salient cleavages. Secondly, even if a party's position can be ascertained, we have to determine which cleavage is more important for the party in determining its coalition behaviour. Again, over the period, the priorities of each party fluctuated. Finally, in the early 1980s, it became difficult to disentangle the respective influence of the two cleavages given that economic aims were used to justify linguistic/communal demands and vice versa.

This leaves us with the question as to what the future trends in Belgian coalition behaviour will be. With the approval of the 1980 constitutional amendments, some would argue that this has depoliticised once more the community cleavage. While it might be an exaggeration to go this far, the formation of a Christian-Social + Liberal coalition in 1981 whose priority has been economic and fiscal policy rather than community policy suggests a return to the forms of coalition behaviour that characterised the late 1950s and early 1960s. However, it would be foolhardy to predict any long-term developments from the post-1981 events. If the regional executives and assemblies are given real political powers, it is not inconceivable that parties will come to concentrate their attention on the regional rather than the national political arena. If so, future research will have to focus attention on both the regional and national levels as well as the relationship between the two.

Appendix. Abbreviations

Political parties:

Christian- Social party(ies)	CVP	Christelijke Volkspartij (Flemish Christian-Social Party)
	PSC	Parti Social Chrétien (Francophone Christian-Social Party)
Socialist party(ies)	BSP	Belgische Socialistische Partij (Flemish Socialist Party)
	PSB	Parti Socialiste Belge (Francophone Socialist Party)
Liberal party(ies)	PVV	Partij voor Vrijheid en Vooruitgang (Flemish Liberal Party)
	PLP	Parti de la Liberté et du Progrès (Francophone Liberal Party)
Community or Regionalist Parties	VU	Volksunie (Flemish)
	FDF	Front Démocratique des Francophones (Brussels)
	RW	Rassemblement Wallon (Walloon)

Trade unions:

ACV   Algemeen Christelijk Vakverbond (Flemish Christian)
ABVV Algemeen Belgisch Vakverbond (Flemish Socialist)
CSC   Confédération des Syndicats Chrétiens (Francophone Christian)
FGTB Fédération Générale du Travail Belgique (Francophone Socialist)

Party factions:

ACW   Algemeen Christelijk Werkersverbond
NCMV   Nationaal Christelijk Middenstand Verbond
BB   Boerenbond
CEPIC   Centre Politique des Indépendants et Cadres Chrétiens
MIC   Mouvement Chrétien des Indépendants et des Cadres
MOC   Mouvement Ouvrier Chrétien
DC   Démocratie Chrétienne

Notes

1. Belgium is an overwhelmingly Catholic country. In a 1983 survey, nearly 80 per cent of respondents claimed to follow the Catholic faith (Institute for Marketing Research survey, 1983). As in many other Catholic countries, the major clerical–anticlerical conflict has revolved around the question of control and finance of Catholic schools.
2. The PLP went through two name changes in the 1970s as a result of party mergers. In 1976 it became the Parti des Réformes et de la Liberté Wallone (PRLW) when it was joined by a splinter group from the RW. In 1979 the PRLW fused with the Brussels Parti Libéral (PL) to form the PRL (Parti Réformateur Libéral). To avoid confusion, the label PLP has been used throughout this chapter.
3. The Boerenbond equivalent in Wallonie, the Alliance Agricole (AA), carries little weight within the PSC. This is not surprising given the relative unimportance of agriculture in what is largely an industrialised region.

References

Axelrod, R. 1970, *Conflict of Interest: a theory of divergent goals with application to politics.* Chicago: Markham
Budge, I., Robertson, D. and Hearl, D. (eds.) Forthcoming. *Ideology, Strategy and Party Change.* Cambridge University Press
Ceuleers, J. 1980, De splitsing van Belgische Socialistische Partij. Een B te veel. *Res Publica, 22* (3): 373–82
Debuyst, F. 1967, *La Fonction parlementaire en Belgique.* Brussels: Centre de Recherche et d'Information Socio-Politiques
Delpérée, F. 1983. *Chroniques de crise 1977–1982.* Brussels: Centre de Recherche et d'Information Socio-Politiques
Delruelle, N., Coenen, J. and Maigray, D. 1966. Les problèmes qui préoccupent les Belges. *Revue de l'Institut de Sociologie, 39:* 292–341
Delruelle, N., Evalenko, R. and Fraeys, W. 1970. *Le Comportement politique des électeurs belges.* Brussels: Institut de Sociologie de l'Université Libre de Bruxelles
Delruelle, N., Frognier, A.P., Dawance, J. and Grodent, J.J. 1982. L'opinion publique et les problèmes communautaires. *Courrier Hebdomadaire,* no. 966
De Meyer, J. 1983, Coalition governments in Belgium. In V. Bogdanor (ed.), *Coalition Governments in Western Europe.* London: Heinemann
De Ridder, M. 1978. Images of Belgian politics. The effects of cleavages on the political system. *Legislative Studies Quarterly, 3:* 83–108

De Swann, A. 1973. *Coalition Theories and Cabinet Formations.* Amsterdam: Elsevier

Dewachter, W. and Clijsters, E. 1982. 'Belgium: political stability despite coalition crises'. In E. Browne and J. Dreijmanis (eds.), *Government Coalitions in Western Democracies.* New York: Longman, ch. 6

Deweerdt, M. 1981. Overzicht van het Belgisch politiek gebeuren in 1981. *Res Publica, 24* (2): 221–60

De Winter, L. 1981. De partijpolitisering als instrument van de particratie. Een overzicht van de ontwikkeling sinds de Tweede Wereldoorlog, *Res Publica, 23* (1): 53–107

Dodd, L. C. 1976. *Coalitions in Parliamentary Government.* Princeton University Press

Epstein, L. D. 1980. *Political Parties in Western Democracies.* New York: Transaction Books

Frognier, A.-P. 1973. Distance entre partis et clivages en Belgique. *Res Publica, 15* (2): 291–311

1978. Parties and cleavages in the Belgian Parliament. *Legislative Studies Quarterly, 3:* 83–108

Hearl, D. and Rudd, C. 1982. The Belgian election of 1981. *Electoral Studies, 1* (1): 100–6

Hill, K. 1974. Belgium: political change in a segmented society. In R. Rose (ed.), *Electoral Behaviour.* New York: Free Press, pp. 29–197

Höjer, C. H. 1969. *Le Régime parlementaire belge de 1918–1940.* Brussels: Centre de Recherche et d'Information Socio-Politiques

Lemaître, H. 1982. *Les Gouvernements belges de 1968 à 1980.* Stavelot: Editions Chauveheid

Lijphart, A. (ed.) 1980. *Conflict and Coexistence in Belgium.* Berkeley: University of California Press

Lipset, S. M. and Rokkan, S. 1967. *Party Systems and Voter Alignments: cross national perspectives.* New York: Free Press

Lorwin, V. R. 1966. Belgium: religion, class and language in national politics. In R. Dahl (ed.), *Political Oppositions in Western Democracies.* New Haven and London: Yale University Press, ch. 5

Luykx, Th. 1978. *Politieke Geschiedenis van België, Vol. 2: 1944–1977.* Amsterdam and Brussels: Elsevier

Malderghem, R. van 1981. Welke zijn de nieuwe publiek en volksgroepen die de Socialistische Beweging aanspreekt? *Socialistische Standpunten, 2* (81): 87–95

Mughan, A. 1983. Accommodation or defusion in the management of linguistic conflict in Belgium? *Political Studies, 31:* 434–51

Nyholm, P. 1982. Finland: a probabilistic view of coalition formation. In E. Browne and J. Dreijmanis (eds.), *Government Coalitions in Western Democracies.* New York: Longman, ch. 3

Obler, J., Steiner, J. and Dierickx, G. 1977. *Decision Making in Smaller Democracies: the consociational 'burden'.* Sage: London

Petersen, R. L., De Ridder, M., Hobbs, J. D. and McClellan, E. F. 1983. Government formation and policy formulation. *Res Publica, 25* (1): 49–82

Platel, M. 1981. Martens I, II, III, IV. *Res Publica, 23* (2–3): 239–76

1982. Martens IV – Eyskens I – Martens V. *Res Publica, 24* (2): 273–304

Rudolph, J. R. 1976/7. Ethnonational parties and political change: the Belgian and British experience. *Polity, 9:* 401–26

Senelle, R. 1980. *Memo from Belgium No. 189*. Brussels: Ministry of Foreign Affairs

Smits, J. 1982. De standenvertgenwoordiging in de Christelijke Volkspartij an de Parti Social Chrétien. *Res Publica*, *24* (2): 73–127

Special issue of *Res Publica* on 'Particratie', *23* (1), 1981

Zolberg, A. R. 1977. Splitting the difference: federalization without federalism in Belgium. In M. J. Esman (ed.), *Ethnic Conflict in the Western World*. Cornell University: Ithaca Press

7 The Dutch Christian Democratic party and coalitional behaviour in the Netherlands: a pivotal party in the face of depillarisation

(a) The political landscape

The Dutch polity is known as a rather fragmented multi-party system. Ever since the introduction of universal suffrage and proportional representation – both in the aftermath of the First World War – the political system has been dominated by minority parties.[1] Even the largest parties – the Catholic and the Labour parties – never gained more than one-third of the vote. In principle it allowed many coalition figurations.

The five major parties nevertheless determined the course of Dutch politics. Three of them were religious parties:

- the Calvinist ARP (Anti Revolutionary party)
- the Dutch Reformed Protestant CHU (Christian Historical Union)
- the Roman Catholic KVP (Catholic People's party).

The other two represented the secular strata of the population:

- the Liberal VVD (People's Party for Freedom and Democracy)
- the Socialist PvdA (Labour party).

The major parties were closely tied to separate social subcultures, the latter being segregated along religious and class lines. Due to the impact of the religious cleavage, neither of the two secular parties was ever able to mobilise its class base fully. The religious parties jointly controlled at least 50 per cent of the popular vote until 1967. In theory the religious parties could govern alone. But the inter-war period had vindicated that the three parties did not always act in harmony. After the Second World War especially the Catholic KVP was keen on enlarging

coalitions above minimum winning size. Due to the KVP the Socialist PvdA
became accepted as a legitimate governing party in the large coalitions of the
1950s. But with post-war reconstruction coming to an end, consensus began to
evaporate again. At the end of the decade Socialists and Liberals came to exclude
each other from government responsibility. From 1959 onwards, the KVP and
both Protestant parties had to choose cabinets that would be called either centre-
right or centre-left.

Coalitions to the right have predominated over the quarter-century since 1959.
This imbalance is not based strictly on the voters' preference. The Christian
Democrats changed partners more often than elections were held. Until the mid-
1960s, the changing of coalitions without premature elections was accepted as
normal practice. The political climate, however, changed in the 1960s, and also
changed with respect to constitutional norms. The fact that in the parliamentary
period 1963–7 a change of partner without elections occurred even twice was
decisive in this respect. From now on a forthcoming change of coalition partner
had to be legitimised by popular vote. The new practice had been pushed forward
by the parties of the left. Representatives of the Labour party and the new
Democrats '66 were hammering at the need for 'political clarity'. They demanded
that other parties opt for a specific coalition previous to an election, to submit the
composition of government to an electoral decision. The new norm, however,
was unable to change the fact that it was not the elections, but the process after the
elections that decided the political colour of the government. Paradoxically, the
new practice – a crisis of government, resulting in the breakdown of the coalition,
to be followed by new elections – did contribute to the stability of cabinets and
thus to the diminution of the number of elections.

Of course the 'democratic' concerns were also encouraged by the growing
uncertainty about electoral results. Provincial elections in 1966 suggested a
process of electoral change of unknown dimensions. In 1967 both the KVP and
the PvdA lost a good 5 per cent of their votes (see Table 7.1). Political and above
all social changes from the 1960s heralded the end of pillarisation (*verzuiling*) –
the traditional system of political forces or families being rooted in organised
subcultures which lent stability to Dutch politics – and a movement towards a
new and more competitive system. Some parties that had grown up with the
system of pillarisation underwent more or less severe identity crises, as the ties
with their 'natural milieus' loosened.

In these days of electoral uncertainty the secular parties introduced an
offensive strategy, subjecting the centrist confessional parties to the pressures of a
more bipolar setting. The Liberal VVD had, in 1959, introduced the idea of
polarisation by excluding the Labour party as a possible partner in government.
The PvdA opted for this strategy after the coalitional experiences in 1965/6. The
Labour party aimed its polarisation strategy primarily against the confessional
parties. For instance:

Table 7.1 *Electoral results in the Netherlands after 1945 for the five major parties*
Percentages of total votes

	Christian Democrats				Socialists	Liberals
	KVP	ARP	CHU	CDA	PvdA	VVD
1946	30.8	12.9	7.8	(51.5)	28.3	6.4
1948	31.0	13.2	9.2	(53.4)	25.6	8.0
1952	28.7	11.3	8.9	(48.9)	29.0	8.8
1956	31.7	9.9	8.4	(50.0)	32.7	8.8
1959	31.6	9.4	8.1	(49.1)	30.4	12.2
1963	31.9	8.7	8.6	(49.2)	28.0	10.3
1967	26.5	9.9	8.1	(44.5)	23.6	10.7
1971	21.9	8.6	6.3	(36.8)	24.6	10.3
1972	17.7	8.8	4.8	(31.3)	27.4	14.4
1977	—	—	—	31.9	33.8	18.0
1981	—	—	—	30.8	28.3	17.3
1982	—	—	—	29.3	30.4	23.1

- the anti-KVP resolution at the 1969 party congress
- the presentation in 1971 and 1972 of a 'shadow' government by three left parties (PvdA, D'66 and PPR)
- the 'majority strategy' of the PvdA in 1977 which insisted that the forthcoming government (unavoidably with the confessional centre parties) would have a majority of leftist ministers.

The PvdA thus hoped to strengthen the links with its traditional supporters as well as to attract part of the religious electorate. The Socialists also wanted the confessional parties to show their colours, and make an explicit choice for one or the other coalition. But in its desire to break the confessional dominance after 1977 the PvdA distanced itself too much from the centre. The penalty was a huge electoral loss in 1981.

Though both the Liberals and the Socialists thought they could take profit from the electoral decline of the religious parties, this became more true for the VVD (see Table 7.1). The electoral gains of the VVD in the 1970s were to a large part due to the political style introduced by its new leadership. The party sharply criticised the centre-left cabinet of Den Uyl (1973–7). In its campaigns it aggressively politicised many social resentments inherent in an overripe welfare society. In the recent centre-right coalition (1982–6) the Liberals were as provocative as ever, mainly due to activist back-bench pressure.

Polarisation was not something the three confessional parties welcomed. It brought the Christian Democrats into a defensive position, although the dynamics of government formation did leave them enough room for adaptation and accommodation. They sought to reverse the process of their electoral decline through a strategy of concerted action. The Catholic KVP, confronted with the earliest and largest electoral losses, was the first to seek a more intense co-operation with the two other confessional parties. In 1972/3 this process was interrupted abruptly, when the Socialists succeeded in building a centre-left coalition by splitting the Christian Democratic camp. But this event paradoxically triggered the establishment of a single Christian Democratic party (the CDA): a federation with one list in 1977, then confirmed by a merger in 1980. The formation of 1972/3 now seems to be the only time the Christian Democrats had not been pivotal.

In this party system, the making of a coalition remains the crucial moment despite the efforts of the Socialists towards more 'political clarity' and pre-electoral coalition agreements. Of course elections do change the numerical relations of strength between the parties, and they thus present assets for the bargaining processes during the formation. But Dutch voters will never decide on the composition of the government. Decisive in the formation process is the behaviour of the religious centre parties. Traditionally they try to evade clear choices, in order to appease their heterogeneous followings. (The establishment of a single Christian Democratic party made things even worse, since the merger process just infused new life into the traditional differences between the three former parties.) To understand the practical reality of the government formation process, it is therefore essential to explain the behaviour of the centrist Christian Democratic CDA. Before we turn to this, however, we have to look at the theories currently used in explaining coalition-making in the Netherlands.

(b)   Coalition-making in the Netherlands: formal theories

De Swaan divides formal coalition theories into those that only take into account the parties' number of seats and those that also take into consideration their policy positions.[2] As to the first category De Swaan is very explicit: the 'minimal winning' coalition propositions are insignificant for all countries under study, including the Netherlands. The success score of formal coalition theories increases markedly when parties' policy positions are taken into account. The central assumption here is that coalitions will consist of parties adjacent on the policy (or left–right) scale. The proposition can be added that such coalitions will not contain a party that increases the range of the coalition, unless that party is necessary for obtaining a majority. De Swaan, however, stipulates that in the Netherlands the propensity to form 'closed' or 'connected' coalitions is much stronger than that towards maintaining a minimal range.[3] The Catholic KVP always occupied the centre of the Dutch party system. In this pivotal position it could play parties to its left and to its right off against each other. De Swaan argues that the KVP, in order to play the pivotal role also in cabinet, preferred oversized coalitions. A similar proposition, advanced by many commentators on Dutch party politics, is that the KVP demanded the inclusion of the Liberal

Left CPN PSP PPR PvdA D'66 KVP CHU DS'70 VVD SGP BP Right
ARP   GPV CP
CDA   RPF

CPN	Communistische Partij Nederland
PSP	Pacifistisch Socialistische Partij
PPR	Politieke Partij Radicalen
PvdA	Partij van de Arbeid
D'66	Democraten 66
KVP	Katholieke Volkspartij
ARP	Anti-Revolutionaire Partij
CHU	Christelijk-Historische Unie
CDA	Christian Democratic Appeal
DS'70	Democratisch Socialisten 70
VVD	Volkspartij voor Vrijheid en Democratie
SGP	Staatkundig Gereformeerde Partij
GPV	Gereformeerd Politiek Verbond
RPF	Reformatorisch Politieke Federatie
BP	Boeren-Partij
CP	Centrum-Partij

Figure 7.1 Party ideological continuum in the Netherlands

and/or Protestant parties as a counterweight to the Socialists' presence in the alliance.

The pursuit of large coalitions, however, succeeded mainly in the 1950s, and can also be explained by the tradition of the politics of accommodation.[4] The 'minimal connected winning' proposition may provide a satisfying rule of thumb for describing coalition-building in the Netherlands. Yet, considering some characteristics of the Dutch party system, one ought not be surprised at this. Daalder once classified the Dutch system as non-polar and centre-based, with the largest party right in the centre of a left–right continuum.[5] One could add that practically all major parties occupy rather central positions on this continuum, while the many splinter parties can be found at the extremes. Parties in a coalition are thus connected readily. Seldom does a new party, and then only for a short period of time, invade the centre of the party space. For instance, DS'70 joined the centre-right government in 1971 only for numerical reasons: the governing parties saw their majority disappear in the 1971 election, and could remain in office only by allying with this new party. D'66 joined the centre-left government of 1973, together with the PPR, due to the commitment of the PvdA to its junior progressive partners. And D'66 joined a centre-left government again in 1981, in this particular case to 'connect' the two major parties CDA and PvdA whose relationship was chilly.

So, one might ask, what exactly did we gain with formal theorising? It is De Swaan himself who concludes that the 'minimal connected winning' rule does reveal the options open to the party leaders, but it allows no definite prediction to be made.[6] To explain the particular coalitions that have been built one has to take a look inside the parties. And it is questionable whether formal coalition theories are of any use in this respect.

The experience of the formation processes from the Second World War onwards clearly indicates that the outcome of coalition-building is predetermined within the ranks of the confessional parties.[7] After the war they, particularly the KVP and the ARP, found themselves at the centre of the socio-economic policy dimension, which is the predominant dimension in the Dutch party system.[8] The reason for the Christian Democrats to occupy that middle-ground position has been the heterogeneity of their following with respect to socio-economic issues. The different socio-economic strata among the religious electorate all had their representatives in the confessional parliamentary parties, due to the formal links between the parties and the social organisations. This meant that the flexible, centrist stance of the Christian Democrats was the result of considerable strife within both the KVP and the ARP. Depillarisation, however, severed the ties between the political parties and the social organisations. The confessional parties suffered large electoral losses too. Their merger restored the dominant position they had in the 1950s and 1960s. Both depillarisation and the merger process, however, could not but change completely the intra-party processes in the confessional parties. Obviously it is not enough to allude simply to the centrist character of the confessional parties in relationship to the dimensionality of the party system. Through the years both this dimensionality and the centrism of the Christian Democrats were subject to fundamental changes.

(c) Coalitions, cabinets, crises

Overviewing the long list of post-war cabinets and their varying internal composition, one will not see immediately why the cabinets of the 1950s are called 'large' ('broad-based'). No more than later cabinets do they include all 'relevant' parties. The reason that ARP and VVD were missing in some of the Drees cabinets, however, had more to do with particular policy questions concerning the decolonisation of Indonesia and New Guinea. The idea of a coalition between the five major parties really was in the minds of the political leaders involved in the formation processes. That idea evaporated only after both the Liberals and the Socialists began to exclude each other.

Looking at post-war Dutch politics in retrospect it is tempting to view 1958 as marking the end of a period; since that year, it seems the PvdA has no longer been a regular coalition partner.[9] Many commentators claim that the Catholic party was willing to share the leadership of the country with the Socialist party only if it

Table 7.2 *Life and composition of Dutch cabinets, 1946–82*

Years of duration	Cabinet	Status (where other than normal)	Elections	Length of cabinet formation (days)	Composition	Combined cabinet support (% of total votes)	Crisis
1946–8	Beel		1946	47	KVP — PvdA —	59.1	
1948–51	Drees		1948	31	KVP — CHU PvdA VVD	73.7	×
1951–2	Drees			50	KVP — CHU PvdA VVD	73.7	
1952–5	Drees		1952	69	KVP ARP CHU PvdA —	77.9	
1955–6	Drees			16	KVP ARP CHU PvdA —	77.9	
1956–8	Drees		1956	122	KVP ARP CHU PvdA —	82.7	×
1958–9	Beel	Interim/caretaker		10	KVP ARP CHU —	50.0	
1959–60	DeQuay		1959 (early election)	68	KVP ARP CHU — VVD	61.3	×
1960–3	DeQuay			10	KVP ARP CHU — VVD	61.3	
1963–5	Marijnen		1963	70	KVP ARP CHU — VVD	59.5	×
1965–6	Cals			46	KVP ARP — PvdA	68.6	×
1966–7	Zijlstra	Interim/caretaker		38	KVP ARP — —	40.6	
1967–71	De Jong		1967	49	KVP ARP CHU — VVD	55.2	
1971–2	Biesheuvel		1971	69	KVP ARP CHU — VVD DS'70	52.5	×
1972–3	Biesheuvel	Interim/caretaker		22	KVP ARP CHU — VVD —	47.2	
1973–7	Den Uyl		1972 (early)	163	KVP ARP — PvdA D'66 PPR	62.9	×
1977–81	Van Agt		1977	208	CDA — VVD	49.9	
1981–2	Van Agt		1981	108	CDA PvdA D'66	71.0	×
1982	Van Agt	Interim/caretaker		17	CDA — D'66	41.9	
1982–6	Lubbers		1982 (early)	54	CDA — VVD	52.4	

were a matter of 'urgent necessity'. They understand these words as a sort of magic formula. The formula was first used by Nolens, the political leader of the Catholics, during the cabinet formation of 1926 when some political leaders gave serious consideration to the idea of a coalition with the Socialists. The opinion that the time was not yet ripe prevailed until 1939, when the circumstances (the threat of war) were very different.

Obviously, co-operation with the Socialists was 'urgent' again immediately after the war. The coalition between the KVP and the PvdA at that time lasted for more than ten years before it became less solid. The crisis of 1958 did not come as a surprise after so many years. The confessional parties have been governing with the Liberals for 19 years out of the 25 since. But does that testify to a natural preference of the religious parties for the right? And does it mean there were only two or three occasions when the necessity to govern with the Socialists was indeed that 'urgent'? In our opinion there is as much evidence for the proposition that the confessional centre parties changed front permanently. Viewing the formation of the three centre-left coalitions since 1958 in the light of 'events' that made those (and only those) coalitions 'urgent' appears to be very eclectic and misleading. Developments within one formation period especially can hardly be explained with this formula. The centre-left coalition from 1973 to 1977, for instance, would have been prolonged in 1977 had not the PvdA asked too much in the final stage of the formation process.

Decisions on the political colour of the next government are made only after lengthy negotiations. A better perspective on this process is provided by the proposition that formations are very indeterminate at their beginning. With each formation the choice is which side the centre parties will turn to this time. The need to accommodate the Socialist party, and the progressive movements behind it, may be one of the arguments to be weighed inside the confessional parties, but it is only one among other motives.

We need to add one other proposition. This proposition is that the change of partners occurred more often after cabinet crises than it did after regular elections. In the latter case the existing coalitions tended to be prolonged. For the party in opposition (PvdA or VVD) there may thus be more need for a cabinet crisis than for a large electoral victory.[10] The same is true, of course, for the faction(s) in the Christian Democratic parties that want(s) to change partner.

Cabinet crises, however, are not as easily provoked nowadays as they were before. The cabinet of De Jong (1967–71) was the first post-war cabinet to sit out the normal four-yearly parliamentary period without formal interruption. The cabinet of Van Agt (1977–81) was the second, and the cabinet of Lubbers (1982–6) has a fair chance too of completing its term. One explanation is of a policy-related kind. Since the economic recession, problems of governability have increased markedly. Between the parties in the first cabinet of Van Agt consensus grew on the need for restrictive policies. The cabinet of Van Agt II, on the other hand, lasted for hardly a year due to profound differences between the CDA and

Table 7.3 Dutch cabinet crises, 1951–82

Years	Cabinet	Crisis year	Cabinet	Locus of Crisis		Party crisis		Dissident Party	Divisive issues
				Cabinet	Parliament	Intra	Inter		
1948–52	Drees	1951	Restored		x	x		VVD	1951 decolonisation policy
1952–6	Drees	1955	Restored		x	x		PvdA	1955 housing policy
1956–8	Drees	1958	Breakdown		x		x	KVP	1958 tax policy
1959–63	DeQuay	1960	Restored		x	x		ARP	1960 housing policy
1963–5	Marijnen	1965	Breakdown	x			x	All parties	1965 broadcasting policy
1965–6	Cals	1966	Breakdown		x		x	KVP	1966 financial/budgetary policies
1971–3	Biesheuvel	1972	Breakdown	x			x	DS'70	1972 financial/budgetary policies
1973–7	Den Uyl	1977	Breakdown	x			x	KVP–ARP	1977 land policy
1981–2	Van Agt	1982	Breakdown	x			x	PvdA	1982 financial/economic policies

the PvdA on policy priorities (budgetary cutbacks vs. unemployment policies).[11] The idea that a rigorous policy is necessary consolidates the current cabinet of Lubbers, notwithstanding its bad performance in the polls. The time-horizon for a coalition is tending to go beyond one parliamentary period due to a growing bipolarity on socio-economic matters. It partly explains why the Christian Democrats have abandoned – at least for a while – their centrist stand on this predominant dimension.

The starting-point for another explanation – of Dutch cabinets becoming more stable – is the process of electoral change, notably since the 1960s. Cabinet crises were low-risk in the 1950s and early 1960s, when electoral turnover was very limited. With the electoral changes from 1967 onwards, and the new habit of crises being followed by elections, matters became different. When we consider the continuation of their political careers as the top priority of elected politicans, we can imagine that they are unwilling to risk the life of 'their' cabinet if the following electoral results are likely to be uncertain.[12]

The shift of the 'locus' of cabinet crises from parliament to the cabinet (see Table 7.3) might be interpreted as evidencing the crisis-evading behaviour of the parliamentary parties. This shift, however, has nothing to do with the calculations of the individual MP. Political leadership has shifted relatively from parliament to the cabinet. (If this process should be pin-pointed at some particular time it would be 1970–1, with the formation of the cabinet of Biesheuvel. This cabinet was prepared in secret by the parliamentary leaders of the parties which constituted the cabinet of De Jong (1967–71), and it was those leaders who would form the core of the cabinet of Biesheuvel.[13]) Once, in the 1950s and 1960s, it was the party leaders in parliament who decided on matters of coalitional life and death. Nowadays, this political responsibility is more diffused. The parliamentary parties now secure themselves against this loss of power by demanding very detailed programmatic statements buttressing the forthcoming coalition.

Government formations in the 1970s and 1980s took rather long. The length of the negotiations, however, provided the Christian Democratic leaders with the time necessary to form the political will in their party – to join either a coalition with the Liberals or one with the Socialists. The history of coalition-making in the Netherlands indicates that the Christian Democratic will has sometimes been moulded by external circumstances, such as the need for post-war recovery, or the existence of an economic recession. It was also said that the nerve to force a cabinet crisis is diminishing – and without such a crisis it is more difficult to change partners. Yet, near-crises are in the air rather constantly.[14] Whether they become real mainly depends on the balance of power in the Christian Democratic ranks.

(d)   Depillarisation and the Christian Democratic party

The gradual erosion of Christian Democratic power – as indicated by the poor performance at the national elections of 1967, 1971 and 1972, and confirmed by the formation of the cabinet of Den Uyl in 1972/3 – made it necessary for the Christian Democrats to reorientate their centrist–pivotal position in Dutch politics. In order to understand how this process of party change did affect the dynamics of coalition-building, it is imperative to make a careful analysis of the way in which the unification of the three confessional parties into one single party proceeded. Depillarisation, both at the cultural–ideological and the structural–organisational level, and the offensive strategies of the Liberals and the Socialists, provide the background against which these internal party changes are to be analysed.

Christian Democracy in Western Europe is currently considered as a post-war political phenomenon. Most theories have connected the growth of Christian Democratic parties after 1945 with the transformation of confessional 'Lager-parteien' into deconfessionalised 'catch-all parties'.[15] Developments in the Netherlands were quite different. The confessional parties came to dominate politics at a much earlier stage. Due to the cleavage structure of Dutch society the religious parties were able to get a mass following well ahead of the Socialists and the Liberals. Their electoral success appears to have been dependent upon an unequalled degree of pillarisation and organisational control by the confessional elites. This control lasted for many years after the Second World War. But in the end the Netherlands did not escape post-war social change. Moreover, the commotion of the late sixties and early seventies was not confined to the turbulences that were experienced elsewhere in the Western world. Depillarisation (*ontzuiling*) profoundly upset the political system, and the most radical changes affected the confessional parties.

In the major confessional party, the Catholic KVP, the Church and the clergy had always played a prominent role. The organisational edifice of the Catholic pillar was largely dependent upon their support. This turned out to be a main disadvantage when the Dutch Catholic Church or province began to disintegrate in the 1960s. From the Second Vatican Council onwards, and the liberalisation that was institutionalised by Pope John XXIII, changes spread fast through the Dutch Church province. In the Netherlands the Catholic Church made a volte-face from ultra-montanism to ultra-modernism. The coincidence of this change with the electoral losses of the KVP is particularly striking. The Catholic party elite was not able to stop the electoral disaster. Within a period of ten years (1963–72) the KVP lost almost half its vote.

The significance of structural depillarisation is stressed by a comparison of the losses of the KVP with the electoral results of CHU and ARP. The Calvinist ARP was known as a well-organised party. Moreover, the Calvinist pillar was not as dependent on Church and clergy as the Catholic party was. While the KVP suffered severe losses, the ARP remained at a stable level of approximately 9 per cent of the total vote. The Dutch Reformed CHU, on the contrary, lost as many votes as the KVP did. In fact, the CHU was hardly a party in the modern sense. It is particularly difficult to characterise the CHU. Let us quote instead a prominent CHU leader who once said that the partisanship of the CHU 'is more an attitude to life than a political choice – the CHU is a circle of friends, slightly lethargic, and conservative as well'.[16]

The traumas of depillarisation, and particularly the unprecedented electoral destabilisation, stimulated the unification of the three confessional parties. Everything pointed to deconfessionalisation – a dramatic erosion of the politically relevant dimension of religion.[17] The loss of power of the Christian Democratic parties seemed irrevocable unless they co-operated. And very soon, as they came to recognise, a merger into one single party was inevitable.

The idea of a merger originated in the late sixties, but was not effectuated completely until 1980. Considering the fast-spreading electoral change, the merging process has taken a long time. The delay can be explained by the bargaining dynamics that enter into every merger process. The dialogue between the three confessional parties was not an easy one. For instance, in the CHU milieu an aversion against ARP 'fanaticism' as well as a fear about Catholic predominance prevailed. Differences of identity and differences in resources the parties had at their disposal determined the course of the bargaining process. It is obvious that the three parties involved would not give up their autonomy just like that; elements of the old leadership as well as basic parts of the original ideology had to resurface in the new party. The party with the strongest identity as well as the largest and most stable electoral support had the best chances to come out of the merger with the greatest benefit.[18] However, all three parties engaged in the making of the CDA party lacked some of these resources. The KVP still had the sheer power of numerical strength; despite the electoral losses it suffered, the Catholic party retained the largest constituency of voters. The ARP was considerably smaller, but it was a far better-organised party and rooted in a vital and solid subculture. This ARP identity appeared to be a major determinant of the merger process. The CHU was obviously the worst off with regard to its bargaining resources.

In the discussion on the ideological profile of the new CDA party, the question of what the C-reference to 'Christian' stood for was crucial. As to the way this ideological discussion proceeded, the following decision moments can be distinguished. A first decision to be made was the choice between a party firmly rooted in political principles and a party that relies primarily on a political programme. Traditionally all the confessional parties in Dutch politics have always been parties of principle; but it was uncertain whether the new Christian Democratic party should continue on that course, or choose the alternative direction and become a programme party. A second (although directly related) decision concerned the alternatives of an open or a closed party. An open party is prepared to admit everyone as a member who will adhere to its political programme, irrespective of his/her personal source of religious, ethical or ideological inspiration. A closed party operates in precisely the opposite way, admitting as members only those individuals pledging allegiance to its religious, ethical and ideological principles. A party of principle will thus also tend to be a closed party, and a programme party will at the same time tend to be an open party.

With regard to both these decision moments, the first CDA party convention can be considered as a typical example of how these bargaining confrontations proceeded.

The first CDA party convention was organised in August 1975 and continued the ongoing discussions over ideology. KVP leader Andriessen started the series of speeches. With regard to the party foundation he stressed two points. He had great difficulty in connecting the adverb 'Christian' with 'politics' or 'party', because of the pretensions which are suggested by this epithet. This view, he immediately added, was not meant to imply that the CDA would not be a Christian party. Second, Andriessen stated that the CDA would not be a closed group of Christians and that there should be a place in the party for everybody with (whatever kind of) CDA sympathies. With this argument Andriessen tried to amalgamate the principle character with the programme feature of the CDA, at the same time making an overture to the open-party model. ARP leader Aantjes was the next speaker. His speech had a sharp accent to it. He had a twofold vision on the relation between the party of principle and the open party. The CDA wanted to be both. But between both features there were tensions and, according to Aantjes, even inconsistency. The ARP accepted the idea of an open party, but the ARP was also strongly in favour of the party of principle model – the Gospel should guide political activism. Hence, both features should be done justice. The open party and the party of principle had, as it were, their boundaries in each other. Aantjes ended his speech by discussing the political relevance of Matthew 25, from which he deduced a complete and, most important, a progressive policy programme for a Christian Democratic party. In making this connection, he faithfully applied the old ARP tradition of the principle–programme–policy trinity. The CDA convention finally approved a resolution that party members, and by implication their representatives, were to accept the Gospel as the guide for political activism, and to propagate this principle by means of the programme and the policy they were to advocate.

After this party convention, there arose intense internal discussions within the ARP. In September, the CHU leadership wrote a letter to the ARP, in which the ARP efforts to monopolise the ideal of firmness of principle were bitterly criticised. The ARP party convention, however, reaffirmed that the formulation of political principles would be decisive for the character of the CDA. Meetings continued and there were conferences in October and November 1975. The KVP, the ARP and the CHU finally 'agreed to disagree' about the question of whether CDA representatives were personally expected to accept the Gospel as the sole guide for their political deeds. At the same time, the conclusion was drawn that this disagreement should not delay the establishment of a single CDA list any longer in view of the next parliamentary elections.

This intra-party diversity is of particular importance for the position of the

Christian Democrats with regard to the building of governmental coalitions. In fact, the confrontation between KVP, ARP and CHU was a controversy about the traditional Christian Democratic centre-party position as well. The views that KVP leader Andriessen put forward at the August convention clearly signified that he preferred the CDA operating as an opportunist as much as ever. On the premise of being a programme party the CDA could freely choose a coalition partner at any time, depending on what the issues of that moment made necessary. Aantjes' reply to Andriessen made it clear that the ARP approach went in an opposite direction. Aantjes pleaded for the new CDA to become a party of principle with a distinctly progressive orientation, and advocated the prolongation of the centre-left coalition. The CHU, on the other hand, though keeping aloof from the ideological disputes, never made a secret of its preference for a coalition with the Liberals.

A brief chronicle of the crucial stages in the development of the CDA since the famous 'agreement to disagree' formula in November 1975 will confirm the vitally important interplay between the coalitional behaviour of the Christian Democrats and the internal diversity of their party.[19]

In the course of 1976 the first common meetings of the parliamentary groups of the KVP, the ARP and the CHU were held. Initially these meetings proceeded in a harsh atmosphere, but gradually the climate improved – especially after the breakdown of the cabinet of Den Uyl early in 1977. The elections in May 1977 subsequently had encouraging results for the CDA: 1 parliamentary seat gained (up to 49). The progress of the Socialists was, however, much larger: 10 seats (up to 53). The elections were followed by a long cabinet-formation period. First, there was an attempt to form a coalition with the Socialists that failed. Finally, there was an agreement between the CDA and the Liberals to form a government: the cabinet of Van Agt I which could count on a majority of only two seats in parliament. But the birth of this VVD–CDA coalition created severe tensions within the Christian Democratic parliamentary group. When the coalition agreement with the VVD was ratified in November 1977, seven so-called 'loyalists' appeared, six of them belonging to the ARP 'blood-group' and one out of the KVP ranks. These loyalists refused to accept any responsibility for the establishment of the new cabinet – although they did not want to prevent it either. One of these loyalists was Aantjes, ARP leader and the first vice-chairman of the CDA parliamentary group.

Meanwhile, the preparations for a complete merger between the three parties continued. At the beginning of 1978 a so-called 'Foundations' committee was appointed. This committee published its report six months later. This report stated that everyone should assume *a priori* that all CDA members had pledged a personal and genuine allegiance to the basic Christian Democratic principles, the 'Foundations'. The report was accepted at the party conventions of the KVP (unanimously), the CHU (unanimously) and the ARP (127 to 50 delegates). The feelings of relief within the KVP and the CHU stood in marked contrast to the suspicions that remained in the ARP. Within the latter party a movement arose to postpone the CDA merger. The programmatic disagreement about the policies of the centre-right government of course contributed to the growing discord. The nuclear arms debate in December 1979 showed a government using its ultimate power to survive – causing a big commotion in the CDA parliamentary group. A number of prominent Christian Democrats decided to resign from the party. Nevertheless, these incidents did not have any consequences for the CDA merger as such. In October 1980, the three parties officially merged into the CDA.

During the first years of the party's existence it was soon to become apparent that the problems stemming from the internal ideological diversity had not been solved definitively. For a long time the 'Foundations'-related discussion had overshadowed the programmatic differences of opinion – but now the latter disagreements came into full daylight, not in the least as a result of the behaviour of the loyalists. The loyalist group regularly questioned the policy of the cabinet of Van Agt I, thus indirectly contesting the coalition with the Liberals. They compared the plans and achievements of the government with the ideals and noble intentions that were laid down, for instance in the 1980 election manifesto. Not only the leftist versus rightist inclinations of the CDA were at stake in these controversies, but also the 'ethics' of mutual attitudes and behaviour within the party (discipline of the parliamentary group, dissident voting, etc). The ARP loyalists simply claimed that they were carrying through the Anti-Revolutionary tradition of constantly emphasising the trinity of principles, programme and policy. In this way what was originally a rather abstract 'Foundations' discussion gradually turned into a much more real-life, hence increasingly delicate, 'political course' controversy.

Despite the behaviour of the loyalist group the cabinet of Van Agt I remained in office and completed its normal four-year term. In May 1981 regular elections were held. The results of these elections constituted a modest success for the CDA: they lost only 1 seat, while the Liberals lost 2 and even the Socialists fell back from 53 to 44 seats. The CDA had become the largest party. The governing coalition, however, lost its slight majority. A coalition with the Socialists was necessary, although the policy distance between the two parties had grown. A third party, D'66, joined the coalition in order to 'connect' the two major parties. Right from the start, the new government had to cope with severe internal tensions between the coalition parties – especially concerning economic policy issues and nuclear armament problems. Ultimately, in the spring of 1982, the cabinet broke down because the Socialists did not accept the new budget proposals and left the coalition. This short intermezzo of a CDA coalition with the Socialists had two features. First, the coalition survived for such a short period of time that the programmatic discord within the CDA with regard to the cabinet and its policies could not resurface. Second, the anti-Socialist mood in the CDA was considerably increased by this coalition fiasco, which gave the right wing of the party the upper hand once again.

The elections of September 1982 did not benefit the CDA: again a loss of 3 seats (from 48 to 45). This time the VVD gained 10 seats (from 26 to 36), and the PvdA 3 (from 44 to 47). In the new CDA parliamentary group less loyalists returned (during the process of candidate nomination some of them had been given a rather low place on the list). The remaining loyalists were firmly warned against any dissident behaviour. The fall of the last cabinet made it clear that the CDA could only attempt to achieve a coalition with the Liberals. The new government immediately presented itself as a team of strong leaders in favour of a no-nonsense policy. They underlined their agreement, especially on the terrain of economic policy and the nuclear armament problem. In parliament the CDA group adopted slowly but certainly that same moderate conservative stance. Former loyalists like Scholten (ex-ARP) and Dijkman (ex-KVP) criticised the 'rightist' course of the party, and showed dissident behaviour intermittently.

Their dissidence did not have any immediately serious consequences for cabinet policy, but obviously it had enormous symbolic impact, not least because of the publicity in the press. Scholten and Dijkman stuck to the original CDA election manifesto, whereas the majority of the parliamentary group considered the coalition agreement with the VVD of paramount importance. In the subsequent controversy the conflicts that had marked the earlier debates were all repeated. The 'leftist' interpretation of the party manifesto by Scholten and Dijkman, however, caused a lot of confusion and a gigantic communication problem within the CDA. The controversies escalated in the autumn of 1983. The majority of the parliamentary group did not succeed in appeasing both loyalists. Ultimately, other CDA politicians refused further co-operation with the dissidents. Scholten and Dijkman in the end could do nothing but resign from the CDA group. Now they operate as an independent group in parliament.

The typical internal diversity of the CDA that is of crucial importance for its position with regard to national government coalitions is in fact threefold:

(1)   philosophical and cultural differences that separate religious groups – Catholics, Dutch Reformed and Calvinists – and, immediately connected with this, the 'blood-group' cleavage that can be regarded as an expression of the political parties that constitute the origins of the CDA – the KVP, the CHU and the ARP;

(2)   the contrast between progressive and conservative confessionalism;

(3)   left versus right tendencies with respect to socio-economic problems.

There should be no misunderstanding: the internal diversity of the Christian Democrats is not something that has suddenly surfaced at the end of the 1960s or ten years later when the KVP–ARP–CHU merger was definitively sealed. That diversity is a factor that has characterised the confessional camp in Dutch politics of old. Therefore, it is important to remember the essential difference in the nature and breadth of that internal diversity before and after 1970. The philosophical and cultural crisis that secularisation and depillarisation have brought about, and that has persisted since the 1960s, has changed the differences and contrasts mentioned above – from a latent and mainly subcutaneous type of variety into manifest and rather disease-like divisions urgently requiring some form or other of therapy. It is primarily structural depillarisation that has led to these changes: internal control and the preservation of hierarchy, as well as a balanced distribution of power keeping all these different currents within the Christian Democratic sphere in check, have become increasingly difficult, if not impossible. The centrifugal pressure within the CDA is therefore much higher than anything the former KVP, CHU or ARP had to cope with. And at present there is the constant threat of crippling conflicts between interest groups, of dissidence, of the formation of factions, of schisms and of all the other symptoms of disintegration.

With regard to the 'C' component of the CDA identity – Christian, Confessional – there are two internal dividing lines: progressive vs. conservative confessionalism, and the triptych of religious groups – Catholics, Dutch Reformed and Calvinists. Conservative confessionalism equals theocracy. What is of essential importance is the belief in the Rule of Divine Justice. Justice, Truth and Legitimacy can be inspired only by God, and the Revelation is their basis. The Divine Justice is the sole foundation of the state, family, marriage and conscience. Without this foundation, there is no understanding of justice, authority, duty, morals or wisdom, and social life would be impossible. The Divine Justice is the supra-temporal root of all life and the durable essence of all humanity: the Justice of Creation. God's Revelation through the Bible discovers that justice. The progressive reading of the Gospel stands in sharp contrast: completely renouncing the original creation-related revelation or justice ideas, it considers both Creation and Law as determined by an orientation towards the future and the salvation that is to come. The belief in Creation has been replaced by the faith of Salvation. It is the motive of the Exodus – emancipation and liberation from oppression – that should at present dictate the interpretation of the biblical message. God's people are no meek herd (not any longer), and have engaged in a never-ending march towards solidarity, equality and freedom. One should never forget that God has promised salvation – no more poverty or oppression – and this will inevitably entail fundamental changes in society. In this view, the conviction at the centre of conservative confessionalism, that there is some kind of creation-given immutable and eternal Justice, can only lead to maintaining and defending the status quo.

The second dividing line within the CDA with regard to the C-symbol that should reflect its Christian identity is the confrontation between denominations as well as the corresponding 'blood-group' architecture of the party. How this denominational and 'blood-group' related variety may indeed transform itself into an internal conflict has already been demonstrated here in the programme vs. principle – and open vs. closed – party debate that has never been really solved (the 'agreement to disagree' of November 1975 still applies). This party-profile controversy is closely related to a second typical example: the discussion concerning the appropriate way for CDA politicians to express their religiousness – a constant and explicit profession of faith (a so-called 'testimonial' attitude) or in a rather discreet fashion, relying on the implicit, but no less distinct or meaningful, Christian significance of one's actions and decisions (the so-called 'behavioural' mode). Is it sufficient to know that something is done or decided by a member of the CDA to be confident that it will therefore be automatically a genuinely Christian deed? Or should Christian Democratic politicians scrupulously plan and justify everything they undertake by some sort of biblical exegesis? The 'behavioural' approach is specifically Catholic–KVP, the 'testimonial' authentically Calvinist–ARP.

Making matters even more complicated – in any case, less easily manageable from the point of view of safeguarding the internal cohesion and integration of the party – is the fact that there is some sort of overlap (and thus mutual reinforcement) of the progressive–conservative confessionalism dividing line, and the contrasts that separate denominations and 'blood-groups' within the CDA. The actual configuration is schematised by the continuum below – ARP–Calvinist: progressive; KVP–Catholic: conservative; and the CHU-Dutch Reformed rather in a 'middle of the road' position.

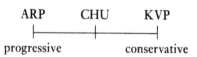

Another basic component of the CDA identity is the 'D'-factor – *Democratic* party, party of the *People*. This means that each time some socio–economic issue appears to be at stake, there is a third dividing line within the party: the opposition between a left and a right wing. Traditionally, an important feature of confessional parties in Dutch politics has been the heterogeneity of lower-, middle- and higher-class groups amongst its supporters. The former, KVP, CHU and ARP were confronted by this phenomenon, and that same pattern of mixing all kinds of social strata and classes has been integrally transferred to the CDA – and it still proves to be an element of major importance. The internal heterogeneity of totally different socio–economic groups has led to the constitution of a leftist and a rightist tendency within the CDA. And once again there appears to be some overlap between two dividing lines: left vs. right, and the triptych of ex-KVP, ex-CHU and ex-ARP 'blood groups'. In its turn this can be illustrated by a continuum schematisation:

ARP   KVP   CHU
├──────────┼──────────┤
progressive   conservative

The left–right positions of the CDA 'blood-groups' are inevitably no more than a rough sketch, and as such they will not completely correspond to every real-life situation. In fact matters are not that neat or crystal-clear, and their implication is rather that the driving force behind the left-wing of the CDA will mainly originate from the ex-ARP tendency, while the basis of the rightist side seems in general relatively more ex-CHU oriented.

Progressive versus conservative confessionalism, and the left–right division: the result is a very nice model with two axes.

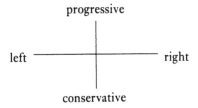

Taking a good look at the CDA, however, it appears that both axes are probably not perpendicular. No doubt the figure below is much closer to reality.

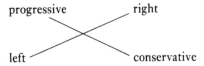

Returning to the 'blood-group' architecture of the CDA, that model will imply this kind of internal party map.

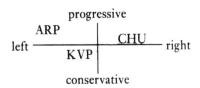

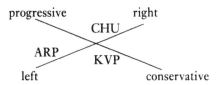

Once the Christian Democrats had decided upon a merger strategy and began working towards its achievement, they had virtually denied themselves any possibility of polarisation. The CDA's lack of polarisation potential in particular deserves close attention, as it may seriously hamper the party in confrontations with both its Liberal and Socialist rivals, and could thus put it in a more vulnerable position. And it goes without saying that within the context of coalition-building the PvdA and the VVD will be only too pleased to try to exploit such a weak and vulnerable position of the Christian Democratic party. The way the socio-economically based polarisation under the impulse of the VVD and the PvdA has succeeded in reducing Dutch politics to a pure left–right configuration cannot be stressed enough. One means of defence open to the CDA could be to try to thwart the left-right polarisation by the Liberals and the Socialists (and thus possibly succeed in partially neutralising it) by initiating an alternative variant of polarisation, viz. along the religious–philosophical dimension in Dutch politics, regenerating the opposition between secular and Christian groups. But until now such a religiously–philosophically based 'Christian vs. secular' polarisation has not been attempted by the CDA. And the reasons for this are not merely fortuitous.

The 'C'-related profile of the CDA, the Christian-confessional identity it is supposed to symbolise, does not emerge within present-day politics – either at the level of views on policy, or with regard to party programme, electoral platform, ministerial decisions or government measures. This is a general observation, but it is particularly striking when one analyses the way preparative discussions, negotiations and the entire building process operate in view of the formation of coalition government. It is a phenomenon that characterises the whole post-war period of Dutch politics. Since 1945 neither the origin and causes of government crises and the resignation of cabinets nor the issues and crucial policy problems that were at stake during the formation of a new coalition were ever of a religious or confessional nature.

The factor that has no doubt played a major role in suppressing the confessional profile of the CDA, and has thus prevented any polarisation along that dimension, is the internal division of the party. Up till now, any real progress towards a significant consensus and substantial equanimity has proved impossible to achieve. And any forthcoming change in this situation appears most unlikely. The incidents and troubles that have paved the long and painful road towards the CDA merger during the 1970s (and which are still fresh in the minds of the present party leadership – that should always be kept in view) have dramatically highlighted those elements of internal division as well as the risk of tragic feuds they entail. During that period, it has become clear that the achievement of a single and uniform confessional profile is an issue that does not lend itself to any pacification or constructive compromise – even so much as a peaceful and rational discussion seems out of the question. Apparently, the only solution for these internal divisions is: (a) to avoid in every possible way that these matters will be touched upon ever again, and (b) to leave constantly enough room for several (and sometimes considerably differing) definitions and modes of identification with regard to the concept of 'Christian' and 'religious'. This fragile internal cease-fire can only be maintained as long as the idea of a singular and uniform confessional CDA profile is forsaken. And since it is precisely such a singular and uniform type of profile that appears impossible, what can be considered as its superlative, viz. a polarisation of the religious–philosophical cleavage, is clearly completely illusory.

But even without the handicap of its internal division, an explicit profiling of the CDA's confessional identity would still remain far from evident. What can indeed be considered in this respect as a second major obstacle is the simple fact that present-day Dutch politics will no longer allow a confessional party to translate its religion- and philosophy-related profile into concrete and straight-forward policies. In recent years there were only a few exceptions that did not match that pattern of deconfessionalised, secular–neutral post-war politics – e.g. the controversy over birth control and abortion, the legalisation of pornography, sexual permissiveness, the institutionalisation of non-marital family structures, the gay movement, women's liberation and euthanasia. But otherwise the nature and breadth of politics at present do not offer many opportunities for the Christian Democrats to live up to their claim (and one of their basic reasons for existing?) of a confessional identity – the capacity to represent and defend religion the political way.

No polarisation of religious–philosophical differences; not even a sufficiently solid basis to achieve a genuine and explicit confessional profile: what this means is that the present configuration leaves the CDA no alternative. The only way to demarcate itself *vis-à-vis* the other political parties in Dutch politics is a deconfessionalised demarcation *vis-à-vis* both the PvdA Socialists and the VVD Liberals.

The position and the profile of the PvdA and the VVD are exclusively determined by the polarity between left and right. Seeking a demarcation *vis-à-vis* the Social Democrats and the Liberals will therefore compel the CDA to position itself somewhere along that same left–right continuum. And this dual demarcation implies automatically a centre-party position. One could argue that this has always been the case, but a major element of change is that at present most of the identity and profile of the CDA solely rest on that position along the left–right continuum. The CDA has been forced to reduce considerably (if not let go completely of) the confessional component of its original profile – and thus an essential cross-cutting complement of its left–right related position has disappeared. In other words, the CDA has become a more genuine type of centre party.

Unfortunately, this metamorphosis has also brought more to the forefront what it is in general that makes a centre-position in such a tripartite configuration so easily awkward and uncomfortable: the near-complete dependence on the strategy and the actions of both rival parties. A centre position *per se* represents very little in a tripartite configuration. The main elements it comprises are determined by both its rivals. What the CDA in its metamorphosed form of a centre party stands for is nothing authentically CDA any more. It will always be merely an odd mixture of anti-PvdA and anti-VVD elements.

A second type of disadvantage of this recent, more genuine, left–right related centre-party course of the CDA is directly related to the Liberal–Socialist polarisation dynamics that seem to dominate Dutch politics completely at present. For a centre-party position will probably only be beneficial and indeed viable for the CDA as long as both PvdA and VVD extremes of the left–right confrontation remain fairly stable and fixed. But polarisation represents precisely the opposite: the PvdA and VVD positions are 'cut loose', and the Liberals and the Social Democrats grow more apart, eventually making the gap between left and right totally unbridgeable. An unbridgeable left–right cleavage means there is no longer any need – nor is there really any space left – for a party that may provide a centre-party compromise and pacification approach.

Polarisation implies that there is no 'centre' remaining between left and right. With regard to its coalitional behaviour, this means that the CDA is now reduced to only two options: a Liberal vs. a Socialist ally. In this way polarisation will confront the CDA with the inevitable choice of changing into either a leftist or a rightist party.

However, each of these coalition models will lead to the frustration and discontent of some important group within the CDA; and it will thus always entail the risk of internal stress and internal conflicts within the CDA. For the limitation to only two coalition variants is not cross-cutting the internal dividing lines of the CDA between leftist and rightist wings, between progressive and conservative tendencies, and between 'blood-group' factions; on the contrary, there is a near perfect congruency, and this will automatically result in frustration and discontent within the CDA ranks. The symbiosis of the internal divisions of the CDA, and what would correspond to that in terms of the support for a coalition with either the Liberals or the Socialists, can be schematised as follows:

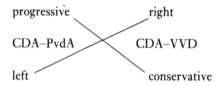

(e)   The CDA and its coalitional behaviour: a conclusion

Numerical strength once allowed the confessional parties to play a decisive role in the making and breaking of Dutch coalition governments. The 'antithesis' opposed them against the secular parties, and this was stronger than the profound religious differences between the three parties. The fact that cabinets during the inter-war period could still stumble over religion-related conflicts did not change that basic solidarity. The Christian Democratic experience with that kind of crisis rather taught them not to stress religious matters too much. It explains also why, for instance, the Catholics were so keen on large coalitions after the war.

In the post-war party system the confessional parties acquired their 'natural' centrist position: the religious dimension was toned down; socio-economic issues became increasingly important. The heterogeneous following of the religious parties (i.e. KVP and ARP) necessarily made them act rather moderately on (re)distributive policies. After all, both the working-class following and the adherents in the higher strata had to be accommodated. The working-class faction had a strong hold in the KVP and the ARP. In the period of pillarisation, close linkages existed between the political party and the whole range of subcultural organisations. The spokesmen of the Catholic and the Protestant trade unions were said to give the KVP and the ARP their 'social face'. In questions of coalition formation they had a strong say, sometimes as strong as the exponents of the other factions. In fact, this balance within the Christian Democratic parties made each formation process indeterminate at the start. This is not to say that the 'social' wing of the KVP or the ARP always preferred a coalition with the Labour party. There were occasions when the Labour party was viewed rather as a rival than a close ally. The decision in 1959 not to prolong the coalition with the Socialists had much to do with this competitive mood. Leading politicians in the ARP, for instance, wanted to prove that the Christian Democrats could pursue a 'social' policy as well without the PvdA.[20] In general, however, the situation was such that the working-class representatives in the confessional parties were the leading figures among those Christian Democrats who favoured a centre-left coalition.

Political developments in the 1960s totally upset the pillarised party system. Electoral change appeared to be disastrous for the religious parties. The CDA merger, a defensive strategy to adapt to the changing circumstances, immediately restored the pivotal position the Christian Democrats occupied before. The events of the formation in 1972/3, when the three parties became divided rather unexpectedly, are now viewed as a mere accident. Social change, however, was lasting and ultimately this would have an enduring impact inside the political parties. The centrist behaviour of the Christian Democratic parties – as far as it is determined by their internal composition – would be different in kind from then on.

Structural depillarisation had irrevocably loosened the ties between the political parties and the social organisations. One of the far-reaching effects was that the working-class presence within the Christian Democratic parliamentary parties was narrowing. But matters got even worse. The same processes of social change provoked a merger between the trade unions. In this case, however, it was that of the Catholic and the Socialist trade unions growing together. The voice of the remaining smaller Protestant trade union was – in the 1970s – heard less and less by the CDA leadership.

The confessional parties alienated themselves not only from the trade unions but also from the voters. Party identification declined; parties lost their hold on the increasingly volatile electorate. At the same time, depillarisation made the link between the voters and their representatives more direct. From then on, politicians were held more responsible for their behaviour – this related in particular to the ambivalent policies of the centrist parties. The Labour party especially tried to increase this kind of pressure on the Christian Democrats by stirring up the issues that were brought forward through several social movements such as the peace movement, the squatters, or the protest against nuclear energy.

More important than the pressure from the left parties and movements may have been the way in which the Churches have reacted on these issues. Despite processes of secularisation and deconfessionalisation in political and social life the Churches still play a role in the process of opinion formation, especially with regard to issues that could easily be discussed in ethical terms. The Churches issued statements on the traditional realm of marriage, sexuality and so on, and also formulated opinions on macro-ethical questions pertaining to world-wide problems such as war and armaments.[21]

This growing interest of the Churches in practical political matters may have had something to do with a diminishing faith in the Christian Democratic party as the exponent of religious principles.[22] A typical example is the Churches' sponsoring of the Interchurch Peace Council (IKV) and its reflection and action on the problems of peace and disarmament. The Churches did not turn their backs on the IKV even when it engaged itself in more politically loaded confrontations with the government. Nevertheless, there is a discrepancy between the views and attitudes of the Church leadership and the rank and file Church members – precisely with regard to the involvement of the Churches in 'purely political' matters. In its turn, this has stimulated the emergence of organised counter-pressures in recent years.[23]

The weakening of the position of the trade unions in the Dutch political system has made the factionalism inside the Christian Democratic party ever more dependent on the religion-related confessional positions of the CDA leadership. The 'ethical' issues of the 1970s and their mediation through the remobilised Churches further triggered the factionalisation on that confessional dimension. For several reasons, already indicated throughout this chapter, the position of the current 'left wing' inside the CDA is much weaker than the position of the trade unionist left wing was in the 1950s and 1960s. In fact, these factors seem to confirm the current rightist course of the CDA. But, as we have demonstrated extensively, it is doubtful whether this will be a definite orientation.

Notes

1. For a better understanding of the peculiarities of the Dutch party system, the reader is referred to the various writings of Hans Daalder, e.g. Daalder 1979. For a more detailed account of the party system in combination with the problem of coalition government and government formation, the reader should consult Andeweg *et al.* 1980 and Vis 1983.
2. De Swaan 1982: 231.
3. *Ibid.*, p. 233.
4. See Andeweg *et al.* 1980; Lijphart 1975.
5. Daalder 1971.
6. De Swaan 1982: p. 231.
7. See Maas 1983.

8. See Lijphart (1982), who found the socio-economic dimension predominant over the religious dimension in ten Western democracies.
9. Daudt 1982, for instance.
10. Vis 1983: 162.
11. Contrary to Gladdish 1983.
12. Van den Berg and Visscher (1984), who analyse cabinet stability at the individual level (the MP) and not in terms of party competition.
13. See De Jong, Prime Minister, interview (1982).
14. For instance, nuclear missiles, 1979; oil embargo Southern Africa, 1980.
15. Irving 1979.
16. Kruisinga 1983: interview.
17. See Andeweg 1982.
18. See De Rijk 1982.
19. An historical account of the merger process can be found in two reports from the Christian Democratic parties (ARP, 1980; CDA, 1980); the two reports are summarised by Hans van Mierlo in his paper for the ECPR sessions at Salzburg (1984): 'The merger of the Dutch Christian Democratic Party as a case of party-internal coalition making'.
20. Maas 1983: 53.
21. Everts 1983.
22. Riedstra 1983.
23. Everts 1983: 215–16.

References

Andeweg, Rudy B. 1982, *Dutch Voters Adrift: on explanations of electoral change, 1963–1977*, University of Leiden
Andeweg, Rudy B., van der Tak, Theo and Dittrich, Karl 1980. Government formation in The Netherlands. In R. T. Griffiths (ed.), *The Economy and Politics in The Netherlands since 1945*. The Hague: Martinus Nijhoff, pp. 223–49
ARP 1980, *Van Woudschoten tot Hoogeveen, documentatie over de grondslagendiscussie in het CDA*. The Hague
CDA 1980. *De groei naar het CDA: momenten en impressies uit dertien bewogen jaren*. The Hague
Daalder, Hans 1971. Cabinets and party systems in ten smaller European democracies. *Acta Politica*, 6: 282–303
 1979. The Netherlands. In Stanley Henig (ed.), *Political Parties in the European Community*. London: George Allen and Urwin, pp. 175–208
Daudt, Hans 1982. Political parties and government coalitions in The Netherlands since 1945. *The Netherlands Journal of Sociology*, *18*: 1–23
De Jong, P. 1982. Interview in Haagse Post, 25 December
De Rijk, Martijn 1982. Het CDA: het moeizame ontstaan van een brede centrumpartij. *Socialisme en Democratie*, *39*: 333–40
De Swaan, Abram 1982. The Netherlands: coalitions in a segmented polity. In Eric C. Browne and John Dreijmanis (eds.), *Government coalitions in Western democracies*, New York: Longman
Everts, Ph. P. 1983. *Public opinion, the churches and foreign policy. Studies of domestic factors in the making of Dutch foreign policy*. Leiden: University of Leiden
Gladdish, Ken 1983. Coalition government and policy outputs in The Netherlands. In Vernon Bogdanor (ed.), *Coalition Government in Western Europe*. London: Heinemann

Irving, R. E. M. 1979. *The Christian Democratic Parties of Western Europe.* London: George Allen and Unwin

Kruisinga, R. *et al.* 1983. Interviews with Christian Historical political leaders in *Haagse Post*, 30 July

Lijphart, Arend 1975. *The Politics of Accommodation; pluralism and democracy in the Netherlands.* Berkeley: University of California Press, 2nd edn.

    1982. The relative salience of the socio-economic and religious issue dimensions: coalition formations in ten Western democracies, 1919–1979. *European Journal of Political Research, 10:* 201–11

Mass, P. F. 1983. *Kabinetsformaties, 1959–1973.* The Hague: Staatsuitgeverij

Riedstra, Siebe 1983. *Negen kerken in de vuurlinie; vredesdiscussies binnen de kerken 1980–1982.* Amsterdam: VU Boekhandel/Uitgeverij

van den Berg, Joop and Visscher, Gerard 1984. Politieke stabiliteit in de betrekkingen tussen kabinet en Tweede Kamer, *Beleid en Maatschappij, 11:* 223–32

Vis, Jan 1983. Coalition government in a constitutional monarchy: the Dutch experience. In Vernon Bogdanor (ed.), *Coalition Government in Western Europe.* London: Heinemann

8 Coalition or Fianna Fail? The politics of inter-party government in Ireland

(a) Introduction

Each of the five coalitions that have formed in the history of the Irish state has been the only alternative to a single-party (Fianna Fail) government. There can be no doubt that this is the single most salient feature of the politics of coalition in Ireland. In the first place it means that Ireland is a member, with Norway and Sweden, of that small group of countries in which coalitions and single-party governments tend to alternate in office. In the second place, it is an idiosyncratic member even of this exclusive club. Fianna Fail, the institution of single-party government, is a populist party of the centre-right, and has always refused to share power with anyone. This means that the coalitions that must form to replace it in office, unlike those in Norway and Sweden, have always needed to span the entire ideological range of Irish politics. While the ideological range of mainstream Irish politics is much narrower than that to be found in most European democracies, this nevertheless means that coalition members have been forced either to put up with or to forget considerable policy differences if they wanted to remain in power.

The normal processes of coalition bargaining are severely constrained in Ireland. Bargaining power in coalition negotiations is usually denominated, ultimately, in threats to bring down the government. Such threats depend upon the existence of viable alternative coalitions. In Ireland, there have never been alternatives to the coalition that formed, because of the implacable refusal of the largest party in the system to share power with anyone. This means that, at the bottom line, the only threat available to the members of each Irish coalition has concerned whether this will take place without an intervening election (though this has never happened in practice) or whether it will happen as a result of electoral gains made by Fianna Fail in the face of the collapse of a coalition government. (Such gains have been made in the wake of each of the four coalition collapses that have so far taken place.) Crucially, therefore, all threats made by coalition members in Ireland contain an element of bluff. If such threats are carried out they stand to damage the threatener as much as, if not more than, the threatened. This single, and overwhelmingly salient, feature of Irish coalition politics renders the assumptions of most conventional coalition theories inoperative.

(b)   A brief history of coalition in Ireland[1]

The roots of the Irish party system can be found in the bitter divisions of the Civil War. These have established the central basis of party competition in the state as a contest between Fianna Fail (the anti-Treaty faction, with a more vigorously republican image for most of the period) and Fine Gael (the pro-Treaty faction with a more unionist image from which it has been recently trying to escape).

Ireland has had 21 general elections since the formation of the state in 1922. The results of these are given in Table 8.1. For the first half of its existence the country had a multi-party system with a tradition of single-party (though often minority) government. The early dominance of Cumann na nGaedheal (to become Fine Gael) was replaced with a long period of Fianna Fail incumbency. The latter 'won' six successive elections between 1932 and 1944. This was followed by the first period of coalition politics, from 1948 to 1957, a situation that was made possible by a surge of electoral support for small parties, notably Clann na Poblachta who won ten seats in 1948, the first election that they contested. This surge was in part a response to the inability of Fine Gael to mount a challenge to Fianna Fail. (Fine Gael's vote fell from 35 per cent to 20 per cent during the period of Fianna Fail's incumbency.) The result was the first 'Inter-Party' government comprising *everyone but* Fianna Fail and a few independents. The post of Taoiseach (Prime Minister) was filled by John Costello, a member of Fine Gael, but not its leader.

Power alternated between the Costello coalition and Fianna Fail until Fianna Fail, led for the last time by De Valera, won a decisive victory in 1957, with only the fourth absolute majority of seats that had thus far been recorded. This heralded a 16-year period of Fianna Fail one-party government. While, formally, the party was short of a parliamentary majority in 1961 and 1965, it was able to rely on secure support from closely aligned independents.

The second period of coalition government, and the one on which the bulk of this chapter will concentrate, began in 1973, with the formation of a Fine Gael–Labour coalition government. The aftermath of the 1954–7 coalition had caused Labour to lose both votes and seats, and to adopt an anti-coalition stance. During the period of Fianna Fail incumbency it had steadily gained support. This reached its highest level ever, at 17 per cent of the vote, in 1969. Continuing

Table 8.1 *Votes cast and seats won in Irish elections, 1923–82*
Government parties identified by *

Date	Percentage of votes					Number of seats						Win- ning thre- shold (seats)	Net govern- ment major- ity (seats)
	FF	FG	Lab- our	Far- mers	Other	FF	FG	Lab- our	Far- mers	Other	Total		
1923	27	39	11	12	11	44	63*	14	15	17	153	77	−27
1927 (June)	26	27	13	9	25	44	47*	22	11	29	153	77	−59
1927 (Sept.)	35	39	9	6	10	57	62*	13	6	15	153	77	−29
1932	45	35	8	2	11	72*	57	7	5	12	153	77	−9
1933	50	31	6	0	14	77*	48	8	0	20	153	77	+1
1937	45	35	10	0	10	69*	48	13	0	8	138	70	0
1938	52	33	10	0	5	77*	45	9	0	7	138	70	+16
1943	42	23	16	10	9	67*	32	17	13	9	138	70	−4
1944	49	21	12	11	8	76*	30	12	11	9	138	70	+14
1948	42	20	11	5	22	68	31*	19*	7*	22*	147	74	−13ᵃ
1951	46	26	11	3	14	69*	40	16	6	16	147	74	−9
1954	43	32	12	3	10	65	50*	19*	5*	8	147	74	+1
1957	48	27	9	2	14	78*	40	12	3	14	147	74	+9
1961	44	32	12	2	11	70*	47	16	2	9	144	73	−4
1965	48	34	15	0	3	72*	47	22	0	3	144	73	0
1969	46	34	17	0	3	75*	50	18	0	1	144	73	+6
1973	46	35	14	0	5	69	54*	19*	0	2	144	73	+2
1977	51	31	12	0	7	84*	43	17	0	4	148	75	+20
1981	45	37	10	0	8	78	65*	15*	0	8	166	84	−6
1982 (Feb.)	47	37	9	0	6	81*	63	15	0	7	166	84	−4
1982 (Nov.)	45	39	9	1	6	75	70*	16*	0	5	166	84	+6

Notes: ᵃ No government majority because not all 'Others' supported the government.

FF = Fianna Fail (The party, as Sinn Fein, abstained from Dail 1923–7. Constituted as Fianna Fail in 1927 partly in order to allow it to participate in Dail.)

FG = Fine Gael (Cumann na nGaedheal 1922–33)

Farmers: Including Clann na Talmhan which entered the coalitions of 1948 and 1954.

Other: Small parties and independents, including Clann na Poblachta, which entered the 1948 coalition in the Dail.

Fianna Fail rule, however, led once more to a reassessment of coalition, while the adoption of the 'Just Society' programme by Fine Gael appeared to narrow the ideological gap between the two parties. Negotiations between them started and had progressed far enough for them to fight the 1973 election on a 14-point joint programme, agreed in detail only after the election was announced. (It should be noted that the Single Transferable Vote electoral system used in Ireland encourages coalition formation before, rather than after, elections – see below.)

The period since 1973 has seen an alternation of coalition government and

Fianna Fail single-party government at every election. The defeat of the outgoing coalition in the 1977 election, which the two parties fought on a joint programme, led to a change of leader in both parties. It also led to considerable scepticism in Labour ranks about the benefits of participation in government with Fine Gael. A response to this was that, in 1981, the Labour leader was bound by the party conference to clear any future coalition deal with a special delegate conference. Both parties fought the election on independent programmes. They just passed Fianna Fail's seat total and formed a coalition (ratified by the Labour conference) with the support of a few independents. This support was soon withdrawn, leading to a defeat in the Dail, by a one-vote margin, for the coalition's tough budget of January 1982. The government fell and a new election was called.

Once more, there was a majority neither for Fianna Fail nor the coalition, but this time Fianna Fail nosed ahead in terms of parliamentary seats. It formed a government with support from the Workers' party and independents. One of these independents, Tony Gregory, exacted a high price for this support in terms of benefits for his inner Dublin constituency, clearly both appreciating and exploiting his pivotal role in the proceedings. In doing this he outflanked the Workers' party, who held an equivalent position but did not manage to extract any serious concession from Haughey. This fragile government fell quickly, and yet another election, the third since June 1981, was held in November 1982. Once more, the Labour party conference had bound the leadership to ratify any coalition at a special delegate conference.

The election produced a legislative majority for the combination of Fine Gael and Labour. The parties' leaders negotiated, produced a joint programme of government, and the coalition was once more ratified by the Labour delegate conference. Since then it has survived a series of confident predictions of its imminent demise. Disagreements between the parties have been well publicised. A steady decline in their support at the polls, however, has caused the leaderships of both Fine Gael and Labour to fear the consequences of yet another election. In public, therefore, each has made much of the need to 'see things through to the finish' rather than to 'cut and run' in the face of unpopularity in the opinion polls.

In the period since 1948, therefore, there have been twelve governments in Ireland, five of them coalitions and seven Fianna Fail one-party governments. Fianna Fail has steadfastly refused to share power with other parties, preferring, when necessary, to rely on outside support from independents. This sets the main rule of the coalition game in Ireland. When the opposition parties wish to oust a Fianna Fail government, they are offered no choice between alternative coalitions. They face a tough but straightforward decision between the respective costs and benefits of government and opposition.

In general, coalition has been kind to Fine Gael. It increased its vote share from 20 per cent to 27 per cent during the period of the inter-party government and increased this again from 35 per cent to 39 per cent during the recent period of coalition with Labour. In contrast, Labour lost vote share on both occasions, most notably in the recent period. In the last election that it fought outside the shadow of coalition, it reached its highest ever vote share of 17 per cent. This has since slumped to 9 per cent. While it may be something of an exaggeration to claim that the battlefield of Irish politics is littered with the corpses of Fine Gael's former allies, it certainly does seem to be the case, given the demise of Clann na Talmhan and Clann na Poblachta, that coalition has operated much more to the benefit of Fine Gael than anyone else.

Formal coalition politics in Ireland has thus been heavily constrained by the refusal of Fianna Fail to share the cabinet table with any others. There have, however, been a number of minority situations in which Fianna Fail has been forced to rely on outside support in the Dail if it wished to take office. This has led to a series of *informal* links between Fianna Fail and the other parties that certainly form part of the background context of coalition politics in Ireland.

In the early period of the state, for example, support for Fianna Fail, and opposition to Cumann na nGaedheal, came mainly from Labour. The first Fianna Fail government, in 1932, was dependent on Labour support. It lasted eleven months and was followed by an election giving Fianna Fail its first overall majority and a government that lasted $4\frac{1}{2}$ years. In the minority situation that followed the 1937 election (which also saw the adoption of the current constitution) Fianna Fail once more formed a government with Labour support. This support was withdrawn eleven months later, and the subsequent election once more saw a majority Fianna Fail government that lasted a full five-year term. Since then, Labour has not maintained Fianna Fail governments in office. Minority Fianna Fail administrations have been secured by independents (in 1943, 1951, 1961, 1965 and 1982) or by the abstentionism of Sinn Fein (in 1957).

The issue of informal Labour support for a Fianna Fail government was raised once more, however, in 1982. Policy concessions were offered by Charles Haughey to the Labour leader in exchange for support for the ailing Fianna Fail government, although the possibility of formal coalition was explicitly ruled out. One prominent member of the Fianna Fail front bench did attempt to secure an agreement for a formal coalition with Labour as part of an attempt to force Haughey out of the Fianna Fail leadership. (For a discussion of these events see Smith 1983.) Labour, however, did not entertain such proposals, mainly because the ousting of Fianna Fail from office had been the main thrust of the public utterances of its parliamentary leaders for some time, and it feared the electoral consequences of such a fundamental volte-face.

Thus, while formal links with other parties have always been an anathema to the Fianna Fail leadership, there has been quite a history of informal contact. Labour has been the main focus of this, often being in a position to secure a minority Fianna Fail administration. Certainly the hypothetical possibility of a Fianna Fail/Labour coalition must be regarded, given all of this, as much more likely than a grand coalition between Fine Gael and Fianna Fail, whose traditional rivalries are one of the defining characteristics of the Irish party system.

(c)   The institutional dimension

There are two important constitutional constraints on the politics of coalition in Ireland. The first is the doctrine of collective cabinet responsibility, and the second is the electoral system.

The doctrine of collective government responsibility is specified in the 1937 constitution (Art. 28.4.2) and became entrenched in the political culture as a result of the period of single-party government leading up to 1948. This doctrine imposes a particular strain on coalition governments, in which ministers belonging to one party may lose a debate in cabinet on an issue close to their hearts, and then be forced to defend their apparent volte-face to a sceptical media and public. This can on occasion place them in an almost untenable position as far as their personal credibility is concerned and has the effect of forcing parties that lose policy debates in cabinet to pay a high public price. While Irish coalition governments have always presented a less unified front than their single-party alternatives, and while the doctrine of collective responsibility has often been bent, it has rarely been broken (see Chubb 1974).

Given the superior weight of Fine Gael in recent coalitions, therefore, the doctrine has often placed Labour ministers in the embarrassing position of being forced in public to defend policies, such as public spending cuts, instigated by Fine Gael in the face of active opposition by Labour.

This situation was exacerbated during the early period of coalition with Fine Gael by the fact that Labour ministers almost never met before cabinet meetings to plan a co-ordinated strategy, and did not sit together as a bloc at the meetings themselves. This obviously further undermined the bargaining position of the party and has led it to emphasise an essentially defensive role in the politics of coalition. Labour much more commonly presents itself as the party tempering the 'worst excesses' of Fine Gael policy, rather than as the instigator of new policies of its own. The doctrine of collective cabinet responsibility does not enable the party to be too explicit on this matter. The message that the Labour leadership tries to get across, however, when yet another policy unpopular with its voters is announced, is one of 'if you think *that* is bad, you should have seen what it was like before Labour ministers got to work on it'. Whether this argument cuts much ice with voters, however, is another matter.

The overall effect of the doctrine, however, is to raise the stakes of any policy conflict between the parties. This must be set in the context of a political system in which policy differences play a lesser role in mainstream politics than in most West European countries, but it is a significant constraint on the coalition game nonetheless.

Related to the matter of collective cabinet responsibility is the emerging convention that coalition negotiations conclude with the publication of a Joint Programme for Government. In 1973, this was a brief and general 14-point document agreed between Fine Gael and Labour *before* the election. In 1977, the parties agreed a more elaborate Joint Programme before the election, but it had no effect since the coalition was defeated. In 1981, a Joint Programme was issued *after* the election, but had little effect since the coalition fell quickly. But in 1982 a relatively detailed document was agreed after the conclusion of coalition negotiations, and forms part of the political context of a coalition that has now been in office long enough to implement some of its proposals.

The consequence has been that the 1982 Joint Programme for Government has been an increasing bone of contention between the parties. Specific measures in it were quickly identified by the media as either 'Labour' or 'Fine Gael' proposals, and the effectiveness of Labour cabinet ministers in particular has been increasingly discussed in terms of their ability to enact 'their' parts of the programme. The introduction of an income-related property tax (albeit at very modest levels) was claimed as an early success. However, a number of specific policy proposals have caused considerable problems: these include legislation on divorce, family planning and local radio. Promises in the Joint Programme have run into heavy opposition, especially from Fine Gael back benchers, and consequent long delays. Increasing pressure has built up on Labour to deliver on its policy planks in the Joint Programme, so that it can demonstrate that participation in coalition provides tangible benefits.

This experience highlights an interesting (and presumably generalisable) tension between the need to score victories in coalition *formation* negotiations, and the need to *deliver* on these victories subsequently. The existence of a coalition implies a joint programme, and this programme is a political battlefield. Yet the joint programme does not seem to have any formal institutional status in the sense of binding a coalition government circumscribed by the doctrine of collective cabinet responsibility. In addition, of course, the state of the nation's finances invariably turns out to be much worse than anyone could possibly have imagined, once the incoming government starts going over the books. New issues arise, and many other excuses present themselves for any failure to adhere to previously announced policy packages.

The logic of this, of course, is for the coalition parties to produce a very vague Joint Programme. Labour's problem in Ireland, however, is that a vague programme may not be sufficient to convince its special delegate conference (see below) that coalition is worth while in the first place.

The Irish Single Transferable Vote (STV) electoral system is unique in major European countries. By offering voters the chance to provide a ranking of candidates (and thus, implicitly, of parties) it offers them a chance to influence the fate of parties other than that of their first choice. STV, of course, is specifically designed to do this, but it does have a major impact on coalition politics in Ireland. It provides significant inducement for parties to form coalitions before an election rather than after it. This enables the respective party

Table 8.2 *Percentages of total terminal vote transfers between Labour and Fine Gael, 1948–82*

Year	Fine Gael to Labour	Labour to Fine Gael
1948	37	24
1951	54	41
1954	46	48
1957	70	37
1961	22	34
1965	55	53
1969	33	35
1973	71	72
1977	72	59
1981	87	56
1982 (Feb.)	69	60

Note: Terminal vote transfers from a party arise when no other candidate from that party is still in the running to receive them.

Source: Vincent Browne (ed.), *Election '82* (Magill Publications, Dublin, 1982). Figures not calculated for November 1982.

leaders to advise voters to give lower preference votes to coalition partners, and can have a significant impact on the number of seats won by the parties, taken together, for the same number of first-preference votes.

The effect of the possibility of coalition on the transfer patterns of Fine Gael and Labour voters can be inferred from Table 8.2. This gives the percentages of votes in terminal transfers (i.e. those occurring when no candidate of the original party is left in the running) going from one coalition party to the other. In the first coalition period, 1948–57, two other coalition parties were available to receive transfers, so transfer rates appear relatively low. For the period of Labour's hostility to coalition, 1957–69, transfer rates were low, at around 40–45 per cent on average. For the period of Fine Gael–Labour coalition, 1973–82, the average transfer votes were 75 per cent from Fine Gael to Labour, and 62 per cent from Labour to Fine Gael. Vote transfers between Fine Gael and Labour were higher when they fought as a prospective or incumbent coalition. Despite the fact that Fine Gael transferred votes to Labour at a higher rate than Labour transferred to Fine Gael, the latter was the net beneficiary. Labour, the weaker party, had greater numbers of votes available for transfer as more of its candidates were eliminated. Thus, while explicit or implicit electoral coalitions helped both parties, Fine Gael was almost certainly the greater net beneficiary.

Such transfer patterns have probably had a make-or-break effect on governments. Comparing Tables 8.1 and 8.2, it can be seen that, in 1969 when Labour's hostility to coalition was at its height and Labour/Fine Gael transfer rates very low, Fianna Fail lost votes and gained seats. In contrast, given the electoral pact of 1973 and correspondingly high transfer rates between coalition parties, the 1973 election saw Fianna Fail gain some votes yet lose the election. The 1973 coalition lost votes but gained power. The number of seats 'swung' by inter-party transfers is probably very small. But in the delicately balanced electoral politics of recent years, those few seats may have made all the difference.

Indeed, the overall effect of STV has been to produce a remarkable sequence of what would, in other systems, be regarded as knife-edge results and 'hung' parliaments. This has led, as often as not, to governments with formal legislative minorities. Table 8.1 also shows the net government majority (excluding outside support) for each election since 1923. From this, the balance of forces can be seen to be very delicate throughout the period, and there have even been two situations (1937 and 1965) when Fianna Fail controlled exactly half of the seats. In terms of conventional coalition theories, the key 'pivotal' group was, as often as not, the 'others'. In reality, of course, this was not a group at all but a heterogeneous array of small parties and independents, which in no circumstances could act as a unified bargaining actor. The result has been that the effective 'winning' threshold of legislative votes for any given government has often been rather less than half of the seats in the Dail. This in turn means that governments which might look most precarious on paper are in practice relatively secure. Such messy situations are not amenable to straightforward analysis by formal theories. Yet they are the rule rather than the exception in Irish politics.

While the doctrine of collective government responsibility and the STV electoral system are the main constraints on the coalition game in Ireland, a further factor has a bearing on the mounting sense of urgency sometimes felt by the 'out' parties over the need to oust Fianna Fail from office. Many senior appointments are traditionally matters of political patronage. Particularly when patronage appointments are permanent, this means that the shadow of a former government continues to be cast, even after it has left the spotlight of office. The 'party men' may still fill key positions in the bureaucracy, the judiciary (and, in particular, the Supreme Court) or in the semi-state bodies (of which there are so many in Ireland). In this important way, the payoffs of office continue to flow even after a government is defeated.

In particular, after the 16 straight years of Fianna Fail one-party government that started in 1957, the opposition parties were acutely aware of the need for them to gain control of the patronage system in the face of the ever mounting tally of Fianna Fail appointments to important positions. The longer the opposition waited before they assumed power, the deeper the shadow of Fianna Fail appointees over their eventual administration. In periods when governments alternate frequently as they have recently, this may not be a significant factor. But when one party controls the system for a lengthy period, it increases pressure on the opposition to take office at almost any cost.

Once a coalition is in power, however, patronage appointments may instead be a source of friction between the government parties. They provide another external and 'objective' measure of the relative power of the coalition partners, since each can be judged on the basis of how many of 'their' people they succeed in placing in plum jobs.

One of the most important recent examples of this was precipitated by the appointment of Peter, Sutherland, a Fine Gael nominee, to one of the coveted EEC Commissionerships with effect from January 1985. Sutherland had been Attorney General, and it became important for Labour to be seen to place someone in this key position. (The office of the Attorney General can have an important impact on the flow of legislation to the Dail.) In this instance, Labour succeeded in 'capturing' the post at the eleventh hour, but the controversy surrounding it illustrates the effect that a patronage system can have on coalitions.

It provides yet another currency in which coalition payoffs can be denominated, while the unpredictable nature of the vacancies concerned can put a strain on relations within the coalition at any point during its tenure of office. This is, however, an aspect of the coalition payoff that the rules of the game do not allow to be discussed in explicit terms. Thus a Labour leadership, for example, could not go to a delegate conference and argue in favour of coalition on the basis of the patronage appointments that can be captured. It goes without saying that every appointee is staunchly defended by the government as quite the best person for the job. Such appointments, however, are chalked up prominently on the informal scoreboard that is kept on the relative performance of coalition parties and can sometimes (as was the case with the recent Attorney Generalship) even be crunch issues.

(d)   What motivates politicians to enter government?

All formal theories of coalition behaviour make assumptions about the motivations of the actors. The two most common of these assumptions relate to the desire of parties for office in and for itself (referred to below as the 'power' motivation) and their desire to enact certain policies (the 'policy' motivation). Obviously these analytical distinctions blur when it comes to political practice, so that no party system can be described exclusively either as a policy- or a power-seeking system. Many other types of motivation may be important. Nevertheless, viewed as general tendencies, the distinction between power-seeking and policy-seeking types of motivation does provide a useful scheme within which to describe the various actors in a coalition-bargaining system.

In general terms, given the fact that the Irish party system is currently characterised by competition between two parties that differ little in their basic philosophies, Ireland must be classified as first and foremost a power-seeking coalition system. The only one of the major parties that does not fit neatly into such a classification is the Labour Party. John Whyte's famous characterisation of the Irish party system as 'politics without social bases' still largely holds true

Table 8.3 *Percentages of respondents within each occupational category expressing a first preference for the three main parties*

Party	Fianna Fail			Fine Gael			Labour		
Percentage of each occupational category voting for party[a]	ABC1	C2	DE	ABC1	C2	DE	ABC1	C2	DE
Nov. 1974	32	43	51	28	14	10	14	24	22
Nov. 1975	29	38	37	33	23	20	14	19	22
Dec. 1976	41	42	51	29	27	12	6	11	16
Oct. 1977	45	53	56	21	14	12	9	7	13
Jan. 1979	41	47	40	24	11	13	7	14	19
Nov. 1979	29	41	35	39	23	21	4	12	19
Nov. 1980	30	34	33	32	25	19	6	11	18
Nov. 1981	29	36	36	38	35	29	6	4	10
June 1982	30	39	42	39	31	22	6	7	8
Nov. 1983	27	43	42	41	28	19	6	5	10
Oct. 1984	42	43		36	24		2	9	

[a] ABC1 = non-manual; C2 = skilled manual; DE = semi- and unskilled manual.
Sources: Irish Marketing Surveys, 1974–83; Market Research Bureau of Ireland, 1984.

today (Whyte 1974). Table 8.3 reports 'snapshot' views of the class basis of party support in Ireland at broadly yearly intervals over the ten-year period for which opinion polling has systematically been conducted. We can immediately see a clear picture of two big parties attracting support from right across the social spectrum. As a consequence of Fine Gael gains made across the board over the entire period, most of these at the net expense of Labour, both main parties now out-poll Labour in every occupational category. Fianna Fail and Fine Gael are each clearly 'catch-all' parties, though Fianna Fail is rather more working class, and Fine Gael is rather more middle class; social profiles have been maintained over the years. The key role of class in Irish party competition, however, is that the two big parties are dependent on support from *all* classes, and cannot afford to alienate *any* with their policies. This means that the ideological basis of competition between them is very weak, particularly with regard to the socio-economic dimensions of party policy that dominate so many West European coalition systems.

The continuation of the 'Northern Ireland problem', however, *has* preserved a distinction between the two big parties on the issue that is the *raison d'être* for their separate existence. It is fair to say that Fianna Fail maintains a more republican popular image on this matter, and is associated with a tougher line on Northern affairs. The most recent evidence for this can be found in the various parties' positions in the debate surrounding the New Ireland Forum. The Forum brought together the three main parties in the Republic and the Northern SDLP in an attempt to produce a common policy line on Northern Ireland. Fianna Fail (more specifically their leader, Charles Haughey) made a clear attempt to distance itself from a final report that canvassed three solutions to the problem (a unitary state, a federal/confederal solution, and joint authority held by Britain and Ireland). Fianna Fail's emphasis on a unitary state was actually a departure from their traditional line under De Valera (which backed a federal solution) and the move was clearly made to maintain some distance, on the republican dimension, between them and the other parties (see Bowman 1983 for a detailed account of the development of Fianna Fail policy on this issue). Images of republicanism do, therefore, provide a policy difference between Fianna Fail and Fine Gael.

Even on socio-economic policy, there is some difference between them, though this is very small when measured on a European scale. On the economic front Fianna Fail, as the more genuinely populist party, has retained an affinity for demand management and Keynesian economics in general. Of the two big parties, it is the one *less* inclined to make a virtue of fiscal rectitude, and of the public spending cuts that usually accompany such a stance. Such politics tend to be unequal in their social impact, and Fianna Fail sees itself as having the most to lose electorally from such division.

Fine Gael, on the other hand, is at least nominally more of a convert to the general European trend towards supply-side economics and monetarism in general. Recent Fine Gael Finance ministers have adopted quite a tough fiscal stance in public, although, while the party is in coalition with Labour, there may be some public posturing on this matter in the knowledge that such policies will be 'watered down' in cabinet. Until very recently, Fine Gael has advocated the elimination of the budget deficit – a source of major friction within the coalition. This policy has recently been abandoned, however, in favour of phasing it out over a period, and in practice the economic policies of Fine Gael and Fianna Fail have differed very little.

On the social front, Fine Gael's 'Just Society' programme of the late 1960s represented a move to a more reforming position on a number of issues. On such matters, it is fair to say that Fianna Fail is more conservative. As the most overtly populist party, its need to maintain working-class support is reflected in social policies that reflect the views of Irish working-class voters, who are more heavily influenced by the Church on such matters than their middle-class counterparts. Recent surveys, for example, show that working-class respondents cite Church influence on their thinking on nearly every social issue more frequently than those from the middle class (see Market Research Bureau of Ireland, 1983. The Irish Marketing Surveys poll of August 1984 shows working-class respondents to be quite clearly more conservative on the issue of reforming family planning legislation).

The ostensible liberalism of Fine Gael has been emphasised under the leadership of Garret Fitzgerald, though this is more evident as a public relations strategy than in the policies that have actually been enacted. Fine Gael, too, is a catch-all party and its freedom of action on social issues is constrained by a conservative wing whose views are among the most traditionalist in the country.

On the face of it, then, there are three dimensions of very modest policy difference between the two big parties, each of which relates more to image than to reality. On these dimensions, Fianna Fail tends to be portrayed as more republican, more Keynesian and more socially conservative than Fine Gael. The overwhelming generalisation that *can* be made about the policies of the two parties, however, is that policy differences between them are *much* less than can be found in most European countries, and that most policies are treated by each as expendable resources in the pursuit of power. (One of the most spectacular examples that demonstrates this 'flexibility' of policies concerns the parties' handling of the issue of domestic 'rates' (local property taxes) in the 1973 election. The 14-point joint electoral policy package of Fine Gael and Labour contained a promise to abolish rates. Fianna Fail had previously said that this was simply not feasible. Shortly before polling day, however, Fianna Fail leader Jack Lynch announced that he too would abolish rates if he became Taoiseach.)

Labour fits less easily into this general description, being in the peculiar position of being a 'labour' party that runs third in popular support in what ought to be its natural constituency, the working class. Effectively, it is a social democratic party. Its economic policies are more Keynesian than those of Fianna Fail, though it has been forced to defend the fiscal rectitude of Fine Gael when in coalition. Labour has a reforming social policy and a tradition of nationalism, though the image of the latter has faded somewhat in recent years. Thus, Labour could be seen as being closer to Fianna Fail than Fine Gael on the nationalist and economic dimensions that separate the two big parties and closer to the liberal wing of Fine Gael on social policy. The fact that it is more Keynesian than Fianna Fail, yet more liberal than Fine Gael, makes Labour an uneasy coalition partner, in policy terms, with either of the big parties, though Fianna Fail's intransigence over coalitions has forced Labour to deal exclusively with Fine Gael.

The key distinction between Labour and the others, however, is the much more intense motivation at certain levels in the party towards the implementation of certain policies as opposed to the simple gaining of power. This, however, should not be exaggerated. The former leader, Michael O'Leary, left the party and immediately joined Fine Gael, while the current leader, Dick Spring, is no ideologue. But, certainly at the level of party activists and of some public representatives, there is a strong feeling that it is important for Labour to articulate its policies unequivocally, even if this does mean staying out of government. For some, this represents a longer-term strategy of building an independent basis of electoral support to allow future interventions in government to be more effective. For others it represents a belief that the putting of 'pure' Labour policies before the electorate is more important than *any* participation in government.

Thus, the classification of Labour as a power- or a policy-oriented party is ambiguous. It has gone into coalition and compromised its policies quite drastically in the process. But it is the one of the three parties of government that maintains, at the activist level, the firmest commitment to its own policies.

Overall, however, it must be said that Ireland, in comparative terms, is a power system rather than a policy system. There is a high level of personalism and clientelism at the local electoral level, and the prize of a government post or a ministerial Mercedes is highly valued. Whether members of the government actually succeed in doing more favours for constituents than their rivals is an open question. Nevertheless, they are popularly perceived as being able to do more and, in an STV system that forces every deputy to nurse his or her local constituency very carefully, the payoffs of power seem most attractive.

(e)   The central–local relationship in Irish coalition politics

Irish local government has traditionally been weak, a situation exacerbated by the abolition of domestic rates (property taxes) in the 1970s and the abolition of agricultural rates in the 1980s. The former was the result of the inter-party policy auction referred to above. The latter was the result of a Supreme Court decision on the unconstitutionality of the anachronistic valuation system that was used. In 1982, a ceiling was also placed on the allowable level of the final major independent source of local authority revenue, commercial property rates. A very large, and usually represented as inadequate, part of local authority revenues thus comes directly from central government, and the consequent lack of independence for local councils has undermined both their power and their political relevance.

In addition, the central party bureaucracies retain considerable control over the validation of candidates for local elections, though this last point does mean that local electoral success is commonly seen as the first step in a national political career. Furthermore, a surprising number of national politicians insist on retaining seats on local councils in order to protect their local electoral position in the Dail.

Strong links certainly exist, therefore, between local and national politics, but power and influence tend to flow from the top down rather than from the bottom up. What goes on at local level has little influence on, and sets few precedents for, national government. Thus, while local coalitions often exist, these are in no sense 'laboratories' for potential future alliances at Leinster House. This means, for example, that while a Fianna Fail/Labour coalition was formed to control Dublin County Council in 1984, this is widely held to set no precedents whatsoever for coalition politics at the national level.

(f)   Internal party influences on coalition politics in Ireland

In chapter 2 of this book it was argued that, in reality, parties comprise a number of types of actor, each with potentially different motivations in the coalition process. Thus, the party leader and the front bench might have different views to those of the back benchers or party activists. In general terms, the closer someone is to the rewards of government, the more enthusiastic we might expect him or her to be about the benefits of coalition.

We have already mentioned the way in which the way the STV electoral system works in Ireland can be perceived by both voters and politicians to operate in favour of those who can do good turns for their constituents. This can create strong motivations to go into government among those who expect to be ministers. In addition, it tends to be the case that STV encourages parties to put up candidates in each constituency who reflect the various 'wings' of the organisation.

The recent history of Fianna Fail candidatures, for example, shows a strong tendency for the party to reflect both the pro- and anti-Haughey factions in each constituency. In the same way, Fine Gael's liberal and conservative wings are often balanced on a single ticket. In each case, this results from an attempt to attract the maximum first-preference vote from some party candidate in the hope that lower preferences will transfer to other candidates of the same party. Obviously, we would expect those candidates identified with the leadership to have different views about the benefits of getting into office. It is clearly the case in the 1982 Fine Gael/Labour coalition, for example, that those most hostile to co-operation with Labour were the more conservative, 'out' wing of Fine Gael. Similarly, those in Fianna Fail who, in early 1982, did contemplate formal coalition with Labour were clearly identified with the anti-Haughey faction and saw coalition as part of a ploy to oust him from the leadership. As for Labour, the resignation from the 1982 coalition cabinet of one of the party's most senior politicians, Frank Cluskey, did not exactly open a new split in the party. Nevertheless, it established a potential party leader who was both inside the Dail and outside the government, providing a focus for a potential anti-coalition move against the Labour leadership.

Notwithstanding all of this, the two big parties in Ireland do operate much more as unified actors in the coalition process than many of their European counterparts. This has a lot to do with their organisational structure.

Fianna Fail, for example, has always been a party tightly run from a centre located in the parliamentary party, with a further concentration of power in the leader of the day. The national executive almost always comprises a significant majority for the leader. This owes something to the personality of Fianna Fail's founder and leader for almost forty years, Eamon De Valera. It is also due to the manipulation of ambition by the leader of the day. The party has held power for the greater part of the period since the foundation of the state. Thus, the inclusion or exclusion of individuals from the cabinet and the appointment to, or relegation from, the front bench in the brief periods of opposition are powerful levers in the hands of the leader. Fianna Fail has stressed discipline in all the years it has formed governments, though the seventies and eighties are noteworthy in that what was formerly regarded as the impossible – the appearance of splits in the monolith – did seem to be emerging. The Ard Fheis of the party (its annual conference) has its agenda, or 'Clár' as it is known, completely in the control of the parliamentary party, which can delete and rank order items for debate. Its Youth Section (Ogra Fail) has no constitutional independence. While it is represented on the national executive, representatives are co-opted, not elected.

Fianna Fail, then, does come very close to being a party that may be viewed as a single actor. The most recent dramatic evidence of this came with the expulsion of one of the most senior figures in the party, Desmond O'Malley. In the wake of Haughey's interpretation of the New Ireland Forum as calling unequivocally for a unitary state in Ireland, O'Malley asked that party policy on Northern Ireland be debated internally within the party. (As we mention above, official policy had hitherto emphasised the federal option rather than that of the unitary state.) O'Malley was bounced out of the party within days of his request, after Haughey not only managed to force a vote on his expulsion, but successfully insisted that the vote be on the basis of a public show of hands rather than a secret ballot. This opened potential O'Malley supporters to the prospect of intense personal pressure from their local constituency organisations, in which support for Haughey remains strong.

Earlier challenges to the Haughey leadership had been handled in similar ways, with the leader's close links to the grass roots being used to put extreme pressure on parliamentary representatives both from the bottom up and the top down. (The most celebrated instance of this, 'The Night of the Long Phone Calls', is well documented in Smith 1983 and Joyce and Murtagh 1983.)

Fine Gael has never ruled alone, but has come close to the point where it can realistically hope to do so. Its structure reveals the same level of parliamentary control as that of Fianna Fail. The leader, Dr Fitzgerald, gained stronger formal control, if anything, than the leader of Fianna Fail when he pushed through a new constitution for the party a few years ago. There, however, the similarity ends. Until the seventies, there was a social democratic ginger group in the party that sought to overthrow the conservative hegemony. A reputation for managerial effectiveness and intellectual ability in a party hostile to ideas brought Dr Fitzgerald to the leadership. There now exists a conservative minority view among Fine Gael deputies that is shared by the majority of the membership. This confronts a centrist or social democratic leadership supported by a young activist minority within the membership. The party is thus in reality less united than Fianna Fail. Nevertheless there is never a real challenge to the coalition proposals of a leader.

Resentment among the lower levels of the party hierarchy takes two real, if insignificant, forms. The first is the suspicion that Fine Gael is being forced by Labour to make concessions in the direction both of economic redistribution and of liberalism on social issues. The second, more widespread resentment is built around the disappointed expectations of those overlooked for office. The favoured tactic of those disappointed in Fine Gael, when they seek to direct animus at a leader insensitive to their ability, is to espouse traditionalism. Overall, however, little violence is done to the facts by regarding Fine Gael as a unitary actor for coalition purposes.

Labour is far more open to divisions. Its constitution stresses the supremacy of branch delegates meeting in conference. The parliamentary party controls just a majority, at best, on the national executive, or Administrative Council as it is known. In the modern period tensions have existed on a permanent basis between the activist, policy-oriented and ideologically committed minority and the clientelist-minded public representatives and their supporting branches.

Getting a coalition package accepted in the party has never been impossible for any leader, but it has always been difficult. This has led to an enormous tension between every recent leader of the parliamentary party and the left. Indeed, as we mentioned above, it has even led to the extraordinary defection of a party leader, not to resign in weary despair but to join Fine Gael without further ado. Labour's Administrative Council is, under its constitution, much stronger than the national executive of either of the two larger parties. The Youth Section, too, is much more independent. It has its own conference, its own executive and the right to elect representatives to the Administrative Council. The same is true of the Labour Women's National Council. The major trade unions are also affiliated to the party and represent a particular view. The chairman and officers of the Labour party are elected by annual conference, not by the parliamentary party, which nevertheless anxiously seeks to influence elections to these offices.

To summarise, the matter of whether or not to go into coalition exposes all party leaders to potential challenges, either from the back benches or from the rank and file. Beyond this, nevertheless, both Fianna Fail and Fine Gael can plausibly enough be represented as unitary actors in coalition negotiations. This arises from the considerable control exercised over the two parties by their respective leaders. In contrast, Labour comprises a number of discrete tiers, each with an autonomous power base. These tiers often have different views of coalition, with the leadership typically being more in favour than the others. Since a proposal to go into government must be agreed by a party conference, the need to 'get the leader through the party conference' has been a factor in coalition negotiations, particularly in relation to the agreed policy package.

This situation obviously creates an imbalance in the structure of coalition bargaining, though it need not, of course, act to Labour's disadvantage. A skilful Labour leader could indeed exploit the need to sell a coalition to his more recalcitrant colleagues, and attempt to use it to extract further concessions from potential partners in government. There is little evidence that this has taken place in practice, a product, no doubt, of the ubiquitous fact that Labour has no one to talk to but Fine Gael if it wants to sit at the cabinet table.

(g)   The socio-political context of coalition in Ireland

We have already discussed the broad social dimensions of party support when arguing that policy motivations are rather low among the big Irish parties. This arises precisely because their social bases are quite diffuse, as can be seen by taking another look at Table 8.3. Unfortunately, no full-scale election study has yet been conducted in Ireland, so we do not have access to the material on the more detailed socio-economic correlates of individual voting that exists, for example, in both Britain and the United States. Relying on the regular work of two commercial polling organisations, Irish Marketing Surveys and the Market Research Bureau of Ireland, however, we see strong evidence for the 'politics without social bases' thesis.[2]

The general features that these results highlight include the remarkable cross-class appeal of Fianna Fail and the developing weakness of Labour even within its 'natural' constituency, the working class. It can also be seen that Fine Gael's election successes of the eighties owe much to a broadening of its class appeal among all categories of manual occupations. This makes its social base look more than ever like that of Fianna Fail, though Fine Gael's middle-class emphasis does still remain to a limited extent.

It is most important to emphasise, however, that the apparently weak social basis of party politics in Ireland does not reflect a low level of partisanship on the part of the electorate. Quite the converse is true. Voters are often intensely partisan. Strong traditions of party support run through families, can be found in national and local newspapers, in local communities and so on. It is probably true to say that most people in a given local area know the partisanship of most of their neighbours very well and that the level of party identification, if it were to be measured in a full-scale voting study, would be high. Table 8.1 shows, whatever about opinion poll results, that actual voting patterns at elections are remarkably stable, with contests being won and lost on the basis of very small shifts in support. Fianna Fail's vote has been outside the range 44–48 per cent only twice in the eleven elections since 1950, for example. Fine Gael's vote has been only slightly more volatile, though it has shown a tendency over the period to increase at the expense of the smaller parties.

However, the strong party loyalties that do exist are not well structured in terms of traditional socio-economic variables. They manifest themselves in personal loyalties to party leaders and political candidates, in attitudes towards the general political and administrative competence of the parties and in general political styles. Quite possibly, if in-depth research on the topic were ever to be funded, these factors would be found to tie in systematically with socio-economic variables, but the material to do this, quite simply, does not exist at present.

One matter on which reasonable data do exist in opinion polls, however, concerns the attitudes of the various party supporters towards the coalitions that have formed. It was noted in chapter 2 in this book that such attitudes, and in particular the electoral fate of coalition members that they portend, can be crucial to the performance of a coalition in office.

In a system in which the electorate has become accustomed to being presented with a choice between 'the coalition' and Fianna Fail, it is difficult to assess public response to the matter of 'coalitions' in general. Fianna Fail has typically put up the same arguments against coalition (in terms of instability, indecisiveness and unrepresentativeness) that have been deployed by Labour and the Conservatives in Britain. However, each of its attempts to change the electoral system from STV to simple plurality voting, on the basis of these arguments, has been rejected by the electorate in constitutional referenda. These rejections have taken place even during periods when the level of public support for Fianna Fail has been high. This can be taken as evidence of a willingness on the part of the electorate to prefer multi-party politics over one-party government at the same time as they prefer one particular party over all the others.

With regard to the specific Fine Gael–Labour coalitions of recent years, the evidence of public attitudes can be seen in Tables 8.4–8.6. The figures justify Labour's more lukewarm attitude to coalition throughout the period. Its supporters are clearly less well disposed to the idea of their party sharing government than those of Fine Gael.

Table 8.4 shows the results of quarterly polls taken by Irish Marketing Surveys for the period of the first Fine Gael–Labour coalition, after the beginning of regular polling in Ireland in 1974. Respondents were asked both for party preferences (though they were offered 'coalition' as an option) and for their attitude to the continuation of the coalition. In the first place, it can easily be seen that supporters of the coalition parties were much more inclined to express a specific preference for their party than for 'the coalition' in general.

Of those who did express a preference for 'the coalition', most were almost certainly Fine Gael supporters. Evidence for this can be found by comparing Table 8.4a with Table 8.1. The June 1977 poll was taken immediately before an election. The prediction of a 40 per cent first-preference vote share for coalition parties preceded an actual vote share of 43 per cent for them. But the predicted 21 per cent and 11 per cent vote share for Fine Gael and Labour respectively turned into actual vote shares of 31 per cent and 12 per cent. This is consistent with almost all of those who expressed a preference for 'coalition' in the survey actually voting for Fine Gael in the election.[3]

Table 8.4b shows the attitudes of the supporters of coalition parties towards the continuation of the coalition. (Fianna Fail supporters, not surprisingly, were overwhelmingly hostile.) This provides further evidence that 'coalition' supporters were predominantly Fine Gael, since there is very little difference in the attitude of these two groups towards the continuation of the coalition government. Both 'coalition' and Fine Gael supporters were overwhelmingly in favour of this. At the beginning of the period, Labour supporters were also very much in favour of the coalition, but this level of support declined significantly during the life of the government. In mid-1975, over 80 per cent of Labour supporters wanted the coalition to continue. By April 1977, shortly before the election, this figure had declined to less than 60 per cent. At the same time, around 90 per cent of Fine Gael supporters backed the coalition. Labour voters'

Table 8.4a *Electoral support for parties and coalition party supporters' attitudes to the continuation of coalition, 1974–7*

Date of poll	Percentage first preference votes				FF	Percentage wanting to see coalition continue		
	FG	Labour	'Coalition'	Total for coalition		FG supporters	Labour supporters	'Coalition' supporters
	1	2	3	1 + 2 + 3	4			
Nov. 1974	16	12	9	37	45	86	80	92
Feb. 1975	21	12	7	40	45	91	77	93
Mar. 1975	19	9	9	37	42	94	83	93
Aug. 1975	19	11	8	38	44	86	81	88
Nov. 1975	21	11	12	44	38	86	80	92
Feb. 1976	17	10	7	34	48	90	66	92
June 1976	16	10	7	33	49	93	79	91
Aug. 1976	19	11	7	37	45	89	63	95
Oct. 1976	19	9	4	32	49	88	67	86
Dec. 1976	19	10	4	33	49	82	66	84
Feb. 1977	24	11	5	40	41	79	61	91
Apr. 1977	19	9	6	34	47	88	57	84
June 1977	21	11	8	40	47	88	79	83

Source: Quarterly 'omnibus' surveys conducted by Irish Marketing Surveys, Dublin.

Table 8.4b *Coalition parties supporters' satisfaction with coalition performance, 1976–7*
% satisfied – % dissatisfied with government

Date	FG supporters	Labour supporters	'Coalition' supporters
Oct. 1976	+51	+3	+46
Dec. 1976	+40	+5	+30
Feb. 1977	+44	+4	+45
Apr. 1977	+56	+9	+45
June 1977	+75	+52	+69

Source: IMS quarterly polls, Dublin: question only asked since October 1976.

support for the coalition picked up dramatically once the election was announced and the likelihood of losing power loomed large.

The justifiability of Labour's mounting reservations about participation in the 1973–7 coalition government is further underlined in Table 8.4b, which shows the net levels of satisfaction of coalition party supporters with government performance. Net satisfaction rates are very high for Fine Gael supporters but, for Labour, satisfaction and dissatisfaction is evenly balanced (except in June 1977, during the surge of support that marked the onset of the election campaign).

Table 8.5 *Overall party support and coalition supporters' attitudes to coalition,*
1981–2

Date	Percentage first preference votes for				Percentage wanting to see coalition continue of		% satisfied – dissatisfied with government of	
	FG	Labour	Total coalition	FF	FG supporters	Labour supporters	FG supporters	Labour supporters
Oct. 1981	31	9	40	41	86	60	+ 42	− 9
Nov. 1981	33	7	40	39	82	61	+ 42	− 17
Dec. 1981	34	8	42	39	85	50	+ 40	− 23
Jan. 1982	33	8	41	38	89	51	+ 42	− 31
Feb. 1982	32	5	37	37	not asked		+ 45	− 20

Source: IMS monthly polls, Dublin.

Table 8.6 *Overall party support and coalition supporters' attitudes to coalition,*
1983–4

Date	Percentage first preference				Percentage wanting to see coalition continue of		% satisfied − dissatisfied with government of	
	FG	Labour	Total for coalition	FF	FG supporters	Labour supporters	FG supporters	Labour supporters
Feb. 1983	37	7	44	38	not asked		+ 32	− 4
Apr. 1983	36	8	44	38	85	53	+ 29	− 49
Mar. 1983	33	7	40	40	84	56	− 4	− 63
July 1983	33	7	40	40	84	42	+ 17	− 37
Sept. 1983	33	6	39	40	82	59	+ 19	− 22
Oct. 1983	33	8	41	40	80	49	+ 15	− 38
Nov. 1983	33	7	41	41	82	61	+ 22	− 29
Dec. 1983	29	6	35	39	80	54	+ 16	− 40
Jan. 1984	31	8	39	39	84	56	+ 13	− 43
Feb. 1984	32	6	38	40	83	49	+ 37	− 28

Source: IMS monthly polls.

The pattern is repeated for the two subsequent Fine Gael–Labour coalitions of
1981–2 and 1982 to date. The poll figures that are available are reported in Tables
8.5 and 8.6 respectively. These tables show the enduring enthusiasm of Fine Gael
supporters for the continuation of coalition, contrasting sharply with a
progressive decline in the proportion of Labour supporters who are happy with
the prospect. (One period during which the enthusiasm of Labour supporters for
coalition did rise to dizzy heights, however, was that between the election of 1981
and the formation of the government. Polls showed that, having 'beaten' Fianna

Fail, supporters of both opposition parties were keen for them to take office, and this argument carried considerable force in both inter-party negotiations and debates within the Labour party.)

The rate of net satisfaction with government performance remains high for Fine Gael supporters, though it has declined during the most recent coalition. Net rates of satisfaction with government among Labour supporters, however, have declined drastically. By the 1981–2 coalition there was significant net dissatisfaction with the coalition government among Labour supporters, a process that has intensified during the current coalition to a point at which Labour voters are more dissatisfied with the government than Fine Gael supporters are satisfied with it.

Overall Labour supporters are much less sanguine than Fine Gael supporters about their party's participation in coalition. The tendency has been for this dissatisfaction to increase sharply, the longer the experience that Labour has of sharing power. At the popular level, the two coalition parties can be sharply distinguished, therefore. Labour's strong and growing group of anti-coalitionists contrasts quite dramatically with general satisfaction among Fine Gael voters about the effects of sharing power. This provides a clear illustration of the agonising dilemma that has recently faced Labour in its dealings with Fine Gael. To exert sufficient pressure on the government in order to extract the policy concessions that might satisfy Labour supporters that coalition is worth while, Labour must use its bargaining power. Its bargaining power, as is the case for all coalition parties, depends crucially on its ability to bring down the government. Yet to bring down the government and force an election before major policy concessions have been extracted is virtually to ensure electoral humiliation, with potentially irreparable damage to the party. Losing support in the electorate, the party cannot face making the threat that might gain it support.

This position is exacerbated by the fact that Fine Gail, which would be asked to concede to Labour demands, has gained considerably during its period of coalition with Labour, with its essential support base largely unalienated. The response to all of this by the Labour leadership has been to hang on and hope. This hope is at present based more on the possibility of economic recovery, and a general increase in the level of electoral satisfaction with the government as a whole, than on any specific bargaining successes that Labour can claim for itself.

The Irish example, if it can be generalised at all, illustrates a major shortcoming in existing formal theories. Chapter 2 discussed the fact that most of these theories are essentially *static*, in the sense that they cannot accommodate the changing circumstances of an inter-electoral period. Yet, particularly in small party systems where the number of potential coalitions is extremely limited, and particularly when the collapse of a government tends to be followed by an election, the *anticipated* electoral performance of the coalition parties must clearly have a major influence on their bargaining power while in office.

The role of opinion polls in this process, of course, is crucial. While some of the more extravagant claims for the effects of public opinion polling on the democratic process may be hard to justify,[4] their effect on the relative power of coalition partners may well be considerable. Any dynamic theory dealing with the development of coalition politics between elections would clearly need to build in some consideration of the opinion poll support of the respective parties. It is only in this way that the feedback of social attitudes on to coalition performance can be taken into account.

(h) Environmental and external effects on coalition politics

External affairs in Ireland are characterised by three major issues. These concern relations with Britain over the constitutional future of the six counties in the north of the island, relations with the EEC and the issue of neutrality.

Of these, neutrality is the least divisive in party-political terms. Indeed it is a most distinguished sacred cow in Irish foreign policy that the state's formally neutral international stance should be preserved at almost any cost.[5] The issue thus has little bearing on coalition politics.

Relations with the EEC are important, but they do not open up major policy splits between the parties. The issue relates more to government effectiveness than anything else. The performance of ministers in extracting the best possible deal from the Community, and especially from the Common Agricultural Policy, is an important matter, but it does not systematically impinge upon coalition politics to any significant degree.

Northern Ireland, however, is another matter, though its effects on politics within the 26 counties of the Republic are complex. One way or another, the problem has led to the collapse of two of the four coalitions that have so far fallen in the history of the state.

The second coalition government fell in early 1957 as a result of the withdrawal of outside support by the small republican party, Clann na Poblachta, led by Sean McBride. This was precipitated by the internment of republican activists, under the Offences Against the State Act, during the IRA border campaign of that period.

The third coalition, the Fine Gael–Labour government of 1973–7, also fell indirectly as a result of proposed action against the IRA. In the wake of the failure of the Sunningdale Agreement, which involved British and Irish governments jointly on Northern policy, the coalition adopted a tough position on security matters and introduced an Emergency Powers Bill in 1976. The President, Cearbhall O Dalaigh, referred this to the Supreme Court to test its constitutionality. This led to him being described as 'a thundering disgrace' by the coalition Minister of Defence. The failure of the government to take appropriate action over this remark led to the resignation of the President. The ultimate effect was that the coalition Prime Minister, Liam Cosgrave, called an election in June 1976 which he fought on a law-and-order platform. He, and many others, expected the coalition to win, but in fact they lost. On two occasions, therefore, the existence of the Northern Ireland problem caused a coalition to fall, though in each case this was precipitated by government action against the IRA in the 26 counties of the south.

More recently, the New Ireland Forum, which reported in 1984, reflected an attempt to produce a common policy line on the North. The three main parties in the South and the Northern SDLP were the main participants, repeatedly referring to themselves collectively as the 'constitutional nationalist parties'. The agreed line favoured a unitary state for the island, but did not dismiss two other options, a federal/confederal solution and joint authority shared with Britain. The avowed intent was to take the North out of Southern politics, though differences between the parties opened up almost immediately the report was published. Charles Haughey, for Fianna Fail, emphasised the unitary state element in the report, while Garret Fitzgerald, for Fine Gael, stressed the openness of the parties to 'other options'.

The coalition was not divided on the affair which does nonetheless highlight Fianna Fail's determination to retain the republican high ground. Nevertheless, in late 1984, Fitzgerald's handling of the Forum Report in a summit meeting with Margaret Thatcher did represent a serious setback for Fine Gael. Thatcher brusquely rejected all Forum options in the subsequent news conference. Fitzgerald, who had built up considerable public expectations for the Forum, was left with egg on his face. Indeed, the coalition's popularity at the polls plummeted immediately after the unsuccessful meeting.

In general terms, however, it is fair to say that broad policy positions on the North have impinged little on the politics of coalition in the South. Rather it has been the handling of an issue that is easy to fumble that has caused the problems. Furthermore, in no case has the government itself actually split on the issue. Rather, the damage has been done to the coalition as a whole, in much the same way as it would have been done to a single-party government.

If we are looking for factors that are beyond the control of Irish coalitions but which have nevertheless served to divide them, however, we need look no further than the international economy. The coalitions of the eighties have been faced with the task of presiding over a domestic economy forced deep into recession by international forces largely beyond their control. This has, as we have already seen, opened splits within governments on economic policy and has also highlighted an important general dimension of coalition politics that relates to the allocation of portfolios between the parties. In times of major public spending cuts, it can be a serious liability to control a major spending ministry. This is particularly true for one party, given the doctrine of collective cabinet responsibility, when the Finance Ministry is controlled by another. The consequence is that the spending minister concerned may be forced to defend unpopular cuts that he or she has fought vigorously in cabinet, and that are effectively beyond his or her control.

Table 8.7 *Cabinet portfolio payoffs to Fine Gael and Labour in November 1982*

	Fine Gael	Labour
Portfolios	Taoiseach (PM)	Tanaiste (Deputy PM) & Environment
	Foreign Affairs	Health and Welfare
	Finance	Trade, Commerce & Tourism
	Industry & Energy	Labour
	Agriculture	
	Justice	
	Education	
	Defence	
	Gaeltacht & Fisheries	
	Public Service	
	Posts & Transport	
Percentage of portfolios	73	27
Percentage contribution to government majority	81	19
Actual number of portfolios	11	4
Predicted payoff, based on proportionality	12	3
Predicted payoff, based on bargaining power	7–8	7–8

The actual allocation of portfolios in the initial 1982 coalition cabinet is given in Table 8.7. From this it can be seen that Fine Gael, the larger party, controlled the two key positions of Taoiseach and Finance, as they had in previous coalitions with Labour. They also controlled Foreign Affairs, Justice and Agriculture, the high-profile ministries not likely to attract flak as a result of spending cuts. Of the big spending ministries on the front line in times of recession (Health and Welfare, Education and Public Service) senior Labour politician Barry Desmond held Health and Welfare while Fine Gael held the other two. Of these, Health and Welfare is undoubtedly the most dangerous since, particularly on the welfare side, government policy may well involve reducing the living standards of the neediest and most defenceless members of society in times that are already very hard. This is an obviously unenviable position for a Labour minister to be faced with the prospect of defending. The other two spending ministries (Education and Public Service) carry obvious risks of confrontation with highly unionised state sector employees in times of spending cutbacks. Strikes by public sector employees, however, tend to be unpopular with the public at large, so that blame for the consequences of cutbacks tends to be spread rather more widely.

Overall, however, it must be said that the environmental and external dimension has had few direct effects on the politics of coalition in Ireland, even though external relations are crucial to Irish politics. There is a broad policy consensus on the three main issues, while the actual handling of these tends to affect politics in unsystematic and unpredictable ways.

(i)   Conclusion: general features of the Irish case

The politics of coalition in Ireland is clear-cut in a number of important respects. In the first place, the ideological basis of competition between the mainstream parties is very weak. In the second place one party, Fianna Fail, refuses to go into coalition in the confident and realistic expectation that, 'next time', it will once more assume its 'natural' role as the party of government. Given the size of Fianna Fail representation, this means the choice of government is effectively between a coalition and Fianna Fail. Thus, when Fianna Fail 'loses' an election, the other two parties must choose either to govern together or go back to the electorate. And the best that they can hope for if they call another election is to face the same choice all over again.

Indeed, it might plausibly be argued that, until Fianna Fail shows a willingness to share power with others, or until it loses support to smaller parties, Ireland is not really a coalition system at all. Herein lies Labour's weakness and Fine Gael's strength. Labour has never been strong enough to govern alone, though Fine Gael is getting large enough to have reasonable hopes of doing so. Labour, therefore, must take what it is offered by Fine Gael, whether in terms of cabinet seats or cabinet policy. It must take what is offered, that is, if it wants to stay in the government. Yet, to bring down the government courts electoral disaster.

The serious question currently facing the party, however, is whether its support has sunk so low that it has nothing to lose by playing the game to the limit. If the party should embark on a significant period of self-imposed exile from the corridors of power, a potential for genuine *immobilisme* would arise in Ireland. It has been Labour anti-coalitionists' long-term hope that this would force Fine Gael and Fianna Fail into each other's arms. Given the current leadership of the two parties, however, or even given any plausible replacements for them, such embraces look as remote as ever.

Notes

1. Fuller accounts can be compiled from Gallagher 1982, Chubb 1974, Whyte 1980, Farrell 1983 and Manning 1978.
2. Thanks are due both to Des Byrne of IMS and Jack Jones of MRBI for making available detailed results that go well beyond the summaries usually published in national newspapers.
3. Obviously, more complex shifts in support would also explain the two findings, but would depend upon much less plausible last-minute switches in allegiance between each of the three main parties.
4. For a discussion on this matter, see, for example, Clemens 1983 and Laver 1984.
5. While all parties have a formal position which accords Ireland's neutrality an extraordinary importance, they differ on its content (i.e. whether it is conditional or unconditional, whether it includes ideological as well as military neutrality and so on).

References

Bowman, John 1983. *De Valera and the Irish Question.* Oxford University Press
Chubb, Basil 1974. *Cabinet Government in Ireland.* Dublin: Institute of Public Administration

Clemens, John 1983. *Polls, Politics and Populism*. Aldershot: Gower

Farrell, Brian 1983. Coalitions and political institutions: the Irish experience. In Vernon Bogdanor (ed.), *Coalition Government in Western Europe*. London: Heinemann

Gallagher, Michael 1982. *The Irish Labour Party in Transition 1957–82*. Dublin: Gill and Macmillan

Irish Marketing Surveys 1974–84. *Monthly Omnibus Surveys*. Dublin

Joyce, Joe and Murtagh, Peter 1983. *The Boss: Charles J. Haughey in government*. Dublin: Poolbeg Press

Laver, Michael 1984. Surveys *of* politics or surveys *as* politics. *Parliamentary Affairs, 37*: 106–9

Manning, Maurice 1978. The political parties. In Howard Penniman (ed.), *Ireland at the Polls*. New York: American Enterprise Institute

Market Research Bureau of Ireland 1983. *21st Anniversary Poll*. Dublin

Smith, Raymond 1983. *Charles J. Haughey: the survivor*. Dublin: Aherlow Publications

Whyte, John 1974. Ireland: politics without social bases. In Richard Rose (ed.), *Political Behaviour, a Comparative Handbook*. London: Collier Macmillan

   1980. *Church and State in Modern Ireland 1923–1979*, 2nd ed. Dublin: Gill and Macmillan

GEOFFREY PRIDHAM

9 Italy's party democracy and coalitional behaviour: a case-study in multi-dimensionality

(a) Introduction: the problem of one-dimensionality

Any study of coalitional behaviour in Italian politics immediately encounters two very basic problems: the problem of coverage, the fact that this subject, despite its obvious importance to the functioning of Italy's political system, has been much neglected; and the problem of interpretation or the need for explaining the dynamics of what is commonly seen and often dismissed as a complex affair. Of these two, the key problem is that of interpretation; but looking briefly at both of them assists in developing a viable approach.

The main outcome so far of this neglect of Italian coalition politics has been to reinforce the popular image of confusion and encourage one-dimensional views. Judgements have either resorted to general assumptions, such as the typical comment of one journalist that 'Italian governmental politics are a bizarre and Byzantine game whose details are followed only by the immediate players, while the rest of the world finds it difficult even to pretend to take an interest,'[1] or they have focussed on particular aspects and usually institutional procedures. For instance, one summary of the process of coalition formation in Italy commented as follows rather satirically:

> Rather than rolling up their sleeves and energetically giving the country a new government, the politicians bow to a form of protocol . . . Moving with liturgical deliberateness, the Italian President consults for one week with all living former Presidents, all former Prime Ministers, all party leaders . . . The crisis is not over when the President designates the man most likely to succeed. This man will, anyway, accept the mandate 'with reservations', and then he begins the cycle of consultations, first with his own party and then with those parties which hopefully will join the coalition . . . If the premier-designate has succeeded, he informs the President and then begin

198

more consultations over the division of Cabinet seats and the Government's programme. When the premier-designate does not drop his 'reservations', the entire series of consultations begins again.[2]

This picture of Byzantine complexity is one that frequently coloured early academic writers on Italy, such as Giovanni Sartori's comment on Italian parties in his essay on polarised pluralism in European politics: 'The net result is a Byzantine and undecipherable party system whose end product is over-complication and confusion; at least this is how the polity must look to the ordinary voter . . . the complexity of the political system is in itself a powerful agent of alienation.'[3]

Coalitions have been the rule in post-war Italian politics, with the 43 governments in the forty years since 1945 ranging from minority administrations, often with external or parliamentary support from extra parties, to usually oversized coalitions of up to five parties, and hence there has been a tendency towards heterogeneity. In terms of the numbers of coalitions as well as the variety of coalition formulas applied, Italy must be reckoned as a rich field for coalition research. However, the problem of raising academic interest to somewhere near the level of importance of this subject in political reality has remained despite a greater popular concern for aspects of Italian politics which clearly relate to it. One need hardly mention the widespread and rather sudden consideration given to the PCI and its strategy of the 'historic compromise' in the mid-1970s, once its increase then in electoral support made its projected alliance with the Christian Democrats more of an immediate prospect. The challenge of the 'historic compromise' featured very prominently in the deluge of publications on 'Eurocommunism', and rekindled interest in consociational democracy theories about cross-party elite co-operation. But this intense interest soon subsided once the electoral fortunes of the Communists declined, and the 'historic compromise' strategy was eventually abandoned. More recently, a growing concern over the country's 'governability' and more broadly 'the Italian crisis' has focussed attention on a problem to which coalitional behaviour must obviously be central. The very stability of the system is therefore linked to this subject. It soon becomes clear that the subject of Italian coalitions is potentially broad because it relates to different features of the country's system, and that is possibly why it has been treated segmentally, if at all.

This continuing neglect of coalition research on Italy has remained even though considerable work has been carried out on the political parties. As one recent survey of the state of literature on this subject commented: 'The Italian political parties are constantly the object of debate and analysis – in the newspapers, in journals and in books; an archive that were to collect all that which has been written on this matter would start to acquire enormous proportions.'[4] Yet, the question of coalitional behaviour in Italy has surfaced in some work here, though usually in relation to specific aspects. As space does not allow for any detailed treatment of the literature on this point,[5] the discussion will simply identify any suggestions which point towards the kind of multi-dimensional approach we are taking.

Firstly, the question of party strategies has been highlighted particularly with reference to the PCI from Togliatti's 'Italian road to socialism' to Berlinguer's 'historic compromise', and this was so even before the rise of popular interest in 'Eurocommunism'. But a necessary distinction has to be drawn between party strategies as a general proposition and actual coalitional relationships, without discounting the former as a determinant of the latter. For instance, this work on the PCI has concerned itself only minimally with that party's actual coalitional experience (1945–7 and again, informally through its support of the Andreotti governments, during 1976–9).

Secondly, the importance of ideology (rated high by formal coalition theories in the case of Italy) has largely been confirmed, for example by survey work on political attitudes,[6] although it is evidently a factor that requires finer tuning with respect to actual coalitional behaviour (e.g. degrees of intensity and articulation in party ideology, salience at different levels of political activism from leadership downwards). Thirdly, attention given to the theme of 'convergence' between the main parties since the 1960s has focussed only on the national legislative level,[7] even though the persistence of social, economic and political cleavages between parties is related to this and indeed has been the principal reason cautioning against viewing this elite-level 'convergence' (as during the 1976–9 parliament) as tantamount to a form of consociational democracy. Di Palma has preferred the term 'political syncretism', a practice adopted to alleviate the perennial lack of alternation in power in Italy and essentially different from the 'Anglo-Saxon' notion of a clear distinction between government and opposition.[8] Fourthly, particular contextual factors of relevance to coalitional behaviour have been analysed in the general work on Italian parties. The most obvious example is the role of internal party factions (*correnti*). Detailed research has investigated the main ruling party, the DC, where Zuckerman has stressed the various *correnti* as its key determinant in the DC's manoeuvres as a coalition actor.[9] More recently, looking back at the period of the 'National Solidarity' governments of 1976–9, Tarrow[10] has noted that in pursuing its strategy an organised mass party has 'to mediate between its internal life and its political behaviour', meaning that the leadership cannot ignore the party base and that it might indeed be constrained by it (an obvious lesson to be drawn from the PCI's mistakes during this forlorn alliance experiment).

If there is any common denominator to these lines of pursuit indicated in the literature for studying coalitional behaviour in Italy, it must be the need to consider this within the party system as a whole – that is, individual political parties as coalition actors must be seen as both socio-political and institutional forces. One may go even further by arguing that such a comprehensive approach is compelling because of the nature of the system in that country. Italy's political system is most commonly described as a *partitocrazia*, often translated as 'party state' or more literally 'party-ocracy' or 'party power'. According to this definition, the parties are seen as playing the central part in formulating and deciding policy and acting as the principal agents in mobilising public support for their proposals and actions as well as reflecting different sectoral or popular demands. They not only 'populate' the state but also penetrate society, for the extent of partisan allegiance in Italy is such that the political parties separately and together predominate in public life in most conceivable ways. The term *partitocrazia* is particularly justifiable because it takes the discussion way outside the formal institutional structures, for in Italy's case the institutions are weak and informal processes are very important. Hence, the term 'party democracy' is preferred as the English version of *partitocrazia*. In recent times, the presence and control of the parties in the Italian 'way of life' have somewhat weakened in the face of an unfamiliar and apparently increasing public disaffection with the performance of government, but nevertheless the term in question is still very applicable.

It is clear, then, that the main problem of interpretative approach to coalitional behaviour in Italy is met by examining this subject within her system of 'party democracy'. We now take this discussion one stage further by considering the value of formal coalition theories for the Italian case before looking closely at the different dimensions under review.

(b)   The limited relevance of formal coalition theories for Italian politics

The foregoing discussion has implied that formal coalition theories have possibly a limited applicability to the Italian case. Their focus on governmental posts and/ or policy payoffs and more broadly on coalition formation and formal institutional procedures as well as their assumption of rational decison-making make them too one-dimensional for Italy, not least because they ignore other significant determinants of coalitional behaviour. Conceivably, formal coalition theories are that much less applicable to Italy than most other West European countries because of the 'complexity' of Italian coalitional situations noted in the Introduction to this chapter. Italian coalitions are indeed complex as such, but – and this is the leitmotiv of the present chapter – they are not necessarily inexplicable.

As predictive instruments, the formal theories in particular have been found wanting. Minimal winning cases hardly apply in Italy, simply because 'unnecessary' coalition members have been the rule rather than the exception. In his study looking at Italian coalitions up to the late 1970s, Marradi also found that no less than 23 included at least one member party that could have been dropped on merely arithmetical grounds, and that 20 of these cases also added to the coalition's range on the continuum; he claimed that such results challenged both the size and range principles.[11] Marradi goes on to show that Riker's and

Gamson's theories stressing the size of actors are hardly applicable at all; there had been no open minimum winning coalitions in Italy since 1946, and only 5 closed minimum winning ones out of 40.[12] However, the formal theories have highlighted some important features and especially the salience of ideology in Italian coalition politics. Italy, when included for mention by the formal theories, has generally been seen as a country where ideology has a high rating, although this has been assumed without adequate differentiation between the prominence of ideological rhetoric and appeals and its actual behavioural motivation. Moreover, recent research on Italian party elites has indicated a qualitative decline in their cross-party ideological perceptions of each other,[13] the sort of consideration not accounted for by the static nature of the formal theories. Nevertheless, as Axelrod demonstrated in reference to Italy, integration of the concept of ideological distance improved significantly the predictability of coalitions.[14]

In view of the need for a broader explanatory framework than that offered by the formal theories, it is worth while at this point identifying salient characteristics of coalitions in Italy, especially those that are somewhat peculiar to that country. The following should be mentioned: heterogeneity, oversizedness, informal variations, the importance of party factions and, of course, the absence of alternation in power. Just to illustrate therefore the importance of party-political determinants which are located or stretch outside the institutional framework, some (though not all) of the reasons for the above-mentioned characteristics are listed, in the same order: the effects of social fragmentation and different ideological traditions and party identities; consensus-formation around the central position of the DC not merely for majority-building, but also to reinforce that party's control over power, with an additional argument sometimes that national solidarity requires cross-party co-operation; the lack of a clear-cut government/opposition divide and use of this for bridging (or circumventing?) ideological divisions; internal ideological divisions and the related rivalry for the control of patronage; and ideological reservations towards the PCI combined with external pressures from allied countries, notably the USA, and a determination by the DC not to be displaced in power.

In the light of this characterisation, we are more able to specify those determinants of Italian coalitional behaviour which do not fall within the orbit of the formal theories. It becomes clear that the formal theories are too formalistic in their view of political parties as strictly institutional actors. So far as Italy at least is concerned, this approach is a limited one because of the very weakness of that country's political institutions in policy-making (the diffuseness of executive power, a heterogeneous and sluggish administrative system, the limited and indeed declining credibility of the political system and, last but not least, the substantial gap between formal structures and 'real' government). While ministerial posts are certainly the object of coalitional bargaining and their occupants are concerned as it were with the everyday politics or administration of coalition maintenance, the most important source of coalition politics is invariably found outside the cabinet in the national party organisations. The key coalitional decisions are taken within the national executive organs of the parties; and the coalition actors with the greatest individual weight and influence are the party secretaries, who, while parliamentary deputies, tend not to enter the government itself. There have been some exceptions to this practice (Craxi as Socialist Prime Minister is a prominent example), but what really counts is their party rather than their institutional position. This 'extra-parliamentary' locus of coalition politics should not be underestimated; in fact, it leads on to broader questions of party structure, including links between the leadership and party bases.

Furthermore, formal theories deal only with 'governing coalitions', namely with those parties represented in cabinets. So far as Italy goes, this exclusion is unrealistic because of a long-established post-war pattern of both minority governments and 'parliamentary' or 'informal' coalitions (some parties remain outside the cabinet, but they make some form of commitment to support the government externally; e.g. programmatic agreements, agreements to abstain, or the formula of participation 'in the majority', to mention the better known of Italy's subtle variations on the theme of alliances). Such 'informal' coalitions may well be important for the size factor of majority-building (although Italy has tended to indulge in 'oversized' coalitions), while the matter of policy distance can be complicated by one reason for a party opting for external support being disagreement over a particular policy item (partial policy distancing). Certainly, a party providing external support usually has less direct impact on policy-making than one represented in the cabinet, while some minority governments have nevertheless taken important policy initiatives. It hardly needs saying that the less clear-cut divide between government and opposition in Italy, noted before, relativises the difference between 'governing' and 'parliamentary' coalitions. This peculiarity of Italian coalitional behaviour, at least with its multiple variations, arises partly from the absence of alternation in national politics; but it also reflects on the limited attraction of ministerial office and, more broadly, the heterogeneity inherent in Italy's multi-party system.

The formal theories' assumption that political parties are unitary actors in the coalition game fails to convince in the case of Italy simply because of the prevalence and indeed visibility of highly organised internal party factions. Going by past experience, there has even been a tendency for factional behaviour to intensify as a direct result of government involvement, linked as this has been with intra-party rivalry for patronage. In underlining how much the factional aspects of coalitional behaviour link this with extra-parliamentary as well as parliamentary party developments, Zuckerman has concluded that formal coalition theories are questionable in understanding the Italian case, not least because studies which focus solely on party interactions fall short of a complete explanation. In particular, he has argued that such formal theories 'have been of little value in analysing cabinet behaviour' since 'cabinets frequently dissolve without the rupture of the inter-party parliamentary alliances', specifically because of factional politics.[15] In general, factional politics also draws attention to vertical relationships within party structures, since the *correnti* in the various parties owe much of their individual weight to their numerical strength at the base as well as to their clientelistic roots at that level. It might also be added that the question of factional politics challenges the implicitly elitist assumptions of the formal coalition theories in the sense these take for granted that parties are manageable entities automatically supporting their leaders' strategic choices.

From looking at the formal coalition theories in explaining coalitional behaviour in Italy, it may be deduced that their *a priori* assumption of rational decision-making by coalition actors is very open to doubt. Predicated on leading politicians possessing complete information, this assumption does little justice to the nature of party politics in that country. Above all, the formal coalition theories are static in their focus on points of coalition formation rather than seeing formation and maintenance as *together* part of a coalitional process. It is relevant to point out that the inter-party mediative role of Prime Minister-designate in Italy hardly ceases with the successful formation of his government, for it then becomes a regular and major element in his performance as head of government.[16] Moreover, the Italian case does not lend itself easily to the deterministic approach of these theories because of unpredictable factors affecting the survival or not of Italian cabinets. One attempt at an exponential survival model for Italian governments, taking a probabilistic and dynamic perspective, came to the view that the causes of cabinet downfall were varied and complex and basically indeterminate. It was therefore held that a theory of political reliability able to model this indeterminacy would yield better explanatory results.[17] This analyis, however, did not consider the kind of party-political determinants which, as we have seen, are necessary in any explanation of coalition politics in that country.

It has been found that those formal coalition theories dealing with policy distance are far more relevant to the Italian case than those concerned with the size principle. But, it should be emphasised, this is not simply a matter of agreeing on a policy package, embarking on government and fulfilling policy objectives, as formal theories commonly postulate. A whole variety of constraints or determinants may operate whether during coalition formation or during coalition maintenance. So, if anything, the key to understanding Italy's coalitional behaviour lies 'inside the parties' in the broad sense rather than merely 'inside the institutions'. There is clearly a need for a different approach here than that offered by the formal coalition theories.

Lawrence Dodd, arguing for a more differentiated handling of coalitional behaviour, starts with the hypothesis that 'the impact of party systems on cabinet durability is a much more complex and multivariate process' than previously supposed, and likewise his conclusion that there are three party-system variables which play a determining role in coalition formation and maintenance – namely, cleavage conflict, fractionalisation and stability – is very pertinent to the case of Italy. He also provided an explanation for oversized cabinets as most likely to emerge from unstable and hyperfractionalised parliamentary party systems.[18] Giovanni Sartori's thesis of 'polarised pluralism', while postulated for Western-type party systems, is really an extrapolation from the Italian example itself.[19] It is, however, somewhat dated in placing the PCI at one 'extreme' of the ideological spectrum, for since he wrote in the mid-1960s that party's evolving strategy has promoted its own legitimacy and integrated it more within the political system, with the consequence that it has formed many more alliances (sub-nationally) over the past decade. Nevertheless, Sartori's emphasis on different forms of polarity may be seen as a variation on policy-distance theories which, as previously noted, are broadly relevant to Italy. In fact, he takes this approach further. What matters for Sartori is not merely the existence of poles, but the intensity of divisions between them and in particular whether their interactive dynamics are centripetal or centrifugal, with obvious implications here for system stability. He also usefully identifies 'different majorities' or issue cleavages – economic, political (i.e. commitment to the system, international alliances) and religious – which do not necessarily harmonise, and this highlights problems of cohesion within actual coalitional relationships. Altogether, this focus on the specific nature of polarisation is an important contextual argument for the Italian example in helping to explain, for instance, the unusually prominent role of the small parties and especially the pivotal position of the PSI as well as being very relevant to the absence of alternation in power. Despite the datedness in Sartori's view of Italian politics, his categorisation of Italy as an example of an extreme multi-party system with peripheral turnover still has some truth.

We now look more closely and systematically at the determinants of and constraints on coalitional behaviour within the context of Italy's party democracy, and see how far the different dimensions presented in this book unravel the complexity of the subject.

(c) Historical patterns of Italian coalitions

Coalitions have been very much the norm in post-war Italian politics because of the multi-party system combined with proportional representation as the voting method. Coalition arrangements have varied with oversized coalitions being prominent, though interspersed with minority governments, and, as we have noted before, a practice of 'informal' or 'parliamentary' alliances. In general, Italian coalitions have been heterogeneous not merely because numerically multi-party (with usually three to five parties: see Table 9.3, 'Results of national elections', p. 208), but also as the parties involved have reflected social fragmentation to some degree. This summarises descriptively the salient characteristics of Italian coalitions when looking at their history (for the

Table 9.1 *Coalition formulas in Italy, 1945–86*

(For details of individual governments and their composition, see Table 9.2, p. 207	

1945–7	Cross-party governments, including DC, PCI and PSI (De Gasperi)
1947–57	Centre-right governments, including DC, PSDI, PLI and PRI (De Gasperi, Pella, Fanfani, Scelba, Segni)
1957–63	Mainly DC minority governments (Zoli, Fanfani, Segni, Tambroni, Leone)
1963–72	Centre-left governments, based on DC/PSI co-operation (Moro, Leone, Rumor, Colombo)
1972–3	Centre-right governments (Andreotti)
1973–4	Centre-left governments (Rumor)
1974–6	Minority governments led by the DC (Moro)
1976–9	'National Solidarity' governments under the DC, with wide party support including especially the PCI (Andreotti)
1979–80	Centre-right government (Cossiga)
1980–6	Five-party coalitions (Forlani, Spadolini, Fanfani, Craxi) or *pentapartito* – DC/PSI/PRI/PSDI/PLI

[Parties involved in coalitions, other than the DC and PCI, have been: Socialists (PSI), Social Democrats (PSDI), Republicans (PRI) and Liberals (PLI). The names of the main Prime Ministers are given in brackets in this table.]

composition of Italian cabinets 1945–85, see Table 9.2, p. 207); but it is also useful to identify here those patterns that may throw light on the dynamics of coalitional behaviour in this country.

First of all, it is possible to recognise successive coalition formulas linking together different cabinets, thus providing some continuity within the picture of short-lived and often unstable governments, as Table 9.1 shows. The most constant theme in the whole post-war period has been the uninterrupted presence and also the dominance or centrality of the DC as the numerically strongest coalition partner, though one lacking an absolute majority (except in the 1948 parliament, but even then it continued to form centre-right coalitions). This central position of the DC, numerically within governments and ideologically within the left–right spectrum, would seem to place it in a classic pivotal role for determining one against other coalition options.

In fact, as Sartori argued, there has been peripheral rather than major turnover in government members dictated by the maintenance or reinforcement by the DC of its power bloc. Put crudely, a weakening of the DC's position in both institutional (i.e. parliamentary seats) and socio-political terms (in the face of social change or increased recognition of the need for bridging social fragmentation) has persuaded it to enlarge 'the area of government', to use a term from Italian coalition vocabulary. This was the significance of the 'opening to the left' or centre-left formula in the early 1960s, with the inclusion of the Socialists as coalition partner, as well as the move towards informal co-operation with the Communists a decade later. These were the two examples of new departures in coalitional strategy in the post-war period, with only the latter opening up the

Table 9.2 *Composition of Italian cabinets, 1945–86*

Period of office (Number of months)	Prime Minister	Parties in the cabinet
1. 6–11/45 (5)	Parri	Action Party, DC, PCI, PLI, PSI, PDL (Democratic Labour)
2. 12/45–7/46 (6)	De Gasperi	DC, PCI, PSI, Action Party, PDL, PLI
3. 7/46–2/47 (6)	De Gasperi	DC, PCI, PSI, PLI, PRI
4. 2–4/47 (3)	De Gasperi	DC, PCI, PSI
5. 5/47–5/48 (11)	De Gasperi	DC, PSDI, PLI, PRI
6. 5/48–1/50 (20)	De Gasperi	DC, PSDI, PRI, PLI
7. 1/50–7/51 (17)	De Gasperi	DC, PSDI, PRI
8. 7/51–6/53 (23)	De Gasperi	DC, PRI
9 7/53 ($\frac{1}{2}$)	De Gasperi	DC (external support of PRI)
10. 8/53–1/54 (5)	Pella	DC (external support of PRI, PLI and Monarchists)
11. 1/54 ($\frac{1}{2}$)	Fanfani	DC
12. 2/54–6/55 (16)	Scelba	DC, PSDI, PLI (external support of PRI)
13. 7/55–5/57 (22)	Segni	DC, PSDI, PLI (external support of PRI)
14. 5/57–6/58 (13)	Zoli	DC (external support of Monarchists and MSI)
15. 7/58–1/59 (7)	Fanfani	DC, PSDI (external support of PRI)
16. 2/59–2/60 (12)	Segni	DC
17. 3–7/60 (4)	Tambroni	DC
18. 7/60–2/62 (18)	Fanfani	DC (external support from PSDI, PRI, PLI)
19. 2/62–6/63 (16)	Fanfani	DC, PSDI, PRI (external support of PSI)
20. 6–11/63 (6)	Leone	DC
21. 12/63–6/64 (7)	Moro	DC, PSI, PSDI, PRI
22. 7/64–1/66 (18)	Moro	DC, PSI, PSDI, PRI
23. 2/66–6/68 (27)	Moro	DC, PSI, PSDI, PRI
24. 6–11/68 (5)	Leone	DC
25. 12/68–7/69 (6)	Rumor	DC, PSI, PRI
26. 8/69–2/70 (6)	Rumor	DC (external support from PSI and PSDI)
27. 3–7/70 (3)	Rumor	DC, PSI, PSDI, PRI
28. 8/70–1/72 (17)	Colombo	DC, PSI, PSDI, PRI
29. 2–6/72 (4)	Andreotti	DC (external support from PRI, PSDI and PLI)
30. 6/72–6/73 (12)	Andreotti	DC, PSDI, PLI (external support from PRI)
31. 7/73–3/74 (8)	Rumor	DC, PSI, PSDI, PRI
32. 3–10/74 (7)	Rumor	DC, PSI, PSDI
33. 11/74–2/76 (15)	Moro	DC, PRI (external support from PSI and PSDI)
34. 2–7/76 (5)	Moro	DC (external support from PSDI)
35. 8/76–3/78 (19)	Andreotti	DC (abstention from PCI, PSI, PSDI, PRI, PLI)
36. 3/78–3/79 (12)	Andreotti	DC (external support from PCI, PSI, PSDI, PRI)
37. 3–8/79 (4)	Andreotti	DC, PSDI, PRI
38. 8/79–4/80 (8)	Cossiga	DC, PSDI, PLI (abstention of PSI and PRI)
39. 4–10/80 (6)	Cossiga	DC, PSI, PRI
40. 10/80–6/81 (8)	Forlani	DC, PSI, PSDI, PRI
41. 6/81–8/82 (13)	Spadolini	PRI, DC, PSI, PSDI, PLI
42. 8–11/82 (3)	Spadolini	PRI, DC, PSI, PSDI, PLI
43. 12/82–8/83 (8)	Fanfani	DC, PSI, PSDI, PLI
44. 8/83–6/86 (34)	Craxi	PSI, DC, PRI, PSDI, PLI

(The party of the Prime Minister is given first among the list of cabinet participants.)

Table 9.3 *Results of national elections in Italy, 1948–83*

Year	Total seats in Chamber of Deputies	Christian Democratic party (DC) Seats	% of vote	Communist party (PCI) Seats	% of vote	Socialist party (PSI) Seats	% of vote	Social Democratic party (PSDI) Seats	% of vote	Republican party (PRI) Seats	% of vote	Liberal party (PLI) Seats	% of vote
1948	574	305	48.5	183	31.0 (with PSI)			33	7.1	9	2.5	19	3.8
1953	590	263	40.1	143	22.6	75	12.8	19	4.5	5	1.6	13	3.0
1958	596	273	42.4	140	22.7	84	14.2	22	4.5	6	1.4	17	3.5
1963	630	250	38.3	166	25.3	87	13.8	33	6.1	6	1.4	39	7.0
1968	630	266	39.1	177	26.9	91	14.5 (with PSDI)			9	2.0	31	5.8
1972	630	267	38.8	179	27.2	61	9.6	29	5.1	15	2.9	20	3.9
1976	630	263	38.7	227	34.4	57	9.6	15	3.4	14	3.1	5	1.3
1979	629	262	38.3	201	30.4	62	9.8	20	3.8	16	3.0	9	1.9
1983	630	225	32.9	198	29.9	73	11.4	23	4.1	29	5.1	16	2.9

(The above list includes only those parties that have acted as coalition partners; other parties include the neo-Fascist MSI and the Radical party.)

prospect of alternation. If one accepts some expositions of DC strategy by Aldo Moro (his party's principal strategist during both experiments), he saw the 'National Solidarity' formula as preparing the way for eventual alternation in favour of the PCI, though not as an immediate prospect; while the centre-left formula was on the other hand an attempt by the DC to drive a wedge between the two parties of the left and hence secure its own hold over government. Moro's acceptance of the possibility of the PCI as governing party was conditional on qualitative changes in that party, not so much in its policy outlook as in its traditional nature as a party (attachment to the democratic system, relationship with Moscow, its own internal organisation). Such new departures in coalition formulas have been preceded by some movement by the parties of the left rightwards along the left–right spectrum, indicated by significant policy shifts (e.g. on the EEC and NATO). This is also true of the *pentapartito* formula with the re-entry of the PSI into government at the start of the 1980s, following Craxi's deliberate movement of his party to a centrist position in order to challenge the dominance of the DC, now electorally weakened, within government. Craxi's appointment as first Socialist Prime Minister in 1983 involved what is called *alternanza*, or changing the political balance within a given coalition formula (the term has also been used to describe a partial change of coalition partners, though limited by the perpetuation of the DC in power), as distinct from *alternativa*, or complete change in dominant coalition partner, which corresponds with what is usually called 'alternation'. Whether the practice of non-DC prime ministers (the first being the PRI leader Spadolini in 1981–2) becomes a tendency and politically encourages more substantial turnover in Italian coalitions remains to be seen.

Looking back over the past forty years, the most conspicuous pattern has been the absence of alternation. Italy is virtually unique in this respect in Western Europe, and this has become a subject of increasing debate among political commentators in Italy. Some of them have linked this problem with the whole question of system stability.[20] It is also of course related to the theme of ideology in Italian coalition politics because of, specifically, ideological reservations towards the PCI which have persisted throughout the whole post-war period despite that party's strategic evolution and expanded role in regional and local government. While the question of ideology also surfaces under other dimensions, it may be said here that the historical dimension confirms broadly the assumption of coalition theorists that ideology plays a prominent part in Italian coalition politics.

The prevalence and practice of coalition politics since the war suggest that attitudes inherent in the coalitional game have become embedded in the Italian way of political life. A typical speech by an Italian politician invariably gives ample attention to his party's actual or prospective alliance relationships with other parties, quite apart from the usual inter-party polemics that, for instance, mark electoral competition. The long experience of coalitions and of different formulas applied have, it appears, conditioned the behaviour of individual parties concerned, their positions and inclinations, certainly at the elite level. On this matter of traditions of party co-operation, the evidence suggests both positive and negative consequences. An accumulated habit of governmental co-operation, bearing in mind the strong continuity in Italian elite personnel, can facilitate coalition formations, though not necessarily coalition maintenance. Certainly, once a particular formula has been tried, its own legitimacy may no longer be disputed: the return of the PSI to government in 1980 in no way caused the controversy that accompanied the 'opening to the left' in the early 1960s; and, it has been argued, the 'National Solidarity' alliance of 1976–9 has set a precedent for governmental co-operation with the PCI in the future. On the other hand, the PCI's bitter disillusionment with this experience might well condition it against any repeat of this formula. Similarly, the PSI had felt 'burnt' by its centre-left coalition with the DC in the 1960s (disappointment over the failure of projected reforms – the major justification on its side for this formula – and loss of popularity through its evident subordination to the DC). In the latter case, this very experience produced a determination under Craxi's leadership from 1976 to undercut the DC's dominance in government, and this has clearly coloured the *pentapartito* formula. In general, the question arises of how much individual party identity might be affected by the extensive practice of coalitional arrangements, but this really points to other dimensions; indeed, the historical dimension can only identify broad points of reference, and obviously some of these require further and more precise examination.

Referring again to successive coalition formulas, if there has been any recent trend it has been one of growing instability in alliance relationships. The decade and more from the early mid-1970s has been characterised by rapid experimentation with differing formulas in place of a medium-term continuity as before. This conforms with the emergence of the 'Italian crisis' or the problem of 'governability' during the same period, thus underlining again the central importance of coalitions in Italy's political system. It is significant that this instability and growing effectiveness of alliance relationships have, among other things, led to a more urgent debate about the need for institutional reform in Italy since the end of the 1970s, which leads us straight into the next dimension.

(d)   The institutional framework of Italian coalitions

While the weakness of Italy's political–institutional structure has warned us against too formalistic an approach to coalitional behaviour there through concentrating on institutional procedures, nevertheless various questions relating to this institutional framework have to be broached.

The first problem here is how far formal structures actually determine or constrain coalitional behaviour. The Italian Constitution of 1948 is remarkably sparse in outlining government functions, and it provides no real clue to the conduct of coalition politics. As it has developed, the most visible institution, the presidency of the Council (Prime Ministership), is relatively weak in that it has provided mediative rather than innovative leadership,[21] so that its potential as an agent for coalitional cohesion and performance is strictly limited. Partly this is due to the unwieldiness of Italian cabinets (they include all ministers and usually comprise around 27 members) and the absence of collective responsibility, but it is also a result of the very heterogeneity of coalitions and the time demands on the Prime Minister to settle the frequent conflicts between coalition partners. One might add the general problem of the cabinet's limited political weight. Attempts on occasions to strengthen the formal executive by deliberately including all relevant party secretaries in the cabinet have usually failed; certainly any attempt to institutionalise such an arrangement has been a non-starter.

Different proposals for institutional reform in the past half-decade have concentrated on such predictable matters as strengthening the constitutional powers of the Prime Minister, the possibility of directly electing the President, tightening up parliamentary procedure to expedite government business and also electoral reform. But, so far, nothing of importance has changed and not merely because of the overall sluggishness in the Italian system, but more pointedly as party interests have inevitably come to the fore and the mutual checking manoeuvres that characterise Italy's multi-party coalitions have tended to work against reform. In short, not merely has the system inhibited its own improved functioning, but more particularly coalition politics has prevented that. It is therefore more a case of the weakness of the political structures placing them at the mercy of coalition politics rather than the formal structures constraining or determining the operation of coalition politics to any considerable degree. A good example of this, from the positive viewpoint of change actually occurring, is the inauguration of regional governments and assemblies across the country in 1970. This was a belated implementation of a provision in the 1948 Constitution which had been obstructed essentially by the DC's reluctance to allow thereby Communist governments in some parts of Italy; but this was overcome by PSI pressure during the centre-left coalition of the 1960s.[22]

In general, then, it cannot really be said that the institutional structures have the effect of binding the parties together and promoting their effectiveness in government. Similarly, on a more specific matter, the formal procedures of government formation do not really encourage rationality. Deriving from the 1948 Constitution but also more from an accumulation of conventions, they are highly elaborate and one might even say ritualistic (as above in note 2). While they provide for wide consultation during the coalition formation process, they are hardly conducive to efficiency. Since the formation process usually takes several weeks, if not sometimes longer, there is ample opportunity for the impact on the process of internal divisions within parties or for different and sometimes contradictory manoeuvres by certain parties so that 'accidents' may occur. Just to complicate matters, in recent times, there has been a new tendency to include industrial, business and trade union leaders in the overall consultation before governments are formed – a reflection among other things of the increasing power and autonomy (from the parties) of the trade unions from the early 1970s, and more generally of the mounting problems of economic management. Neo-corporatist practices have begun to impinge on Italian coalition politics.

Constitutional regulations may be seen as providing little more than a technical backdrop to the process of coalition formation. A further point arising here is that the frequency of government formations (the average life of a government is ten to eleven months) has in effect created more scope for the President's role in that process if not also sometimes in coalition maintenance. Incumbent presidents have occasionally even sought to influence events in favour of a particular coalition formula, although this has not always been publicly visible. In recent times, the decline in governmental effectiveness has focussed interest that much more on the role of the presidency. This is also because Pertini (in office 1978–85) has shown an unprecedented firmness in dealing with conflictive coalition partners, but it has to be seen as more a matter of an individual incumbent rather than a source of previously untapped institutional strength.

Finally, various points arise from looking at the institutional framework of Italian coalitional behaviour and they reinforce a sceptical view of it. Firstly, taking the style of bargaining, any fine distinction between coalition formation and coalition maintenance is not possible. This has clearly to do with the limited life of coalitions and the frequency of formations, but it also refers to the practice of 'renegotiating' items of coalition policy that intermittently occurs during a government's lifetime, sometimes even leading to a 'government crisis', though not always the formal collapse of a coalition. This certainly, in the case of Italy, emphasises the need to consider 'formation' and 'maintenance' together as part of an ongoing coalitional relationship. Secondly, there is no insistence in Italian politics – as there is, for instance, in West Germany – that governments should automatically have to command formal majority support in the legislature, an attitude encouraged by the general expectation on a government's investiture that it will probably be short-lived. Furthermore, in the case of oversized coalitions, these have more often fallen as a result of internal policy disagreements, the withdrawal of support for the cabinet by one or more parties in government, or factional infighting within the DC rather than the erosion of a formal parliamentary majority in, say, the British fashion. Quite often, government collapses have not led to the ending of a coalitional relationship as such (coalitional formulas have, as we noted earlier, persisted through several successive formations), while some government collapses/coalition re-formations have amounted to a little more than cabinet reshuffles, as in the UK, with the same Prime Minister in office. Only recently have government collapses more than before begun to question coalitional relationships, and this reflects the growing instability in such relationships. Altogether, the problem here is the heterogeneity of alliances – whether these take the form of 'executive coalitions' or 'parliamentary coalitions' (including informal support) – rather than the existence or not of formal majorities. Thirdly, there is a special feature of the Italian situation, known commonly as *sottogoverno* ('sub-government'), or patronage on a mass scale, which derives from holding political office and inevitably enters coalitional behaviour. Because of this, the allotment of cabinet posts does indeed have interesting consequences – in particular, which party obtains which posts, for some offer more patronage possibilities than others. It is a process involving appointments also to such agencies as state-controlled banks, industrial companies and especially the large state corporations. Paolo Farneti has even written that 'in Italy there have always been two governments, that which is an expression of the parliament and that which is generated by the party in power, namely *sottogoverno*'.[23] This represents part of what Sartori has called the 'invisible' side of Italian government (though in the light of mounting scandals somewhat less 'invisible' than before), and it is always implicit in coalitional bargaining. The point here is that, while such patronage is transmitted via institutional channels, it is essentially handled by the political parties operating beyond those channels.

Overall, the discussion in the introductory chapter of the relationship between arithmetical considerations (the respective parties' strengths in the legislature) and political considerations (a variety of, looking to the other dimensions which follow) is particularly useful with respect to Italy. It is clear that the former – the focus of many formal coalition theories – cannot be treated in isolation, not least because so many determinants of coalitional behaviour are located outside the institutional corridors of power. All this underlines the distinction made between formal structures and 'real' government in Italy; or, as Guiseppe Di Palma has commented, her political system lacks 'institutional persuasion' as it does not possess a certain momentum of its own which can regulate the flows and pressures of political life.

(e) Motivation in Italian coalitional behaviour: problems of strategy, ideology and power

This is the least straightforward of the dimensions when looking at Italy, both because it involves a mixture of different motives and also because they interrelate closely. There is consequently an ambiguity about their individual importance at given points of time. This dimension will be approached from a number of angles, thereby providing some insights without necessarily definitive answers.

Perhaps the obvious starting-point is the crude but searching question of power versus policy, one of the most common of the *a priori* assumptions raised by the formal theories. Is policy seen as a means for acquiring power (the 'cynical' school of thinking), or vice versa, with policy and its implementation being the overriding consideration? Or, alternatively, are these two motives viewed somewhat independently with the need, in concrete coalitional situations, for a trade-off between them? It is tempting to argue that the power motive prevails in the light of the habitual cynicism that seems part of Italian political thinking and even culture.[24] It is commonplace among governmental elites, and it is illustrated by the subtle and suggestive vocabulary used in the coalition game by politicians and their friends – or enemies – in the media, intimating darkly that matters of principle are always pliable.[25] Furthermore, the immobilism that has long characterised the operation of the political system has a discouraging effect on innovative policies. But this general question is of course conditional upon what is understood by 'power' in the Italian context.

In Italy, 'power' cannot simply be equated with office-holding in the cabinet, even though ministers enjoy some prestige and the trappings of office inevitably entice (one might also add that now there are personal inconveniences with tight security precautions against the threat from terrorism). This equation cannot be made because power in the sense of the location of decision-making is diffuse, and hardly concentrated in the cabinet. As we have seen, power in Italy's *partitocrazia* also lies in the hands of the party secretaries, who usually remain outside the cabinet, so that the distribution of cabinet portfolios is not as acute as some formal coalition theorists would assume, though at the same time it is not by any means neglected. There is the other special aspect to 'power' in Italian coalition politics relating to *sottogoverno* whereby cabinet posts (or certain ones) are seen as offering access to resources rather than formally being identified with policy-making. In other words, power given its special definitional twist in the Italian case seems to be the predominant motive *as a general proposition*, so far in the discussion.

If access to and – given coalitional dictates – the sharing of the benefits of power is the key motive, does this therefore mean that all combinations of parties are possible as coalition partners? The immediate answer is in fact no, and here we have to turn to party-specific motives and the relevant question of ideology. One general possibility restricting the open choice of combinations, noticed in some other West European countries, is that some parties might be hostile to coalitions as such. This is true of the small Radical party, which has set itself up against all the 'established' parties and is purist about certain issues like civil rights and open government. The neo-Fascist MSI (Italian Social Movement) is excluded as not being a legitimate coalition partner by all the other parties for obvious historical and ideological reasons. But the most important case in question is the PCI, though for a complex of reasons. To say that ideology has divided the PCI from the other parties (though possibly less so from the Socialists) is true as a general statement, telling us that full governmental co-operation with the parties of the centre and the right would be difficult if not impossible. In fact, it has not occurred except during the special circumstances of the constituent period of 1945–7.

But it does not as such tell us much more than this. We have to pursue more carefully party-specific motives. So far as the PCI is concerned, one predominant motive has been its desire to avoid isolation in Italian politics and for its own full legitimation as a political force. Hence, it has been very committed to the concept of alliances and it of all the Italian parties has spoken most decidedly of having a strategy, from Togliatti's 'Italian road to socialism' through Berlinguer's 'historic compromise' to the Democratic Alternative of the 1980s. But, when it comes to actual coalitional choices, the position of the PCI has been less clear-cut. On the important question of its willingness to govern and share power, the PCI has on the one hand linked its own legitimation with being accepted as a governing party and it has actively sought this role, both in demanding national government participation during the 1976–9 parliament and in leading or participating in coalitions regionally and locally. Yet, the PCI has at the same time insisted on its radical aims and long-term revolutionary goals, and it has encapsulated this position in its slogan 'Party of Government and Struggle' (*Partito di Governo e Lotta*). In short, the PCI has linked its governmental co-operation to the question of basic policy objectives, thus suggesting that policy comes before power as such, which fits with what we know of the PCI as a distinctly programmatic party (a category happily accepted by PCI interviewees). Nevertheless, there remains an element of ambiguity in the PCI's attitude to power. While this has been seen by itself as a means to its legitimation, the party has been cautious about the actual prospect of power. Indeed, since the disillusioning experience of its support for the Andreotti governments in the late 1970s, the PCI has become more rigid about its preconditions for government participation, and it seems more content for the time being to concentrate on its role as opposition. And if the Democratic Alternative strategy departs in any way from the 'historic compromise', it is that the PCI now excludes governmental co-operation with the DC.

This discussion of the strategy of the PCI, as the most ideologically minded of the possible coalition actors, confirms that ideology as a 'pure' motive in Italian coalition politics is hard to sustain. It is evidently there as a factor, but it is hard to measure exactly. For instance, it is possible to say that to some extent 'ideology' is in the eye of the beholder. The other parties view the PCI, in the context of alliance politics, as adhering to an ideology which presents a barrier to full co-operation, and of the PCI's traditions as a party its relationship with Moscow is highlighted. But there is an element too of party interest or calculation in this 'ideological' view of the PCI, notably in the case of the DC. Its anti-Communism has habitually provided the DC with an important argument for maintaining its own power bloc (this has consistently reappeared in the DC's electoral appeals), and it is a common denominator with its allies in the centre and on the right.

In reverting to the power versus policy argument, we come to the verdict that the PCI is on the other side of the balance between these two motives from the other parties because it *is* a different type of political party. This is reflected in the fact that its leaders and activists employ a different style of political language (dialectical, programmatic and Marxist) which is alien to the cynical coalition vocabulary mentioned earlier. By contrast, the DC emerges as first and foremost a power-motivated party prepared at almost all costs to preserve its role in the state. Conceivably, its policy drive was more evident in its early period such as under De Gasperi, when some crucial policy directions were established. But over time the DC's desire to maintain power for its own sake has overwhelmed other considerations, even though one or two of its factions (notably on its left) could be said to retain something of a programmatic outlook.

In other words, while this seems to lead us to the conclusion that ideology is indeed very much present in Italian coalition politics, that it can be divisive and hence restrictive on the scope for coalition partners, it also tells us to pursue further the interlinkage between ideology and other forms of motivation. We might also note a time dimension variable here, for the parties of the left have shown a willingness to adapt their positions on key issues (such as foreign policy) at least in part for the sake of new alliance possibilities: i.e. strategically motivated policy convergence. There is also evidence (see again note 13) that ideological perspectives among the various political elites have lessened with time, and they are certainly much less intense than they were during the height of the Cold War in the late 1940s and the 1950s. Behind all this lies the question of the real motivational force of ideology. For, while ideological appeals have continued to be common in political rhetoric, parliamentarians have shown a marked capacity for inter-party accommodation and this includes the PCI both before and after as well as during the 'National Solidarity' period of the later 1970s. It is this kind of consideration Samuel Barnes had in mind when he commented: 'Ideology is a weapon of particular importance in inter- and intra-party struggles, and is also a useful analytical tool in discussing some aspects of Italian politics; but it can easily confuse rather than clarify the reality of the Italian situation.'[26] Two additional aspects of the motivation dimension in Italian coalitional behaviour should offer some insight into this problem: the dictates of Italy's multi-party system and the question of policy distance.

To state the obvious, since Italy has a multi-party system the individual parties are ultimately dependent on each other for translating their strategies into action (actual coalitions or alliances). A categorisation may be made here for multi-party systems between: (a) leading parties, though dependent on others for forming coalitions – so far, only the DC because of the exclusion of the PCI from heading any national government (but it has performed this role at the sub-national levels); (b) pivotai parties, specifically the PSI, taking advantage of this exclusion of the PCI, although also weakened by its numerical inability to 'make up' a majority alone with the DC (in this crucial sense different from the West German FDP); and (c) smaller parties, basically dependent, playing a supplementary or satellite role in relation to the leading party. If one were to focus on the dynamics of this multi-party setting, the question of direction or movement in individual party strategies would arise. Here, the relationship between arithmetical and political considerations is once more useful. It may be hypothesised that what may be arithmetically possible is not necessarily politically feasible; equally, what may be politically desirable – on the party of intending coalition partners – may not be arithmetically possible. For instance, Berlinguer and other PCI leaders argued after the 1983 election that the 'numerical conditions' now existed for a 'democratic majority' without the DC (following the latter's severe drop in voting support), but this proved politically a non-starter because the DC and PSI, albeit with their different motives, were set on a reproduction of the *pentapartito* formula. In similar fashion, though with the parties taking different strategic courses, a new edition of the centre-left was numerically possible after the 1976 election (which this time saw an unprecedented electoral breakthrough by the PCI), but the PSI, wishing to repudiate the, for itself, unhappy centre-left experience, had already come round to demanding the entry of the PCI into government as a precondition for its own participation. This was linked to the apparent electoral legitimacy granted the PCI's strategy of the 'historic compromise'. The result was, as is known, the informal 'grand coalition' of all three parties plus others.

From this, one interesting conclusion is possible. Given the dynamics of individual party strategies, the left–right ideological spectrum has to be applied with some flexibility as a yardstick for assessing coalitional options, particularly with respect to the degree of space between the different parties. Such mobility within the ideological spectrum, reflecting the reality of Italian coalitional situations, is not easily accommodated by the formal coalition theories. There is even the peculiarity in Italy whereby parties may leapfrog each other on the spectrum in what is known as the *salto di quaglia* (the 'hop of the quail') – an act of heresy in the eyes of the formal coalition theorists! Specifically, this might arise over a particular policy area which may be defined in left–right terms, but this leads us into our final aspect of motivation.

The question of policy distance was identified earlier as having a relevance to Italian coalitions, but it has already become clear that it cannot be treated in any bland manner – in looking, empirically, at the Italian case – nor can it be seen as a static determinant. There may be at given periods divergent and convergent priorities between parties, and these may shift over time. Here, it is useful to take up Sartori's argument in favour of different issue majorities. At the time he wrote, he identified three such majorities or issue cleavages over economic, political and religious questions, to which one might now add the 'moral question' that has become prominent (corruption, organised crime and its links with politics) and possibly also civil rights. There is no space here to discuss in any detail the policy positions of the parties on all these matters, so attention will be drawn to some sample lessons on this aspect of motivation.

The religious cleavage is historical, but its intensity has generally lessened with secularisation. Its saliency has become issue-specific, such as over the questions of divorce and abortion which arose in the 1970s, dividing the DC from the lay parties and straining their alliance. The cleavage is obviously lay versus Catholic, but it is difficult to fit this exactly into left–right terms: the Liberals, then very much on the right of the spectrum, took a 'progressive' line in accordance with their anticlerical tradition; while the Socialists were more intransigent towards the DC over both issues than the Communists, who acted cautiously both because of their large Catholic base and also their strategic concern for convergence with the Christian Democrats. As a cleavage with more continuous saliency, international affairs saw a convergence (declining policy distance) between left and right in the 1960s and 1970s, but from the start of the 1980s the greater East–West tension has left its mark on inter-party relations in Italy. This occurred simultaneously with the PCI's break with the 'National Solidarity' formula, though the two events were not connected, helping to sharpen the conflict which followed. But this has produced a differentiated reaction on the part of the PCI: while it has established links with the new peace movement in Italy, clashing with government policy (the protest against US missiles has generally 'internalised' defence matters and increased polarisation), the PCI has nevertheless distanced itself further from Moscow over the Polish crisis of 1981, so that altogether it is not possible to talk of an outright case of widening policy distance in this area.

It is evident that different issue cleavages occasion different intensities, which may increase or decline over time; also, that issue majorities vary between parties and may even split the government camp and straddle the government/ opposition divide. However, the cleavage over the 'moral question' is essentially between those parties which have been continuously in government and have had opportunities for abusing patronage and those which have not (i.e. first and foremost the PCI). It is a straight government/opposition divide rather than a simple left–right one, although it does again link with the PCI's sense of identity as the party of 'clean hands' and hence its legitimacy. Finally, the basic traditional cleavage over economic policy has not been as clear-cut ideologically as in many West European countries because of a practice of government intervention under the DC. The PCI has developed an alternative economic approach to deal with the recession which concentrates on a return to full employment and the removal of regional imbalances; yet, during the 'National Solidarity' period the party adopted the idea of 'austerity', involving sacrifices to avoid economic collapse. This met with keen resistance from the party base, while the PCI's own position in negotiating with the Andreotti governments at that time suffered from its lack of specific proposals in the field of economic policy.[27] There was evidence on this issue that the dynamics of polarisation operated against elite accommodation.

In general, therefore, while ideology is certainly relevant to the study of Italian coalitional behaviour, it does require differentiated handling. For, if ideology involves the systematic ordering of policy priorites, it also runs up against the fact that the saliency or urgency of policy areas is to a significant extent determined by the impact of events; furthermore, the translation of these policy priorities is also subject to compromise with coalition partners. In other words, power together with 'events' may be said to modify ideology, just as earlier we found that policy commitment could modify the power drive. One may therefore speak of a trade-off between power and policy, but the interplay between the two is not a simple one in Italy's case. Plainly, there is party variation on this matter, not to mention a time scale to the intensity of ideology, also different 'issue majorities' requiring a flexible use of the policy-distance framework, ideological concerns not always being free from instrumental considerations, while individual strategic aims other than policy are relevant.

We may say, then, that the left–right spectrum is still valid as a framework, but that it has to be qualified on a number of grounds. Polarisation does exist in Italian politics, but it has to be viewed dynamically, not statically, and it does require some specific handling. The final thought on this complex side of Italian coalitions must be that, while 'power' and 'policy' are conceptually neat, in practice they are closely interrelated and they are not exclusive of other forms of motivation.

(f) Horizontal/vertical channels of coalition politics

The essential point here is that sub-national (i.e. local and regional) coalition politics invariably enters the strategic considerations of national party leaders, for even local alliance arrangements outside the larger cities are monitored. So far as the national–horizontal level is concerned, we have already established that the key coalition actors are the party secretaries and other leaders within the parties' national executive organs. We now begin to look at the lower reaches of Italy's *partitocrazia*.

The point of departure for looking at vertical channels must be the nature of the state structure in Italy, as providing opportunities for coalition politics. For most of the post-war period, Italy has had a centralised system which became modified from 1970 with the introduction of regional administrations and assemblies across the country – the 15 'ordinary regions' were added to the 5 'special regions' created soon after the war. Other sub-national units are the 94 provinces and of course the communes, of which there are more than 8,000, ranging from large cities like Milan and Rome to villages. It is important to note, however, the lack of real policy autonomy enjoyed by these different structures with respect to national government, especially in the financial dependence of the former on the latter. This is still generally true, even though in 1977 there was a transfer of certain powers from the national to the sub-national levels in such fields as public works and agriculture and control over some public agencies.

Despite this institutional limitation, sub-national politics has habitually been an important arena for coalition operations for reasons of party strategy.[28] But this has not necessarily meant that coalition formulas sub-nationally have followed the same pattern as nationally, if only because the myriad of sub-national units against the background of territorially variable party strength has made that impossible. For instance, the introduction of country-wide regional structures – together with the metropolitan cities, the most visible and prestigious of these units – significantly enlarged the scope for coalitional differentiation. It also provided a new synchronic outlet for power-sharing by the PCI, since its road to Rome was blocked. As a result, there has over time been much more variety of coalition formulas in sub-national politics,[29] including alternation in power with the formation of many administrations of the left from the mid-1970s (primarily PCI + PSI) as well as some co-operation between the Communists and the small centre parties. The impact of ideology has been less acute sub-nationally, although it has been sufficient to prevent formal coalitions between the DC and PCI except in certain smaller and usually insignificant localities.

This raises two questions about vertical channels of coalition politics concerning the nature of national intervention in the regions and communes and the possible effect of coalitions at this level on national coalitional behaviour. In general, there has been direct intervention by national parties when coalition formation or maintenance has involved a prestigious unit (a large city or a particular region), or when the case in question has become controversial or beyond the control of the regional or local party structures (such as a 'crisis' in an important city which might have repercussions on national alliances). The parties have to varying degrees regionalised their own structures following the devolution of the state, but their national leaderships have done their utmost to keep control of the reins of sub-national coalitional behaviour where necessary.[30] Another feature has been experimentation in sub-national coalitions for reasons of party strategy. For instance, the centre-left formula was first introduced in the three large cities of Florence, Milan and Genoa at the start of the 1960s before it was formally adopted nationally in 1963. However, the administrations of the left in most cities and several regions have not led to a repetition of this process, because of the problems of alternation in national politics already discussed. What happened in the later 1970s was a reproduction of the 'National Solidarity' formula in many regions, particularly in the South, where severe economic and social conditions were seen as a compelling argument. But these arrangements were abandoned in the wake of the PCI's withdrawal of support for the Andreotti governments nationally in 1979. Even so, the PCI has seen its role of government in the regions and cities as a major element in its overall strategy.

It is difficult to argue that sub-national coalitions have had any autonomous effect on the national level, seeing that coalition actors in the former case have had their hands tied more often than not by their national leaders. Apart from its value for experimenting with new coalition formulas, sub-national politics has nevertheless had indirect effects on or implications for party strategies and for prospective coalition arrangements in Rome. In this sense, the PCI's increased role in governing the cities and some regions (outside the traditional 'Red' areas of central Italy) during the 1970s and sustained reputation for efficient and prudent performance have promoted its legitimacy and potentially its strategic objectives. By contrast, the DC's mismanagement of city government and notorious implication in corrupt practices have contributed to its general problems of credibility in recent times, which in turn have begun to affect adversely its electoral support. Hence, indirectly its local role might weigh against the DC in coalitional arrangements in Rome (it already has in losing it the prime ministership to the Socialists in 1983). Meanwhile, the PSI has played a centre–periphery pivotal role by maintaining coalitions with the PCI sub-nationally, while at the same time rejoining the DC in national government. Altogether, sub-national coalitions have their own importance, but essentially within the framework of general party strategies. Vertical channels operate more top-down than bottom-up, but this question must be pursued further under the next dimension.

(g) The internal party dimension: elite control or elite constraints?

So far we have established that *generally* political authority over coalitional behaviour altogether lay with the national party leaderships, but attention has also been drawn to the importance of factional politics within parties. While the first focussed on actual coalition formation and maintenance and left aside internal party processes over strategic or coalitional options in a broader sense, the second problem raised more directly the basic question of parties as unitary actors or not. The internal party dimension will accordingly be examined from three angles: if the national leaders' authority tends to carry over coalitional behaviour, how is this exercised within the party structures? What about internal divisions over party strategy or coalitional options, either at the national–horizontal level or within vertical channels? And what about bottom-up vertical influences within party structures that 'informally' might act as a constraint on elite behaviour such as by the law of anticipated reactions? In other words, the question of parties as unitary actors relates to the problem of elite control or otherwise.

Firstly, the nature of party structures as a variable in coalition politics has been raised by Groennings, maintaining that the more centralised they are the stronger are parties as coalition actors.[31] This point might be taken one stage further by arguing the same for party leaders in relation to their followers. But how does this work out with the Italian parties, and can we start to categorise them as unitary actors or not? There is certainly a wide disparity between the parties on this count, with the PCI superior in its structural articulation and bureaucratic control and the small parties at the other end of the scale in both respects. The DC as the other mass organisation operates internally by means of more informal procedures, while its formal structure is much less bureaucratic than that of the PCI. Its factions (*correnti*) in particular act as vertical channels of control, as they have also done within the PSI, although the latter's machine has in the past functioned rather loosely. The PSI is in fact an apt example of Groennings' point. While under the centre-left it did suffer from loose internal control within its organisation, weakening Nenni's position as coalition actor *vis-à-vis* the DC, Craxi chose deliberately to tighten up his party's structure to weaken his internal opponents, in this way strengthening the PSI's weight when it re-entered government with the DC in 1980.

As to specific structural elements, it is worth remembering that the national executive organs of the parties (such as the central committees of the PCI and PSI and the national council of the DC) include many sub-national level leaders, who may help to influence party strategy and also transmit decisions downwards. Party congresses provide clues about the internal positions of party leaders, and are an occasion for expounding and even debating strategy before the activist body, although more concerned with broad strategy than actual coalitional options. In the case of the PCI, control by means of its bureaucratic machine is assisted by a strong sense of party solidarity among the membership. With the other parties, whose actual structural mechanisms for control are weaker, governmental office with its patronage facilities may help to cement the authority of the leadership. In general, it may be suggested that a long coalitional experience conditions a party's followers to that particular game; whereas, by contrast, the PCI's own lack of that experience makes it more difficult for that party as a whole to operate in actual coalitional situations, at least at the national level. In other words, the PCI has structural strengths and weaknesses in this respect, and both were illustrated by the 'National Solidarity' experiment of 1976–9.

Secondly, since it is obvious that organisational control cannot be separated from political authority, we must consider what happens when there are differences within the leaderships over strategy. We have already seen the negative effects this has on a party's effectiveness as coalition actor in contrasting the leaderships of Nenni and Craxi in the PSI, but this question needs further discussion beyond leader-personalities. The best example here is clearly the DC because of its long history in government and the importance of its institutionalised factions. As noted, its *correnti* act as vertical control mechanisms, but they are also rival channels of power and patronage. It follows that the internal balance of the *correnti*, what form of intra-party coalition or of divisions exist between them, is crucial to the translation of the DC's strategy into coalitional choices. There has even been evidence of cross-party inter-factional links, such as between DC *correnti* and individual leaders of other parties, of an informal nature. It has been known over the past decade that certain DC leaders, and behind them their *correnti*, have preferred a coalition with the PSI, while others have leaned more towards an arrangement with the PCI. During the 'National Solidarity' governments, the DC was led by an internal coalition called the 'Area Zac' (named after the then party secretary Zaccagnini) of several *correnti* 'open' to an alliance with the Communists, including *morotei* and *andreottiani* (the *correnti* of the two most prominent DC leaders supporting that strategy). Subsequently, Zaccagnini's position was weakened by the assassination of Moro, the most skilled of the party leaders in weaving inter-*correnti* alliances within the DC, and in 1980 he was replaced by a different internal coalition which favoured a coalition with the PSI. The only party in Italy where factions do not predominate internally is the PCI. However, to claim that the PCI is simply or unreservedly a case of a unitary actor in its relations with other parties is difficult, if not a travesty of its internal processes, if one considers the differences that have emerged over actual choices as well as party strategy in general within the national executive organs. This problem was intensified by the PCI's rapprochement with power during its external support for the Andreotti governments of 1976–9, as witnessed in the lively debates in the central committee over the decision to demand full entry to the government in December 1977.

Thirdly, when such differences arise at the top of party structures they can percolate downwards, especially if there exist rival organised channels like the *correnti*. For instance, the territorial variation in the balance between the DC *correnti* is one key as to why that party may prefer one coalitional option in one locality and a different one elsewhere. But what about vertical influences the other way? This is very difficult to measure, not least because such influences may be indirect or even confidential within party ranks. However, certain relevant indicators are present, notably levels of activism or passivity within party structures.

The general passivity of the DC membership, together with a certain deference in the activist body over grand questions of strategy, tends to moderate the effects of divisiveness from factional politics, although implicitly there were signs during the 'National Solidarity' experiment, for instance, that the anti-Communist belief system that pervades the DC base acted as a sort of constraint on those party leaders pursuing an entente with the PCI. The PCI is a party with a stronger activist base, and this factor emerged publicly in relation to alliance politics in 1978–9. Growing restlessness and discontent within the membership over the meagre policy results from supporting Andreotti began to percolate upwards through intermediate level party functionaries. This combined with trade union militancy over the government's austerity programme and electoral setbacks for the PCI from 1978 to force the party leadership's hand in withdrawing support from Andreotti early in 1979. It is an interesting case of where the party leadership failed to carry the activist body over an alliance relationship, despite the PCI's strong organisational machine.

It may be concluded that party elites cannot automatically take for granted their followers' acquiescence in their coalitional choices and that they take a risk if they do, for successful party leadership involves cultivating vertical as well as horizontal links within party structures. This problem is, however, less in the case of the small parties, which have low memberships as well as weak and unarticulated structures and depend more on the personal authority of the main leader. This dimension reflects too on the broader question of how far parties are unitary actors, as clearly the stronger its elite control the more effective a party's performance as coalition partner. But, equally, no leader is free from actual or potential internal constraints, and these may condition his behaviour towards other parties; indeed they may also be exploited by them.

(h)   Socio-political factors in Italian coalitional behaviour

We are now moving to what may be called the 'deeper' side of Italy's *partitocrazia* in considering parties and their social bases, and how this relationship might affect their coalitional behaviour. Behind this, the broad question of political culture appears, for, as Groennings has said, public values and norms have a bearing on coalition formation in, for example, 'influencing the parties' views of their compatibility and thereby affecting their motivation'.[32] It is possibly a fair assumption that the prevalence of coalition politics in Italy ever since the war has habituated the public to its practice; on the other hand, the constant picture of Byzantine intrigue conveyed by the media would reinforce any impression of elite opportunism. In fact, the recent trend has been of a growing public criticism of political elites. This may be related to basic changes in mass political behaviour since the late 1960s (participatory demands, increasing issue consciousness and a more critical awareness of political activity); it has been encouraged by mounting evidence of scandal and corruption, and it has begun to express itself through a new volatility in electoral behaviour. This last feature makes the calculations of political actors more difficult, for previously Italy has been remarkable for its high level of voting stability.

In examining this socio-political dimension, the factors which may have a bearing on coalitional behaviour are really probabilistic rather than ascertainable. However, there are a variety of indicators which point once more to possible indirect constraints on elites. In the first place, politicians choose to interpret public opinion in certain ways. On a particular point, it has long been a common assumption among political elites in Rome that the public does not take kindly to a party which is seen to initiate the collapse of a coalition. This may well induce the kind of evasive political language we noted earlier in Italian coalition politics, but there have been frequent signs that this has restrained some party leaders, particularly if an early election is one likely outcome of a government crisis. More broadly, party leaders have in certain circumstances (economic crisis, political situations of overriding national importance) argued the need for wide social consensus at the base of coalitional options. This societal reason behind 'over-large' coalitions was present during the immediate post-war constituent phase following the defeat of Fascism; and it reappeared with the 'National Solidarity' experiment, occasioned as this was by the breakdown of previous coalition formulas but against a background of the growing recession.

Both examples were forms of semi-consociationalism, but they were temporary because, whatever reasons or justifications were presented, they ultimately conflicted with party interests and the dynamics of polarisation, as the end of 'National Solidarity' illustrated. There has been a curious vicious circle about politicians' behaviour on this question: consociational beliefs among them have served as a motive in coalitional options out of a concern for political stability, and yet the very social fragmentation which lay behind these beliefs has itself prevented institutionalisation of the 'grander' version of over-large coalitions. There is therefore a complex interplay between political and societal considerations, as shown already before by the differentiated picture of issue cleavages. While the parties' bases tend to be structured around traditional socio-economic variables, and interest groups have operated via their allied parties in exerting influence on the coalitional process, this pattern has in recent times begun to loosen up with social change and also political discontent growing. In general, the onset of the recession and increasing social tension have made it more difficult for the parties to maintain or control a social consensus. Accordingly, party leaders have found less room for manoeuvre in their coalitional options.

Greater unpredictability in public reactions to political events and party behaviour over them has made the calculations of coalition actors even more difficult. The old problem of the low level of political information among the public generally remains, despite the growth in issue consciousness, although it could be said to generate at worst a passive form of cynicism. Nevertheless, the rise of issue consciousness does suggest heightened risks for coalition actors, as survey evidence shows that the more Italians read about politics the more intolerant they become of political elites.[33] The quality papers usually report in much detail on the day-by-day manoeuvres of coalition politics in Rome, but the Italians are not avid readers of political reporting.[34] Also, with few exceptions the papers are linked to party or economic interests, so that a distorted picture is conveyed. Moreover, the very complexity of Italian coalition politics – its multi-dimensional nature, as explained in this chapter – is in any case virtually impossible to project with any objectivity to what is still a fairly unsophisticated public.[35] Opinion surveys as published do report regularly on the standing of the parties and the popularity of different political leaders, but only intermittently on how coalitional arrangements affect either of these,[36] so they cannot be considered a dependable source for politicians to make calculated risks in coalition politics. All this confirms the scepticism about rationality in coalitional behaviour, if one brings into the discussion parties' relationships with the electorate. With multi-party systems like the Italian one, this has always been a questionable thesis and in the light of changes in mass behaviour just discussed it must be even more open to doubt. The Italian political scientist Paolo Farneti, writing at the end of the 'National Solidarity' governments and in the run-up to the 1979 general election, commented on this as follows:

> The voters cannot at all think about voting in a way that would facilitate the formation
> of governments; rather on the contrary. As is only natural, they vote for the party with

which they identify, or for reasons of ideology or self-interest, or for both of these (as is so in the majority of cases). In the event of a party with which its voters identify giving signs that it wishes to form alliances, the voters of that party penalise it heavily, because the voters want those parties with which they identify to come to power by themselves and not by means of the arrangements and the compromises that necessarily characterise coalition governments.[37]

Klaus von Beyme has gone further by arguing that 'the paradoxical results of elections in some European multi-party systems indicate that the burden of rationality is too heavy for many voters: a vote given for a certain party does not necessarily increase its chances of entering the government; it may even diminish them'.[38] It is useful here, using the arithmetical factor again, to distinguish between statistical dictates set by the electorate in their 'unwisdom' and political signals sent out by them by means of electoral movement. Both may have an effect on coalition formation and even coalition maintenance. A prominent example of the former must be the rise in PCI support in the 1976 election, which required the DC to reach an accommodation with that party in the new legislature. This same result also reflected positively on the PCI's credibility, thus signalling to the other parties that an agreement with it was less likely to have negative repercussions. In fact the PSI took this message, and refused to co-operate in government unless the PCI were involved. Another example was Andreotti's formation of a centre-right coalition in 1972–3 (with the inclusion of the right-wing PLI and the exclusion of the PSI) as a direct attempt to check the alarming rise in voting support for the neo-Fascist MSI at this time, threatening as it did the (more right-wing) electoral base of the DC. More recently, the DC's acquiescence in the PSI's demand for the prime ministership in 1983 was an outcome of the former's unprecedented drop in support in the election of that summer. Evidently, it has more often been electoral movement rather than election results as such which has occasioned change in coalitional arrangements in Italy, seeing that the importance of the second is diminished by the tendency for over-large coalitions.

   This discussion of the socio-political dimension suggests there is still much truth in Samuel Barnes' dictum that there is a basic dichotomy in Italian politics between the policy game and the electoral game.[39] Nevertheless, the linkages between the two, not always clear and often indirect though they may be, are such that what goes on inside the *palazzo* cannot in reality ignore activity in the *piazza* of Italian politics.

(i)   Environmental and external influences on Italian coalitions

It is already apparent that the most important environmental or external factor affecting Italian coalitions, especially over the past decade, has been the international economy. The odds against government success have lengthened so that, combined with the weaknesses of the Italian political system, we have a scenario hardly conducive to easy coalitional relationships: hard decisions have to be taken, if such decisions are not for reasons of coalitional convenience postponed, and these involve establishing priorities which are likely to alienate one party from another in government, if not altogether lower their electoral prospects. The social and political consequences of the austerity programme of the Andreotti governments of 1976–9 are just one example of where a significant initiative at cross-party co-operation came unstuck. The conclusion may therefore be drawn that policy immobilism and hence coalition deterioration, if not disintegration, are the likely outcome of operating under such difficult circumstances as economic crisis; whereas policy dynamism and coalition survival, if not harmony, are more probable in times of economic growth, if we look back to the period of De Gasperi. This is a law applicable to many other countries, except that with Italy the system's own deficiencies exacerbate this problem.

There is one other particular external influence over Italy's coalitions deriving from her nature as a 'penetrated system' or one where domestic and international factors interrelate closely with possibly two-way effects. We are talking about international constraints from efforts by some Western allies of Italy, above all the USA, to influence coalitional options in Rome specifically against the political left. Such intervention, invariably channelled through the country's embassy in the Italian capital, has been motivated by considerations of ideology and international strategy, the latter because of Italy's geopolitical location in the Mediterranean. It is one of the more arcane factors in Italian coalition politics, to which prime ministers or some ministers, particularly of the DC, have been privy, although on occasions such external influences have become semi-public. Notably, this happened during the 1976 parliamentary election when the prospect of a PCI role in government was taken seriously abroad. Kissinger, then US Secretary of State, warned Italian voters of the 'serious consequences' if this should happen. Normally, however, pressure has been exerted privately on leaders of the centre-right governing parties, though with what actual effect it is usually difficult to ascertain. Certain examples are, however, common knowledge, especially the effective US veto over Socialist participation in government in the later 1950s. Arthur Schlesinger, adviser to President Kennedy, who eventually lifted that veto in the early 1960s because of the PSI's break with the PCI, summed this up:

> The policy of the United States before Kennedy had been one of purposeful opposition to the opening to the Left. The reasons were clear enough: the Eisenhower administration did not trust Nenni; it believed him to be a neutralist if not still at heart a fellow traveller; and it did not want social and economic reform in Italy.[40]

Less is known as yet about the attempts by the American and also some West European governments to exert influence over the PCI question a decade later. Andreotti, in his published diary on this period, is uninformative and somewhat scathing about external pressures, although Kissinger in his memoirs makes no secret of his mistrust for 'the wily Moro' and his 'sponsorship' of a growing PCI influence on the Italian government. In one aside, he remarked that 'these trends ... were hotly contested inside and outside the US government' and quoted from a State Department memorandum to President Nixon urging that Washington 'keep the problem under close scrutiny, and continually assess the means of using our resources to make our view known in a discreet but effective fashion'.[41]

In general, it should be pointed out that if such external pressure were influential it remained one among several different determinants and constraints in Italian coalition politics. So far as we know, such pressures have been applied by means of subtle or less subtle threats about links between Washington and Rome, appeals to Western solidarity, the financing of Italian parties of the centre-right (as the Lockheed scandal revealed) or simply the blandishment of leading Italian politicians (who are invariably given red-carpet treatment on visits to the USA). Such external influence may, however, operate more by the law of anticipated reactions. Italian leaders have tended to go out of their way to consult American leaders or officials in Washington at times when new coalitional options are under consideration in Rome. Bettino Craxi was, for instance, assiduous in cultivating the Reagan administration during the years before his appointment as Italy's first Socialist Prime Minister.

(j)   Conclusion

The multi-dimensional approach adopted by this book has been found very applicable to the Italian case of coalitional behaviour; indeed, all seven dimensions have been found relevant in their various ways, and therefore useful in unscrambling what is undeniably a complex example of this political phenomenon. Certainly, interlinkages between the different dimensions have surfaced in the discussion, such as ideology and its interplay with other factors. This has been particularly pertinent for understanding the PCI's alliance relationships with other parties, as involving not just a problem of ideology but also its nature as a party in other respects. Again, the arithmetical factor – the focus of much formal coalition theory – has appeared under various dimensions, emphasising its interplay with a variety of political determinants. In short, this chapter has proceeded by accepting conceptually that coalitional behaviour, at least in Italy, is an inherently complex affair. One is reminded of the judgement of one student of Italian politics that in the real world behaviour arises from the interplay between the 'pulling' environment and the 'pushing' attitude,[42] except that with coalition politics there are additional angles, as outlined in the discussion of dimensions above.

Despite its central importance to the government of that country, the subject of coalitional behaviour in Italy has long been an area neglected in research. It soon becomes clear, however, that the main problem in studying this subject is not so much lack of evidence as the lack of a comprehensive interpretative approach, for too often in the past judgements about Italian coalitional behaviour have been one-dimensional. The key to such a multi-dimensional approach lies in the all-embracing nature of Italy's *partitocrazia* or 'party democracy'. This is really obvious when looking at how this country's system actually operates; in fact, some of the literature on the political parties has begun to indicate such an approach, although more on specific aspects than as a broad interpretation of the problem. In other words, the answer to Italy's complex coalition politics lies with the various political parties acting separately and together; that is, any understanding of this subject has to proceed from an examination of what happens inside the political parties in the full sense rather than merely inside the state institutions as such. An outside view of the subject may well give the impression of backstairs intrigue among political elites, but in reality party leaders are subject to a multiplicity of different influences and determinants. They are less free to do what they prefer than is commonly assumed, although admittedly in applying the multi-dimensional approach presented here there is substantial room for variation between the parties.

In applying the different dimensions, certain ones have been more straight-forward than others and, perhaps predictably, the most difficult to assess has been motivation. This has demanded careful and differentiated handling, particularly on the central question of the power motive as against the policy motive, although generally the conventional left–right spectrum is still valid as a framework. It is this major feature of ideology in Italian coalition politics where the formal theories have most of all pointed in the right direction. Otherwise, they have offered very limited mileage in a close analysis of the Italian case because here they have been found to be too narrow in focus (especially in viewing political parties as no more than institutional actors), too formalistic and deterministic and above all too static in their approach to the subject. Some of their assumptions are not very applicable or are very simplistic, as over such matters as parties as unitary actors, party motivations as being broadly similar and of course rationality in coalitional decision-making. In conclusion, therefore, a dynamic model of Italian coalitional behaviour that attempts to steer a course between theoretical elegance and political reality has to incorporate the full implications of Italy's party democracy.

Notes

Thanks are given to Luigi Graziano of Turin University for his careful criticisms of the original draft of this chapter, as well as to other members of the ECPR workshop for their helpful comments. This chapter draws on the author's own research project on Italian coalitional behaviour, primarily based on elite interviews with party and government leaders, parliamentarians and party organisers at both national and regional/local levels. The results of this project are to be published as *Political Parties and Coalitional Behaviour in Italy: an interpretative study*, by Croom Helm, London, in 1987.

1. *The Times*, 7 May 1982.
2. *Guardian*, 26 January 1972.

3. Giovanni Sartori, 'European political parties: the case of polarised pluralism' in J. LaPalombara and M. Weiner (eds.), *Political Parties and Political Development* (Princeton University Press, 1966), pp. 153–4.
4. Mario Caciagli, 'Partiti e sistema partitico in Italia: un trend report', paper presented to ECPR standing group on Southern European Politics, Barcelona, November 1982, p. 1.
5. For a detailed discussion of this, see chapter 1 in the author's forthcoming book mentioned above.
6. E.g. R. Putnam, *The Beliefs of Politicians: ideology, conflict and democracy in Britain and Italy* (Yale University Press, 1973). See also Paolo Farneti, *Il Sistema dei Partiti in Italia, 1946–1979* (Il Mulino, 1983).
7. Giuseppe Di Palma, *Surviving without Governing: the Italian parties in parliament* (University of California Press, 1977).
8. Giuseppe Di Palma, *Political Syncretism in Italy: historical coalition strategies and the present crisis* (University of California Press, 1978).
9. Alan Zuckerman, *Political Clienteles in Power: party factions and cabinet coalitions in Italy* (Sage, 1976). See also his *The Politics of Faction: Christian Democratic rule in Italy* (Yale University Press, 1979).
10. Sidney Tarrow, 'Historic compromise or bourgeois majority?: Eurocommunism in Italy, 1976–1979' in Howard Machin (ed.), *National Communism in Western Europe* (Methuen, 1983), p. 141.
11. Alberto Marradi, 'Italy: from "Centrism" to crisis of the centre-left coalitions' in Eric C. Browne and John Dreijmanis (eds.), *Government Coalitions in Western Democracies* (Longman, 1982), p. 55.
12. *Ibid.* pp. 53–5.
13. E.g. work by R. Putnam and R. Leonardi on regional party elites, published as *La Pianta e le Radici: il radicamento dell'istituto regionale nel sistema politico italiano* (Il Mulino, 1985). Also, Geoffrey Pridham, *The Nature of the Italian Party System: a regional case-study* (Croom Helm, 1981).
14. R. Axelrod, *Conflict of Interest: theory of divergent goals with applications to politics* (Markham, 1970), p. 198.
15. Zuckerman, *Political Clienteles in Power*, p. 35.
16. See Sabino Cassese, 'Is there a government in Italy? Politics and administration at the top' in R. Rose and E. Suleiman (eds.), *Presidents and Prime Ministers* (American Enterprise Institute, 1980), pp. 171–202.
17. C. Cioffi-Revilla, 'The political reliability of Italian governments: an exponential survival model,' *American Political Science Review*, June 1984, pp. 318–37.
18. Lawrence C. Dodd, *Coalitions in Parliamentary Government* (Princeton University Press, 1976).
19. See above, note 3.
20. E.g. see Giuseppe Tamburrano, *Perche solo in Italia No* (Laterza, 1983).
21. See above, note 16.
22. See Pridham, *The Nature of the Italian Party System*, chapter 1(c).
23. Paolo Farneti, *Diario Italiano* (Rizzoli, 1983), p. 51.
24. On this, see Putnam, *The Beliefs of Politicians*.
25. See Geoffrey Pridham, 'Party politics and coalition government in Italy' in Vernon Bogdanor (ed.), *Coalition Government in Western Europe* (Heinemann, 1983), pp. 216–17.
26. Samuel Barnes, 'Italy: opposition on left, right and centre' in R. Dahl, *Political Oppositions in Western Democracies* (Yale University Press, 1966), p. 317.
27. Grant Amyot, *The Italian Communist Party* (Croom Helm, 1981), pp. 215–16.
28. See Geoffrey Pridham, 'Parties and coalitional behaviour in Italian local politics: conflict or convergence?' *European Journal of Political Research*, September 1984, pp. 223–41.
29. According to a study of the Cattaneo Institute, Bologna, there were in the mid-1980s as many as 65 different combinations of parties in alliances administering Italy's more than 8,000 *comuni* (see Arturo Parisi (ed.), *Luoghi e Misure della Politica* (Il Mulino, 1984).)
30. See Pridham, *The Nature of the Italian Party System*, passim.
31. S. Groennings, *The Study of Coalition Behaviour* (Holt, Rinehart and Winston, 1970), p. 454.
32. *Ibid.*, p. 453.
33. Interview with Ennio Salamon, director of Doxa Institute of Public Opinion Research, Milan, 18 May 1984.
34. *Ibid.* Of the roughly 40 per cent of Italians who read the daily newspapers only 10–15 per cent pay attention to the political coverage, according to Salamon.

35. According to Salamon, the average Italian does not understand the 'specific aspects' of coalition politics because he 'has the impression of a difficult language, a very difficult language', in reference to the style of coalition terminology.

36. Doxa has published only a few special reports on this question, and these have been reported briefly in the political weeklies. The weekly *Panorama* publishes fairly regular reports from Demoskopea on the standing of the parties, however.

37. Farneti, *Diario Italiano*, p. 167. This is a collection of articles by the author in the weekly *Il Mondo* during 1976–80. The quotation is from an article dated 23 March 1979.

38. Klaus von Beyme, 'Governments, parliaments and the structure of power in political parties' in H. Daalder and P. Mair (eds.), *Western European Party Systems: continuity and change* (Sage, 1983), p. 343.

39. Samuel Barnes, *Representation in Italy: institutionalised tradition and electoral choice* (University of Chicago Press, 1977), p. 134 and *passim*.

40. Arthur Schlesinger, *A Thousand Days* (Mayflower Dell, 1965), p. 677.

41. Henry A. Kissinger, *The White House Years* (Weidenfeld and Nicolson, 1979), pp. 920–1.

42. See Putnam, *The Beliefs of Politicians*, p. 3.

IO *Party coalitions in the first democratic period in Spain, 1977–1982*

(a) The neglect of coalition studies in Spain

In 1977, after a dictatorship of some forty years, Spain agreed to a democratic system. The passing of a system based on the denial of liberties and competitive elections to another dominated by political parties and electoral results was, as is well known, peaceful, having been attained by means of a pact between reformist groups of the Franco regime and the parties of the democratic opposition.[1]

Immediately following the elections of 15 June 1977, the Cortes proceeded to work on the Constitution in a climate of general consensus; at the same time, the main parties signed the so-called Moncloa Pact of 1977, which was of a political, social and economic nature. Simultaneously, the problems related to autonomy began to resolve themselves with the adoption of devolutionary measures negotiated between the government and nationalist or regionalist groups.

Thus, the idea of a pact, negotiation, agreement, consensus, etc. came to form the substratum upon which the Spanish constitutional system has been built, and caught the immediate attention of all political observers, who were surprised at the breadth of this policy of collaboration between parties and social forces of widely differing tendencies.

However, although every study has indicated the importance of this policy to the consolidation of the democratic system, the subject of cross-party alliances has been studied only in an indirect and practically marginal way in the context of studies on the party system. Paradoxical though this may seem, it is not absolutely strange. In Spain, it is not only democracy which is young, but also political science. The latter has devoted its attention primarily to the study of a system of rapidly changing parties with profound regional variations and, to this end, it has focussed particularly on the analysis of electoral results and the right–left axis.

This is an area which has a sound empirical basis, with less exhaustive data than its European counterparts, but with comparable techniques. On the other hand, it does not have at its disposal scientific monographs on the parties, since the mechanisms for relating parties, interest groups and the electorate are practically unknown. In this context, the policies adopted by the parties have not been studied in detail and, to be specific, the subject of cross-party alliances has been more or less ignored. Consequently, any reference to this subject has to be found in an indirect and descriptive way in studies purporting to explain the alternatives to, and perspectives on, the party system.[2]

At any rate, perhaps this oversight on the part of political scientists in their neglect of cross-party coalitions is not due simply to the magnitude of tasks facing them in Spain. It may also be that there has been a belief that authentic coalitions have never actually existed in Spain. Until the present time, the governments of the Unión de Centro Democrático (UCD) during 1977–82 have been as monocoloured or one-party as that of the Partido Socialista Obrero Español (PSOE) from 1982, therefore seeming to render useless the various formal theories on cross-party negotiations.

That, in effect, has been the case. Because a long list of governments, whether minority, majority, coalition or monocoloured, has not been available, it is impossible to say whether or not the assertions of formal theory are being fulfilled in Spain. However, abandoning the methodological contributions made by these theorists does not help us to understand the effects of the dynamics of collaboration and opposition between the various Spanish political parties. This is why it is absolutely essential to try to examine in the closest detail the various components of coalition politics in Spain, trying to assess its different dimensions in order to understand the first steps of the democratic system.

The consensus politics of the constituent period during 1976–8 was the result of an informal coalition. It was not presented in the form of a government alliance; no express and binding agreement existed in parliament; at no institutional level had the different parties adopted a stable compromise which would avoid producing serious tensions, and yet a 'grand coalition' did exist. Its limits were imprecise (and later on we shall show in what way the different parties participated), but it was clear that it did employ a certain method of policy-making which strengthened the desire for negotiation between the leadership of the parties, and which demobilised the activist bases, the electorate and the interest groups in order to facilitate the adoption of specified decisions.

Consequently, if we are to understand this situation of informal coalition, we should ask ourselves not how the coalitions were formed, but rather how the decisions were taken. Thus, with this change of perspective, it may perhaps be useful to take into consideration the models of coalitions based on games theory in order to see to what extent it can provide us with clues to help us understand the internal dynamics of cross-party collaboration–opposition and also the extent to which its contribution is limited.

(b)   Along the paths of formal coalition theory

It would be a mistake to think that the period when the Constitution was being written up is characterised by only one type of cross-party relationship, the so-called consensus one. Actually, in Spain, the term 'consensus' does not convey a precise concept; instead, it points to a certain spirit which has been used to focus upon some specific problems. To understand this spirit, it is necessary first to construct a general overview of the formation in parliament of the majorities needed to shape the Constitution, and then to make a detailed study of the different kinds of cross-party relationships.

Above all, it is necessary to clarify that the term 'consensus' has no legal significance, since it refers to the way in which a political process develops, while the approval of a certain legal text consists of a legal procedure. The intermediate step between politics and law is made in parliament in accordance with one rule: the formation of majorities. A close observation of these majorities helps us to appreciate the different coalitions which form within the consensus dynamic. (On the strength of the parties in the Spanish parliament (Cortes), see Table 10.1, p. 235.)

Thus, in the Cortes elected on 15 June 1977, the seven parliamentary groups present[3] could ally themselves hypothetically in 127 different ways – according to the combinatorial formula $2^{np} - 1$ (where np indicates the number of parties or parliamentary forces) – and out of these 127 alliances, 63 got an absolute majority of votes in the Congress of Deputies (lower house of the Cortes). Therefore, any legal text could be approved by any of these 63 numerically possible alternatives.[4]

One should be aware, in any case, that this number is only an indicative figure, because parliamentary procedure offers in fact greater flexibility than merely showing positions in favour or against an issue. In principle, the parties can vote, becoming part of the majority or minority, but they can also attenuate their positions by abstention or by absence. Of course, abstention or absence involves a correlative decrease from absolute majority to simple or relative majority, and so it can be said that groups which abstain or are absent have allowed approval and thus form part of the majority alliance without necessarily altering the existence of those 63 mentioned alliances. Nevertheless, even if this appraisal is mathematically correct, it will not be so in practice unless it signifies a reduction in partisan stances.

Another complexity to be added to the previous one is the procedural fact that the parties can vote on a given issue at different times. Thus, one parliamentary group can be against a proposal in the standing committee and accept it in the plenary session; or it can vote first for its own amendment, against a certain regulation, and after this has been rejected, join with the majority vote which has

Table 10.1 *Results of Spanish national elections, 1977–82*

	1977		1979		1982	
	%	seats	%	seats	%	seats
UCD	34.7	165	34.3	168	7.1	12
PSOE	29.2	118	30.0	121	48.4	202
PCE	9.2	20	10.5	23	4.1	4
AP	8.3	16	5.8	9	26.2	106
PSP	4.5	6	—	—	—	—
CiU	2.8	11	2.6	8	3.7	12
PNV	1.6	8	1.5	7	1.9	8
UDC	0.9	2	—	—	—	—
ERC	0.7	1	0.7	1	0.6	1
EE	0.3	1	0.5	1	0.5	1
Ind.	0.3	2	0.3	1	—	—
FN	—	—	2.0	1	0.5	—
PSA	—	—	1.8	5	0.5	—
HB	—	—	0.9	3	1.0	2
CDS	—	—	—	—	2.9	2

drawn up the proposal. Finally, the parties can make their positions more flexible by playing the double game of presenting an amendment and then retracting it before it can be put to a vote or by suggesting 'in voce' amendments.

None of these activities denies as such the validity of the assertion that the Congress could establish 63 different alliances to obtain a majority, but they indicate how difficult it would be to make an effective study based on the formal criteria of the theory of alliances. In fact, the wording of the Constitution cannot be compared with the formation of a government in which, with all of their pertinent subtleties, the conceptions of the formal theories could be applied in the belief that majority and opposition are mutually exclusive in allotting ministerial positions, thus allowing those alliances called 'minimum winning coalitions' to be formed.

Our problem can be framed precisely in opposing terms: that the logic of a constituent period forces one to look for the broadest coalitions possible. Nevertheless, the affirmation that 63 possible alliances could be formed is not completely useless, especially at that time in Spain when relations between parties had not yet been defined. It is helpful, then, to know what consequences can be deduced from the fact that in the Congress it was possible to make 63 different alliances to form a majority.

In this sense, the most important proof here is evident in its paradoxical nature. The number of majority alliances hypothetically possible in a parliament does not depend on the distribution of the seats among the groups (for example, if three parties obtain representation, there should be exactly $2^{3-1} = 4$ possible governments independent of how the seats are divided up among the parties), and logically it would seem that the figure which we have been repeating has no bearing on how the internal dynamic of the Congress is structured. Nevertheless, this is not the case, and the actual distribution of theoretical alliances is highly significant: for out of the 63 majority alliances, in 61 the UCD presence was necessary.

We are now no longer in a formal realm. For the moment we apply an abstract and timeless formula, voluntarily leaving aside the complex interplay of political factors which led the UCD to direct the process of transformation from an authoritarian system to a democratic one, we run against the fact that the parliamentary power of the centrist party was so strong that it became indispensable for any legislative solution which arose. In other words, there were no majority alternatives. The government party could choose between 61 different strategic options, and it should be emphasised that it could do so without fear of being left on the margin. In fact, the other two majorities – (PSOE, PCE, AP, MC, Mx) and (PSOE, PCE, AP, MC, PNV, Mx) – are outflanking, and break the basic rule on (ideological) connection or adjacency which should exist among the participants of an alliance, and thus would occur infrequently and when dealing with less important matters.[5]

Before beginning a detailed study, we already have one of the requirements for the formation of a parliamentary majority in Spain: the obliged consent of the UCD, since its lack of support would veto any possible decision. It can be concluded, therefore, that the Constitution which resulted from the constituent period is that which the centrist party wished or permitted. The projects of the other groups could not attempt to substitute the position of the UCD; the UCD's capacity to veto meant that other parliamentary groups were only effective if they presented a model which could be integrated with the UCD model.

Thus, the dynamic of the whole constituent process did not develop as a bipolar confrontation in which two poles – even being unequal in size – were trying to achieve hegemony. This point should be emphasised, because it is possible to imagine other combinations in the Congress with the same political groups in which, due to a greater equality between the two principal parties, one of them would not have been absolutely necessary in all of the combinations.

The alliances possible in 1977 were an extension of the UCD. In fact, this is the principal contribution of the formal theory. Whereas the classic analyses of the Spanish party system discussed to what extent there existed a two-party or a multi-party system, the formal alliance theory explains the strengths and weaknesses of the parties at the moment of decision-taking. Driven to take effective action (because they could not absent themselves from such an important process as the working out of the Constitution), they were obliged to reach an agreement with the UCD because in no way could they ignore it. The explanation for this period cannot be found in the confrontation between two sides, but instead in the structuring of a parliamentary negotiation by the UCD based on the cross-party compromises which they wished to reach.

This does not imply, however, a hegemonic situation in the governing party since, as it did not have the absolute majority of the members of the Congress, it was forced to look for alliances; with, of course, the relative freedom to orient them in the direction that it desired. In a chamber of 350 members, 166 of the representatives, as the UCD had, would normally have been enough to create a homogeneous government,[6] but the UCD could not act alone to establish the constitutional system. Therefore, we should return to the list of the 63 alliances to see what options were open to it.

(c) Hypothetical coalitions and the historical dimension

Naturally, it is impossible to comment, even briefly, about each one of these coalitions and we are limited to those which *a priori* seem to have the most political relevance to the period in question. The reduction which we propose (real for the centrist party) does not deny that in certain concrete ways those alliances excluded could not appear at particular times; but we are trying to emphasise the large axes – still at a hypothetical level – around which a cross-party dynamic could be structured.

Therefore, we shall eliminate to begin with those alliance agreements which are not sufficiently connected through intermediate parties: thus, for example, the union between the UCD and PCE and all of those following a similar scheme. We also believe that Minoría Catalana (MC) and the Partido Nacionalista Vasco (PNV) can be identified and compared in their desire to regulate the political system based on their common nationalist ideology; thus, those alliances in which only one of these parties participates should be excluded, that is those such as UCD–MC or UCD–PNV. In the same way, we shall eliminate all of those in which the Grupo Parlamentario Mixto (Mx) is present, since its inclusion would not indicate the political direction we are looking for.

In this way, initial complexity is limited, although the following basic alternatives remain:

```
AP–UCD
UCD————————PSOE
UCD–MC–PNV
AP–UCD————————PSOE
UCD————————PSOE–PCE
AP–UCD–MC–PNV
UCD–MC–PNV–PSOE
AP–UCD————————PSOE–PCE
AP–UCD–MC–PNV–PSOE
UCD–MC–PNV–PSOE–PCE
AP–UCD–MC–PNV–PSOE–PCE
```

The first of these alternatives, the agreement between the UCD and AP, had 182 representatives, which makes it the smallest of the mentioned coalitions. Nevertheless, this coalition can be considered in terms of some socio-political coincidences which parliamentary members in both groups shared.[7] In fact, only in these two groups could representatives who had formed part of the political elite during Franco's regime find a place, thus enabling them to remake old alliances.

Having belonged to the Francoist elite has a bearing on two different areas which, however, were interconnected due to the peculiarities of that organic system. In the first place, these two groups shared the 38 representatives who had previously been *procuradores* (representatives) in the Cortes. The figure is important if we keep in mind that it represented 10.8 per cent of the House,[8] while, for instance, the third party in the Congress, the PCE, had only 5.7 per cent of the seats. In the second place, in these two groups 30 representatives (8.5 per cent of the Congress) can be found who had held some position by direct designation of Franco. In addition to these two political factors, it should be added that the majority of the representatives who were on boards of directors in the business sectors were members of UCD and AP.[9]

Nevertheless, these facts should not be considered the sociological basis which mechanically brought the AP and UCD together, apart from the fact that this itself implies a political decision in which other types of reasoning intervene; the same variables which indicate a sociological affinity also indicate that the two groups had internal differences. Up until now we have spoken about the areas they had in common; but what was essential for one group, for the other represented only a small part numerically. Thus, the 'ex-procuradores' represented 81 per cent of the AP and only 15 per cent of the UCD, and those representatives who had held positions directly designed by the dictator were 62.5 per cent of the AP and only 12 per cent of the centrist party. Therefore, the socio-political analysis should not be exclusively focussed upon this coalition option: the rest should also be considered.

A second type of alliance could be situated – and here we are speaking generally for reasons we are about to explain – on the right of the political spectrum, widening the agreement between the AP and UCD (which, more than right-wing, should be considered a restructuring of Francoism) to the Minoría Catalana (MC) and to the PNV, or else putting these two groups together and excluding AP, which would give it a more centrist character. Nevertheless, after pointing out these possibilities we should stop to consider that the terms 'right' and 'left' were ambiguous during that time.

What use is it to classify as right-wing parties which were divided in terms of their evaluation of Francoism? Should the electorate supporting the MC and PNV during that time be considered right-wing? Spanish politics was not exclusively determined by the right–left axis, and the influence which the relationship between the centre and periphery had over this duality must be taken into consideration. Thus, we can immediately appreciate how difficult it was for the nationalist groups to unite with the UCD (especially if the AP was included) in a country where the theme of state structure was vehemently discussed.

This contraposition between the state or national parties and the regional parties opens up another range of possible coalitions in which the four national groups are present (or at least some of them), but in which the nationalist parties are excluded. In the broadest terms, this agreement would include *aliancistas*, centrists, Socialists and Communists, while in the narrowest it could proceed to break away from one or both of the two extremes. This large alliance makes sense in terms of the contraposition mentioned between the centre and the periphery; it is only necessary to remember the similarity of interest which could arise in questions like the composition of the Senate or the legislative powers of the Cortes in relation to those of the autonomous communities.

In this type of alliance, which ranges from right to left and leaves the regional parties to one side, the agreement between UCD and PSOE stands out by itself. It concerns a biparty alliance based on common interests shared by, and stemming from the size of, these two large groups. The fact that, together, they have more than 81 per cent of the seats and that, in some way, both were the only two parties with any possibility of forming a government allowed them to lessen their differences, which doubtless existed on other questions. The pact between UCD and PSOE may be based upon an identical way of conceiving the structure of the houses, the formation of the parliamentary groups or the relations between the government and the parliament. This, then, is a coalition to which one should pay special attention.

Due to their nationalist character, the MC and the PNV could fit in with the previously mentioned coalitions, fulfilling in particular the function of bridging the gap between the right and the left; thus, for example, in the case of an agreement between the UCD–MC–PNV–PSOE. Naturally, if we keep in mind all of the aforementioned combinations, in mitigating the confrontation between right and left and nationalist polemics by virtue of the necessities of the constituent process, we arrive at the largest coalition of all: AP–UCD–MC–PNV–PSOE–PCE. But the difficulties of this coalition are also obvious, and therefore it was difficult for this agreement to prevail.

This hypothetical overview, considering possible alliances, has helped to show that the UCD faced different formulas with which to overcome its minority position. This is something which must be kept in mind, because to a greater or lesser degree all these formulas were present at some time or in relation to some particular issue. The formal theory of alliances has suggested an abstract number of possible combinations, which could subsequently be reduced by applying various criteria of proximity or relationship. In the case of Spain, the newness of the political system and of the party system has made it especially difficult to apply these criteria, which are largely abstract, until the system itself has become firmly established.

An example of this difficulty can be seen in the questions 'Which of the parties was closest to the UCD? Was it the AP, since both parties derived from the Franco system? Or the PSOE, because they both sought a moderate electorate? Or the nationalist parties, because they occupied a central position?' These questions could not be answered *a priori*. In fact, in order to understand the alliances which were established it is necessary to make use of a multi-dimensional analysis in which the different cleavages which pass through the party system are taken into account.

The historical dimension of the problem (some leaderships had been formed within the Franco system and others within the opposition), the horizontal/vertical dimension (centrist and nationalist parties) and the sociological dimension of the parties' electorates, for instance, intermingle and combine in various forms to produce or impede collaboration between the parties in this initial phase. However, it is important to take into account that, on the axis of the motivational dimension, the various political actors showed their willingness to reach the fullest possible agreement in an effort to overcome the obstacles which the remaining dimensions represented in contrast to this willingness.

The formal theory has nothing to tell us about this and, consequently, it is necessary to study the operation of the different dimensions of those coalitions which were hypothetically possible.

Indeed, the utilisation of different alliances was vital to the understanding of the informal coalition politics of the constituent period. A grand coalition ranging from the AP to the PCE, including the nationalist parties, was not possible. The only way in which all the parties could participate was by the formation of different alliances depending on the issue at stake. This allowed all the parties to participate in the climate of general consensus, which allowed work on the Constitution to proceed. However, this did not prevent certain strategies from prevailing over others, as we will try to show in the following pages.

(d)   Coalitional behaviour and the overriding motivational dimension

Initially, after the first elections in 1977, the two large parties, the UCD and PSOE, tried to impose their majority by using it as a way of coming to agreements. They were the two most relevant parties in parliament. Their clear electoral victory, facilitated by distortions in the electoral law,[10] gave them 81 per cent in the Congress and any agreement between these two groups made interventions by other groups merely testimonial to this. The UCD could look for other allies but, because of the nature of their programmes, such agreements were difficult to achieve. On the other hand, a terrain of common agreement between the two large parties became a pattern which made them the only ones able to govern, and the only truly nationalised ones. So it was possible to confirm the biparty parliamentary system which reinforced the biparty tendencies which the voters had chosen.

It meant, therefore, that political life revolved around two poles, the government party and the opposition party, which reinforced this biparty system as much as possible. The UCD, nevertheless, was not consolidated enough. Having been created from very diverse political tendencies – liberal, Christian

Democrat, Social Democrat and Francoist – and unified through the figure of Suárez,[11] this party was not homogeneous enough to confront the PSOE which, although it was going through a period of restructuring,[12] had a programme, an ideology and a much more consolidated tradition. The first step in moving towards eventual bipartisanship had to consist of converting this electoral federation of the UCD into one parliamentary group, and then getting rid of all its integral parties, making them into one party. In 1977 this task was easy; not only because of the existence of a strong opposition, but also because of the non-existence of another centrist party, like a Christian Democratic or Liberal one, which made it difficult for the groups which composed UCD to find external points of attraction.

On the left, the same thing happened with the Partido Socialista Popular (PSP). The weakness of its parliamentary representation kept it from disputing, in the future, the Socialist terrain of the PSOE for whom the PSP votes were necessary to beat the government party in new elections. Soon, integration between them would be achieved.

Consolidation of the UCD and reinforcement of the PSOE are the two basic elements in this bipartisan strategy which tries to take space away from the remaining parties. To this end, the first problems in the functioning of the Cortes were resolved by way of an agreement between UCD and PSOE. Thus, when the steering committee was elected, only these two parties got representation. The same thing happened when the subcommittee of parliamentary rules was named. But this strategy was most evident during the debate about the requirements necessary to constitute a parliamentary group. The figure of 15 representatives as the minimum number to form a group, agreed upon by the PSOE and UCD, essentially attempted to reduce the voice of the PSP, forcing it to integrate with the PSOE or with the mixed group, and to limit the influence of the Catalan and Basque members, who were forced to become a single parliamentary group. Parliament then began to form along a biparty model, although the reality of Spain was much more complex due to national, regional and ideological problems.

But resistance to this process was also evident. To make the other parties into satellites was complicated because they had ample forms of support: for instance, nationalist ideology, influence in the trade unions or penetration into the state organisms. The MC and PNV, the PCE or AP could not be kept on the sidelines without producing a serious crisis during the constituent period, which was also characterised by economic difficulties.

Soon, therefore, a new kind of relationship among the parties appeared, characterised by political consensus; that is, by searching for agreements in which all parties could participate, although one should remember that revolving around these agreements were majority and minority positions, and tensions continued to exist between the parties. In fact, together with recognising that all the parliamentary parties had to participate in working out the Constitution, there were attempts by the UCD to guarantee its political domination and attempts by the PSOE to reinforce its role as an alternative; while the remaining parties tried to ensure their function as necessary partners in dialogue.

The first symptoms of this concerted manner of solving relations among the parties manifested themselves in the elaboration of the parliamentary regulations. We have already pointed out that the subcommittee in charge of the first draft had revealed a bipartisan tendency; nevertheless, after an amendment that had been presented by the Communist group, a regulation was approved which took into consideration many of the amendments presented by the minority groups in an attempt to achieve unanimous votes. As a result of this new agreement, the number of components on the steering committee grew to make room for an AP and PCE representative. Similarly, the number of representatives necessary to form a parliamentary group was reduced, which made it possible to divide the Basque–Catalan minority into two parliamentary groups (although this reform was not sufficient to enable the PSP to have their own group).

These were the first landmarks of a period which has been characterised by the word 'consensus', and which would have its prime moments during the drafting of the Constitution and the Moncloa Pacts. With this the party system loses its bipartisan rigidity. Consensus politics makes it more difficult for the PSOE to present itself as a substitute for the UCD in power. Indeed, if the seriousness of the political, economic and social problems demanded a unifying policy approach, the pretensions of the Socialist alternative lost much of their validity. With consensus, the PSOE found itself in the middle of a range of forces which, for different reasons, could find ground for common agreement and move in that direction. Thus, the UCD reinforced its position as the leading party by weakening the PSOE alternative, and in turn the PCE overcame the danger of being left out, by accepting the dominant bipartisanship while gaining credence before broad sectors of the electorate as a party of the system.

The consequences of a consensus policy in its formative influence on the party system do not end here. The possibility that parties with very different origins and ideologies could collaborate on the same approach allowed them to consider themselves as adversaries rather than enemies. But, apart from this undoubtedly positive fact, the way in which agreements were made, negotiated directly by the party leaderships, has caused two less beneficial circumstances: the reinforcement of internal tension inside the parties, and denial of the electorate's participation in the support of party programmes. In this respect, there was a tendency to cut elite–militant–voter links,[13] as well as to encourage a certain distance between society and state which was later expressed in an increase in abstention.

At the same time, the consequences of the consensus were shaping the course of the future functioning of the party system. Nevertheless, this came about in a contradictory way. On the one hand, in many cases the Constitution demanded the prolongation of a consensus atmosphere; on the other, some aspects (the electoral law, censorship motions, etc.) were reinforcing the biparty nature which the UCD and PSOE propagated.

This double dimension, consensus–bipartyism[14] was also present within the autonomous regional framework. While in the Constitution this problem was assimilated by looking for an agreement between the parties involved, when the pre-autonomous regime was generally applied, the government reinforced the biparty aspects of the Spanish political system in all those regions where UCD or PSOE hegemony could not be disputed. The special cases of the Basque Country and Catalonia were resolved in a different way. In Euskadi, the agreement between the UCD and PSOE to leave the PNV off the Basque Council presidency became a symbol for this biparty policy. In Catalonia, the figure of President Tarradellas was used to form a government of unity. To summarise, the formation of the autonomous policy did not cause any problems for the national parties in the party sphere; no nationalist party could assume a position of power from which it could oppose the decisions made by parties acting on the national level.

The requirements of the constituent period had given the Spanish party system a marked peculiarity. Although the tensions between the parties had not disappeared, they found themselves within the framework of the consensual elaboration of the Constitution, of the agreed-upon definition concerning autonomous regional policy and the existence of governments of unity in the autonomous system. Nevertheless, once the Constitution was approved, the nature of the relations between the parties changed. In December 1978, a new phase began which would question the direction of the political process and the competition between the parties.

This is the significance of the general election in 1979. In reality, the peculiarity of the constituent process allowed the government to choose between calling for new elections or submitting to the investiture motion. The decision of the UCD in favour of the first possibility reflected its desire to obtain a larger majority than it had had in the 1977 legislature. This became a polemical issue. On the one hand, municipal elections had not yet been called; on the other, some sectors, especially the Communists, strongly insisted that the elections were unnecessary and that the consensual policy should be continued. In spite of these arguments, the UCD and the PSOE wanted to be the protagonists of a new phase – the former, to govern more easily and without having to negotiate; the latter, to make its alternative proposal a reality. In this context, the nationalist parties and the PCE were the most reticent about calling new elections because the two large parties were likely to be the only beneficiaries.

In any case, the general elections in March 1979 – which we will not analyse here[15] – did not modify in any spectacular way the relations between parties. In spite of the growth of the Partido Socialista de Andalucía (PSA), Euskadiko Eskerra (EE) or Herri Batasuna (HB), the Congress of Deputies maintained a similar distribution of forces. In these conditions, the UCD did not have an absolute majority, even though it was the number one parliamentary party and, together with the PSOE, continued to dominate with 81 per cent of the House. On the other hand, the municipal elections, one month later, marked a fundamental change in the electoral behaviour of the citizens, since the Socialists, Communists and nationalists were clearly the winners.

Each election had given different results. The legislative elections confirmed the UCD and, in general, the political spectrum of the country; the municipal ones gave strength to parties outside the government (except the AP). But both the first elections as well as the second ones fulfilled the same objective: the rupture of consensus politics and the attempt to achieve a hegemonic position. On 30 April 1979 Suárez obtained the investiture and the UCD formed a homogeneous minority government with votes from his party, the AP and PSA. In local government the opposite situation could be seen, the Socialist–Communist pact enlarged to the nationalistic parties where necessary, which took the UCD out of the leadership in practically all of the important cities. Finally, many of the governments of unity in the pre-autonomous regions disappeared, either because of the autonomous regional elections (Catalonia, Euskadi) or because of inter-party conflicts (Valencia, Canary Islands).

The general climate, then, was one of confrontation. The way in which the UCD had resolved the investiture motion indicated not only their desire to form a single government, but also their desire not to compromise themselves with any one legislative agreement. Thus, the government, for each law, would try to come to a pact with another group (nationalists, AP or Socialists) which would allow them to obtain a majority without this following any particular pattern. This policy of the UCD, which needed collaborating parties, could not become assimilated to the consensus approach because it did not imply a negotiated action on the part of the UCD, but instead a previous decision between its internal tendencies and the subsequent support of some other party, depending upon the tendency of the internal winner.

The UCD's pretension to lead the system from a minority position and as a party with little cohesion turned out, however, to be difficult, because it was limited by two types of party confrontation. On the one hand, the UCD was opposing the left on economic, social and ideological matters. On the other hand, the demands of the autonomous regions made relations difficult with the nationalist parties which had similar sociological bases and similar programmes, without the UCD being sure that it would appease the left on this issue.

In any case, it was not in parliamentary politics that the government encountered its principal difficulties. The minority position of the left and their division made it possible for the UCD to govern without any great problem (for example, the controversial Statute of Teaching Centres was approved by 187 votes to 127).

The key to the weakness of the government led by the UCD without any legislation pact can be found outside the parliament. Autonomous regional policy played a predominant role which would have repercussions in the Cortes and in relations between the ties on a national level. The establishment of the autonomous communities would also influence the relations between parties at all regional levels and, finally, the whole Spanish party system.

The elections in March 1980 in Catalonia and Euskadi had opened the doors to one-party governments like those of Convergència i Unió (CiU)[16] and the PNV. Thus the old governments of unity disappear while the PSOE and the UCD see their influence reduced. From then on, the autonomous policy is carried out between two differentiated actors. The nationalist parties make demands and the UCD government concedes or refuses them. When the nationalist parties become protagonists in the regional party subsystems and when the consensus disappears, a radical change has taken place; the centre–periphery confrontation becomes a problem exclusively for the UCD, unlike the situation during the formulation of the Constitution when all of the parties had assumed the two extremes of the problem.

That is why the UCD, acting alone, sought to try to decrease the autonomous regional tension, deciding that the government would not support any initiative which led to extensive autonomy among the remaining pre-autonomous regions. Thus, by making the problems of the regions into a central issue, the failure of the UCD's autonomous policy called into question the UCD as a whole, and not only in certain regions. The referendum for autonomy in Andalusia sparked this situation off. From the very beginning, the decision by the national UCD put the Andalusian UCD into crisis (for example, the resignation of the Minister Clavero Arevalo), but when, on 28 February 1980, the autonomous forces were able to triumph in all the provinces except Almeria, the crisis extended to the whole party and to the government itself, which had to rationalise the autonomous conflicts as a question of state.

In this climate, Suárez decided to remodel the cabinet; but the tensions between the different 'families' in the UCD delayed adopting his strategy, and forming a new government was slow and difficult. Finally, on May 2 1980 the new Suárez government was announced; an occasion the parliamentary parties took advantage of to force a debate in the Congress which the UCD did not want. During this debate, the PSOE, without previously consulting other groups, presented a motion of censure. The results of this motion, which can be seen in Table 10.2, p. 246, show the isolation of the UCD, which lost the AP and PSA votes which had supported it at its investiture.

The censure motion presented by the PSOE signified the definitive presentation of this party as an alternative, moving away from any kind of consensus strategy, and highlighted the fact that the UCD had lost support from minority groups. From this time onwards, the UCD crisis became more and more violent among its different internal tendencies. It must be emphasised that an important part of the internal conflict was caused by the need of the government party, which did not have a majority, to look for pacts with other

10.2 *The crisis of the UCD governments: parliamentary votes, 1980–1*

	Investiture of A. Suárez government, 1980				Censure motion against A. Suárez government, 1980				Investiture of L. Calvo Sotelo government, 1981			
	Yes	No	Abstained	Absent	Yes	No	Abstained	Absent	Yes	No	Abstained	Absent
UCD	168				166				165			
PSOE		116		5	120					117		2
PCE		23			23					23		
AP	9						9		9			
MC			8			7	1		9			
MV		6		1				7		7		
PSA	5				5					4		1
Mx	2	4		3	4	5		3	3	7		3
Total	184	149	8	9	152	166	21	11	186	158		6

groups. This encouraged a conflict between those who wanted to move towards the right and those with more centrist positions.

In fact, as the leaders of the parties had been abandoning the consensus approach, there became visible one of the essential problems of the young Spanish democracy: the lack of internal cohesion of some parties. For various reasons, the UCD and the PCE, which had played an essential role in the search for agreements during the constituent period, were faced from 1980 with serious internal tensions, which in their turn made the production of new global or partial agreements even less attainable. The internal crisis and the external crisis fed upon each other continuously and in an increasingly serious way, as can be seen by the resignation of Suárez and the unsuccessful attempt at a *coup d'état* on 23 February 1981, at the precise moment when the parliamentary representatives were carrying out the investiture of Calvo Sotelo.

The UCD had not succeeded in defining clearly an ideology and policy approach which would place it between the right and the left, between centralism and autonomy; for this reason, each issue developed into an occasion for dissent between the internal tendencies and ended by splitting the party.

Thus, when the early elections of 1982 were called, a group of UCD parliamentary deputies joined AP; another formed the Partido Demócrata Popular (PDP), which presented itself as an electoral coalition with the former; one section remained in the UCD; Suárez had formed his own party, Centro Democrático y Social (CDS) and a final group, after having created the Partido de Acción Democrática (PAD), had merged with the PSOE.

For its part, the PCE was locked in an internal crisis which resulted in the expulsion of some of the more reformist sections (*renovadores*) and splits by groups which favoured a more traditional form of Communism. Basically, this situation was the consequence of the adoption of a Eurocommunist programme which necessitated important changes, especially in the transition from clandestine to legal status. However, to understand the significance of the controversy generated within the PCE, perhaps unlike other Communist parties which have also experienced these two phenomena, one has to take into account that the ideological renewal coincided with the adoption of a consensual policy which increased the feeling of uneasiness between some of the activist groups within the PCE.

Thus, without rival from the right or from the left, in the 1982 elections the PSOE won a landslide electoral victory,[17] forming a one-party government which could count on the support of the majority of parliamentary representatives. Since then, the Spanish political system has been characterised much more by the attempt to reconstruct the parties or to form other new ones than by the question of inter-party coalitions.

(e) Conclusions

After this rapid description of the agreements and conflicts between and within the parties, it is evident that, in a comparative study, the case of Spain presents certain peculiarities deriving from the form of transition from a dictatorship to a democratic system. In the abstract, in democratic countries, we can observe different levels of coalition (governmental, parliamentary, regional and local) or different objectives (access to positions of power, influence over policy-making, etc.). These distinctions are of relative importance in the case of Spain because, basically, the coalitions were established in a less concrete form, although having greater influence; what was sought was a pact to establish and consolidate democracy.

Consequently, it is essential to understand the mechanisms of this pact. However, one cannot achieve this understanding by applying the mathematical models of formal coalition theory. The evidence of this impossibility in a country in which coalitional behaviour had an extremely imprecise nature (minority governments with a multi-directional climate of consensus) has ruled out the use of these models by researchers into the Spanish political transition. As a consequence, it has been found preferable to explain the political dynamics in terms of evolution of electoral results and the ideological distance between the parties.

However, the far-reaching nature of this constituent pact – unable to be studied from formal theory, and pushed aside in classic studies of the party system – forces us to keep in mind, as a central variable, the formal and informal coalitions between the parties which were evident in their decisions. The period 1977–82 is characterised not only by the relative positions of the parties (by their number of votes, by their place on the left–right axis, by their sociological composition, etc.), but, essentially, by the strategies developed by each group. As an example, we can cite the major part played by the PCE – out of proportion to its small number of seats in parliament – in proposing a government of national concentration.

If, as seems clear to us, the party system cannot be viewed separately from coalitional behaviour, the correct way to understand this forces us, conversely, to take into consideration all those elements of the party system which affect coalitions. So, methodologically, the overall proposals which consider the different dimensions of coalitional behaviour are more explanatory than those based on mathematical models, since there exists a continuous link between the alliances and the party system.

This connection leads us to observe the formal and informal Spanish coalitions from a double perspective of contrasting effects. On the one hand, consensus politics served to establish the democracy while, on the other, it contributed to the aggravation of the internal crises of some of the parties. This double effect of building up and breaking down was produced because alliance policy weakened, simultaneously, the risk of cleavages in the party system and the very identity of some of the parties.

In fact, the grand coalition of the constituent period was difficult to maintain. Historically, some groups proceeded from the Franco system, and others from the democratic opposition; sociologically, some were left-wing and others right-wing; territorially, some were centralist and others autonomist. The party leaders, however, pressed for agreements with the remaining parties in order to democratise the system. In this way, a dimension which we might call 'motivational' was imposed on the other dimensions, reducing their effectiveness. The negotiations between the party leaders did not take into consideration the immediate, short-term benefits (a situation which forms part of the basic hypothesis of the formal theory) which had occasioned the negotiations and alliances, in accordance with more or less classic models, but remained subjected to a long-term strategy.

However, these dynamics directed by the leadership had a logical tendency to reduce the points of reference and identity between the electorate, the activists and the party leaderships. These effects surfaced in a spirit seen in the general use of the term of 'disenchantment' (*desencanto*), and in a growing abstentionism at elections (although this should not always be interpreted as a protest against consensus policy); and also in the manifestation of internal tensions within the parties.

The parties in Spain – and the UCD in particular – were not unitary actors. Under these conditions, in a combination of mutual interaction, the internal dimension of the parties hindered coalition policy, at the same time as diminishing the necessity for a constituent pact, any attempt at coalition policy aggravating the crisis of those parties which needed an alliance. The UCD, which was in government without a parliamentary majority, and the PCE, on the sidelines and in the process of ideological transformation, fell victims to this process. On the other hand, the PSOE, the AP and the nationalist parties, which occupied much more clear-cut positions, managed to retain a greater degree of internal stability, which was clearly appreciated by the electorate in 1982.

The 1982 election was the culmination of a process which indicated that the exceptional coalition of 1977 was being replaced by cross-party relationships with a clear distinction between the majority and the opposition. All the characteristics that had led to the UCD being in a good position to reach agreements with all the other parties in the first phase of Spanish democracy turned afterwards into an obstacle to establishing this majority because it was so strongly divided. Consequently, a realistic theory of coalitions is vital to a clear understanding of the relationship between the party system and the political system in Spain.

Appendix. *Party full names*

UCD   Unión de Centro Democrático
PSOE Partido Socialista Obrero Español
PCE   Partido Comunista de España
AP   Alianza Popular
MC   Grupo parlamentario de la Minoría Catalana
Mx   Grupo parlamentario mixto
PNV   Partido Nacionalista Vasco
PSP   Partido Socialista Popular
PSA   Partido Socialista de Andalucía
EE   Euskadiko Eskerra
HB   Herri Batasuna
PDP   Partido Demócrata Popular
CDS   Centro Democrático y Social
PAD   Partido de Acción Democrática
CiU   Convergència i Unió
UDC   Unió Democràtica de Catalunya
ERC   Esquerra Republicana de Catalunya
Ind   Diputados independientes
FN   Fuerza Nueva

Notes

1. R. Morodo, *La transición política* (Tecnos, Madrid, 1984); J. Santamaría, *Transición a la democracia en el Sur de Europa y en América Latina* (CIS, Madrid, 1982); R. López Pintor, *La opinión pública española: del franquismo a la democracia* (Centro de Investigaciones Sociológicas, Madrid, 1982).
2. A. Bar, 'El sistema de partidos en España', *Sistema*, 47, 1982; M. Buse, *La nueva democracia española. Sistema de partidos y orientación del voto (1976–1983)* (Unión editorial, Madrid, 1984); J. De Esteban and L. Lopez Guerra, *Los partidos políticos en la España actual* (Planeta, Barcelona, 1982); J. J. Linz (ed.), *Informe sociologico sobre el cambio político en España (Informe FOESSA)* (Ed. Euramérica, Madrid, 1981); J. J. Linz, 'La frontera sur de Europa: tendencias evolutivas', *Revista Española de Investigaciones Sociológicas*, 9, 1980; J. J. Linz, 'The new Spanish party system' in R. Rose (ed.), *Electoral Participation* (Sage, Beverley Hills and London, 1980); F. J. Llera Ramos, 'Caracterización sociopolítica del sistema de partidos de la Comunidad Autónoma Vasca y Navarra', Revista de Estudios Políticos 20, 1981; J. M. Maravall, *La política de la transición (1975–1980)* (Taurus, Madrid, 1982); R. Morodo (ed.), *Los partidos políticos en España* (Labor, Barcelona, 1979); G. Di Palma, 'Destra, sinistra o centro? Sulla legittimazione di partiti e coalizioni nel Sud Europa', *Rivista Italiana di Scienza Politica*, 2, 1978.

3. There were actually eight parliamentary groups with the following names: the Unión de Centro Democrático Parliamentary Group, the Socialists in Congress PG, the Socialists from Catalonia PG, the Communist PG, the Alianza Popular PG, the Minoría Catalana PG, the PNV–Vasc PG and the Mixed PG. Nevertheless, we have reduced these options to seven, because logically the general criteria were similar between the two Socialist groups of the PSOE. On the other hand, it is problematic to include the Mixed group; it should be taken into consideration that this group was represented as a group on permanent commissions, and at the beginning it was principally composed of representatives from the Partido Socialista Popular, which made its intervention coherent.

4. The formula is 2^{np-1}, from which 64 coalitions are formed; but we have to correct it because it does not point out that, in the case of an even number of the seats, the two blocks could be equal in number. Indeed, this was the situation during the first period when an alliance between UCD and the Basque group came to 175 representatives, the same number present in the agreement between the rest of the groups.

5. Although the theory of alliances is too formal for our work, the principle of spatial proximity discussed by R. Axelrod in *Conflict of interest: a theory of divergent goals with applications to politics* (Markham, Chicago, 1970) and A. De Swaan in *Coalition Theories and Cabinet Formations* (Elsevier, Amsterdam, 1973) should be kept in mind.

6. The UCD had 47.5 per cent of the representatives, which, as has been pointed out by J. C. Colliard, shows a borderline case between a quasi-majority government and a majority government. See J. C. Colliard, *Los regímes parlamentarios contemporáneos* (Blume, Barcelona, 1981), p. 354 and especially diagram 6, p. 139.

7. The references we make to these socio-political coincidences should not be taken for sociological determinism. They are simply facts which should be taken into consideration together with or beside the global political structure. With respect to this, see the commentaries made by J. Meynaud in 'Introduction: présentation générale des parlementaires', *Revue Internationale des Sciences Sociales*, 4, 1961.

8. M. Baena and J. M. García Madaria, 'Elite franquista y burocracia en las Cortes actuales', *Sistema*, 28, 1979, p. 18. This article is useful for information on the parliamentary personnel in the 1977–9 legislature; nevertheless for a more specialised study of this theme see also J. Condomines, 'Los Diputados españoles. Primeros análisis a partir del fichero ESDIP', *Universidad y Sociedad*, 2, 1982.

9. B. Diaz Nosty, *Radiografía de las nuevas Cortes* (Sedmay, Madrid, 1977).

10. F. De Carreras and J. M. Vallés, *Las elecciones* (Blume, Barcelona, 1977); Centro de Investigaciones y Ticnicas Políticas, *Ley electoral y consecuencias políticas* (Madrid, 1977); D. Nohlen, *Sistemas electorales del Mundo* (Centro de Estudios Constitucionales, Madrid, 1981); and *Revista de Estudios Políticos*, 34, 1983.

11. L. García San Miguel, 'The ideology of the Unión de Centro Democrático', *European Journal of Political Research*, 9, 1981; and C. Huneus, 'La Unión de Centro Democrático, un partido consociacional', *Revista de Política Comparada*, 3, 1980–1.

12. Maravall, *La política de la transición*, J. F. Tezanos, *Sociología del Socialismo Español* (Tecnos, Madrid, 1983).

13. For the consequences of the direct relation between political leaders and public opinion, see I. Molas, 'Sur les attitudes politiques dans l'après-franquisme', *Pouvoirs*, 8, 1979, especially p. 18.

14. The continual interference between consensus and bipartyism during the constituent period cannot be accounted for by consociational democracy models.

15. See J. de Esteban and L. López Guerra, *Las elecciones legislativas del 1 de marzo de 1979* (Centro de Investigaciones Sociológicas, Madrid, 1979).

16. J. Marcet, *Convergència Democratica de Catalunya. El partit i el moviment polític* (Ed. 62, Barcelona, 1984).

17. J. M. Vallés, 'Las elecciones legislativas del 28 de octubre de 1982: una aproximación de urgencia', *Revista de Estudios Políticos*, 33, 1983.

II Coalitional theory and practice in Scandinavia

(a) The Scandinavian area and coalition politics

In line with our re-evaluation of classic coalition theory and the need for a broader-based approach to the subject, the unity of the Scandinavian area (Denmark, Norway and Sweden) has a special attraction. Treating the Scandinavian area as a single entity enables a cross-national comparative analysis to be undertaken with greater assurance than between countries with less similarity. Furthermore, the Scandinavian area is a rich 'laboratory' for coalitional research. This area offers the broadest possible range of types of coalition and of nuances in coalitional behaviour. At the same time, it offers numerous examples of cases where the process of government formation *could* have followed the precepts of classic coalition theory, but in fact did not; with the prospect of holding office, parties often did not choose to do so. With the potential for forming closed minimum winning coalitions, the parties – perversely from the point of view of traditional coalition theory – preferred other alternatives, such as minority coalitions or minority governments, with or without stable external support. This must be strong prima facie evidence that classic theory has overrated the importance of certain dimensions, such as propensity to hold office, size and even contiguity, whilst not adequately integrating other factors related to the party system as a whole into the analysis. This is how the general mandate for the book seems to apply to Scandinavia, whose relevance to our common theme lies in these basic facts, which we shall attempt to amplify, codify and evaluate.

We shall first attempt to substantiate, at least at the level of a working hypothesis, the concept, basic to our analysis, of the unity of the Scandinavian area as follows. A number of elements in both the political systems and the political cultures of the three countries are very similar:[1]

(1)   All three countries have effectively unicameral legislatures elected by fairly strict systems of proportional representation, introduced in the 1910–20 period to preserve a multi-party system which was already in existence. The forms of proportional representation used in each country nevertheless show variations, with implications for the various party systems.[2] In practice, the Danish system is both the most proportional and the most favourable to very small parties, with a threshold of 2 per cent of the votes cast. Sweden has a threshold of 4 per cent, while Norway has no fixed threshold, but the nature of the system tends to set an effective threshold of over 4 per cent unless the votes cast for a party are relatively concentrated in one or two constituencies. The Norwegian electoral system is the least open to new entrants and potentially the most biased against smaller parties, which may be seriously underrepresented unless their support is heavily concentrated in one or two constituencies.

(2)   Parliament has remained the cockpit or essential focus of political life, especially in its committees and inter-party negotiations. This is a function of the absence of clear parliamentary majorities, in itself a consequence of the party and electoral systems.

(3)   The three countries are homogeneous societies, with a high standard of living and well-developed welfare states; the three countries also share a type of political culture which can be characterised as 'consensual democracy'. They have a marked preference for decision-making by broad consensus and compromise, which can ensure long-term continuity in policy. Indeed this characteristic has scarcely diminished during the brief periods of majority government in the various countries.

(4)   All three countries have rather similar party systems, with a number of common characteristics: dominant Social Democratic parties, with signifi-cant political forces to the left of the Social Democrats; several fiercely competitive 'bourgeois' parties (at least three in each country), which from time to time face the threat of radical populists (KRF in Norway in the 1930s; the Danish Justice party in the 1950s and the Progress parties in Denmark and Norway in the 1970s). All three countries have a long tradition of multipartism, going back to the First World War period. The Danish party system has always been the most complicated and became even more complicated during the 1970s. The Swedish party system has remained the most simple and unaffected by the seismic shifts of 1973 in both Norway and Denmark. Despite national variants, new entrants and departures, a working five-party system exists and indeed has existed for some time in all three countries, which could be schematically represented as shown in Table 11.1.[3]

Table 11.1 *Structure of the five-party systems in Scandinavia*[a]

Party/Groupings	Denmark (%)	Norway (%)	Sweden (%)
Far left	SF DKP } 5–15 VS	SF NKP } 3–11 SV	VPK 4–6
Social Democrats	S 26–42	NAP 35–48	SAP 42–50
Centre	RV CD } 4–15 (since 1973)	S 6–11 (Nye Folkeparti 3)	C 9–5 FP 6–24 ——— 31–35
Rural conservative	V 11–27 KRF (1973) 4	V 3–13 KRF 8–12	KDS 1.5
Urban conservative	KF 6–24	H 11–32	M 11.5–24

[a]Abbreviations are explained in the appendix at the end of the chapter.

This schematic presentation naturally ignores some of the nuances and some very small parties, as well as the recent irruption of the populist right FRP in Denmark and Norway (up to 13.8 per cent in Denmark), but it is a broadly accurate representation of the party systems and shows the relative stability within these countries and close comparability of the *rapport de forces* between the various groupings across the three countries. It is important to note that stability is much more evident between the two blocs (Socialist and bourgeois) than within them, where, as the table below shows there have been considerable transfers between parties within each bloc, especially within the bourgeois bloc. Comparing the balance between the blocs, the following range is obtained in each country for the post-1945 period:[4]

	Socialist	Bourgeois
Denmark	(36.7) 41.2–50.2	49.8–58.8 (63.3)
Norway	43.1–52.9	47.1–56.9
Sweden	47.8–53.1	46.9–52.2

The Danish 1973 results are a special case, as indeed are the next lowest result for the Socialist bloc obtained in 1975. A more normal range would be indicated by 43.3 (1968) – 50.2 (1979). Due to the high fragmentation of the extreme left in Denmark, there have rarely been Socialist majorities (1966–8). Comparatively, the Danish balance of party forces has been the most fluctuating and the least favourable to the Socialist parties. Whilst the Social Democrats have always been the largest party in parliament, and naturally the largest party in their bloc, all three Swedish bourgeois parties have at one time or another been the largest party within the bourgeois bloc; two of the three main Danish bourgeois parties have held this position and the rank order between all three has frequently shifted; in

Norway the Hoyre has remained the largest bourgeois party since 1945, but its degree of dominance has shifted considerably, while the Liberals have almost totally disappeared and the other two bourgeois parties have been struggling to maintain their relative position.

Of course, there are inevitably limitations to any comparison. There are quite naturally differences between the three countries' political systems, but these are mostly matters of degree. The Swedish and the Norwegian party systems are less fragmented than the Danish, but the same basic patterns of cleavage and the same broad topology are evident. Perhaps, during some of the period, the Norwegian and Swedish systems have approached bipolar systems with a single dominant pole. However, since 1977 convergences between the three systems have been even more evident than earlier. Thus, despite the variations, the broad comparability remains very strong, and offers a basis for the regional analysis undertaken in this chapter.

(b) The applicability of formal coalition theories

How does coalitional practice in Scandinavia relate to formal theoretical concepts? As we have seen, the political systems in each country and their respective party systems are relatively similar. The same can be said of the basic procedures and norms of behaviour relating to government formation. It is therefore possible to construct a topography of the various types of government which have been formed in the three countries since 1945. Ten categories can be identified:

(1)   Single-party majority government
(2)   Oversized majority coalition (closed)
(3)   Oversized majority coalition
(4)   Minimum winning coalition (closed)
(5)   Minimum winning coalition
(6)   Minority coalition with fixed support
(7)   Minority coalition
(8)   One-party government with fixed support
(9)   One-party government with 'negative' support
(10)   One-party minority government

Most of these types are self-explanatory, or well-known categories from the literature on coalitions. However, some explanation is required in respect of categories (4) and (5) and categories (8) and (9). Categories (4) and (5) in fact blend the two key concepts in coalition theory: size and distance as critical dimensions. Both are rather rare in Scandinavia. The 'closed' category is identified only when a government contains the minimum winning combination *and* its components are contiguous along any accepted distance continuum. On the other hand, discussion about 'fixed' or 'negative' support for a minority coalition or for a one-party cabinet is very characteristic of Scandinavia; indeed, as we shall see, it is perhaps the principal key to understanding government formation and maintenance in the region. Fixed support gives a government a solid, active legislative majority. Negative support guarantees only freedom from no-confidence motions. The parties which provide 'negative support' may lack any cohesion together and may not offer any positive legislative support (Denmark 1979–82 or Norway 1973–81 are good examples). It will also be obvious that the ten types of government have been ranked in descending order of apparent strength and survival potential.

There have been 37 changes in government in Scandinavia since 1945, a change being defined not as a change in Prime Minister, nor as a formal change required by an election, but as a change in nature of the parliamentary basis of the government. Thus, there have been 15 such changes in Denmark, 11 in Norway and 11 in Sweden. Denmark has seen two centre-left majority coalitions (7 years); four minority Social Democrat governments (20 years); one majority bourgeois coalition (3½ years); two minority bourgeois governments (5 years); one S–V coalition (1½ years); two one-party bourgeois governments (3½ years). In Norway, there have been: one majority NAP (Labour) government (16 years); four minority NAP governments (12 years); two majority bourgeois coalitions (6 years); one minority bourgeois coalition (1 year); one single-party bourgeois government (1 year). Sweden has seen one SAP (Social Democratic) majority government (2 years); one centre-left majority coalition (6 years); four minority SAP governments (26 years); two bourgeois majority coalitions (4 years); one bourgeois minority coalition (1 year); and one one-party bourgeois cabinet (1 year). The most obvious and paradoxical trend in these statistics is the predominance of Social Democrat or Social-Democrat-led governments (76.9 per cent of the time), despite the fact that there has been a bourgeois majority in the Scandinavian parliaments for 52.1 per cent of the time and an absolute Social Democrat majority for only 5.1 per cent of the time.[5]

Turning to each of the 'new formations' of governments in each country, according to the definition given above, Table 11.2 sets out the salient data: outcome of the formation process, Prime Minister, duration in office by years, parliamentary basis, category following the scheme set out above, response to the question of whether a minimum winning closed coalition could have been formed. A 'Yes' to that question involves more than a mechanistic judgement, but implies also that such an outcome was politically feasible at that particular time. A 'Yes?' implies greater doubt. Indeed, one complication arises out of the foreshortening of the political spectrum, at least in respect to government formation over much of this period, due to the presence of parties which were either mild anti-system parties (Communists and FRP) or were for other reasons not considered *koalitionsfähig*, such as the Danish and Norwegian SF or the

Table 11.2 *Categorisation of governments in Scandinavia, 1945–82*

Formation	Form of government and basis of support	Could a closed minimum winning coalition have been formed? Parties needed for?
Denmark		
Kristensen (V) 1945–7	One-party minority, negative RV/KF support	Yes? VKR[a]
Hansen (S) 1947–50	S minority, negative DKP + RV	No
Eriksen (V) 1950–3	Minority VK coalition, with S + RV 'toleration'	Yes? VKR
Hansen (S) 1953–7	S minority (+ RV), variable geometry majorities[b]	No
Hansen (S) 1957–60	Majority S + RV + DR coalition, probably not closed	No, unless S + RV + DKP
Kampman (S) 1960–4	Minimum winning closed S + RV + one Greenland member	—
Kampman (S) 1964–6	S minority, negative RV + SF	Yes? RV + S + SF
Krag (S) 1966–8	Minority S, with fixed SF support except on foreign policy	Yes S + SF
Baunsgaard (RV) 1968–71	Majority VKR coalition: closed minimum winning	—
Krag (S) 1971–3	S minority with fixed SF support	Yes S + SF
Hartling (V) 1973–5	One-party (V) minority, variable geometry legislative majorities	No
Jørgensen (S) 1975–6	S minority, variable support	No
Jørgensen (S) 1976–8	S minority, with fixed support from small centre parties	No
Jørgensen (S) 1978–9	Majority SV minimum winning, but not closed	No
Jørgensen (S) 1979–82	Minority S, negative blocking support and variable geometry legislative majorities	Yes SV or RV + S + SF (closed)
Schlüter (KF) 1982–	Minority bourgeois, closed (KF + V + KRF + CD), with RV toleration, except on defence policy	Yes? RV + S + SF
Norway		
Gerhardsen (NAP) 1945–61	Majority NAP	—
Gerhardsen (NAP) 1961–3	Minority NAP cabinet, with negative SF support	Yes NAP + SF
Lyng (H) 1963	Minority bourgeois (closed): H + V + S + KRF	Yes NAP + SF
Gerhardsen (NAP) 1963–5	NAP minority, negative SF support	Yes NAP + SF
Borten (S) 1965–71	Closed, but not minimun winning majority coalition (H + V + S + KRF)	No, unless NAP + S

Table 11.2 (cont.)

Formation	Form of government and basis of support	Could a closed minimum winning coalition have been formed? Parties need for?
Bratteli (NAP) 1971–2	NAP minority, negative toleration from the bourgeois pro-EEC parties	No
Korvald (KRF) 1972–3	Minority anti-EEC bourgeois (V + KRF + S) with negative NAP toleration	NO
Bratteli/Nordli/ Brundtlund (NAP) 1973–81	Minority NAP, with negative SV support and variable geometry majorities	Yes? NAP + SV
Willoch (H) 1981–2	Minority one-party, with fixed S + KRF support	Yes H + S + KRF
Willoch (H) 1982–	Oversized, closed bourgeois coalition H + KRF + S	Yes? NAP + S
Sweden		
Hansson/Erlander (SAP) 1944–51	SAP one-party minority, with negative VPK support	Yes SAP + VPK
Erlander (SAP) 1951–7	Closed oversized coalition: SAP + C; for a short period it was minimum winning	No (SAP + VPK)
Erlander (SAP) 1957–68	One-party SAP minority, with negative VPK support and variable geometry legislative majorities	Yes SAP + VPK or SAP + C
Palme (SAP) 1969–70	SAP majority	—
Palme (SAP) 1970–3	SAP one-party minority, with negative VPK support and variable geometry legislative majorities	No?
Palme (SAP) 1973–6	SAP minority, with negative/fixed (FP) support in 'tied' Riksdag	Yes SAP + FP
Fälldin (C) 1976–8	Oversized, closed majority M + C + FP	Yes SAP + FP
Ullsten (FP) 1978–9	One-party bourgeois minority, with SAP toleration	Yes SAP + FP
Fälldin (C) 1979–81	Oversized, closed majority M + C + FP	Yes SAP + FP
Fälldin (C) 1981–2	Minority bourgeois coalition C + FP with M negative support	Yes SAP + FP
Palme/Carlsson (SAP) 1982–	One-party SAP minority, with VPK negative support	Yes SAP + VPK

[a]VKR = Danish usage for designating the three-party Venstre–Konservativ–Radikale Venstre coalition. (Other abbreviations are explained in the appendix to this chapter.)
[b]Shifting voting coalitions, from issue to issue, with some common core component.

Source: V. Bogdanor (ed.), *Coalition Government in Western Europe* (Heinemann, London, 1983), ch. 4, 'Coalition formation in Scandinavia' by P. Pesonen and A. H. Thomas. Evaluations of the coalitions by the author.

other Danish far left parties and DR before 1957. Some of these parties thereby became 'prisoners' with no margin for manoeuvre and no ability to command concessions. It is a constant difficulty, and indeed a matter of almost subjective judgement, how to integrate these factors into the general scheme.

Returning to our earlier classification of types of government, our analysis of the individual formations involving changes produced the following breakdown:

Single-party majority	2
Oversized closed coalition	7
Oversized majority coalition	1
Minimum winning closed	2
Minimum winning	1
Minority coalition + fixed support	2
Minority coalition	3
One-party government + fixed support	4
One-party government + negative support	12
One-party government	3

(These types of government may be explained chronologically, as shown in Table 11.2.)

There is, as already indicated, a broad spread of categories of government, with various types of minority government being the most characteristic, with 24 cases altogether. In only 3 cases were minimum winning coalitions actually formed and of these only 2 were closed. One other coalition (the 1957 DR + RV + S coalition in Denmark) might also be considered as minimum winning, but probably not closed. One of the minimum winning closed coalitions (SAP + C in Sweden) only conformed to the requirement for part of its term of office, since later an alternative 'smaller' coalition would have been possible. If this result is compared to the number of cases where an outcome of a minimum winning closed coalition was even moderately feasible, the predictive value of formal coalition theory is shown in all its limitations. There were a mere 4 cases at a maximum out of a possible 23.

Some preliminary comments arising out of these results are necessary before moving on to attempt a more conceptual analysis. It should be underlined that the concept of a minimum winning coalition, let alone a closed coalition, lost all meaning in the fragmented Danish and Norwegian legislatures between 1973 and 1977. Classic theory likewise seems to take almost no account of other dimensions related to the party systems: the extreme reluctance in certain countries and time periods (mostly Sweden and Norway) to form longer-term formal coalitions or even formal alliances 'across the middle', bridging the Socialist–bourgeois cleavage; the existence, already noted, of small prisoner parties at a position in the party system which gives them no leverage, although their votes can be 'used' to offer protection against a motion of no confidence. On the other hand, the 'support parties' are often precisely those that classic coalition theory would designate as coalition partners. This should not be seen as a vindication of the theory, since it fails to explain why no coalition was in fact formed.

Closer examination of the actual out-turn in the numerous government formation processes tends to confirm this view even more strongly. The key issue always has been: can the Social Democrats govern and do they wish to do so under the conditions prevailing? Bourgeois alternative coalitions have been slow to form, even when parliamentary arithmetic favoured them. Even when formed, they have been unstable, ineffective (even in the eyes of their own voters) and liable to premature collapse. In fact, of the eight bourgeois coalitions formed in Scandinavia since 1945, four have met that fate. Indeed, the failure of bourgeois coalitions to form and of bourgeois governments to meet the expectations of their electorates may go far to explain the seismic upheavals in at least the Danish and Norwegian party systems in the 1970s and the emergence of protest parties such as the Norwegian and Danish FRP and the KRF. The immediate impact of these parties was dramatic, though not very deep in significance, but it cannot be denied that they undermined the stability of the party systems concerned for a period of time. Of perhaps more long-term consequence to these party systems – and this includes Sweden – the failure of bourgeois coalitions has led to the long-term decline of many of the smaller bourgeois parties and the emergence of a distinct *bourgeois* vote as such – a floating vote – moving between bourgeois parties, now favouring one of them, now another, according to which currently seems to offer the most credible pole of opposition to the Socialist bloc. Thus, RV was favoured in Denmark in 1968; Venstre in 1975; Center in Sweden in 1976 and the Conservatives in all three countries since 1979. This may suggest a regrouping within the bourgeois bloc, but does not necessarily imply more stable coalitions. Indeed the contrary may result, as the diminished centre parties fight to maintain their identity. This analysis reinforces the view that traditional theory is too one-dimensional and that the understanding of coalitional behaviour in Scandinavia must lie in the party systems viewed more broadly rather than merely in relation to formalistic concerns about the size of and distance between parties at the parliamentary level.

(c) The need for a broader approach to Scandinavian coalitions

More recent work on Scandinavia, both general and specifically on the area of coalitions, has largely confirmed these assessments and, from a basis of detailed empirical work on the three countries, has begun to focus on the new dimensions which require analysis and to bring out the full complexity of the coalitional behaviour to be observed in Scandinavia. Here, we carry the study of coalitional behaviour in that area further by identifying more directly those dimensions, while at the same time continuing to use some of the basic concepts of earlier theory.

This more recent literature[6] had tended to focus more heavily on Denmark

Table 11.3 *Elections in Scandinavia since 1945*

Number of seats won by parties

Denmark	1945	1947	1950	1953 (I)	1953 (II)	1957	1960	1964	1966	1968	1971	1973	1975	1977	1979	1981	1984
VS	—	—	—	—	—	—	—	—	—	4	0	0	4	5	6	5	5
DKP	18	9	7	7	8	6	0	0	0	0	0	6	7	7	0	0	0
SF	—	—	—	—	—	—	11	10	20	11	17	11	9	7	11	21	21
S	48	57	59	61	74	70	76	76	69	62	70	46	53	65	68	59	56
RV	11	10	12	13	14	14	11	10	13	27	27	20	13	6	10	9	10
LC	—	—	—	—	—	—	—	—	4	0	—	—	—	—	—	—	—
CD	—	—	—	—	—	—	—	—	—	—	—	14	4	11	6	15	8
KRF	—	—	—	—	—	—	—	—	—	—	0	7	9	6	5	4	5
DR	3	6	12	9	6	9	0	0	0	0	0	5	0	6	5	0	0
V	38	49	32	33	42	45	38	38	34	34	30	22	42	21	22	20	22
KF	26	17	27	26	30	30	32	36	35	37	31	16	10	15	22	26	42
DS	4	0	—	0	—	—	—	0	—	—	—	—	—	—	—	—	—
FRP	—	—	—	—	—	—	—	—	—	—	—	28	24	26	20	16	6
U	—	—	—	—	0	0	6	5	0	0	0	0	0	0	0	0	0
Slesvig Seat (German Minority)	—	0	0	0	1	1	1	0	0	0	0	0	0	0	0	0	0
N. Atlantic	1	1	2	2	4	4	4	4	4	4	4	4	4	4	4	4	4
Total seats	149	149	151	151	179	179	179	179	179	179	179	179	179	179	179	179	179

Norway	1945	1949	1953	1957	1961	1965	1969	1973	1977	1981
SF/SV/SFP	—	—	—	—	2	2	0	16	2	4
NKP	11	0	3	1	0	0	0	—	0	0
NAP	76	85	77	78	74	68	74	62	76	66
S	10	12	14	15	16	18	20	21	12	15
KRF	8	9	14	12	15	13	14	20	22	10
V	20	21	15	15	14	18	13	2	2	2
NFP	—	—	—	—	—	—	—	1	0	0
H	25	23	27	29	29	31	29	29	41	54
FRP	—	—	—	—	—	—	—	4	0	2
Total	150	150	150	150	150	150	150	155	155	153

Sweden	1948	1952	1956	1958	1960	1964	1968	1970	1973	1976	1979	1982
VPK	8	5	6	5	5	8	3	17	19	17	20	20
SDAP	112	110	106	111	114	113	125	163	156	152	154	166
C	30	26	19	32	34	35	39	71	90	86	64	56
FP	57	58	58	38	40	43	34	58	34	39	38	21
M	23	31	42	45	39	33	32	41	51	55	73	86
Total	230	230	231	231	232	233[a]	233	350	350	349	349	349

[a]One other.

Abbreviations are explained in the appendix to this chapter.

than on the other two countries, especially in the wake of the seismic election of 1973. A full survey of the literature on coalitions, or that relevant to them, would be beyond our scope. But what does the trend of the literature generally seem to indicate? Work on Scandinavia in the last two decades has emphasised the continued survival of the broad contours of consensual democracy, despite the apparently rather dramatic changes in the party systems, though these are often held to be more apparent than real. Emphasis has of course been placed on the changing party system and its relationship to changing patterns of social and electoral behaviour. Much attention has been paid to the importance of a set of established behavioural norms, which condition political action, arising out of the political culture and the party system. The phenomenon of minority governments and their survival through 'assymetrical' issue salience, giving rise to variable geometry voting coalitions (foreign policy vs. domestic policy majorities) has also attracted attention. All these issues, which have been treated both in single-country studies and in a comparative framework, are not primarily concerned with the study of coalitional behaviour, but do shed considerable light upon it.

Two recent works, specifically on coalitions, both deal with Scandinavia or individual countries within the area. Browne and Dreijmanis[7] deal with Denmark only and Bogdanor[8] has two chapters which deal with Scandinavia as a whole. Both works point in the same general direction. Their analysis underpins the thesis which underlies this chapter: the need for a broader-based analysis of coalitional behaviour. They – and this author concurs – contribute to a general scepticism about traditional coalition theory. They point to the fact that there are too many exceptions to the classical model; too many riders; too many factors of considerable complexity which the classic theories simply do not take into account. As the concluding chapter in the Browne and Dreijmanis work makes clear, they are seeking to suggest new directions for analysis. Bo Särlvik in his comparative and stimulating essay in the Bogdanor volume goes farthest towards codifying these complexities into an analytical framework which recognises, as he puts it, that 'coalitional politics does not only take the form of coalition governments', and relates the coalition game to the party system.

Our analysis of the empirical situation in Scandinavia and the thrust of other recent work suggest the need to develop an approach to coalitional behaviour that can integrate within itself the diversity of the observed phenomena and offer some framework for understanding the processes that are being observed in Scandinavia. This would in turn require a broad-based analysis, incorporating a number of additional dimensions to those of size and contiguity, which would enable the effective analysis of coalitional behaviour within the framework of the Scandinavian party systems.

The most relevant dimensions would appear to be those relating to:

(a) *the political culture:* historical experience; the nature of the political culture; consensual tendencies;[9] behavioural norms arising out of the political culture.

(b) *motivation:* policy *v.* office-holding; party strategy in the long and the short term.
(c) *electoral considerations:* voter movements and party rivalry.
(d) *internal party factors:* role of non-parliamentary actors; coalitional politics as part of faction infighting inside parties.

These dimensions will now be examined in turn.

(d) Political culture and behavioural norms in Scandinavian coalitions

The importance of the political culture as a key dimension to coalition behaviour is evident from our discussion of what has actually happened in the process of forming governments in Scandinavia. There is a broad and well-understood range of norms of behaviour, arising out of historical traditions; shared experience among political elites of making fragmented party systems function in a pragmatic manner, and traditions of working together between certain parties (such as between the S and RV in Denmark, or the four 'NATO parties' in Denmark or the Social Democrats and the Center in Sweden), which make negotiations easier. Even norms of 'coalitional behaviour', as distinct from formal coalition procedures, are well known and well understood in all three countries, involving an infinite range of subtleties in behaviour: co-operation as support parties; legislative as distinct from executive alliances; variable geometry alliances; passive support or 'toleration', sometimes by abstention in key votes. All have their own well-understood rationales and pay-offs.
based policy-making, which can ensure a significant degree of continuity. This arises out of the consensual nature of these societies. The welfare state; the Swedish social reforms of the 1950s; foreign policy; military policy; tax reforms (Denmark in the 1960s and Sweden in 1981–2); energy policy – the examples are legion – have all been issues on which, despite their inherently controversial character, or perhaps because of it, broad-based consensus and continuity, anchored in large majority constellations, transcending the traditional bloc cleavages, have been sought. Governments have often reached out beyond the confines of their own parliamentary support to seek such broad majorities.

One can identify therefore a series of both formal constitutional rules and behavioural norms favouring consensual policy-making as well as the survival of minority governments, which in turn encourage, indeed require, a consensual approach, especially in the fragmented legislatures that have characterised Scandinavia since the mid-1960s. Among these are the provisions for an abrogative referendum on legislation passed by the Danish Folketing, if demanded by one-third of its members; the lack of any provision to dissolve the Norwegian Storting for resolving a political crisis; the rather strict PR electoral systems; the key role of parliamentary committees; the essentially 'negative' form in which the parliamentary principle is expressed (governments do not need a positive 'investiture' by parliament). All these tend to promote a form of pragmatic, co-operative democracy, in which parliament is the key forum, both in its committees and in the permanent inter-party negotiations and deals which generate broad-based support for most measures.[10]

The stark distinctions between being in government and in opposition, so characteristic of more 'adversarial' political systems such as Britain or France, have been greatly watered down in Scandinavia. On many issues, the 'opposition' may enter the majority and even part of the usual 'majority' may be found in opposition. For instance, the Swedish tax reform of 1981 was carried by the opposition SAP and the majority centre parties, against the majority Moderaterna and the VPK; in Denmark, at present defence policy is partly made by the four 'Old' parties (the four traditional parties – S, RV, V and KF) and partly by an alliance of the left and the RV, which otherwise forms part of the 'majority' of the Schlüter minority coalition. Responsibility and power are consequently diffuse and shared, which is an important matter in respect to unpopular measures. Furthermore, as a result, political competition has its rough edges worn off and in practice is considerably *nuancé*. The coalition 'game' is thus far from being the only game in town. The issue of who forms the government, whilst remaining perhaps the most central issue, is not the only issue and may, for some actors, not be the most salient issue. Here, one leads directly to the motivation dimension which, viewed comprehensively, looms extremely large in any analysis of Scandinavian coalitional behaviour.

(e)　*Motivation in Scandinavian coalition politics: variations on a broad theme*

We shall now turn to look at the motivation of parties in the coalitional process, but it does need defining carefully. The debate about policy-oriented motives vs. office-holding is in some respects a gross over-simplification, but it is nevertheless a convenient peg on which to hang the discussion, or at least as a starting-point for our analysis here.

Ian Budge has argued that not only do parties tend to pursue policy-oriented goals as such, but that they do so according to priorities or salience preferences.[11] He identifies as motives system defence, left–right polarisation and sectoral interest related to a party's electoral base. His analysis is borne out in Scandinavia, if one adopts a broad definition of system defence goals. Such considerations link in closely with theories of Scandinavian consensual behaviour. The traditional key actors in the political system behave in such a way as to give priority to system and consensus maintenance goals. This may involve parties in seeking not to hold office, but to wield influence through their negotiating position as part of the majority or, more accurately, the variable geometry majorities which minority governments find for their various policies. It may mean defending the existing system of political norms and values; the foreign policy of the state or the constitutional arrangements, rather than the particular concept of defence of the stability of the democratic system, which has not even appeared under threat, except perhaps in the immediate post-liberation period in Norway and Denmark or in the 1973–5 period in Denmark.

Defence of norms of consensus behaviour on defence policy, on Swedish neutrality, on entry to the EEC, on the Danish constitutional reforms of 1950–3; and even of consensus itself in the difficult 1973–5 period in Denmark and Norway has been an important determinant of party behaviour and hence coalition politics. These issues rather than left–right polarisation have been the most salient, as Budge again suggests. This does much to explain the fact that the balance between blocs has not been the key factor in coalition behaviour. It also does much to explain the frequency of types of minority arrangements, which cover the whole range from participation in a minority government, through minority coalitions to a whole range of relationships between parties which can vary from mere abstention and therefore 'toleration' to formal pacts for external support, such as that between S and SF in Denmark between 1966 and 1968. Consensus can exist on the best type of government required to carry out certain agreed policy objectives: for example, the revision of the Danish Constitution in 1953 was considered to have a better chance under a bourgeois coalition; the bourgeois parties supported minority governments in Denmark and Norway in the 1971–3 period in order to ensure EEC membership, although this failed in Norway. The 1982 tax reform in Sweden was carried out across the Socialist–bourgeois divide by a broad Center–Folk–SAP voting coalition, excluding both the Moderates and VPK.

Informal or issue-based alliances 'across the middle' are frequent, as parties do not appear to give an overriding priority to the bourgeois–Socialist divide. Both the Social Democrats and the bourgeois parties show this behaviour. This is in part tactical – to undercut or isolate competitors within their own bloc; in part it also represents a genuine commitment to the norms of consensus and in part it lies in the creation and acceptance of variable geometry voting alliances or even agreements, based on non-reciprocal saliency on alliances varying across domains, the classic example being the Danish and Norwegian Social Democrats leaning towards the far left in domestic policy issues and to the centre–right on defence and foreign policy issues.[12]

The formal procedures and norms of coalition formation processes vary from country to country, on such matters as the effective role of the monarch, the degree of elite domination of the process, the role of non-parliamentary actors, but one norm is constant: progress by exclusion. (In some countries non-parliamentary actors (perhaps we could specify the non-parliamentary party organs and party-linked interest groups) play a significant and visible role, whereas in others they do not. This may even vary from one party to another. There are no formal rules.) The size and strategic position in the political system occupied by the Social Democrats are such that the key prior question is always:

do the Social Democrats wish to hold office? If so, with whom and at what price? If not, who else wants to hold office and indeed who does not? Can others form a government, or must the Social Democrats form the government? Sometimes more parties are reluctant (or appear so) to hold office than are prepared to do so. 'Pre-cooked' coalitions, as in Denmark (VKR) 1968–71; Sweden 1976–8 and 1979–81; and Norway 1965–71 often fail to work well, as the real predisposition of parties to govern, the real policy differences and the concealed strategic differences have not been treated in the fire of real coalition negotiations.

Of course, when looking at the three countries it may be argued that the policy orientation of parties arises ultimately out of the party system structures, which remain relatively stable, despite recent upheavals, or at least that the former may well be influenced by the latter. Movements between the blocs remain small, although movements within the blocs are often significant. The movement of votes follows a clear, predictable logic, which has become more fluid in recent years, but it nevertheless broadly retains its predictable character. A certain continuum and positional nexus exist between the parties, identified clearly in 'distance' analysis in parliamentary votes and the attitudes of voters as identified both by attitudinal surveys and in the direction of movements between parties. This relatively stable continuum and the divisions between bourgeois parties have given greater leverage or margin for manoeuvre for certain parties. The Social Democrats, as the largest party, faced with 'captive' far left parties and a divided and fiercely competitive bourgeois bloc, have enjoyed considerable margin for manoeuvre. The centre parties (RV, FP, Center) have also enjoyed some margin for manoeuvre between the tightly balanced blocs.

The key problem has been that of bourgeois disunity based on strategic considerations. One or more bourgeois parties may consider that it or they could obtain more policy leverage as an external supporter of a Social Democratic government. Other things being equal, the Social Democrats will usually seek to retain power, even at the risk of considerable compromise. This was the motivation for the Danish 'triangular' government in 1957–60 and the SV government in 1978, or the decision of the Danish Social Democrats to remain in power after the 1981 election. The same motive applied to the SAP decision to remain in power in Sweden in the balanced 1973–6 Riksdag. Apart from the obvious cases of Denmark in 1945 and Norway in 1972, the Social Democrats have never sought not to form a government when they could have done so, although one might include the 1973–5 period in Denmark. The record of the bourgeois parties is altogether less consistent. These parties have often sought to avoid forming part of a coalition for a variety of reasons.

Strategy for the bourgeois parties especially involves maintenance of the party's relative weight within the bourgeois bloc; profile maintenance; and improving the party's range of options, as this will in turn (irrespective of its size) increase its bargaining power, all of which are considerations ignored by formal coalition theories. The last of these concerns will lead a party to seek influence maximalisation (often a policy, rather than an office-holding orientation). For the Social Democrats, and usually the Conservatives because of their size (or in the case of the Conservatives because of their unfavourable position without much leverage, to the far right of the political spectrum), office-holding will usually also represent the maximum influence position. Not least because of the possibility of their commanding the Prime Minister's post and the majority of key cabinet posts, with the attendant media attention and their dominance over the state machine, such considerations played a major role in decisions by S to remain in office in Denmark in 1981 and in Sweden between 1973 and 1976, for example. Only very strong countervailing electoral or political arguments (as in Denmark in 1945 or Norway in 1972) will lead these larger parties to seek opposition by choice. For the other parties a 'coalitional arrangement' of one type or another may actually offer greater policy leverage than participation in government, without the attendant costs in terms of electoral unpopularity arising from certain measures.

Positional strategy can thus be seen both in parliamentary and electoral, if not broadly political terms. This positional strategy, linked with profile maintenance, is a major feature of the bourgeois parties' behaviour and especially of the smaller bourgeois parties. For them, relative strength *within* the bourgeois bloc and profile maintenance *in relation to* the other bourgeois parties have been major determinants of their behaviour, often dictating their approach to coalitional relations or to break-up of coalitions or coalitional arrangements. Coalitions may fail to form because one party would dominate the coalition, because one party would presumptively lose its profile in the coalition, or because a potential partner would be an 'inner member' rather than a 'pivotal member' in terms of policy space. Parties can be pivotal not only in the arithmetical sense (i.e. in a 'swing position') but can, especially if they are centre parties, hold a pivotal position in terms of the potential coalition's space continuum. Such a pivotal party may be able to exhibit a higher profile than 'inner parties' in the continuum. The Radikale Venstre or the Swedish Center or Folk parties are typical examples of such 'strategic' parties, which have a key position but which must also take into account the need to change their coalitional alliances in order to maintain their leverage and their profile.

Given this internal rivalry within the bourgeois blocs, a party may also enter a coalition to deny another party entry to government, or to balance the presence of another party and parties. The creation of the bourgeois coalition in Norway in June 1983 followed this pattern. The KRF entered the coalition in order to secure its influence and forced a reluctant Senterparti to follow suit, despite the common preference of both individual parties to remain outside a formal coalition after the 1981 election. Likewise, the 1957-60 triangular coalition in Denmark (S–R–RV) was, in its origin, basically a purely negative alliance to prevent a VK (Venstre-Konservativ) coalition being formed, as seemed most likely immediately after the 1957 election.

(f)   Coalition politics and electoral considerations

Parliamentary manoeuvring by party leaderships must, however, take account of the electoral consequences of decisions on coalitional behaviour. Indeed, concern with profile maintenance and preference for less binding forms of co-operation than formal coalitions are evidence of this basic fact. Electoral reaction, or prospective electoral reaction, represents a constraint on the freedom of action of parties, which may vary over time and from party to party, especially in the bourgeois camp. Without entering into the complex debate about voter rationality, it is clear that voters in the three countries have shown themselves able to react with sufficient coherence, the complexity of the party system notwithstanding, to send clear messages to party leaderships.

Voter reaction and potential reaction weigh most heavily on the bourgeois parties. Shifts between the blocs are mostly small – less than 5 per cent. Such shifts, important as they are, rarely in themselves constitute a decisive factor in determining a party's behaviour, although, as in Norway in 1965 and 1969 and in Sweden in 1976, they represented the essential precondition for turning the prior choice of the bourgeois parties into reality. Yet, the situation of Denmark, with an almost permanent bourgeois majority, and the failures of the Swedish and Norwegian bourgeois coalitions amply illustrate the fact that the mere existence of a bourgeois majority in the parliament is no guarantee of a bourgeois majority coalition.

Voter shifts within the Socialist bloc have rarely had a determinant impact on the behaviour of components of that bloc. The exchanges of votes between SDAP and VPK in Sweden (up to some 2 per cent) have had little discernible effect on the strategy of either party in recent times. In Norway, the 'seismic' EEC election of 1973 saw a major shift of votes from NAP to the far left SV alliance, but the SV gains did not come uniformly from the NAP, as the fact that the 1969 bourgeois majority disappeared attests. As usual, it was bourgeois disunity which made an NAP minority government virtually inevitable, whatever the outcome of the election. The loss of votes by S to SF in Denmark is a possible exception, in that it was at least one of the major factors dictating a change in the previous Social Democratic policy of non-co-operation with SF. Again, the competition between several parties of the far left in Denmark has perhaps prevented SF taking up a more open and co-operative stance.

It is, though, mainly in the bourgeois camp that voter shifts or the threat of them have been of the most significance. This is most evident in Norway and Denmark, where the 1973 elections completely restructured the party system, but the same trends are evident to a lesser degree in Sweden. Until the early 1970s the Scandinavian party systems remained rather stable. Each bourgeois party had a secure electoral base, built on a core of sociologically or ideologically distinct voters. Movements of voters did occur, but not in enough magnitude to upset the system or to threaten the existence of any of the parties. The 1970s and 1980s have seen a much more fluid electorate, caused by a variety of factors, ranging from tax revolts and, in Norway and Denmark, the EEC debate. Even so, the bourgeois parties have retained a degree of differentiation, which may guarantee their continued existence, but no longer ensures their strength or their place in the party system. However, a more specifically bourgeois electorate has emerged, not tied to any one party and ready to float between them in search of the strongest pole among the non-Socialist parties. This has variously been Venstre in Denmark in 1975, Center in Sweden in 1976 and, since the mid-1980s, the Conservatives in all three countries.

Thus, the potential gains, but also the potential losses, from any given form of coalitional behaviour have greatly multiplied. This may have to some extent increased the room for manoeuvre available to party leaderships, but it has also increased the risks involved. It has become possible to hope that new voters will replace those lost by any given course of action, but at the same time it means that electoral calculations, and especially the likely reaction of a party's voters to a possible alliance, have become more important. We shall turn to look briefly at these voter shifts, at changes in the party system which have resulted, and at patterns of voter perception, in so far as these bear on our theme of coalitional behaviour.

The position of the Danish parties in the spectrum, as shown by the voting behaviour of the parties in the Folketing and the attitudinal dispositions of the voters (both in judging the 'distance' of their parties from other adjacent parties and their movement in response to events) has shown a consistent pattern along a two-dimensional continuum:[13]

This has given at least a relatively clear structure to the interrelationship between parties, which also ensures that in their parliamentary manoeuvring they do not move too far out of step from the electorates. The 1977 elections in Denmark were a very effective illustration of the relationship between parliamentary alliances and electoral changes. The Social Democrats gained 7 per cent net and their small allies also gained net, from outside the so-called 'Forlig'. This Forlig was an agreement concluded in 1976 and renegotiated in 1977 between S and a group of small support parties (KRF, CD, RV), in order to provide a longer-term stable parliamentary basis for the S minority government. These gains, given to both S and its small allies, indicate popular support for the Forlig.[14] This popular support is underscored by the fact that 77 per cent of the voters sought a stable broad-based government, to which the Forlig was the nearest available possibility, and even among Venstre's voters, only 27 per cent supported the aim of their own party, which was to form a bourgeois coalition.[15] The pattern of interrelationships between the three main bourgeois parties has followed the same pattern as in the other Scandinavian countries. In the immediate post-war period, Venstre was the largest bourgeois party; in the 1960s the Radikale Venstre doubled its strength to become the second largest bourgeois party. After a surge in 1975 resulting from its short period alone in government, it was overtaken by the KF, which had consolidated its position as the strongest bourgeois party. These various interrelationships and shifts, seen together with the perceptions of distance of both voters and members of the Folketing (which for the most part coincide), can be represented by the spectrum below. The parties within each area marked have at one time or another in various years acted together to form the parliamentary basis of a government. The patterns thus formed show clearly the importance of distance perception in such co-operation.

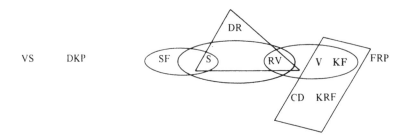

Norway too had seen a stable pattern of interrelationships between the parties and voter shifts until 1973, when there was a marked collapse of the liberal centre under the pressure of the Common Market debate. She has also seen the secular decline of the special interest groups upon which the individual bourgeois parties were based. These groups have declined in size, moved into the towns and become less identified with particular bourgeois parties. The EEC referendum, which split almost all Norwegian parties, and the simultaneous discontent with the performance of the 1965–71 bourgeois coalition, led to a serious increase in political alienation and broke up the old party system, although by 1977 it had settled down into a pattern only marginally different from that which had prevailed previously. The split in the old Venstre into the anti-EEC Venstre and the pro-EEC New People's party, after which both virtually disappeared from the Storting, coupled with the inroads made into the support of several bourgeois parties by Anders Lange's party (later FRP), created a new fluidity in the bourgeois camp.[16] Longer-term analysis of electoral trends also shows that the greater general fluidity in the electorate began to emerge earlier. The NAP has suffered a secular decline among farmers and fishermen to the benefit of KRF and Senterparti, reflecting social and geographical mobility but also a shift in the stable rural population.[17] Even so, it is interesting that the different bourgeois parties' electorates still attached different weights to 'the most important issue' in the 1973 election:[18]

KRF: abortion (47%)
Venstre: abortion (37%)
NFP: taxes (34%) and abortion (32%)
Senter: EEC (31%)
Hoyre: taxes (35%)

Thus, there still remained differences in issue saliency among bourgeois voters and therefore there was still a basis for 'specialisation' among the bourgeois parties. Those who held a restrictive view on abortion moved overwhelmingly to KRF if they moved (+ 8 per cent); those who believed taxes to be too high moved to Anders Lange's party from NAP and Hoyre; those who opposed the EEC moved to Senter and the far left, if they moved. Issues could interact and reinforce each other: the left Socialists' most spectacular gains were among those in favour of freer abortion, but opposed to the EEC (+ 21 per cent) or opposed to the EEC but accepting a high level of welfare expenditure (+ 11 per cent). The liberals only gained among voters (presumably bourgeois voters) who favoured freer abortion, but opposed the EEC (+ 3 per cent). There has thus been a continued basis for three bourgeois parties (Senter, KRF and Hoyre), but the greater fluidity has led to a greater polarisation, with Hoyre now holding a dominant position in the bourgeois bloc, as against the *primus inter pares* position it occupied earlier, with 53.2 per cent of bourgeois seats in 1977 and 65.4 per cent in 1981; whilst the secular decline of Senter, arrested in 1973, has continued. One can foresee a confirmation of this trend, with only KRF remaining as a significant centre party, although on some issues it is to the right of Hoyre. The consequence of these trends has been to make the formation of bourgeois coalitions difficult in the earlier sensitive phase, but now rather easier because of Hoyre's strengthened position. However, although the fluidity of the electorates and variable issue saliency have given party leaderships somewhat greater room for manoeuvre, the old concerns with relative position and profile maintenance continue to manifest themselves.

Sweden likewise had a relatively stable basis for its three-party bourgeois camp, but with some movement between camps and more within camps continuously occurring. As well as the left–right cleavage, urban–rural and materialist–non-materialist cleavages have played an important role in voter perceptions and behaviour. The parties retain a separate base and identity even within the new fluidity. Thus, the Center has only 34 per cent of its voters in towns and only 8 per cent in large towns, against 63 per cent for the Folkpartiet and 62 per cent for the Moderaterna. M and FP voters are more likely to be home owners than SDAP or Center voters. FP voters are also likely to be flat owners (not renters). The FP is more middle-class than Center, with its best electoral support among lower white-collar workers and civil servants who own their own homes in urban areas. Center has 65 per cent of all farmers, who represent 23 per cent of its electorate. Many of its supporters in urban areas are recent arrivals from the country. Center has 12 per cent of industrial workers as against 5 per cent for FP and Moderaterna. FP is a younger and more highly educated party than Centerpartiet.[19]

Looking at changes in Sweden between 1976 and 1979, 5 per cent moved between blocs and 2 per cent between SDAP and VPK. Movement was greatest (25 per cent) among the youngest voters (under 30). Center, a big loser, held on best among its traditional core voters: farmers (90 per cent loyalty), small businessmen (68 per cent) and older voters; and least among young, urban, white-collar voters. Its losses were in all directions, but mostly to Moderata Samlingspartiet, probably on the nuclear energy issue. The FP lost to SDAP and Moderaterna among its 1976 small-town and working-class voters (i.e. marginal groups for the FP) and was most stable among its core younger voters. The Moderaterna did lose voters in some city areas, despite its large net gains (− 13 per cent of its working-class vote to Center; 9 per cent of its rural vote to Center).[20] All parties tended to lose some support among their marginal groups.

Problems of voter perception of distance, elite perception and issue saliency are greatest in the centre in Sweden. There is no difficulty in locating Moderaterna to the right and VPK to the left of the Social Democrats. However, in recent years Center and FP have battled for pre-eminence in the centre and have considered various strategies: using the centre as a bridge 'across the middle' to the left (Center 1951–7 and FP in 1973–6) or leading the bourgeois bloc from the centre (the Fälldin coalitions). Attachment to a party began to decline, at least for the bourgeois parties, in the early 1970s, as shown in Table 11.4.[21] Furthermore, an increasing proportion indicated (1973 and 1976) that they had voted for a different bourgeois party than that of their primary identification.

Swedish parties, like others in the Scandinavian region, sought at times, in the new post–1973 fluidity, to ignore voter reaction, in the hope that voters would either in time 'catch up' with any new strategy or that new voters would compensate for any losses. However, in such a polarised two-bloc system, with the highest class-voting in the Western world, such a strategy may prove to be very high-risk, as Center found in its 1951–7 coalition with SDAP, or as FP found in the 1970s. Yet it can be profitable in another sense: in the short term votes may be traded for the influence that a pivotal party can exercise. This increased influence, arising out of a risky alliance, may possibly in turn increase the profile of the small party and lead to electoral gains. The extent of the risk (and the potential gains, if any) depends in large part on the 'distance perception' that

Table 11.4 *Voter attachment to parties in Sweden*

Percentage

	VPK		SDAP		Center		FP		M	
	1968	1973	1968	1973	1968	1973	1968	1973	1968	1973
Strong	23	26	51	44	29	21	19	27	37	27
Weak	10	20	25	33	24	23	31	24	26	31
Total	33	46	76	77	53	44	50	51	63	58

voters of that small party have of voters of other parties close to it in the spectrum, as well as of its prospective allies. Such an analysis shows the problems and opportunities faced by the Swedish small centre parties. Most SDAP voters consider Center (and not VPK) to be their closest party:[22]

VPK	21%
Center	44%
FP	7%
Moderaterna	2%

While this proportion may have altered somewhat, it nevertheless renders any FP–SDAP alliance problematic, as SDAP could expect to lose votes to both Center and VPK. Center voters lean more towards SDAP than Moderaterna, but most towards FP. Center seems to have broad options: an alliance with SDAP; a centre grouping or a broad bourgeois alliance at least in terms of voter preference:

SDAP	29%
FP	32%
Moderaterna	21%

FP cannot claim the same broad centre position. Its attempts to break out of a position to the right of Center do not seem to have much basis in the perceptions of its electorate. The second preferences of FP voters distribute as follows:

SDAP	9%
Center	55%
Moderaterna	22%

This distribution would seem to show also that any centre-left strategy by the FP must be a high-risk strategy, especially as the Center and the VPK, the likely gainers from FP and SDAP in any such alliance, are parties with the characteristics of protest parties whose voters are the most politically alienated and mobile. Furthermore, on key issues such as taxation, pensions, welfare, unemployment, foreign policy and ideological judgements, FP voters were more negative than Center voters and often almost as negative as Moderaterna voters towards the SDAP.[23] This analysis must, however, leave a question-mark over the appropriate political spectrum in Sweden, which could perhaps be portrayed as follows:

Left   VPK   SDAP   Center
                        FP   Moderaterna   Right

Our analysis points to the fact that even if party leaderships in all three countries enjoy limited room for manoeuvre in their coalitional behaviour, without taking voter reaction, or the threat of it, into account, they cannot escape the constraint entirely. The voters deal the cards with which the parliamentary game is played. They determine the broad contours of the party system. Their perception of distance and contiguity cannot be altogether ignored, either in periods of stability in the party system, or in the rather more fluid circumstances pertaining in all three countries since about 1973. Some parties are, however, more immune from these considerations than others. As we have seen, it has been the bourgeois parties which have been the most influenced by these concerns, at least in so far as their coalitional strategies are concerned.

(g)   Internal party factors and coalition politics

We should consider a final variable: the internal dynamics of the parties that appear as actors in the coalitional game, and the external influences upon them. Classic coalition theory has treated parties as unitary entities, ignoring internal tensions. This may be true of Scandinavia, with its iron party discipline in parliament, if the analysis is confined to the parliamentary level. At times, however, non-parliamentary party bodies and external pressure groups closely linked to parties can exercise a degree of influence on a party's strategy. Where this is so, or where the coalition negotiations themselves become the battleground in factional in-fighting within a political party, these internal dynamics must be taken into account.

It is rare, however, that a coalition should be entered into or rejected entirely for internal reasons. There is no doubt that the Danish Social Democratic leadership, often under trade union pressure, has sought to retain power, and hence access to the patronage and administrative powers of the executive, in circumstances where other groups in the party preferred opposition. This was the case in the 1957–60 coalition which included the Justice party, or in 1971–3 where the party's pro-Market wing sought to retain power to prevent the party opposing EEC membership from opposition, as happened in Britain. Trade union pressure broke up the SV coalition, but seems to have been a major factor in deciding the Social Democratic leadership to reverse its initial preference for opposition after the 1981 election. There is no doubt that the NAP leadership sought to remain in power in the post-1973 period in order to control and dampen down the move to the left which followed the 1973 election. Internal extra-parliamentary pressure prevented the SF leader Aksel Larsen entering a formal coalition in 1966, which was in turn offered by the Social Democratic Party in order to force SF to enter the arena of parliamentary responsibility, and so stem the Social Democrat losses to that party. The right of S then wanted a formal coalition with SF, but the left wanted then, as later, a working parliamentary/ legislative coalition only. In the later 1970s internal pressures inside SF prevented effective RV–S–SF co-operation, which would have offered a stable centre-left majority in the Folketing. In Sweden, internal pressures did much to break the Center–SDAP coalition in 1957, and poor relations between Center and FP in the wake of debate about a merger came from the FP extra-parliamentary party. These problems greatly helped the SDAP minority government from 1973 to 1976. In sum, factions can use coalitions and alliances as weapons in their internal battles. Often moderate leaderships apply the restraint of an alliance to maintain control of their party. Coalitions to the far left have only been contemplated by the Social Democratic leaderships when they have not threatened power relations within the party.

Certainly, parties are by no means monolithic entities in the bargaining process. They are subject to a whole range of internal and external pressures, which the parliamentary leadership will have to take into account. Internal battles and even purely internal motives may be obscure, but do, as we have seen, influence parties, particularly the Social Democrats, in seeking to retain power. The role of pressure groups, such as trade unions, employers' organisations, farmers' organisations and, for the Christian People's parties, the Church, which may have special formal or informal links with certain parties, is not clear. Certainly, these groups have 'access' to and provide input for the making of policy in 'their' party, but have rarely exercised direct influence on their coalitional behaviour. The employers' and farmers' organisations do not seem to have exercised any effective pressure in favour of bourgeois unity in any of the three countries. In Denmark, on the contrary, these groups seem to have preferred Social Democratic government in alliance with smaller bourgeois parties, at least until the mid-1980s. Only the trade unions, as we have seen, represent an important exception. They have always been a force in Social Democratic counsels in favour of retaining power, usually as a minority government, in order to retain control of the very significant patronage and administrative powers of even the weakest minority government. The greatest extra-parliamentary influence thus has lain with internal party bodies and factions, yet even their influence should not be exaggerated. It is a largely negative, restraining influence on party leaderships, which can usually gain easy approval of the arrangements that they have negotiated, although they may have had to incorporate the views of some of these extra-parliamentary actors into their negotiating position at an earlier stage.

(h) Conclusion

Scandinavian coalitional politics is complex and subtle, like a multi-dimensional chess game. The relevant parameters are often numerous, changing and contradictory. The Scandinavian area, which exhibits sufficient common characteristics to permit comparative treatment, illustrates the weaknesses of classic coalition theory. These theories concentrate on a too limited range of factors and party motives, and tend to ignore the wider importance of the party system and indeed of the political culture as a whole. In addition, these theories have concentrated on only one type of political behaviour: coalition formation and the office-holding motive.

In Scandinavia, their analytical and predictive value is limited, since in reality minimum winning closed coalitions, and indeed any coalitions, are as much the exception as the rule. The concerns of political parties seem to be different, being more related to policy influence maximalisation and profile maintenance, which may or may not be best served by seeking office in a coalition. Parties' concerns often seem to be long- or medium-term, rather than short-term, which is understandable in systems where mere seat maximalisation or office-holding may not be the most effective strategy, since election winners may turn out to be the political losers.

Scandinavian experience, then, fits the underlying assumptions of this work, that a broader-based analysis, incorporating a wider range of factors relating to the party system, distance perception, voter trends, party goals and motivation, is necessary. The key questions will always be relative: who will gain? Who will lose, and at whose expense? Will office-holding strengthen a party's relative position in the party system as a whole and within its own bloc? In short, coalitional behaviour is inevitably linked to the evolution of the party system, and should be seen as such.

Appendix. Abbreviations

Denmark

S	Socialdemokratiet	DS	Dansk Samling
RV, R	Radikale Venstre	U	De Uafhaengige
KF	Konservative Folkeparti	FRP	Fremskridtsparti
DR	Danmarks Retsforbundet	CD	Centrumsdemokraterne
SF	Socialistiske Folkeparti	LC	Liberal Centrum
DKP	Danmarks Kommunistiske Parti	V	Venstre
		KRF	Kristlig Folkeparti
VS	Venstre Socialisterne		

Norway

NAP	Norsk Arbeiderparti	SF	Sosialistisk Folkeparti
S	Senterparti	NKP	Norsk Kommonistisk Parti
V	Venstre		
H	Hoyre	SV	Sosialistisk Valgalliance
FRP	Fremskridtsparti (Anders Lange's Parti)	KRF	Kresteligt Folkeparti

NFP	Nye Folkeparti	SVP	Sosialistisk Venstre Parti

Sweden

SAP/SDAP	Socialdemokratiska Arbeiderpartiet	M	Moderata Samlingspartiet
C	Centerpartiet	VPK	Vänsterpartiet Kommunisterna
FP	Folkpartiet	KDS	Kristen Demokratiska Samling

Notes

1. Basic sources for the three countries:
   Denmark: J. Fitzmaurice, *Politics in Denmark* (Hurst, 1981)
   Norway: K. Cerny (ed.), *Scandinavia at the Polls* (American Enterprise Institute, 1977), ch. 2 (pp. 39–72)
   H. Valen, *Valg og Politik* (NKS Forlag, 1981)
   Sweden: S. Holmberg, *Svenska Väljare* (Liberforlag, 1981) Cerny, *Scandinavia at the Polls*, ch. 3.
   In a more comparative perspective, see N. Elder, A. H. Thomas and D. Arter, *The Consensual Democracies?* (Martin Robertson, 1982); and B. Turner and G. Nordquist, *The Other European Community* (Weidenfeld and Nicolson, 1982).
2. V. Bogdanor and D. Butler (eds.), *Democracy and Elections* (Cambridge University Press, 1983), pp. 122–41.
3. On the party systems, see Elder, Thomas and Arter, *Consensual Democracies?*, and Turner and Nordquist, *The Other European Community*.
4. Bogdanor and Butler, *Democracy and Elections*, tables at pp. 144–6
5. Calculations by the author.
6. Much of this literature is highly relevant to coalition behaviour without being specifically related to it. The key works (see note 1) are Valen, Fitzmaurice and Cerny.
7. E. Browne and J. Dreijmanis (eds.), *Government Coalitions in Western Democracies* (Longman, 1982), ch. 4. (A. H. Thomas).
8. V. Bogdanor (ed.), *Coalition Government in Western Europe* (Heinemann, 1983), ch. 4 (Pesonen and Thomas), pp. 59–96, and ch. 5 (Bo Särlvik), pp. 97–152.
9. For an analysis of the consensual concept, see Elder, Thomas and Arter, *Consensual Democracies?* pp. 9–28 and 85–96.
10. E. Damgaard, *Folketing under Forandring* (Samfundsvidenskabeligt Forlag, 1977).
11. See I. Budge, 'Beyond office-seeking: a pure policy pursuing theory of parties in government', ECPR paper, Salzburg, 1984; or I. Budge in *West European Politics*, vol. 7, January 1984.
12. Elder, Thomas and Arter, *Consensual Democracies?*, pp. 85–97.
13. Damgaard, *Folketing under Forandring*, pp. 97–9.
14. See Fitzmaurice, *Politics in Denmark*, pp. 98–100.
15. Ole Worre, 'Folketingsvalget 1977', *Økonomi og Politik*, 52nd year, no. 1, 1978, pp. 18–47.
16. See survey on 1965, 1969 and 1973 elections reported in H. Valen and S. Rokkan, 'The Norwegian program of electoral research', *Scandinavian Political Studies*, vol. 2, 1967; vol. 9, 1974.
17. Cerny, *Scandinavia at the Polls*, pp. 41–4.
18. *Ibid.* p. 59.
19. Soren Holmberg, *Svenska Väljare* (Liberforlag, 1981), especially ch. 13, pp. 351–2 and 346.
20. *Ibid.*, p. 362–77.
21. Cerny, *Scandinavia at the Polls*, p. 83, taken from a nation-wide sample survey (see *ibid.*, p. 73).
22. Distance perceptions taken from *ibid.*, p. 86.
23. *Ibid.*, pp. 100–1. The 1985 election in Sweden, however, vindicated FP's attempt to act as a Social–Liberal counterweight to M in the bourgeois bloc.

12   *Multi-dimensional approaches to the study of local coalitions: some cross-national comparisons*

(a)   Prospects and pitfalls of studying local coalitions

Any general theory of coalitions should help our understanding of coalitional behaviour at all levels, but traditionally most studies have focussed on national coalitions. In contrast, sub-national coalitions have attracted far less public and academic attention, but are equally important for understanding the nature of coalitional behaviour. There are numerically many more opportunities for studying inter-party agreements at the local level than there are at national level, and, by using the local context, it is possible to examine a number of coalitions simultaneously within a single country. Moreover, the study of local coalitions means that we emphasise intra-party relationships among the factors which may influence coalitional behaviour, and therefore no longer automatically view the party as a unitary actor.

A major criticism of traditional coalition theories has been their tendency to look upon political parties as unitary actors, each making rational calculations about the utility of coalition formation. To some extent, this tendency is the result of borrowing and adapting assumptions from earlier socio-psychological and game theory approaches to coalitions where the actor was believed to be both rational and single-minded. In political life, the coalition actor, the political party, does not possess the perfect knowledge and foresight which are prerequisites of rationality and is generally much less single-minded: intra-party conflict is frequently as fierce as inter-party rivalry. There may be relatively few occasions when the party acts with one mind and one voice. Internal conflict can occur between leaders and rank and file members at every party level, and also between levels in the party hierarchy. Examining local coalitional behaviour helps our understanding of vertical party relationships in particular as a determinant of coalitional behaviour at these various levels. The significance of hierarchical party relationships lies in their potential for mutual influence and interdependence: central authorities may sometimes impose their will on local branches or the latter may, in a less hierarchical system, act as a restraining influence on the behaviour of national groupings. Whatever the internal distribution of influence/power, both national and sub-national levels may learn from the successes and failures of coalitional activity at the other level. Such experience may subsequently be one factor in determining the attitudes of actors at each level of government towards prospective coalition partners. Regional and local authorities could, as they have, for example, in Italy, act as laboratories for subsequent national inter-party alliances.

Six countries are covered in this survey – Britain, France, West Germany, Ireland, Italy and the Netherlands. There are, of course, difficulties associated with cross-national comparisons of local coalitional behaviour. Like any comparative study, there is the risk of merely scratching the surface and failing to appreciate important differences between political systems. The unique character of the institutional components and the specific locality-bound nature of party cleavages and political issues add to the difficulties. Constitutional arrangements for sub-national units may, for example, vary within, as well as between, countries. This is perhaps best illustrated by the case of West Germany, where political heritage has ensured, within national boundaries, the survival and development of quite distinctive forms of local government structure. Likewise, the lack of a formal executive (the formation of which is the focus of most coalition study) in some local political systems presents problems, as does the difficulty of mapping country-wide patterns of activism and partisanship. Most important of all, despite the excellent potential, there is a lack of substantial research and data on the subject.

Relatively little attention has been paid to the phenomenon of local coalitions. The sheer number and variety of local authorities would make the collection of quantifiable data a formidable task, but this in itself is not a satisfactory explanation for its almost total neglect by academics. Perhaps the best published work in this area concerns Italy.[1] Since the local political system offers the only opportunity for studying coalitional behaviour in a British setting, there has been some interest in examining local coalition politics in Britain.[2] In general, however, the subject of local coalitions remains under-researched.

Most theoretical work on political parties has referred, if only briefly, to such inter-party agreements and not at all to local politics in this context. Duverger, for example, touches upon the contribution made by internal party structure and ideology in the operation of party alliances (specifically using the example of the Communist party), but concentrates on the impact of electoral systems, the significance of party strength and the possible patterns of coalition which might develop nationally.[3] More recently, Sartori and Lijphart have considered in much greater depth the significance of fractionalisation and elite control respectively as factors in inter-party relationships.[4] A limited attempt to catalogue variables in the formation and maintenance of coalitions – though incomplete and with relatively little emphasis on political parties – has been made by Hinckley.[5] The most ambitious attempt to provide a framework for the analysis of the party dimension in determining coalitional behaviour remains that of Groennings.[6] Although Groennings does not himself apply his framework to particular systems (except, in passing, Norway), let alone local politics, the study is valuable from our point of view in shifting emphasis away from the more traditional concerns of the initial distribution of resources and the size of winning coalitions to wider concerns such as situation, compatibility, motivation and interaction.[7] While focussing only on national politics, these theoretical works nevertheless help us formulate a multi-dimensional approach to the study of local politics.

The framework outlined in the first chapter of this book, in common with Groennings' approach, moves away from a single (horizontal) dimension in coalitional studies towards a multi-dimensional approach which has a particular applicability to local coalitional behaviour. Most of these dimensions – the historical, institutional, motivational, horizontal/vertical relationships, party-internal, socio-political and environmental – may, with varying degrees of significance, be applied to the dynamics of local council coalitions. It is impossible, however, in a relatively brief survey of six countries to attempt to apply them to more than a limited extent in order to test their usefulness for our understanding of coalitional behaviour. We have, therefore, chosen to emphasise the institutional, motivational and horizontal/vertical dimensions, the latter being linked in this case with the party-internal dimension. These dimensions are particularly helpful in explaining the nature of local coalitions; their application to local politics illustrates the value of adopting a multi-dimensional approach for the more general analysis of coalitional behaviour. First, however, it is important to examine the place of political parties in the arena of local politics.

(b) Party coalitions in local government

An analysis of local coalitional behaviour must begin with an assessment of party involvement in local politics, since it is an implicit assumption of the multi-dimensional approach taken in this book that political parties are the primary actors involved in the formation and maintenance of coalitions. In the case of national politics this is a reasonable assumption; it may be less so in the context of local politics. In the context of local government, it should not be assumed that political parties are invariably the primary actors involved in coalitional behaviour. It is perhaps helpful to distinguish between two models of the local political system: community-based local politics and party-based local politics.

Traditionally, political parties have been less involved in local politics than they have at the level of national politics. In many areas, especially rural ones, partisanship may even be considered divisive and inappropriate to the needs of the local community. In West Germany, for example, in view of the country's chequered history, a community-based approach to local politics has been widely encouraged. This community-based model of local politics, with parties playing little, if any, role, survives in less urbanised areas of all six countries. It is particularly well illustrated in France, where dispersed settlement patterns, combined with compact and physically cohesive communities, have militated against the development of strong provincial party organisations.[8]

The alternative pattern of local politics is a system which is party-based. Over the last ten to fifteen years, political parties have become increasingly involved in local government, which can again be illustrated by reference to West Germany.[9] Twenty years ago, confessional issues were primarily the basis of local party differences. Recently, these have been replaced by a more overt form of local party politics, especially, as elsewhere in Europe, in industrial and urban areas. In part this has resulted from the changing economic situation, particularly its effect on local taxes and employment prospects. It is also due in part to the response of national parties to the influence of non-party grassroots movements (*Bürgerinitiativen*). Increased national party involvement in local politics is also evident in the Netherlands. Twenty years ago, it was observed that there was 'a tradition of treating all but the most explosive of matters as non-political and . . . [a] . . . willingness to allow a good deal of independent judgement to those entrusted with authority'.[10] Although co-operation between parties remains common in the 841 Dutch municipal authorities, there has been a sharpening of party attitudes, especially by left-wing parties.[11]

A simple measure of increased party activity in local government is the extent of party involvement in local elections. In Ireland, for example, there has been a significant decline in the number of non-party councillors during the last decade. Similarly in Britain, especially since the reorganisation of 1974, local elections have become more party-dominated with fewer uncontested wards. In the last election prior to reorganisation, approximately 47 per cent of English and Welsh local authorities were controlled by Independents or non-party councillors. Within six years, the proportion had fallen to 21 per cent. In both Britain and Ireland, local elections are now very much a continuation of the national party struggle; in neither country is there much evidence of purely local parties.

There are a number of general reasons why parties have become increasingly involved in local politics. In part, it stems from an electoral requirement of mass parties to organise themselves locally. There follows from this a need for a coherent and cohesive party image which inevitably extends into the arena of local politics. Moreover, the incentive for party involvement in local politics has expanded as the distinction, especially in financial matters, between central and local spheres has become less clear. Left-wing parties have mainly been responsible for the increased involvement of political parties in local politics, as evidenced by Labour parties in Britain and the Netherlands and the Communists in both France and Italy. In general, national party penetration is greatest, and party conflict most intense, in the large cities.

These two models of local politics – community-based and party-based – are to some extent artificially distinguished here for the sake of illustration and explanation. The models are, of course, tendencies rather than pure in form and the two kinds coexist to greater or lesser extent in all six countries. The trend has been towards party-based systems, but this does not prevent the appearance of consensus politics in certain circumstances. In southern Italy, for example, party co-operation has followed deteriorating economic problems and social disloca- tion in the cities.[12] The importance of distinguishing two models of local politics is to understand their significance for the nature of coalitional behaviour or, to be more precise, the strategy behind, and the constraints upon, coalitional behaviour.

In those areas where party activity is weak, there is often a general atmosphere of *allgemeine Koalitionsfähigkeit*: a community-based model implies a good measure of accommodation and co-operation. In such circumstances, coalitions may be more concerned with personal prospects than party interests and are almost invariably loose, *ad hoc*, and not especially ideological. Individuals play a key role in coalition formation. By contrast, a high degree of party involvement in local politics brings with it an approach to coalitions which more closely resembles that which occurs at national level. Individual politicians are aware of partisan interests and may be more disciplined in their attitude and behaviour. Ideological considerations will be taken into account and both strategy towards coalitions and, frequently, the actual pattern of coalitions may mirror those which obtain at national level.

Party coalitions function in a political space and, therefore, unlike coalitions in non-political settings, a measure of ideological or socio-cultural compatibility is usually present in agreements between groups. Although no combination of groupings can as such be excluded as a possibility – especially in single-issue alliances – more durable electoral or governmental coalitions require some measure of mutual acceptability or, at the very least, a recognition of mutual interdependence (especially by captive parties).[13] Infrequently, there may be tactical agreements by parties at the opposing ends of the ideological spectrum to exclude centre parties, the effect of which is to stifle the benefits of those groups which usually occupy a pivotal position. In British local authorities, for example, Conservative and Labour parties sometimes give tacit support to each other in forming a minority administration in order to preclude the involvement of Liberals. Generally, however, it may be anticipated that partnership patterns will recur and be reasonably consistent. Moreover, there may be an in-built dynamism since, as illustrated in France, the more that elections are fought by a given coalition of parties the more credible that coalition formula is likely to become.

The relative consistency of national coalition patterns in Western Europe is also a feature of local coalitions. Sometimes, especially in more partisan councils, these patterns will conform to national ones. On other occasions, coalitions will diverge from those at national level and may even be unnatural in ideological terms. Within some countries there are also distinctive local traditions of inter-party co-operation, e.g. Socialists with Communists in various localities in the 'Red' region of Tuscany. The strength of these traditions may be such that they resist quite strong pressure from higher party levels to conform to national coalition patterns. This is true in parts of both Italy and France. Pridham, for example, has observed how in Italy local Socialist leaders were able to frustrate the attempts by national officials of PSI to apply its new centre-left alliance with the DC in the sixties in those areas with a long tradition of co-operation between PCI and PSI.[14] In those areas where a community-based tradition endures, norms of accommodation and co-operation will be especially forceful.

Traditions of co-operation are built upon personal relationships as well as those between parties, and a measure of personal compatibility between political actors obviously contributes to a successful outcome in coalition negotiations. The less partisan atmosphere which still prevails in many local governments, especially in cohesive rural communities, is enhanced when there is a mutual regard between individual participants. In such cases, an inclination towards personal co-operation can even overcome party competition. Such co-operation can derive from a number of factors. It may reflect a common belief in community-based programmes, particularly in those places where party labels only become really significant at election time. A shared commitment to a pragmatic or flexible political style or common role perceptions will also make alliance-building an easier task. Most simply, personal trust and mutual respect are important ingredients in the making of cross-party agreements. Groennings notes some of the factors that may induce or inhibit coalition formation:

> The positive factors include norms of rationality, willingness to experiment and senses of trust, tolerance and pragmatism. The negative factors include senses of suspicion, parochialism, superiority and self-righteousness, craving for contradiction, the tendency to underscore nuances of abstract principle, and the outlook that compromise is a sign of weakness.[15]

One specific factor which may well affect coalition formation at local level is the relatively intimate environment in which local politics is conducted – an environment where the key actors are frequently in close physical and social proximity. This is, of course, especially the case in cohesive rural communities. At local level, especially in those areas where party penetration remains weak (and this is the case in some areas of all six countries) personal relationships will be instrumental in determining participation in, and the outcome of, inter-party negotiations. Indeed, if the personal relationships have been divisive, negotiations are unlikely to start at all.

The influence of personal relationships between local politicians in formulating attitudes towards coalitions, both positive and negative, can be seen in the example of one British local authority. In the municipal elections of May 1982, the city of Bradford in northern England found itself with a hung council: Labour (previously in power) had 42 seats, Conservatives 42, Liberals 5, Social

Democrats 1. The three major party leaders were quite distinctive characters. The Labour leader was a veteran local Labour politician who saw very clear party divides in municipal affairs. Arguing that he had fought the election on a clear programme, he was not now prepared to compromise with what he considered opposition forces in order to retain control. In contrast, the Conservative leader, a university lecturer who had only recently been appointed leader, was much less rigid in his political views and adopted a considerably more flexible approach in his relationship with fellow councillors and officers. Immediately the election results were known, he indicated his willingness to negotiate with other party groups. The Liberal leader shared his flexible approach to politics and a policy agreement between himself and the Conservative leader was agreed quite speedily. Within a few weeks, the Conservative leader resigned for business reasons. His successor adopted a much more traditional view of party relationships and Liberal–Conservative relations subsequently returned to a more traditional and polarised basis. The episode demonstrates the significance of personal compatibility between individuals in coalition formation and maintenance. While other determinants remained unchanged – for example, the party balance and prior party relationships – the relationship between the respective party leaders was sufficient to initiate a coalitional arrangement and, subsequently, to allow it to founder.

Clearly, the nature of party involvement in local politics is an important determinant of coalitional behaviour at this level. Whilst we assume that there is a high degree of partisanship at national level, this may be less true of local government. Indeed, until recently, political parties played a relatively limited role in local politics. The distinction which can be made between community-based and party-based models is helpful in illustrating the effects of politicisation and increasing partisanship on coalition formation and maintenance.

(c) Institutional dimension

The opportunities for local coalitional behaviour are strongly influenced, if not predetermined, by the constitutional setting in which the political system operates. To take the most distinctive aspect of the constitutional setting, local government is, in general, legally subordinate to national government. This means that bargaining between individuals and parties at this level is constrained by a legal framework which can be altered only by a higher authority. Whereas, for example, a potential coalition partner at the national level can seek a constitutional modification (e.g. a change in the electoral system) as the price of an alliance, this is not possible at local level. The bargaining process is also constrained because of restrictions on what a local authority may do: in some areas it may be required by law to perform certain duties, whilst in others it may be excluded from so doing. Its limited ability to raise and spend money is a further factor which may well inhibit the extent of coalitional behaviour, since there may be less to bargain for between parties. Finally, there is the nature and election of the executive body, if any, in the local council. It is, of course, a matter of some dispute whether 'office' or 'policy' is the greater prize in coalition negotiations. The precise nature of the executive in local government varies both cross-nationally and within some countries, so that in some the positions of mayor and committee chairman or committee representatives will be thought of as considerable prizes, whilst in other councils policy agreements may rank over office allocation as the greater reward.

Sub-national units of government in the six countries assume a variety of forms: four (France, West Germany, Italy and the Netherlands) have regions, provinces or states in addition to their basic local governments. The size, powers and constitutional status of local authorities vary considerably between the countries. In the Netherlands, for example, 22 local authorities have populations of less than 1,000 (only 17 have over 100,000), whilst in Britain 3 metropolitan county councils have populations of over 2,000,000 and only 14 district authorities have less than 40,000. Predictably, the range in size is matched by corresponding differences in budgetary levels. Moreover, there are variations in size, power and constitutional status within, as well as between, countries. In West Germany, for example, two-tier councils exist alongside single-tier units and there are four distinct types of constitution. Some (particularly in Bavaria and Baden-Württemberg) put the mayor in a strong political position and reduce the availability of negotiable posts and offices, while others (notably in Hesse and Schleswig-Holstein) produce a collegiate executive and leave more scope for coalitional activity.

Two interrelated factors – the level of central control and the degree of financial autonomy – are especially significant in determining the status of local authorities, and hence the scope for coalition politics. Increasing control by central governments, often caused by decreasing financial self-sufficiency, is common in West European local government. This issue has dominated local government affairs in Britain in recent times. Similarly, a change in the financing of local government in Ireland in 1977 has meant that local authorities there have become much more dependent upon the Dublin government. The extreme example of central budgetary determination is to be found in the Netherlands, where a mere 6 per cent of municipal revenues derive from local taxes.[16] Of the remainder, 34 per cent is general funding and, significantly, 60 per cent takes the form of funding for specific purposes. Since budgetary issues (i.e. from whom money should be collected and on whom money should be spent) are the very essence of political debate, Dutch local authorities operate in a severely confined political environment. In addition there are various forms of central (and, sometimes, provincial) restrictions on local autonomy: negative limitation (Municipal Law, Art. 194), co-administration (Constitution, Art. 153), preventative (Constitution, Art. 155) and repressive (Municipal Law, Art. 185) supervision. The latter means that locally made decisions can be suspended or annulled by the central government if they conflict with the law or the general interest. It has been estimated that about 70 per cent of all discussion in Dutch municipal councils deals with decisions which need the approval of the central or provincial government.[17]

Italian local authorities are similarly constrained. In official language, Italian local government is generally referred to as 'administrative', the term 'political' being reserved for the activities of central government. Although there has been some devolution of authority since the establishment of regions throughout the country in 1970, the 8,000 communes and the regions have little significant power. In France also, municipal authorities are highly dependent upon central government, and in both countries there have been demands during the past decade, especially from the Left, for greater devolution of power.

Limitations on legal competence, however, do not necessarily restrain political debate; an inability to make and effect policies does not of course inhibit local politicians from expressing opinions on important issues. Local authorities in Britain, for example, have adopted stances on issues like nuclear weapons and British policy in Northern Ireland in the same way as Italian local councils passed resolutions on Vietnam.[18] The important point is that constraints upon the formal powers of local government do not preclude party activity and, therefore, the potential for party coalitions. Coalitional activity may certainly take place in a more limited bargaining arena than at national level and for goals which differ from those in national politics, but these characteristics apart it need not differ fundamentally from other kinds of party coalitions.

There is one further institutional dimension which has a particular effect on coalitions at the local level: the interval between elections. In contrast to some national systems, local elections are held almost invariably at fixed intervals. In Britain, the interval is four years in the case of counties and some non-metropolitan districts and annually (except in a year when the county election is held) in the remaining non-metropolitan and all the metropolitan districts, with one-third of the councillors retiring each round. In the Netherlands and France, the interval is four years and six years respectively. In West Germany, the interval varies (four to six years), as it does in Italy (four to five years). In Ireland, the interval is nominally five years, but this rule was recently suspended and the elections delayed by a further year.

The significance of election intervals for coalitional behaviour is that the more enduring the situation, the greater the incentive to engage in inter-party co-operation. There is sufficient time to achieve policy objectives, and there is time to disengage (if so wished) in order to re-establish separate identities towards the end of the period. The electorate may be less tolerant of a party which refuses to work with other parties and therefore perpetuates governmental uncertainty over a protracted period. Conversely, if parties have to wait only twelve months before another election and anticipate a change of political fortune, there might be a temptation to 'sit out' the balance of power in the hope of a more decisive result next time. In such cases, the long-term interests of maintaining ideological purity outweigh the short-term benefits of temporary power-sharing. This is one particular instance where socio-psychological explanations of formal coalitional behaviour do not correspond with political reality. Much coalitional theory generally assumes that actors will always wish to 'win' the present 'game'. In real political life, 'games' take place in a political context with both past experiences and future consequences and there are occasions when it is better to be wholly out of power rather than partly in power – one instance where the proverb 'half a loaf is better than no bread' does not seem to apply.

The significance of the duration of the power balance is illustrated in British local government since different election periods operate concurrently (one and four years) and, unusual by European standards, there is a possibility that a subsequent election might bring about a decisive result. In the 1981 county elections, seven county councils lost their overall majorities and were faced with a four-year period in which no single party commanded an overall majority. Some political leaders, recognising that the difficult situation was not temporary, were prepared to engage in coalitional negotiations. By British party standards, these were unusual initiatives. The Labour leader in Cheshire, for example, engineered a formal arrangement with the Liberal group, but he faced considerable opposition from members of his own party and the arrangements collapsed after one year. A similar, and seemingly more enduring, deal was struck between Conservative and Alliance groups on the Lothian (Edinburgh) Regional Council in May 1982. In both cases, the electoral impasse would last for four years. In contrast, in local authorities where an annual election takes place the major parties are much more reluctant to become involved in any accommodation with other groups. The political costs seem too great for so short a period and, if it is not possible to take control from a minority position (risking the occasional lost vote), then the likelihood is that parties will be content to avoid any responsibilities for the duration. The consequences of this approach are that there is considerable uncertainty throughout the year and changes of committee chairmanship on a monthly basis are not unknown. It may, indeed, only be resolved by one of the smaller parties taking up the challenge to attempt control. At the present time, for example, in the northern industrial district of Calderdale, the Liberals, who are the third-largest group behind Conservative and Labour, have assumed control of the committee chairmanships, since neither of the two larger groups were willing to take on this responsibility.

The fact that parties are occasionally reluctant to become involved in local coalitions is an illustration of the difference between traditional theoretical approaches to coalitional behaviour and what actually takes place in the real world of politics. In political life, the costs of coalitions have to be offset against the benefits which such alliance may bring. This is especially true in the context of local politics, since some features of the institutional setting – notably the frequent absence of executive offices and a constrained framework for bargaining

– can reduce the incentive for coalition formation. At national level, it is often assumed that government offices are key objectives in coalition bargaining, but at local level no such powerful offices may be available.

(d)   Motivational factors in local coalitions

The prime motivation for political leaders involved in coalition negotiation must be their desire to obtain a particular benefit from the agreement. This is usually access to power through holding a government office or obtaining policy concessions from their coalition partner, or sometimes both. In practice, however, the distinction between 'power' and 'policy' motivations may be artificial, since a prime reason for holding an office is to secure policy objectives. To argue this, of course, may be to neglect the personal, as opposed to the party, motivation of political actors in seeking office. The separation of 'power' and 'policy' is less meaningful in local politics; offices are usually sought (e.g. committee chairmanships and places) as a means of achieving longer-term policy benefits.

There are, however, two notable qualifications to the assertion that policy motivations prevail over considerations of office in the conduct of local coalitional behaviour: the motivations of parties which have suffered long exclusion from office and those which have newly arrived on the political scene. In both cases, their local coalitional behaviour is especially instructive, the former because local power may be seen by the party as a means of compensating for an inability to achieve national office and the latter because new parties often have their first taste of power in local government. In both circumstances there is an understandable temptation to seek a share of power irrespective of the political costs involved.

The strategy towards local coalitions of parties which have been excluded from national office is well illustrated by the British Liberal party, and more recently by the Liberal–SDP Alliance. At the present time the Liberal and Social Democrat parties control a handful of councils and hold the balance of power in a further 19 counties and districts. Officials warn local councillors against being too eager to enter into some kind of deal:

> Balance of power in reality is the toughest position in which any group of Liberal councillors can find themselves . . . Any arrangement involves compromise and the danger is that Liberals may become too clearly identified with another party . . . This is doubly dangerous if the other party is electorally unpopular. Similarly, Liberal initiatives might be interpreted by the media as the other party's initiatives . . . If the Liberals sell out too cheaply you will have little to show for the deal, you get left with the problems.[19]

When the Liberal–SDP Alliance decided to support a Conservative administration in Lothian Region in May 1982, a Scottish newspaper warned that the arrangement 'holds more political risks for the Alliance than the Tories. Lothian has now become their test bed in local politics.'[20] The message is clear: be cautious and retain a distinctive identity. Nevertheless, if the alternative is perpetual exclusion from office, parties often resort to adopting an accommodating stance.

The Irish Labour and Fine Gael parties recognise that co-operation with each other at local as well as at national level is the only way of competing for power with Fianna Fail – the only one of the three parties which can hope to form a single-party government. After a long time in the political wilderness, even a share of power is a great temptation, and since all four of the county boroughs and 19 of the 23 county councils are currently without a single-party majority, Irish local government provides numerous opportunities for power-sharing between these two parties. Perhaps the most vivid illustration of how a party can use the local arena to compensate for exclusion from national power is to be found in Italy, where the Communist party has exploited almost every opportunity to participate in local and regional government.

'New' parties face similar temptations, and the question of how to react to the opportunities of local coalitions is one now facing the Green party in West Germany. The extent of the electoral success of the Green party at local level can be seen by recent election results in North Rhine-Westphalia. In 1979 the Greens polled a mere 0.21 per cent of the vote which won them 42 local government seats; in September 1984 they captured 1,249 seats with a 6.13 per cent share of the vote and now have five deputy mayors in the region. In the Hesse Landtag the nine representatives of the Greens have held the balance of power and in December 1982 they sided with the SPD minority government when the numerically superior CDU made a bid for power.

The Greens in West Germany have generally been cautious and even divided when faced with the possibilities of power-sharing, with attitudes ranging from fundamental opposition through limited involvement to active participation. Even where they are willing to participate in inter-party arrangements, they are careful to maintain an independent visibility, preferring written coalition agreements and frequently insisting that the negotiations leading up to the agreement are made public. Although this procedure is not without precedent in West Germany (for example the 'Vereinbarung zwischen SPD und FDP für die Jahre 1979–1984', Cologne), the tactic has the virtue of publicly maintaining party integrity. It also contrasts with the often elitist nature of alliance formation between other parties – an aspect of coalition behaviour which is widely disapproved of by the German electorate. The approach taken by the Greens, however, does have the disadvantage of reducing the trust (which is a prerequisite of many other inter-party agreements) between itself and other parties.

(e)   Vertical/party-internal dimensions

Relationships between coalitional behaviour in local and national political arenas will be largely determined by the structure of political parties. A highly centralised party will be able to formulate national coalitions with only minimal reference to subordinate party levels. Moreover, it will have the ability to discourage 'deviant' local coalitions, or indeed any participation in local coalitions, and, if it wished, encourage the testing of experimental sub-national alliances prior to their adoption at national level. Where the party structure is less centralised, local coalitional behaviour will be freer and sub-national levels more able to affect national coalitional behaviour.

In all six countries, deviant coalitions do occur at local level – in the case of Britain, any local coalition must be deviant by virtue of the absence of coalitions at national level. The implication of this is that, on a vertical as on a horizontal plane, parties are not wholly unitary actors since in none of these countries is their coalitional behaviour entirely uniform. In each country, local coalitions are not simply a replica of national alliances. Again, it is worth noting that this is especially true in rural communities, where national parties are less able and, perhaps, less concerned to discipline local party branches.

National party policy towards local coalitions and the degree of party centralisation naturally varies. Despite the existence of deviant local coalitional behaviour, there are powerful centralising forces. In most parties, structural relationships are weighted towards cohesiveness and centralisation and even where the local party retains a high degree of autonomy, local activists are inevitably influenced by national coalition patterns. It is hardly surprising that local coalitions will often conform with those at national level, even where it is not an obligation upon local parties.

All three Irish parties have distinctive attitudes to coalitions as such, which spill over into the local setting: one is a negative view (Fianna Fail), the other two (Fine Gael and Labour) are positive. Of the latter two, Fine Gael is the more centralised and decisions reached in Dublin are readily accepted in the municipalities. In practice, distinction between the parties is a little artificial, since throughout the country there is strong adherence to central policies whenever potentially controversial issues are being discussed. Much of the business of local government is not conducted on a partisan basis, but when sensitive issues do occur, such as the allocation of committee places and the annual budget, party lines are observed. This discipline is both imposed by the centre and volunteered by the locality. The incentive for the latter is occasioned by the fact that in Ireland, like many other countries, membership of a local council is an important career stepping-stone for many aspiring national politicians. This is an important factor in explaining why local politicians often conform voluntarily to national strategies.

The four main parties in Britain may be categorised in the following way: Labour and Conservative are well organised and largely centralised; the Social Democratic party is centralised but has a weaker organisation; and the Liberal party is decentralised.[21] Of these four parties, only the latter two have given much thought to coalitional strategies at both local and national levels. Not surprisingly, the policy of both is to exploit opportunities for local power-sharing, although with caution.[22] Of the other two parties, Conservatives avoid any nationally imposed view, whilst Labour comes close to attempting to prohibit involvement in local coalitions. Clause 6 of the Model Standing Orders for Labour Groups stresses that, when in opposition, Labour groups should avoid taking on any committee chairmanships and most local groups have interpreted this as meaning that they should refrain from taking chairmanships when they are not in a majority situation.

In West Germany, none of the main parties stipulate policies towards local coalitions, although all would maintain that the party's principles would need to be observed in any local arrangement. In practice, all parties consistently engage in local coalition activity of varying degrees of formality. The real influence of national parties is manifested through the tendency of local parties to imitate coalitions in Bonn. In the Netherlands, the party system is much more hierarchical, but communication between party levels is poor and party cohesion fragile. National parties frequently stress the need to preserve separate identities and the more aggressive attitude of Labour nationally has been reproduced at local level. Even this, however, has failed to have much impact on the traditionally consensual approach of Dutch municipal government. It has politicised rather than polarised Dutch local government.

Central determination of local political behaviour in Italy has been extended in recent years, most significantly by the Communists. Both DC and PCI have sharpened their policies towards coalitions, although a weaker organisation and more fractionalised structure in the former have meant that central policies have been more easily resisted by powerful local leaders.[23] In the case of both parties, national strategies take precedence over local preferences, although the party bureaucracy can be frustrated when attempting to impose such strategies locally. In the DC, elite control is aided by weak activism at lower levels and in the PCI by a highly organised national structure. Central control of smaller parties is reduced by the need to respond to local circumstances and, in particular, the locally dominant party. Thus, for example, the PSI carefully avoids any limitations to its freedom of action in selecting local coalition partners. Indeed, the existence of local party strongholds militates generally against all parties adopting too rigid a national strategy towards local party groups.

The most forceful central determination of local coalitional behaviour is to be found in France. The bipolarisation which has been seen at national level has also occurred at the lower levels of French political life. Originally, the impetus of the left to organise itself in the localities stemmed from the need to contend with Conservatives and Radicals in local government from which the Senate was elected. The extent of bloc organisation at the local level can be judged from the fact that in the 1983 local elections the centre-right *majorité* presented a single list in 200 of the 225 towns with populations over 30,000 and the left in 204 such towns. The latter figure compares with 60 out of 159 in 1965 and 124 out of 193 in 1971.[24] Party organisation and cohesion, previously poor, has been significantly strengthened, especially on the left.

Local alliances involving the Socialist party (PS) have been modified by the strategy of left-wing unity adopted by the Congrès d'Epinay in 1971. At every subsequent election, the party has followed a policy of collaboration with forces of the left. As a consequence, at the 1977 French municipal elections PS broke off all its alliances with the centre or anti-Gaullist right-wing parties, some of which had existed for thirty years. Instead PS systematically applies a policy of collaboration with other groups on the left – PC, MRG, PSU. Indeed, it is significant that the collaboration between Communist and Socialist has proved more durable at local than at national level over the past decade and survived both the split at the end of the seventies and the more recent one between PS and PCF. The Communists' contribution to this strategy is particularly valuable through its strong grassroots organisation (as in Italy) and association with the trade union CGT. The formality of the arrangement is such that before each election, the Socialist party draws up a strategy, detailing arrangements for joint list negotiations, which is adopted by a national convention comprising delegates from departmental federations. The March 1983 strategy, for example, stated that where it was not possible to form joint PS/PCF lists at first round then the second round must involve proportionate joint lists. If necessary, the party headquarters intervenes in cases of disagreement and always has the final say in the formation of local coalitions. According to PS, local groups have not been involved in any local coalitions outside this national framework since 1977.

The extent of party centralisation is clearly an important factor in determining how free a local party is to engage in coalition negotiations in its own right. Throughout these six countries, increasing attempts have been made by the political parties to secure greater cohesiveness in vertical relationships. Whereas party levels previously tended to operate in isolation and relative freedom, fresh discipline now characterises many political parties and a high degree of centralisation, expressed through attitudes to local coalitional behaviour, is most visible on the left, as evidenced in France, Italy and, to a lesser degree, Britain. Nevertheless, no single party has achieved complete control over coalitional activity at every level. To this extent the notion of parties as unitary actors is inappropriate in the context of local politics. This is not to deny that what happens at national level has considerable bearing on the coalitional behaviour of local parties. Rather it points to the value of a multi-dimensional understanding of coalitions where the vertical dimension (in this case from centre to periphery) is only one factor affecting the behaviour of the parties in local politics.

(f)   Concluding comments

In this survey, it has been possible to apply only selected aspects of the multi-dimensional model to the study of local coalitional behaviour, but this should not be taken to imply that other features of the model are irrelevant to the processes of local coalitional formation and maintenance. It is clearly the case, for example, that the local media, local bureaucrats, interest groups and the electorate – all facets of the environmental dimension – will influence the attitudes and behaviour of local politicians towards coalitions. The purpose of the multi-dimensional approach is to highlight the superficiality of traditional, single-dimensional approaches to coalitions. The distinction which is made in it between the various dimensions is not intended to suggest that they operate in isolation from each other.

The dimensions discussed here – institutional, motivational, vertical/party-internal – have been selected for a number of reasons. They demonstrate, for example, the inadequacy of the notion, prominent in traditional theory, that political coalitions are determined on the basis of single-minded rationality, modified only to take account of the ideological considerations inherent in a political context. In local as in national politics, party considerations must be recognised as an important constraint on the assumptions of rationality in traditional coalition theories.[25] However, the multi-dimensional approach goes further in revealing the inadequacy of viewing parties as unitary actors as well as recognising forces outside the party sphere. One particularly useful feature is the perspective associated with the vertical dimension: in studying the local arena, the significance of the vertical dimension, together with its associated pressures and implications for both national and subnational levels of government, is emphasised. It becomes clear that constraints on coalition behaviour already associated with the horizontal (traditionally, national) dimension are also applicable on a vertical plane. Political parties are non-unitary actors in that they are subject both to the forces of fractionalisation on the horizontal (both national and sub-national) level and of alienation in vertical intra-party relationships.

There are, of course, some important differences between national and sub-national levels, including the constitutionally and financially subordinate nature of the local political arena. One obvious distinction is the frequent absence of an executive body in local politics, denying coalition actors the opportunity of negotiating the high-status positions which are often viewed as the prizes in national coalition activity. That coalitions do occur suggests that policy considerations often prevail over those of office-holding in the context of local coalitional behaviour. Perhaps the most significant distinction between national and local politics is the extent of politicisation and partisanship. Whereas we assume considerable party rivalry at the national level, this is not always the case in local politics. While it appears that in most West European countries traditions of community-based politics are giving way to a more politicised, partisan model, community traditions still prevail in some localities. Moreover, strong community ties may re-emerge in a politicised context in the form of a consensual response to economic deprivation or crisis, which temporarily subordinate partisan demands. To that extent, the pattern of politicised, consensual politics at the local level offers a useful insight into the coalitional behaviour of groups governing under pressure. The urban/rural dichotomy appears to be particularly relevant in this context, and is perhaps one feature which merits a refinement of the multi-dimensional approach.

The multi-dimensional model of coalitional behaviour clearly offers an improved approach to the study of coalitions at local as well as national level. Local coalitions deserve considerably more attention from academics than they have hitherto received. They offer valuable opportunities to improve our understanding of the formation and maintenance of coalitions, the ability to study several coalitions simultaneously and within a single national setting being a particularly useful feature of the sub-national arena. Further investigations of local coalitions, using the multi-dimensional approach, promise the possibility of adding significantly to our knowledge and understanding of the nature and dynamics of coalitional behaviour.

Notes

1. G. Pridham, 'Parties and coalition behaviour in Italian local politics: conflict or convergence', *European Journal of Political Research*, vol. 12, 1984, 223–41, and L. Graziano *et al.*, *Archivo ISAP*, no. 2, n.s. (Milan), 1984.
2. See, for example, C. Mellors, 'Coalition strategies: the case of British local government' in V. Bogdanor (ed.), *Coalition Government in Western Europe* (Heinemann, London, 1983) and 'Political coalitions in Britain: the local context', *Teaching Politics*, vol. 13, 1984, pp. 249–59; A. Alexander, 'Coalitions in British local government' and A. Blowers, 'The politics of uncertainty: the consequences of minority government in an English county', both papers presented to the workshop on 'Conflicts and Coalitons in Local Politics', ECPR, Freiburg, 21–25 March 1983.
3. M. Duverger, *Political Parties*, 2nd ed (Methuen, London, 1959), pp. 324–51.
4. G. Sartori, *Parties and Party Systems* (Cambridge University Press, 1976); A. Lijphart, *The Politics of Accommodation: pluralism and democracy in the Netherlands*, 2nd edn (University of California Press, Berkeley, 1976).
5. B. Hinckley, *Coalitions and Politics* (Harcourt Brace Jovanovitch, New York, 1981), pp. 51–64.
6. S. Groennings, 'Notes toward theories of coalition behaviour in multi-party systems: formation and maintenance' in S. Groennings, E. W. Kelley and Michael Leiserson (eds.), *The Study of Coalition Behaviour* (Holt, Rinehart and Winston, New York, 1970), pp. 445–65.
7. *Ibid.*, p. 449.
8. S. Tarrow, *Between Center and Periphery* (Yale University Press, New Haven, 1977), pp. 55–6.
9. See, for example, O. W. Gabriel, P. Haungs and M. Zender, *Opposition in Grossstadtparlamenten*, KAS Forschungsbericht 42 (Knoth, Melle, 1984).
10. Committee on the Management of Local Government, vol. 4, *Local Government Administration Abroad* (HMSO, London, 1967), p. 130.
11. Lijphart, *The Politics of Accommodation*, pp. 196–219. On the attitudes of the Labour party towards municipal politics, see W. van Raay, 'Changes in local pattern of coalition', paper presented to ECPR Workshops, Freiburg, March 1983, p. 3.
12. Pridham, 'Parties and coalition behaviour', p. 229.
13. Groennings, 'Notes towar.' theories of coalition behaviour', p. 451.
14. Pridham, 'Parties and coalition behaviour', p. 234.
15. Groennings, 'Notes toward theories of coalition behaviour', p. 454.
16. A. Hoogerwerf, 'Relations between central and local governments in the Netherlands', *Planning and Development in The Netherlands* (Van Gorcum, Assen, 1981), pp. 215–37.
17. *Ibid.*, p. 218.
18. Pridham, 'Parties and coalition behaviour', p. 228, points out that Italian local councils passed resolutions on Vietnam.
19. Margaret Clay, *Life in the Balance* (Association of Liberal Councillors, Campaign Book no. 7, n.d.).
20. *Scotsman*, 17 May 1982.
21. When the Alliance was formed (between the Liberal and SDP leaderships), the SDP leadership clearly failed to appreciate the difficulties their Liberal colleagues had in imposing that deal at grassroots level, with the consequence that the SDP was frustrated at the slow progress of agreement on seat-sharing arrangements.

22. Clay, *Life in the Balance*.
23. Pridham, 'Parties and coalition behaviour', pp. 230–4.
24. V. Wright, *The Government and Politics of France* (Hutchinson, London, 1978), p. 128.
25. See K. von Beyme, 'Governments, parliaments and the structure of power in political parties' in H. Daalder and P. Mair (eds.), *West European Party Systems* (Sage, Beverley Hills, 1983).

13 Research notes

(a) A note on the empirical analysis of coalition policy

Michael Laver

Formal theories of government coalition formation tend to consider two inputs: the number of seats controlled by a party and its position in the ideological party space. Formal theories of government coalition payoff tend to consider two outputs: the distribution of cabinet portfolios and the policy package agreed by coalition partners. The testing of such theories has been straightforward with respect to seat and portfolio distributions, which are easily ascertainable. The policy positions of both parties and coalitions, however, have presented empirical problems. Until recently, the solution has been to have recourse to experts, who have been asked to locate parties on ideological dimensions. These expert judgements have then been used as input to the analysis. (A recent, and systematic, exposition of this technique can be found in Castle and Mair (1984).)

'Expert'-generated data have severe drawbacks as far as the testing of coalition theories is concerned. By far the most serious of these is that data on party policy positions must be entirely independent of the subsequent coalition negotiations, if such data are to be used to predict coalition formation. In practice it seems likely that expert judgements on policy positions will be highly coloured by the outcome of coalition politics. However much they might be earnestly exhorted to do so, any set of experts would find it very difficult to divorce the fact that two parties went into government together from the possibility, in theory, that they might be moving further apart in policy terms. Crucially, of course, it is impossible to know whether our experts have succeeded, or not, in keeping such matters apart.

The second problem with expert-generated data is that it does not exist in time series form for the full range of European coalition systems. Experts can, of course, be asked for retrospective judgements on party movements over a period of forty years or so. But the problem of divorcing party movements from coalition formations is then almost certainly insuperable. Conventionally, the formation of certain coalitions is used as a prime piece of evidence about the existence of certain movements in party policy.

Recently, however, the European Consortium for Political Research (ECPR) Research Group on Party Manifestos has generated an alternative data set that does provide a quite independent statement of each party's ideological position. The detailed results are reported in Budge *et al.* (1985), but may be briefly summarised.

The ECPR researchers, each a country specialist, engaged in a detailed content analysis of the election manifesto of each party in their system, at each election since 1945. A common, agreed coding scheme with 54 basic categories was used, though researchers were free to add their own country-specific sub-categories. The categories were grouped into general 'issue domains', such as 'economic policy', 'international relations' and so on. A dimensional analysis was first conducted on each domain in order to extract key dimensions.[1] Examples of such dimensions might be 'pro social service expansion' or 'pro law, order and traditional morality'. These 'first stage' policy dimensions (of which there were generally 10 to 14) were then subjected to a further dimensional analysis.[2] The result was a compact spatial representation of party policy positions in the system, as indicated by party manifestos.

This technique enables the calculation of exact co-ordinates for each party at each point in time. Such data obviously represent a major resource for the testing of theories of government coalition formation.

The second stage of the project is to collect equivalent data for coalition policy packages. This stage is currently in progress, applying the same coding scheme to the policy document that is the immediate result of the coalition negotiations. This data will allow the testing of policy payoff theories. When a number of coalitions occur within a single inter-electoral period, it will also allow the development of a more dynamic model of the process.

The selection of party election *manifestos* and statements of coalition policy on *formation* obviously raises the issue of precisely *what* should be taken as the authoritative evidence of party or coalition policy. It might well be argued that it is what parties or coalitions *do* that is important, not what they *say*. Systematically measuring what parties or coalitions do, of course, is a very difficult business, and almost certainly returns us to the realm of generalised expert judgements. Furthermore, the explicit policy statements that will be used have two big advantages. In the first place, they tend to be comprehensive, laying out party or coalition policy on issues that may not arise in the political hurly-burly of a given parliamentary session (but which are no less important parts of party policy for that). In the second place, these are the documents that represent the 'official' public face of the parties or coalitions concerned. They are the documents for which parties and coalitions are held to account at election time, and in this sense can be seen as 'bench marks' of policy.

Obviously, in an established coalition system, in which both parties and voters become accustomed to the making of policy concessions in coalition negotiations, it may be that manifestos anticipate the process and do not reflect 'true' party policy. Manifesto policy might move *towards* that of anticipated coalition partners in this event (in order to facilitate negotiations) or it might move *away* from it (in order to establish a bargaining position). Strategic considerations may operate to shift published policy from 'real' policy in unpredictable ways and we are left, once more, with the published documents as at least some sort of objective bench mark against which subsequent performance may be evaluated.

The ECPR Manifesto/Coalition project, therefore, is in the process of generating a data set that will enable *formal* theories to be tested and explored in a more comprehensive manner than has hitherto been possible. As was noted in the chapter 2, existing tests for formal theories have worked most effectively on a country-by-country basis. It is to be hoped that the new data set, by enabling more elaborate analyses to be performed, will go some way towards increasing the empirical relevance of formal theories for country specialists.

(b)   An events conceptualisation of cabinet stability: a research programme

Eric C. Browne and Dennis W. Gleiber

The defining characteristic of scientific investigation is its goal of exposing the order of the universe. In somewhat less grandiose terms, scientific research seeks to describe, predict and explain observable phenomena by identifying particular observations as belonging to (subsumed under) some more general class of phenomena. The universe becomes orderly when we are satisfied that the phenomena we observe behave in ways that are expected from extrapolations of general models and theories of such phenomena. Thus, planetary motion becomes orderly through the application of classical mechanics and markets are considered 'well behaved' when they are observed to tend to an equilibrium.

In political science, the concept of order is perhaps most frequently identified with studies of political stability. Indeed, this area of research has been the major preoccupation of those engaged in the study of comparative politics. While there has been considerable interest in the stability of political regimes in the so-called developing countries, much of this work has drawn upon insights gained from the study of democratic stability, the focus of which is largely on experiences of the industrialised nations. Within this tradition, much attention has been paid to the stability of governments, since governmental stability is usually presumed to be associated with institutional effectiveness in satisfying the aspirations of the public and, by extension, building or reinforcing the legitimacy of the regime.

A cursory examination of the experiences of cabinet governments has led many scholars to conclude that cabinet instability is not only prevalent in many countries, but is also an undesirable condition which is in need of attention and repair. If we grant the desirability of creating greater political stability by creating more stable governments, we must come to an understanding of the variability in the stability of governments as they exist in nature. To this end, we have embarked upon a research programme which offers a new conceptualisation of the problem of cabinet stability. This project will be described in the remainder of this chapter.

Towards a theory of cabinet stability

'Cabinet behaviour is disorderly.' This statement calls attention to the remarkable variability which is observed among the cabinets of Western parliamentary democracies. Some cabinets come into existence with well-defined policy proposals which are sweeping in their potential for social change and which are swiftly promulgated into law, while others seem content to accomplish little in the way of major reform. Still others seem beset with conflict and controversy, while some encounter little adversity. Some seem to be continuously at the brink of dissolution, and yet endure, while others, which appear to be operating smoothly, succumb suddenly for no apparent reason. How can these disparate experiences be explained?

The major tradition investigating the stability of cabinet governments has conceived the idea of stability as the length of time cabinets endure in office; that is, the longer lasting, the more stable. Thus, researchers have sought the determinant factors which account for variability in the tenure of governments. Generally, these have been conceptualised as either conditions representing varying degrees of multipartism in parliament or cabinet, or as particular manifestations of ideological conflict in the parliamentary/cabinet arena. Statistical models have been estimated by a number of scholars relating these party and party-system attributes with cabinet duration, confined normally to experiences in the post-war period but embracing a large sample of governments in many Western parliamentary democracies (Dodd 1976; Sanders and Herman 1977; Taylor and Herman 1971; Warwick 1979). Reported results of such tests have relied upon coefficients of determination for interpretative purposes and have demonstrated weak statistical associations (normally less than 30 per cent of explained variance), regardless of the measures employed.

In recent work (Browne, Frendreis and Gleiber 1984) we have questioned the adequacy of this specification of the problem, arguing instead that the determinant attributes identified by others may not in any necessary way be related to the longevity of cabinets. Rather, they are more profitably seen as conditions in the immediate environment of cabinets which may or may not contribute to or detract from the ability of cabinet actors to sustain their governments in the face of whatever 'disturbances' as may arise during their tenure. We conceive these disturbances, generically, as 'events', which function as covariates of cabinet dissolution, and posit that the timing of their arrival in the environments of cabinet actors is randomly distributed over the tenure of governments. Some of these events are expected to be of sufficient intensity to bring on the demise of a government (terminal events, or 'no exit' states, such as the death of a Prime Minister), while others may actually enhance longevity (e.g. the success of the Italian football team in the 1982 World Cup matches). The important point here is that events bring on dissolutions of cabinets, not their attributes, and that even the most congenial mix of attributes may not be sufficient to sustain the existence of a cabinet.

A focus on 'events' as terminating agents of governments (as dependent variables) directs our attention away from constant factors in the environments of cabinet actors (e.g. the number of parliamentary parties, the number of cabinet actors, the presence of surplus actors in cabinet, etc.) to those which are variable in their manifestation. In particular, we have been interested in the 'scheduling' of terminal events as they are oriented in time. Because we have at present no data with which to map the events environments of cabinets, we have constructed a 'null' events model of cabinet dissolution and tested it with dissolution data for cabinets in twelve Western parliamentary democracies for the period 1945–80 (Browne, Frendreis and Gleiber 1982).

Essentially, this model assumes that terminal events are the effective agents of dissolution and that they are generated by a random variable with a negative exponential (Poisson) distribution. Our test results demonstrated a strong fit of the distribution of observed dissolutions with that derived from the exponential Poisson model for four of the countries in our sample (Belgium, Finland, Israel and Italy). For the remaining eight countries (Austria, Denmark, Iceland, Ireland, Netherlands, Norway, Sweden and West Germany) the results were equivocal ($.05 > p > .001$), though not sufficient to demonstrate a contrary result. We interpret these findings as supportive of our view that the dissolution of cabinets is modelled by a functional form different from a linear regression analysis, and that the timing of terminal events is uncertain in the experience of cabinet decision-makers and most probably also unpredictable in many (or most) instances.

It is, perhaps, somewhat disconcerting to reach a conclusion that important political phenomena are cogently described as random processes. For, among other things, this would appear to jeopardise, if not confound, our goal of exposing the order which underlies the process of governing. However, such a conclusion would be premature and would depreciate the importance of a stochastic understanding of the phenomenon under investigation.

A way forward

If terminal events, occurring randomly in time, are the effective agents of cabinet dissolution, we shall need to know a great deal more about them than at present if we are to understand why cabinets break down when they do. In the first place, the political environments of cabinet decision-makers are filled with a diversity of events (both terminal and non-terminal) which is almost infinitely large. These comprise the countless transactions which occur both domestically and internationally on a daily basis, some of which will intrude significantly upon cabinet decision-makers as they discharge their governing functions. Theoretically, it is useful to conceive of such events as 'demands' received variably by cabinet actors and calling for some response. This may be anything from satisfying a demand to ignoring it or to rejecting it. Terminal events are conceived as those demands on cabinet actors that they cannot or will not satisfy in a satisfactory way and which, thus, force a decision (by one or more of them) to terminate the existence of a cabinet. The problem, thus, is an understanding of the process whereby terminal events are generated so that their occurrence (arrival in the decisional environment of cabinet actors) can be anticipated.

Presently, our research is proceeding along three related paths, each of which is designed to illuminate the problem in a theoretically meaningful way. First, we have undertaken a project to collect events data for the cabinet experiences of the French Fourth Republic. This is, as it were, a first cut at these data, based on historical and journalistic accounts. What is gained is a chronology of occurrences for various cabinets, susceptible to classification by issue domains and environmental source. With such data we shall be able to assess cabinets in terms of periods of turmoil and calm, and eventually learn something of the dynamics surrounding the progression of covariates (their serial or discrete nature) and the conditions under which they intensify or diffuse. An example of this approach, utilising data collected for the Ramadier government in 1947, is presented in chapter 5 of this volume.

Since we have conceptualised cabinet dissolution as the result of the occurrence of a particular type of event, what we have called 'terminal events', a second strand of our research has focussed directly on them. Again, our initial efforts have been centred on classification, and we have produced one paper which studies cabinet terminations in the Scandinavian countries (Browne, Frendreis and Gleiber 1984). Here, we have considered terminal events as being either discrete or serial in their manifestation, and have attempted to discern the types of terminal events which occur and the various issue domains within which they arise. Dominant, of course, among the events precipitating cabinet dissolutions is the constitutional necessity of holding elections for the renewal of parliament. Additionally, many other dissolutions resulted in the holding of unscheduled elections. There were also several dissolutions brought about by political scandals or the deaths (or ill health) of prime ministers.

With respect to issue domain, events arising from the domestic economy dominated, many associated with union activity. These accounted for half of all dissolutions not brought about by regularly scheduled elections. Finally, it was noted that some variability characterised country experiences with respect to how conflict generated by events will be manifested. In general, more dissolutions were occasioned by disagreements arising among coalition partners than from initiatives led by opposition parties in parliament. Specific dynamics surrounding dissolution involve the importance or not of particular leadership positions, notably prime ministers and heads of state.

The third strand in our research programme is theoretical and methodological, and focusses on the specification of a dynamic model capable of dealing with the seemingly random patterns in the distribution of cabinet dissolutions and the generation of events. Here, we are beginning to investigate the relevance of two approaches, mathematical chaos theory (Browne and James 1985) and catastrophe theory, for application to the problem. Generally, chaos theory proceeds on the assumption that small occurrences (events) have large consequences. From the standpoint of chaos theory, cabinet dissolutions may be able to be modelled as 'rare events' in time which are 'sensitively' dependent on perturbations occurring in their environment. Sensitive dependency in this case indicates the existence of a dynamic process conditioning the downfall of cabinets such that the occurrence of systematically local events may, under certain conditions, create events configurations, or patterns, which have specific consequences for the cabinet according to their *dimensionality*: i.e. they may magnify or cumulate in such a way as to constitute a threat to the stability (persistence) of the cabinet.

The most promising branch of chaos theory for such investigation is fractal geometry, which seeks to identify the dimensionality of some environment of potentially disruptive events which yields the most accurate representation (topography) of that environment. Put another way, fractal geometry offers us a way to discern an appropriate level of detail in the events environment wherein the generation of terminal events for cabinets may be observed. Thus, fractal geometry may allow us to move beyond our current understanding of a Poisson process driving cabinet dissolutions through its reconceptualisation of randomness as sensitive dependency. This construction of the problem can lead to the creation of simulation models, based on varying events configurations and fractal dimensions, for forecasting purposes. A computer algorithm can be developed which will allow us to identify those events patterns, represented through quantitative fractal dimensions, which are most likely to lead to cabinet dissolutions. While such research cannot be expected to produce point-specific predictions, it should yield some forecasting ability based on probability estimates from events data.

Catastrophe theory provides a mathematical framework capable of explaining suddenly changing behaviours (discontinuities in a dependent variable) which result from some set of continuously distributed independent variables. In the case of cabinet stability (duration), the observed condition of the dependent variable is that 'cabinets live until they die'; that is, dissolution is a discontinuity in the continuing existence of a government. Deterministic attributes models of cabinet duration, in effect, give prognoses of longevity based on discrete values which attach to independent variables (attributes) observed at the time of government formation. The form of such prognoses is something like a very gross probability estimate of duration, such that the greater (lesser) the values attaching to attributes at formation, the greater (lesser) the likelihood that the cabinet will enjoy extended duration. As noted, the estimates produced by such models have not yielded acceptable levels of predictive ability.

Among other things, traditional stability (duration) models depreciate the importance of continuous processes occurring over the life of a cabinet. If, for example, cabinets fall as a result of conditions in their environment, are these conditions manifested in the same way, or have they 'changed' during the period the cabinet held office? To consider a simple example, a cabinet is invested at a particular point in time, and the investiture vote may be taken as an indication of parliamentary support for its continuing existence *at that time*. However, examination of roll-call voting indicates that, for the French Fourth Republic governments at least, there is a more or less continuous erosion of parliamentary support for sitting governments until, finally, a discontinuity occurs such that the government is either forced from power or resigns in anticipation of this outcome.

This possibility raises the more general question as to whether cabinet dissolution (or duration time) is a singular or complex phenomenon. While direct measurements of either concept suggest the former, there may in fact be several kinds of theoretically distinct forms of cabinet dissolution. For example, dissolution may occur to fulfil a constitutional requirement that parliament be renewed (so that the government will remain responsive to the citizenry). Alternatively, dissolution could result from economic or political conflict among interest organisations or from other social dissatisfactions which accumulate in society and intrude upon cabinet decision-makers indirectly. Further, dissolution might be effected by seemingly random events, like the death of a Prime Minister or an international crisis. If all these kinds of dissolution processes may plausibly occur over a universe of cabinet experiences, then what is needed is a model which can simultaneously describe *both* continuous and discontinuous changes in the attributes and environment of cabinets; that is, a single dynamic theory. Such a model must allow for multimodal states and discontinuous jumps between such states, based on gradual variations in the independent parameters. Catastrophe theory seems an appropriate framework for such analyses.

Summary

The programme just outlined focusses interest on the general problem of cabinet stability in Western parliamentary democracies. It has particular importance for the study of coalition behaviour inasmuch as a substantial portion of the relevant universe consists of cabinets which are coalitions of political parties. With respect to coalition cabinets particularly, certain implications for stability have emerged from our previous research. The findings of our Poisson analysis have demonstrated distinct cross-national differences with respect to the rate at which cabinets may be expected to fall. More specifically, while the general form of the distribution of duration times (dissolutions) appears to be a negative exponential for all countries in the analysis, the time period (days) over which the distribution extends is shorter in some countries than in others. In the four countries (Belgium, Finland, Israel and Italy) where dissolutions most strongly indicated a random events process (were Poisson distributed), the time period over which cabinets fell was the shortest. To the contrary are those countries in the analysis where the existence of a random dissolution process was only weakly indicated by the data; they fell over a longer interval of time. Ireland had the most pronounced tendency in this direction. What this would seem to suggest is that country-specific factors (particularly institutional rules and norms) might be effective in inhibiting the effect of random shocks on governmental stability. The Irish example might also suggest that the structure of the party system itself could be effective in this way; where single-party majority cabinets can rule as a normal condition (as, say, in Great Britain), we should expect that the cabinet is less vulnerable with respect to its ability to persist than is the case where government by coalition is, because of electoral outcomes and the party system, virtually inevitable. If this is true, then cabinet dissolution in coalition systems might fruitfully be viewed as a mechanism for conflict management, while in single-party majority governance systems, political conflict management might take other forms, as, for example, in periodic cabinet reorganisations.

More generally, we assert that the key to understanding the relative ability of cabinets to persist through time is an appreciation of uncertainty in the environment and the occurrence of chance (improbable) events. This suggests that successful models of cabinet stability will be stochastic in their structure, replacing deterministic attributes models which are based on (often unrealistic) assumptions about the linear nature of relationships among variables. At this point in its development, our research programme is quite exploratory. Our previous research (discussed in part above) has given indication of promise (e.g. cabinet dissolutions are a negative exponential Poisson process in four countries), but the construction of an appropriate events model (possibly building on chaos theory or catastrophe theory) has not yet been accomplished, nor have the data requirements for testing any such model been met. Bringing these tasks to a successful conclusion constitutes our agenda for continuing research on the problem.

Notes

1. The first-stage analysis was a principle components analysis (PA1 in SPSS).
2. The second stage analysis was a varimax rotated factor analysis (PA2 in SPSS).

References

Browne, E., Frendreis, J. and Gleiber, D. 1982. The process of cabinet dissolution: an exponential model of duration and stability in Western democracies. Mimeo

1984. The dissolution of governments in Scandinavia: a critical events perspective. Mimeo

Browne, E. and James, P. 1985. Political disorder: the potential of mathematical chaos theory for the study of political stability. Mimeo

Budge, Ian, Robertson, David and Hearl, Derek Forthcoming. *Ideology, Strategy and Party Change.* Cambridge University Press

Castles, Francis and Mair, Peter 1984. Left/right political scales: some 'expert' judgements. *European Journal of Political Research, 12*: 73–88

Dodd, Lawrence 1976. *Coalitions in Parliamentary Government.* Princetone University Press

Sanders, T. and Herman, V. 1977. The stability and survival of governments in Western democracies. *Acta Politica, 12*: 346–77

Taylor, M. and Herman, V. 1971. Party systems and government stability. *American Political Science Review, 65*: 28–37

Warwick, P. 1979. The durability of coalition governments in parliamentary democracies. *Comparative Political Studies, 11*: 465–98

Index

(The detailed table of contents is seen as performing part of the function of the index, e.g. the role of constitutions and electoral laws may be found under 'institutional dimension' in the various chapters; party factions under the 'internal party dimension'; and party electoral support under the 'socio-political dimension')

For EU product safety concerns, contact us at Calle de José Abascal, 56–1°,
28003 Madrid, Spain or eugpsr@cambridge.org.

www.ingramcontent.com/pod-product-compliance
Ingram Content Group UK Ltd.
Pitfield, Milton Keynes, MK11 3LW, UK
UKHW042149130625
459647UK00011B/1252